Making the Best of It

STUDIES IN CANADIAN MILITARY HISTORY

Series editor: Andrew Burtch, Canadian War Museum

The Canadian War Museum, Canada's national museum of military history, has a threefold mandate: to remember, to preserve, and to educate. Studies in Canadian Military History, published by UBC Press in association with the Museum, extends this mandate by presenting the best of contemporary scholarship to provide new insights into all aspects of Canadian military history, from earliest times to recent events. The work of a new generation of scholars is especially encouraged, and the books employ a variety of approaches – cultural, social, intellectual, economic, political, and comparative – to investigate gaps in the existing historiography. The books in the series feed immediately into future exhibitions, programs, and outreach efforts by the Canadian War Museum. A list of the titles in the series appears at the end of the book.

CANADIAN WAR MUSEUM
MUSÉE CANADIEN DE LA GUERRE

Making the Best of It

Women and Girls of Canada and Newfoundland during the Second World War

Edited by Sarah Glassford and Amy Shaw

UBCPress · Vancouver · Toronto

29 27 26 25 24 23 22 21 20   5 4 3 2 1

Printed in Canada on FSC-certified ancient-forest-free paper (100% post-consumer recycled) that is processed chlorine- and acid-free.

Library and Archives Canada Cataloguing in Publication

Title: Making the best of it : women and girls of Canada and Newfoundland during the Second World War / edited by Sarah Glassford and Amy Shaw.
Names: Glassford, Sarah Carlene, 1978– editor. | Shaw, Amy J. (Amy Jeannette), 1972– editor.
Series: Studies in Canadian military history.
Description: Series statement: Studies in Canadian military history | Includes bibliographical references and index.
Identifiers: Canadiana (print) 20200159569 | Canadiana (ebook) 20200159623 | ISBN 9780774862776 (hardcover) | ISBN 9780774862783 (paperback) | ISBN 9780774862790 (PDF) | ISBN 9780774862806 (EPUB) | ISBN 9780774862813 (Kindle)
Subjects: LCSH: World War, 1939–1945—Women—Canada. | LCSH: World War, 1939–1945—Women—Newfoundland and Labrador. | LCSH: Women—Canada—Social conditions—20th century. | LCSH: Women—Newfoundland and Labrador—Social conditions—20th century.
Classification: LCC D810.W7 M35 2020 | DDC 940.53082/0971—dc23

Canadä

UBC Press gratefully acknowledges the financial support for our publishing program of the Government of Canada (through the Canada Book Fund), the Canada Council for the Arts, and the British Columbia Arts Council.

This book has been published with the help of a grant from the Canadian Federation for the Humanities and Social Sciences, through the Awards to Scholarly Publications Program, using funds provided by the Social Sciences and Humanities Research Council of Canada.

Publication of this book has been financially supported by the Canadian War Museum.

Printed and bound in Canada by Friesens
Set in Helvetica Condensed and Minion by Apex CoVantage, LLC
Copy editor: Deborah Kerr
Proofreader: Judith Earnshaw
Indexer: Timothy Pearson
Cover designer: George Kirkpatrick

UBC Press
The University of British Columbia
2029 West Mall
Vancouver, BC V6T 1Z2
www.ubcpress.ca

We dedicate this volume to our grandmothers, three young women and one girl who did their bit through Canada's Second World War in very different ways:

Lucienna (Wismer) Jones Pattison ~ eleven years old in 1939
Raised on a farm near Amherstburg, Ontario, she knitted quilt squares for British war orphans through the Junior Red Cross, worked as a telephone operator, and married a veteran in 1946;

Mildred (Leverton) Glassford ~ twenty-two years old in 1939
A farmwife living near Turin, Ontario, she returned to teaching in a local one-room school to help meet the wartime teacher shortage;

Mildred (Linforth) Makins Thompson ~ nineteen years old in 1939
A native of Toronto, she joined the Women's Royal Naval Service and worked as a photographer during the war;

Phyllis (Wiseman) Shaw ~ thirty-five years old in 1939
A Toronto housewife, married just a year before the conflict began, she raised her first three babies during the war years.

Contents

Acknowledgments

Our first co-editing experience together (which became the 2012 collection, *A Sisterhood of Suffering and Service*) was so positive that, even before we finished the project, we talked about doing it again. In the end, we took a five-year break, then tore off the dustcovers and cranked up the editorial machinery once more. It's been even more enjoyable the second time around. We work well together because we divide-to-conquer, pick up the slack during hectic or stressful periods of each other's lives, remember things the other has forgotten, and laugh a lot. It's a treat to watch half-baked ideas and "very drafty drafts" transform into smarter, more stylish versions of themselves as they travel back and forth between us. But regardless of whether Sarah was living in Ontario or New Brunswick, Amy in Alberta was always too far away for a casual afternoon chat over coffee. Our first big thank you therefore needs to be directed at Science and Technology for all the digital and telecommunications inventions that have allowed this Arts and Humanities partnership to flourish. Fittingly, our one and only in-person meeting about the book, in the summer of 2018, took place in the Brutalist concrete splendour of Weldon Library, at our mutual alma mater, Western. So, thank you, Science. (Just don't get uppity about it. The Arts matter, too!)

The research, writing, editing, and production of this book took place against a backdrop of broken bones and health complications, relationships formed and ended, demanding jobs and major career changes, geographical relocations, the joys and heartbreaks of parenthood and family relationships, and the varied mini-dramas of daily life. The authors and editors alike have struggled to find time, space, and quiet simply to think, let alone to say something new and important, and to say it well. For these reasons, we would like to thank the authors whose work is represented in this volume for carving out a bit of space in their lives for this joint endeavour, and for making it a priority when it needed to be. We know it has not always been easy, and that makes us appreciate it even more.

There are good reasons some scholars want no part of edited collections or other collaborations: having to co-ordinate schedules, negotiate deadlines, wait for others to finish their work, buy into a collective vision, and take practical steps to integrate one's work into a larger entity can be annoying and frustrating.

Sometimes, the result never transcends the sum of its disparate parts. But, as editors, we enjoy working with authors on their chapters, identifying themes for the larger book, and seeing the volume slowly knit together. We also value the diverse perspectives our authors bring to the table and are proud that they include both women and men, students and more established scholars, scholars who work in a variety of professional settings, and full-time academics who span the early, middle, and senior years of their careers. We hope it has been a good experience for each of them.

We would like to thank the Laurier Centre for Military, Strategic, and Disarmament Studies for its support of this volume, as well as the University of Lethbridge, which provided a research dissemination grant that helped pay for professional indexing. The Social Sciences and Humanities Research Council's Aid to Scholarly Publications Program has made the production of this book possible, for which we are grateful. And finally, we appreciate the many agencies and universities who financially supported the research of our authors.

UBC Press was a natural home for this book because of its strength in Canadian wartime history but even more so because working with the press on our First World War book was such a pleasure. Editor Randy Schmidt capably shepherded us through the acquisition and peer review process, and Michelle van der Merwe offered her expertise on the production side. Copy editor Deborah Kerr kept us from committing egregious crimes against the English language, and the talented Timothy Pearson created a wonderful index for us. Thank you, one and all, for channelling your skills and expertise into this book. It is yours as well as ours.

Everyone involved in this project owes a debt to the oral historians, collectors, attic and basement packrats, librarians and archivists, museum curators, digital exhibit creators, journalists, and others who fashioned, preserved, and passed on a rich legacy of Second World War text, image, sound, and "stuff." Women *make* history all the time, but we cannot write their history without evidence from which to piece it together.

A personal word from Sarah: working on this book with Amy while going back to school and launching into a new profession has been a lifeline. Thank you, Amy, for sticking with it and with me. I'm grateful to all the family members, friends, and former academic colleagues who have supported me as I transformed (often painfully) from full-time academic into full-time archivist. Special thanks to Ryan Kirkby for forging the path I later followed and also to Kristie Jones: our weekly lunches in the FIMS/Nursing atrium were good therapy. I started my Master's of Library and Information Science program at Western feeling defeated but found in my small winter 2017 cohort a peer group whose enthusiasm, sense of humour, and strong work ethic reinvigorated my love of learning and helped me see new possibilities for myself. Jordan Bulbrook, Emily Carlisle, Yu Chen, Tamara Hluchaniuk, Krisandra Ivings, Anne Kosowan, Jennifer Nangreave, Madison Patterson, Nadine Poulos, Erin Unger, Matthew White, and others – thank you. Jonathan Vance was a friendly face from my Western History Department past, just when I needed one, and Robin Keirstead at Western Archives was the best mentor a historian-turned-archivist could ever hope for. As a co-op student and a new grad, I found the Provincial Archives of New Brunswick to be a refuge and a godsend: I learned so much and loved working with so many people I could laugh with. Finally, to my new colleagues at the University of Windsor's Leddy Library, thank you for the warm welcome: I look forward to all the years to come.

A final word from Amy: my thanks to Sarah for her hard work, insights, and grace, and to my colleagues and friends at the University of Lethbridge, with its famously collegial History Department. Finally, thank you to my family for their interest, support, and patience.

Making the Best of It

Introduction
Community, Memory, and Historical Precedent

Sarah Glassford and Amy Shaw

Sue Ward was living with her parents in Vancouver when the Second World War broke out, earning money by singing and playing her ukulele on a local radio station, where she was known as Sunshine Sue. Ward joined the Canadian Women's Army Corps in 1941, embarking on what she later described as being, in unexpected ways, a novel experience:

> I had never known sisters and had few girl friends. There were many of us, depression kids, farm girls, lone city kids, who had few playmates and limited educations. There were no free summer camps or sponsored sports teams in those desperate times. Lifelong friendships blossomed from those exhausting basic training experiences. Thirty strangers were thrown together by no reason other than each had volunteered to help the Canadian Army win a deadly war. City know-hows, country bumpkins, drones and workers, swift and slow, bright and dull, large and small, youth and mature, from both sides of the tracks – we all melded.[1]

When Canadians imagine or recall the deprivations of the Great Depression of the 1930s, its isolating effects are perhaps not what come immediately to mind. Yet, as Sue Ward's account suggests, young women from the British dominions of Canada and Newfoundland who lived through the Second World War had spent their youth or young adulthood in countries wrenched not only by economic depression but also by profound social fractures.[2] Their wartime experiences were inevitably coloured by what they perceived as the contrasts – and in some cases, the continuities – between the two periods. Later in life, countless numbers of them would refer to the forging of new friendships and the creation or renewal of a strong sense of community as being among the war's most lasting impressions on them as individuals. Older women had a greater variety of experience to draw upon when making sense of the war years, and they drew parallels and contrasts with the First World War, as well as the interwar decades.

Whether produced by schoolgirls or homemakers, war charity volunteers or members of the armed forces, office clerks or factory workers, the memoirs and oral histories of female Canadians and Newfoundlanders tend to be upbeat in tone. Peppered with anecdotes of fun and adventure, they are commonly tinged with an obvious satisfaction in the opportunities wartime offered to put their skills and abilities to work – and to earn money, status, or social approbation in the process. Boredom, loneliness, grief, and fear appear, too, but they are nearly always hedged by some degree of happiness. As such, these memoirs reflect the warm glow of nostalgia and the era's emphasis on cheerfulness in the face of adversity. They also reflect the identities of their authors, most of whom belonged to the white, Christian, anglophone majority, seeing out the war from the safety of Fortress North America. Their experiences stand in stark contrast to those of women in Europe, East Asia, and North Africa – and also with those of certain minority groups in Canada, most notably Japanese Canadian women and girls, for whom the war years meant traumatic dispossession and displacement.

Collectively, Canadians and Newfoundlanders faced the outbreak of the Second World War with disappointment and reluctance: memories of the previous war were too fresh for any other response. Yet, they also possessed a clear sense – one that only grew stronger as the war progressed – of being on the right side of history. As J.L. Granatstein and Peter Neary explain, they perceived the conflict as a "good war," in which the whole country pulled together to defend democracy and protect the vulnerable.[3] The villains of the piece (Nazi Germany, Fascist Italy, and later Imperial Japan) were obvious and indisputable. Notably, this framework continues to guide Canadian popular memory today, even as academic historians expose the deep-seated racism that fuelled the Japanese Canadian internment or question the morality of Canadian participation in the fire bombing of German civilians in Dresden.[4]

This powerful popular memory also optimistically interprets the war as a watershed moment in which women broke through a variety of gendered barriers to achieve full participation in society. This interpretation rests heavily upon their highly visible participation in most elements of the war effort and has been carried into the present by iconic propaganda featuring Canada's Bren Gun Girl and America's Rosie the Riveter. Since the 1980s, in part because of this perception, much of Canadian historical scholarship about women and the Second World War has revolved around the single question of whether it liberated them or (less dramatically) at least improved their socio-economic status and opportunities in the long run. The answer tends to be "not really," yet the popular memory persists, bolstered by those cheerful wartime memoirs and their message, either implicit or explicit, that something had fundamentally shifted for women.

This collection revisits the Second World War through a gendered lens, contending that the time has come to think more broadly about women's experiences of it and to ask a wider series of questions. Gender was a crucial factor in determining the parameters of these experiences: the societies in which Canadian and Newfoundland women lived saw gender as a compelling reason to mobilize them for, or exclude them from, a variety of activities. But gender was not *the* defining identity for many women and girls. Instead, their membership – whether voluntary or externally imposed – in a series of communities, sometimes mutually exclusive and sometimes overlapping, determined the narratives, discourses, proscriptions, opportunities, and hierarchies that would shape their wartime experience. Though these communities could be regulatory and restrictive, they were often sources of strength and solidarity in the face of unprecedented challenges brought on by the war. The fellowship, support, and sense of shared endeavour that marked such communities often numbered among the elements that were best remembered by those who lived through the war years.

Membership in such communities was so significant that it practically renders moot the question of whether or not the Second World War liberated women. Liberated which women? In what ways? According to whose standards? And why would we expect it to liberate them in the first place? As Tarah Brookfield and Sarah Glassford conclude, with regard to understanding women and war throughout Canadian history, the liberation question proves "insufficient to grapple with the diverse array of women" who were involved, and "the fact that this question is rarely (if ever) asked of men and war further illustrates its limits as an entry point for understanding gender and war as broadly as possible."[5] The question also becomes inappropriate when applied to the European women and girls who came to Canada as displaced persons after 1945 or to the Japanese Canadians who were dispossessed and interned by their own government. Mary Greyeyes Reid made history by becoming the first Indigenous woman to join the Canadian military when she enlisted in the Canadian Women's Army Corps in 1942,[6] but Indigenous women and girls were no closer to being treated as full Canadian citizens after their participation in the war effort. Newfoundland as a whole experienced greater prosperity as a result of the war, but outport women's limited opportunities and expectations remained remarkably consistent until well after Confederation with Canada in 1949.[7] A more granular approach is clearly required, to do justice to the diversity in the female populations of Canada and Newfoundland.

The women and girls examined in this book are marked by their membership in social groupings defined by age, geographical location, socio-economic class, religion, language, race, ethnicity, and participation in domestic, voluntary, paid, or military forms of labour. The bonds formed between individuals in these groups are an explicit or implicit theme in nearly all the chapters of this

Figure 0.1

Executive members of the Nisei Unit of the Canadian Red Cross Vancouver Branch, c. 1939–41. Left to right: Myea Okamura (vice convenor), Hisa Kato, Kathleen Fujiwara (secretary), Kideko Hidaka (treasurer), and Mrs. Mickey Maikawa (unit convenor). "Nisei" refers to Canadian-born children of Japanese immigrants. Neither these women's Canadian birth nor their Red Cross work would keep them from being interned with other Japanese Canadians in 1942. | Courtesy of the Canadian Red Cross, Public Affairs department.

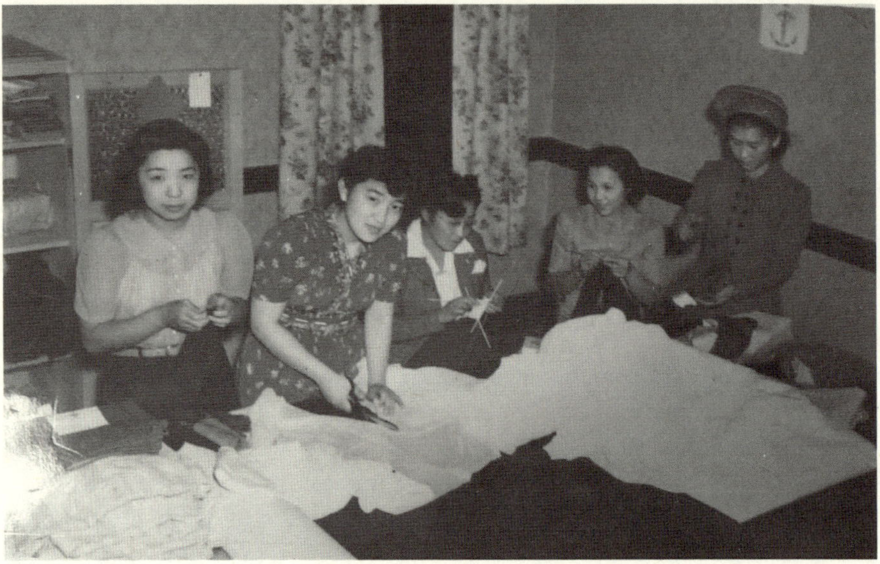

collection. For some women and girls, the war years brought dramatic changes in where and with whom they lived, what they wore and ate, and what work they did. For others, it altered their days more subtly, through the things they bought, participation in war-related charity work, and the emotional strain of having friends and loved ones fighting overseas. In both cases, the war was not only an individual experience but also one mediated by the communities of which Canadian and Newfoundland women and girls were a part.

The two decades of relative peace that elapsed between the First World War (1914–18) and the Second World War (1939–45) were long enough to ensure that a new generation would do the actual fighting in the second conflict but short enough that many, if not most, of those who held positions of power or influence in government, industry, the military, and the voluntary sector had lived through the previous war. They understood and conducted their efforts in the Second World War in light of their First World War experience, striving to reproduce their successes and improve upon their failures. In a similar vein, the experiences of women and girls must be situated within a broader context of change and continuity that spanned the years between 1910 and 1950.

During the First World War, the women of Canada and Newfoundland mobilized themselves to meet wartime needs through voluntary work, military nursing, and new forms of paid employment, earning lavish praise for their efforts and a new public appreciation for their abilities. Many also won the right to vote provincially and/or federally during this period. Yet, these changes often proved disappointingly temporary and were often far from universal. For instance, women who found meaning, enjoyment, and/or a welcome wage increase in their non-traditional wartime employment (such as banking or munitions work) were pressured or forced to leave it after November 1918, to make way for returning servicemen. At the same time, the major national war charities and voluntary organizations that had absorbed the energy and ability of so many women and girls either closed their books or focused on veterans and the needs of peacetime civilian society: in both cases, the authority, urgency, and sense of serving a vital cause were lost, with the result that membership and donations declined dramatically. Meanwhile, some women remained disenfranchised at the federal level, on the basis of their race or ethnicity. The fight for provincial woman suffrage continued into the 1920s in several Canadian provinces and in Newfoundland, which was still a separate British dominion. In Quebec, women suffragists fought an uphill battle until they finally attained the provincial vote in 1940. The First World War had produced profound changes in the lives of women and girls *as individuals*, but it had not led to a revolutionary transformation of their collective place in the political or economic spheres of either Canada or Newfoundland.[8]

It would be a mistake, however, to say that nothing had changed. During the interwar years, women and girls in urban areas of the two Dominions had expectations and opportunities that would have seemed unthinkable during the first two decades of the twentieth century. Cynthia Comacchio explains that, in Canada, "the peer group took on a new importance in the lives of modern youth" and adolescents remained dependent on their families longer than in preceding generations – in part because, for the first time, most of them attended high school, even if only briefly. And although post-secondary education was still overwhelmingly the preserve of young men, by the 1920s a little more than half of Canadian high school students between the ages of fifteen and seventeen were female. Many took advantage of the expansion of girls' sports teams and intramural leagues; others chose "commercial" training (increasingly over the domestic science stream that had been popular before the First World War), which prepared them to work in an office or retail setting.[9] The iconic Modern

Girl of the 1920s – complete with short skirt, bobbed hair, cosmetics, cigarettes, and wide visibility in paid employment, beauty pageants, and motion pictures – was, as Jane Nicholas demonstrates, "simultaneously popular and problematic" in interwar Canada.[10] Although comparable research on Newfoundland has yet to be conducted, it seems reasonable to imagine that similar changes might have occurred in St. John's, at least. Nor were signs of change in female lives limited to the culturally vibrant 1920s: the Depression years increased women's role in many family economies. Wives and mothers doubled-down on their traditional functions of budgeting, stretching, and supplementing available resources, and the number of young women in paid employment increased. As Comacchio explains for the Canadian case, "reflecting the nature of the Depression as a crisis of male breadwinners, the 1931 census saw a definite increase in the cheaper employment of young women, with 25 per cent of those aged fourteen to twenty gainfully employed by comparison to 16 per cent in 1921."[11]

In short, the armistice that was supposed to close an aberrant chapter and enable a return to normality instead ushered in an intense two decades of cultural change, a short-lived economic boom followed by protracted depression, unprecedented political experimentation, and profound social dislocations. But despite the changes and new opportunities of the interwar years, the lives of Canadian and Newfoundland women of the late 1930s bore obvious (and limiting) similarities to those of their predecessors. Keeping in mind the variations and exceptions resulting from socio-economic class, race, ethnicity, religion, age, health, region, and urban or rural location, social expectations of female lives in 1939 still revolved primarily around heterosexual marriage and biological motherhood. Whether a single woman worked or not, she was expected to be a full-time homemaker after marrying. And when she did work, she would receive less pay than men in equivalent positions, have limited opportunities for professional advancement, and be excluded from a wide range of jobs and professions on the basis of her gender. Although a few extraordinary individuals, such as engineer Elsie MacGill, senator Cairine Wilson, and pilot Marion Orr, were pushing into traditionally male preserves, girls and young women were still firmly guided toward the caring and/or service-oriented fields – teaching, nursing, social work, secretarial work, and household science. Others found employment in retail, domestic service, and certain types of traditionally female factory labour. Most women could vote, and a handful had been elected to public office, but government remained overwhelmingly male dominated – as did industry and the military.

Canada's participation in the Second World War wrought dramatic and enduring changes in the country: it ended a decade of economic depression, increased state intervention in everyday life, expanded hydroelectric power resources, established new economic and military relationships with the United States, and created or sundered family or romantic relationships.[12] Even amid this whirlwind of change, the alterations to female roles and expectations were some of the most visible and striking. Large numbers of women went to work in war plants, making everything from binoculars to bombers, while others moved into new areas of civilian employment such as driving buses or working for the railways. Thousands of women picked up the slack and did "men's jobs" on farms across the country. Altogether, the number of women who had paid employment outside the home rose from 600,000 in 1939 to 1.2 million in 1944.[13] By mid-war, this unprecedented expansion was encouraged at the highest levels: in May 1942, a dedicated Women's Division was created in the federal Department of National Selective Service, to help place female workers in the war economy. This was only one of many extraordinary measures the government felt were necessary to fully mobilize the country against the sophisticated Axis war machine.

Although many women combined their new war work with ongoing responsibilities at home, others moved (sometimes across the country) to live in dormitories near factories, providing a desperately needed pool of non-traditional labour that fuelled the economy and contributed in vital ways to the war effort. It is difficult to overstate the impact on Canadian society of this widescale movement of women into unaccustomed roles and spaces. In some cases, their bodies and clothing became subjects of public debate, their increased presence on city streets and public transit seen as a challenge to gender norms.[14] Jane Nicholas shows that women's bodies were linked in complex ways to Canadian discussions of nationalism and nation building in the interwar years, so it is not surprising that they were also a matter of much social significance and public concern during the Second World War.[15]

Despite the fact that increasing numbers of women had already been working during the Great Depression, the dramatic expansion of their paid employment after 1939 was described as a temporary response to the wartime emergency and a necessary support to men's combat roles overseas. Nor was the mobilization of women limited to paid workplaces. Posters urged them to "roll up their sleeves for victory," to "back them up to bring them back," and to "back the attack," whether they did so with a "make do and mend" approach at home or through voluntary work, paid employment, or enlistment in the women's armed services. Women met the challenge, although not always without a certain ambivalence, since there were consequences to their support. As a francophone veteran of the Royal Canadian Air Force (Women's Division) recalled, "when I'd read the casualty lists in the papers, I'd say to myself, 'It's true, I am doing something to help, but the boy I've relieved for overseas duty might very well end up getting himself killed.' So my sentiments were mixed. It was hard to know what was right."[16] In a similar vein, Marlene Epp's chapter on Canadian Mennonite women in this volume reminds us that national mobilization for war created tensions and dilemmas in the lives of pacifist women, even as it opened new opportunities for them.

The Second World War had a dramatic impact on Canada, but its effects on neighbouring Newfoundland were arguably even greater. Devastated by the contraction of international trade after 1929, the export-dependent dominion surrendered its self-governing status in return for a British bail-out and a British-led Commission of Government.[17] The change stung the pride of many Newfoundlanders, and even British assistance could not fend off the rigours of the Depression. The advent of war in 1939, coupled with Nazi Germany's heavy investment in submarine warfare, transformed Newfoundland from a little-known outpost territory subsumed by grinding poverty to a strategic lynchpin in the Allied defence of North America and the Atlantic supply chain. Canada made its own declarations of war on Germany, Italy, and Japan thanks to the greater independence it gained through the Statute of Westminster (1931); however, Newfoundland's participation in the war was still directed by Britain, and was automatically included in their declaration of war. Britain also traded military bases on the island of Newfoundland and in mainland Labrador for American naval destroyers as part of the Lend-Lease Agreement, and it arranged that Canadians would take responsibility for the defence of Newfoundland. Soon, the island and parts of Labrador were overrun with Allied army, navy, and air force personnel. It was a "friendly invasion" that brought steady employment, cash salaries, massive infrastructure investments, motorized vehicles, and cultural novelties such as hot dogs, Coca-Cola, and big-band dances three nights a week. The economy boomed, and Newfoundlanders tasted prosperity on a wider scale than ever before. Due to its fishery-dependent economy, the dominion did not experience the same kind of industrial or agricultural workforce mobilization as in many parts of Canada, but Newfoundland women still found plenty of paying jobs: the Canadian and American bases scattered along the coasts employed large numbers of civilians throughout the war, with women helping to staff administrative, retail, and switchboard positions, among others.[18]

The significance of women's paid labour in both Canada and Newfoundland was matched, if not surpassed, by the movement of women into the armed forces, where they played important and highly visible supporting roles. During the First World War, nursing was the only position for women in the Canadian military – and the Canadian Army Medical Corps was alone among the Allies in enlisting female nurses within the army itself, where they held the rank of lieutenant/nursing sister. Their impressive service ensured that nursing sisters were considered a vital part of the military medical system when the Royal Canadian Army Medical Corps mobilized for the Second World War. As in the previous conflict, the list of applicants far outstripped the available spots, with 4,500 women serving by the end of the war. As Cynthia Toman demonstrates, they were still expected to uphold the social norms of respectable femininity. Nevertheless, both their nursing work and their uniforms changed with the times. She explains that Second World War "innovations in medicine, surgery, and drugs brought opportunities to move closer to the frontlines of war and the frontiers of medical technology, where [military nurses] learned new skills and challenged the established boundaries between physicians' work and nurses' work." The sisters' regular working uniforms of blue cotton dress, white apron, and white veil echoed those of the First World War but were replaced by a more practical khaki uniform of shirt, trousers, and heavy boots when they worked in active theatres of war.[19] However, the subtleties of change were lost on a public already accustomed by the previous war to associating women with caring health work. Ultimately, the expansion of women's military roles *beyond* nursing captured the public's greatest interest, earning praise and censure in almost equal measure.

The cultural proscriptions that had long curbed the enlistment of women into the armed forces had begun to weaken by 1939 – probably helped in part by examples such as Canada's military nursing sisters of the First World War and the 1938 creation of the Auxiliary Territorial Service as a women's branch of the British army.[20] Even before the war began, women in Victoria, British Columbia, organized themselves into a paramilitary unit that evolved into the British Columbia Women's Service Corps. The outbreak of hostilities in 1939 and the fall of France in 1940 spurred the creation of similar units elsewhere in Canada; by mid-1941, some 6,700 women, both anglophone and francophone, were active in dozens of women's paramilitary groups in urban areas from coast to coast. Keen to play a more active role than that offered by voluntary or paid work, they created military-style hierarchies, bought or made their own uniforms, and trained themselves in skills such as military drill, orienteering, marksmanship, and auto mechanics. In 1914, a fledgling women's home guard unit in Toronto had been successfully pressured to disband. By contrast, the Second World War's BC Women's Service Corps, the Corps de Réserve National féminin, and the Canadian Auxiliary Territorial Service (among others) lobbied hard for official recognition by government. When Ottawa chose in 1941 to create its own official women's branches, the paramilitaries provided an initial pool of officers and recruits.[21] Many Newfoundland women, similarly eager to see active service, joined the Canadian women's armed services; others joined the British or American equivalents.

In the end, neither the persistent lobbying of women such as BC Women's Service Corps commandant Joan Kennedy nor a sudden conversion to equal rights feminism moved Ottawa to admit women to the armed forces. Rather, a growing labour shortage combined with the ferocity of the Nazi war machine and France's shocking capitulation in 1940 – followed in December 1941 by the Japanese attack on Pearl Harbor – made it clear to Allied governments that "total war" against the Axis powers would demand, among other things, the sacrifice of social niceties and (some) gendered divisions of labour. Every able-bodied, age-appropriate man must be put to work wherever he was most needed (whether in combat, on a farm, or in heavy industry), and that meant drawing upon women to fill non-combat positions.[22] Accordingly, like Britain, the United States, Australia, and New Zealand,[23] Canada opened the doors of its army, navy, and air force to women – albeit in a limited and controlled way. Separate women's branches of the three services were formed, and women were not permitted in combat roles. Their enlistment was purely for supportive service, framed explicitly as a means of releasing men for combat. Under the terms of the National Resources Mobilization Act of 1940, "all Canadian men *and women* over 16" had to register with the federal government, and by June 1942 it was difficult for anyone, regardless of gender, to take a job of their choosing without permission from a National Selective Service officer. Despite such efforts to deploy Canada's human resources as effectively as possible, debates and measures concerned with conscription for military service explicitly and implicitly meant, in Prime Minister Mackenzie King's words, "conscription of men."[24] Conscripting Canadian women for military service, whether at home or overseas, was unimaginable. Meanwhile, Newfoundland's Commission of Government never contemplated conscripting anyone, choosing instead to encourage voluntary enlistment in the British or Canadian forces.[25]

Despite women's exclusion from combat, their admission into non-nursing military roles marked a highly symbolic change in the opportunities available to them, and opened up a meaningful new avenue for wartime service. The Women's Division of the Royal Canadian Air Force – the RCAF (WD) – was established first, in July 1941. It prepared women for a variety of ground-based jobs, including clerks, drivers, cooks, electricians, mechanics, and engine technicians. Over seventeen thousand airwomen would serve in Canada and overseas during the war. The Canadian Women's Army Corps (CWAC) was set up immediately after the RCAF (WD), in August 1941, ultimately recruiting almost twenty-two thousand women and becoming indispensable to the functioning of the Canadian army. Initially limited to roles such as cooks, laundrywomen,

Figure 0.2

A cheerful send-off for Wren recruits, as they prepare to depart from St. John's, Newfoundland, on 29 August 1943. | Library and Archives Canada, National Film Board of Canada fonds, e000760822.

clerical help, and telephone operators, CWACs were also filling a wide variety of administrative and logistical positions by the end of the war. In Canada and abroad, they were ordnance technicians, mechanics, coders, and signallers.[26] The Women's Royal Canadian Naval Service (WRCNS, also known as the Wrens) was established in July 1942. With a membership of slightly less than seven thousand, it was the smallest of the three branches, its members serving throughout Canada and in Newfoundland, the United States, and Britain. Like women in the land and air forces, the Wrens were assigned a wide variety of support tasks, including signals work, where they staffed shore-based radio intercept stations that were a key means of detecting German U-boats.[27]

Despite the striking symbolism of women's movement into non-traditional paid work and the military, a far greater number of women and girls in Canada and Newfoundland spent the war years engaged in more traditional forms of female labour. Many retained their roles as wives, mothers, and homemakers, feeding, clothing, and otherwise caring for their families. Regardless of their age and marital or motherhood status, and just as their First World War predecessors had done, millions of women and girls took up volunteer work in response to patriotic and humanitarian appeals. They put their executive abilities to work, running local, provincial, and national war charities, relief funds, and voluntary organizations, proving themselves to be creative and indefatigable fundraisers for war-related causes of all kinds. In organized groups and individually, they put their sewing machines and knitting needles to work, creating comforts and supplementary hospital supplies for military personnel and suffering civilians. Some mobilized their communities to voluntarily staff and donate blood in civilian blood drives for military use; others turned their culinary skills to the tasks of staffing canteens for military personnel or factory workers, packing millions of prisoner of war food parcels, planting Victory Gardens, or canning food. They worked within the limits of new regimes of food and gasoline rationing, developed and shared recipes, learned to make do and mend when consumer goods became scarce later in the war, and participated in nationwide watchdog groups to help enforce consumer price controls.[28] Although voluntary work lacked the perceived glamour and novelty of military service, and did not produce vital materiel in the same way that women's munitions and other industrial labour did, it remained a crucial pillar of women's contribution to the war effort. It was also a socially approved way for pacifist women to express their beliefs and for enemy alien and minority women to demonstrate their patriotism.

Canadian women supported many of the same major national organizations as they had during the First World War, particularly the Canadian Red Cross, the Imperial Order Daughters of the Empire (IODE), the Women's Institutes, and the YMCA/YWCA, in addition to local voluntary associations or relief funds established by religious, ethnic, or other affiliations. In Newfoundland, the governor's wife, Lady Walwyn, spearheaded a 1939 revival of the First World War–era Women's Patriotic Association of Newfoundland (WPA), which mobilized outport women from its St. John's headquarters. The WPA co-ordinated much of the voluntary and charitable war work of Newfoundland women and co-operated closely with other organizations, such as the Canadian Red Cross, whose staff were stationed in St. John's.[29] The presence of so many American troops opened another opportunity for Newfoundland women to volunteer: nearly a thousand were recruited to act as hostesses, entertaining American servicemen at dances, parties, sports events, dinners, and outings for United Services Organization (USO) operations in Newfoundland; others were recruited as performers for travelling USO shows.[30]

Lady Walwyn's role in leading the WPA indicates the value placed by Governor Walwyn and the Commission of Government on women's active involvement in the war effort. Ottawa, too, was keenly aware of the significance of women's voluntary and charitable work. In 1940, the federal government created a Women's Voluntary Services Division within the Department of National War Services specifically to help co-ordinate this aspect of the war effort on the home front. By 1945, women were running forty-four branches of the division across Canada.[31] On an individual level, as Ian Mosby shows, government propaganda campaigns, such as those that described thrifty homemakers as "housoldiers" and "kitchen commandos," fostered "a broader feeling of solidarity and individual participation in the nation's mobilization for total war," even if efforts such as Victory gardening were of dubious value in the end.[32]

Although the Second World War is clearly its own unique event and era, it is also deeply and inherently connected to the First World War. In fact, the two are sometimes seen as elements of a larger period of geopolitical strife in Europe, separated by a two-decade pause in the fighting. Similarly, in many ways this book is a sequel to our previous volume on women and the First World War. Scholars often ask the same questions about women's involvement in both conflicts, and students, scholars, and feminists have often sought milestones in the twentieth-century expansion of women's rights within each of the world wars. The heightened intensity of citizens' and governments' responses under the stress of total war presents a valuable opportunity for scholars to explore the operation and disruption of gender norms in both conflicts. For these reasons, even before the positive reception of *A Sisterhood of Suffering and Service* and its efforts to reinsert women into the narratives of Canada and Newfoundland during the First World War, we thought that a similar collection on the Second World War could be useful. Since we conceive of the two books as linked in this larger conceptual sense, and because the structure of the first volume worked so well, we have largely reproduced it here. Readers will find the chapters organized into broad thematic sections, each prefaced by a short introduction. The volume as a whole is buttressed by an editorial Introduction and Conclusion that survey the historiography of women and the war, contextualize the individual chapters, and say something about the place of women's wartime experiences in the larger sweep of women's history and women's lives. A substantial bibliography provides an overview of the existing historiography and a guide to future researchers who we hope will take up new questions in the field.

Beyond the structural similarities, *Making the Best of It* echoes its predecessor by bringing together the wartime histories of Canada and Newfoundland. Their economic, political, and social realities were quite different at the time, but both retained strong ties to Britain and held similar views with regard to gender roles. The war itself brought Newfoundlanders and Canadians into closer contact than ever before, and, in 1949, Newfoundland would become a Canadian province. As Peter Neary explains, "it was the war and its consequences that made Confederation [between Canada and Newfoundland] practical. For Canadians and Newfoundlanders, individually and collectively, the war years constituted a period of mutual discovery that laid the foundation for the common bond of nationhood."[33] Regrettably, we received only a single Newfoundland-related submission, but we have striven to highlight Newfoundland women's experiences throughout the Introduction, the Conclusion, and the introductions to each part of the book. There is much to be learned from a comparative examination of the two countries' experiences.

This volume also sees age as a fruitful category of analysis and singles out girlhood as a distinct subset of female experience. It has benefitted from steady growth in the children's history subfield, allowing us to offer an entire section organized around the intertwined histories of childhood, girlhood, and motherhood. Our definition of "girl" remains flexible, tied to social status as much as to age. One legacy of the First World War was the emergence of a so-called youth culture and of "youth" as a more distinct category in the 1920s, so that girlhood stretched later into the teenage years than perhaps it had prior to the Great War. Girlhood was further prolonged for many Canadians and Newfoundlanders during the 1930s, as the Depression made it difficult to attain coming-of-age markers such as marriage and establishing a separate household. And although some young women became family breadwinners during the Great Depression, their unmarried state and role as daughters of the household ensured that they were still referred to somewhat dismissively as "business girls," "factory girls," or "girls in service" rather than as "working women."[34] These interwar developments significantly influenced young people's worlds, as did the involvement of children and youth in the First World War. Propaganda and mobilization efforts by government and war charities alike emphasized the necessity of sacrifice by, for, and of young people and their participation in a variety of war-related activities.[35] When the war made labour scarce, many young people dropped out of school, eager to trade the limited opportunities of the Depression for a well-paying job (in many cases their first).[36]

The perceived centrality of women's and girls' productive and reproductive roles in sustaining the health of the nation fuelled considerable anxiety. Fears that wartime work and military service would create a post-war generation of unfeminine women – manly, promiscuous, and neglectful of their domestic duties – were rife throughout the war, and Canada was gripped by a full-scale moral panic about the degeneration of youth, especially girls. By means ranging from limitations on who could hold supervisory roles to the tailoring of military uniforms, many government departments and businesses tried to uphold gendered boundaries and subsequently urged (or forced) their female employees to leave their jobs after the war. Concerns about adult women's work and youth degeneration were inherently linked, as Jeffrey Keshen observes, in "headlines about latchkey children and street gangs, and the consequent need to reconstitute so-called traditional values and structures as soon as possible after the war."[37] The intimate connections between women, children, and the well-being of society are explored by Lisa Pasolli in Chapter 3 of this volume.

Making the Best of It does not claim to comprehensively cover the broad range of female wartime experience. The chapters presented here are those that we received in response to our call for papers, and inevitably they do not address all interesting and important topics and groups of people. For example, though we are pleased to have Lisa Moore's chapter, which compares francophone and anglophone girls in Quebec, we would have liked to include something more about francophone women's wartime experiences, both within and outside Quebec – a significantly understudied area. Likewise, we sincerely regret that no chapter explicitly discusses Indigenous women. Perhaps scholars have not concentrated on Newfoundland, Quebec, and Indigenous women during the Second World War because they do not see this period as particularly significant for them. Denyse Baillargeon's *A Brief History of Women in Quebec*, for instance, identifies the 1940 attainment of provincial woman suffrage – the culmination of a long feminist struggle in Quebec – as "the outstanding event of this period" rather than the war itself or any of its impacts on Quebec women.[38] It is also tempting to wonder if the all-consuming questions of nation – whether it be Newfoundland Confederation, post-war Quebec nationalism, or a resurgence of Indigenous activism in the second half of the twentieth century – have pulled scholars' attention away from women's wartime experiences. Regardless of whether or not this is the case, the Second World War histories of Canada and Newfoundland would benefit from future scholarly attention to these groups of women.

Several chapters discuss the influence of socio-economic class on women's wartime lives, but this is not a theme of the book as a whole. And although members of some ethnic and religious minorities are examined here, far more are absent, including Japanese Canadians, whose internment is so powerfully explored by novelist Joy Kogawa and historian Pamela Sugiman.[39] Our editorial policy has been to highlight new themes and questions being asked by historians, rather than to reproduce existing research. We hope the resulting volume will move the historiographical conversation into new territory, while also drawing attention to the many topics that await scholarly study.

Although the contributors to *Making the Best of It* ask new questions, the entire collection owes a great debt to, and is firmly grounded in, a rich historiographical tradition.[40] The literature on Canadian and Newfoundland women and the Second World War, generated over four decades, is the product of many scholars from diverse disciplines. Yet, the undeniable polestar is Ruth Pierson's classic 1986 book *"They're Still Women After All": The Second World War and Canadian Womanhood.* In this pioneering monograph and several articles that preceded it, Pierson connected her own historical moment to a popular perception of the war as a time of important change for women and to her central research question of whether it had liberated them. "We women of the so-called second wave of feminism sometimes look back nostalgically to the Second World War as a period of women's emancipation," she wrote, citing the influence of propaganda photographs of female soldiers and factory workers. "But such images do not give the whole picture."[41] Pierson's interest in researching the topic sprang from a student essay she received in a 1975 women's history class. Written by Shirley Goundry, then a fifty-something feminist activist in St. John's, it tackled the question of why the "feminine mystique" was so widely embraced after 1945, doing so from the perspective of the author's own experience as a young British Columbian woman during the war, especially in light of her service in the RCAF (WD).

Goundry's conviction that women's unprecedented wartime work was always intended to be temporary led Ruth Pierson to the archives, where she sought to test the assertion. "Did this vast mobilization of the female population of Canada lead to a more equal sharing of power and responsibilities between men and women in the public and private spheres of Canadian society? Did war 'liberate' Canadian women from patriarchal divisions of labour and conceptions of proper womanhood?" she asked.[42] These were important and timely questions for feminist historians like Pierson in the 1970s and 1980s, as they engaged in their own struggles to advance women's equality in Canadian universities, homes, workplaces, and public discourse. Pierson ultimately argued that, although the war certainly provided powerful images and examples of strong, capable women doing extraordinary things, second-wave feminist nostalgia for the era was misplaced. No long-term liberation of Canadian women followed the conflict, because none was ever intended, and wartime policy and propaganda worked to keep women in their traditional place as often as it promoted their exceptional efforts. Pierson's conclusions were supported by subsequent work on servicewomen and female war workers by scholars Tina Davidson, Jennifer Stephen, Helen Smith, and Pamela Wakewich. Women's non-traditional wartime activities, they contended, were consistently undermined by measures, discourses, and expectations tied to traditional gender roles and the conventions of respectable femininity.[43]

This line of argument has been revisited and challenged from two directions. First, studies of immigrant and racialized women that began to appear in the 1990s drew attention to the intersections of race, ethnicity, and gender, as well as how they shaped women's historical experiences. In differing ways, Dionne Brand's chapter "'We Weren't Allowed to Go into Factory Work until Hitler Started the War,'" about African Canadian women's employment in war industries, and Pamela Sugiman's oral history research on interned Japanese Canadian women highlight the fact that race had significant – and sometimes violent and oppressive – implications for non-white women in wartime.[44] Sugiman's work in particular demonstrates that the question of whether the war liberated women is not the only one that matters – indeed, it is deeply inappropriate in some contexts. Capturing the diverse experiences of Canadian and Newfoundland women during the war demands an expanded set of questions.

Second, some scholars have suggested an alternative interpretation somewhere between the popular assumption that the war liberated women and Pierson's conclusion that it offered continued oppression dressed as (temporary) liberation. In *An Officer and a Lady*, Cynthia Toman argues that in the unique context of overseas military medicine, nurses "learned new skills and challenged the established boundaries between physicians' work and nurses' work." However, "for the most part those changes failed to transform postwar and non-military settings to any significant degree."[45] In *Saints, Sinners, and Soldiers*, Jeffrey Keshen explains that his attempt to determine whether the war produced any significant or enduring advances for the status of Canadian women convinced him that "the patterns ... are not neat and tidy but as chaotic and at times contradictory as the complex society in which they occurred." Moreover, he suggests that Pierson "sets the bar too high" in terms of what constitutes progress and offers his own "two steps forward, one step back" interpretation that identifies real change during the war years, a post-war backlash, and the ultimate impossibility of fully returning to pre-war norms.[46]

More than thirty years have passed since Pierson opened the historiographical conversation about Canadian women and the Second World War, but it still largely revolves around her question of whether the conflict was good for women in some way. The question has also influenced the historiography of the First World War – the peer reviewers for *A Sisterhood of Suffering and Service* urged us to use it as a unifying thread for the collection. After slightly modifying Pierson's liberation question to whether the First World War "transformed" women's lives, we took the reviewers' advice. In *Making the Best of It*, we freely acknowledge our debt to Pierson's work and aim to continue the conversation. Some chapters explicitly reference her arguments in constructing their own. However, we have also chosen, quite deliberately, *not* to use liberation or transformation or any variation thereof as a unifying theme of the volume. Instead, we weave these questions into the Introduction and Conclusion as part of a broader set of questions about women and war, and leave the contributors to address or not address liberation as they choose. The related issue of whether the war years produced long-term changes for women in Canada and Newfoundland is taken up in our Conclusion.

In the summer of 2014, when Brookfield and Glassford compiled a bibliography of historical publications relating to Canadian and Newfoundland women and war, they found that the works dealing with the First and the Second World Wars were nearly equal in number.[47] This result is surprising, because the historiography for the second war *feels* richer and larger than that of the first. This may stem in part from the far-reaching influence of Pierson's work, which lends a political relevance to Second World War historical writing by implicitly connecting it to present-day gender issues. It may also be related to the greater number of memoirs and other first-hand accounts left by women who lived through the Second World War, as compared to the First World War. If, in a society that privileged the male soldier's voice, they initially felt reluctant to write about their experiences (as was true for women of the First World War), this reluctance clearly wore off at some point. Currently, women also enjoy a much larger place in the popular memory and historiography of the entire Second World War, as compared to the First. But this was not always the case. Their place in the landscape of Second World War history in Canada has benefitted from two related developments of the late twentieth century. The first is the interest and initiative of women's historians, who have sought out and studied the experiences of Second World War women. The second is the dramatic alteration in women's roles and expectations beginning in the 1970s. As women gained access to greater equality, opportunities, and voice in public discourse, those who lived through the war may well have reassessed their experiences – in some cases, to the point of asserting their importance in the historical narrative.

In 1979, when journalist Jean Bruce began her research into Canadian women and the Second World War for what became her popular book *Back the Attack! Canadian Women during the Second World War,* she suspected there was a lot to say about the topic. To her dismay, a symposium organized by the Department of National Defence's Directorate of History that year contained only a single reference to women in fourteen papers, despite being titled "The Second World War as a National Experience." In addition, wartime footage chosen by staff at what was then the Public Archives of Canada and screened for symposium attendees similarly omitted women. Bruce subsequently scoured the archives, interviewed women of the war generation, found "a treasure-trove of material waiting to be discovered," and assembled an engaging collection of photographs, official documents, letters, advertising and propaganda posters, and oral history. She was working on her book when George Robertson's CBC TV documentary on women in the armed forces, *Women at War,* first aired on 11 November 1982. Two years later, the Canadian War Museum mounted a temporary exhibition, Women and War, guest curated by Nancy Miller Chenier. Bruce identified the documentary and exhibition as "the first significant and successful attempts to attract public interest in this long-neglected subject area." The exhibition drew so many visitors – the largest proportion of them under the age of twenty-one – that the museum extended its original one-year run for another full year.[48] By the time it closed in 1986, both Bruce and Pierson had published their books.

The fact that public acknowledgements of those who served or died in the Second World War were most often added to First World War monuments, rather than constructed from scratch, helped perpetuate the absence of women's contributions from public commemorative spaces. A simple "Second World War 1939–1945" plaque added to a monument depicting a First World War soldier, for instance, does nothing to remind observers of the involvement of servicewomen in the second war, let alone the other ways in which women mobilized in wartime. A notable exception is *The Volunteers,* a bronze monument erected by the Halifax Women's History Society. Unveiled on 16 November 2017, it depicts Second World War voluntary work by women of European, African, and Indigenous descent in youth, midlife, and old age.[49] As its recent creation suggests, interest in Canadian women's Second World War history has proliferated since the 1980s, producing a host of celebratory material – from books and TV dramas to keychains and Internet memes. The Canadian War Museum's travelling exhibition World War Women (2018–19) is only the latest example. It uses "artifacts, photographs, documents[,] reproductions, and audiovisual material" to tell the story of Canadian women in the two wars. In the process, it demonstrates that not only are women now considered an important and intriguing part of Canada's world war history, but also that there are good sources with which to study their experiences.[50] Popular memory of women and the Second World War largely revolves around the most visible signifiers of their changing roles and those elements that seem to presage the much greater equality and opportunities enjoyed by twenty-first-century Canadian women: images of strong women doing non-traditional work, such as overall-clad factory workers wielding machinery or uniformed servicewomen driving jeeps. Kelly Saxberg's 1999 National Film Board documentary *Rosies of the North* and the Global Television network's 2012–13 drama series *Bomb Girls,* both about female factory workers building war material, attest to the enduring appeal of this distinctive imagery.[51]

Today's vibrant (if limited) Canadian public memory of women's roles in the Second World War is therefore a relatively recent phenomenon, which owes a great deal to second-wave feminism and the emergence of women's history as a field of study. But Bruce also wrote that a major challenge in her research "was to overcome the self-deprecating attitude of women with remarkably interesting experiences to relate – once I could persuade them to talk. Even when they did consent to be interviewed, several chose not to speak for attribution."[52] Although some women preserved documents and recorded histories of their work – members of the Canadian Red Cross Corps Overseas Detachment are a good example – others had to be convinced that their experiences were of historical significance. Bruce's interviews with reluctant subjects were conducted in the early 1980s, and even the proactive Canadian Red Cross Corps veterans conducted their most extensive preservation and oral history efforts during the 1990s and early 2000s.[53] Perhaps highly publicized commemorative occasions, such as the fiftieth anniversary of D-Day (6 June 1994), and a tendency to reflect as they reached their twilight years helped spur women to assert their place in the larger historical narrative.

That narrative itself offers an interesting point of comparison between the First and Second World Wars. In the histories of both Canada and Newfoundland, the first war is presented as a national coming-of-age, distinguished (for better or worse) by iconic battles in which the flower of a generation was lost. By contrast, the second war features ordinary citizens fighting against the Nazi menace (Japan and Italy usually take a backseat) and two countries relatively small in population playing crucial roles in co-operation with much larger Allies. In these narratives, women's allotted task is to be a source of cheerful patriotism, to step gamely into the breach when manpower runs short, and to keep the home fires burning. As such, they support the themes of communal pulling together and victory over a demonstrably evil enemy.

Not only did women of the Second World War leave more accounts of their experiences than those of the First World War, but they are also present in far more visual sources. A wealth of propaganda posters, photographs, war art, and films made by the National Film Board of Canada allows us to "see" women and girls of this era in greater numbers and offers rich fields for analysis. As discussed above, female factory workers are a central element of Second World War iconography today, with carefully staged photographs of Veronica Foster, the Bren Gun Girl, portraying them as the epitome of cool competency. Other popular images – of Canadian women uniformed and marching in step or working as mechanics and radio operators – support this narrative of women capably taking on unaccustomed roles. The war genuinely opened spaces for women, where they often surprised themselves and others with their abilities – a theme that is woven through a number of chapters in this collection.

Throughout *Making the Best of It,* the authors make use of a wide array of primary sources, showcasing the rich sources that have survived. Photographs, posters, films, legislation, government documents and publications, newspapers and wartime advertising, oral histories, memoirs, diaries, letters, institutional records, memorials, and fiction are subjected to analysis and mined for the insights they offer – sometimes at face value and sometimes in the women's and gender history tradition of reading between the lines and identifying gaps and silences. The results repay the effort.

To highlight some of the clearest points of connection, the chapters in this book are grouped into four parts. The first discusses children, childhood, and parenting during the war. In Chapter 1, Barbara Lorenzkowski focuses on the experience of childhood, especially girlhood, in the Atlantic seaports of Halifax, Nova Scotia, and Saint John, New Brunswick, using oral history to explore what it meant to grow up in these most militarized Canadian cities. For girls and young women in the war years, the harbour represented both a militarized space and a play space: a locale where the extraordinary and the ordinary communed. Children's experiences of the war, Lorenzkowski finds, were shaped by the attitudes in their homes and local environments – the "small spaces" of childhood. They were attuned to the emotions of those around them in a way that was distinctive to childhood.

In Chapters 2 and 4, Claire Halstead and Lisa Moore carry this forward to look at children and teenage girls in school. Halstead examines British child evacuees, concentrating on the impact of their presence on Canadian children and the relationships that developed among them. She argues that the unprecedented circumstances of evacuation enabled evacuees and Canadian girls to establish a non-biological sisterhood in foster homes, friendships at school, and a wartime girlhood within their communities. Moore examines the differences in war exposure and participation at three Quebec private schools for girls, one English, one French, and one bilingual. In the process, she demonstrates not only the differences in how girls from these two linguistic communities viewed the war, but also how their perceptions affected and were influenced by family relationships, friendships, and student-teacher interactions.

In Chapter 3, Lisa Pasolli approaches wartime childhood from the perspective of parents, examining working motherhood and childcare in Canada. Her focus on the federal Wartime Day Nurseries Agreement, and specifically the differing approaches taken in Ontario and Quebec, leads her to argue that the (re)distribution of care between states, markets, and families was a crucial transformation of the war. Pasolli also analyzes the experiences of racialized, poor, and other mothers whose work did not fit neatly into narratives about temporarily doing their bit.

Part 2 of the book considers women's lives on the home front. Unfortunately, few scholars have examined the role of religion in shaping women's wartime experiences – a role that, for women of minority faith groups in particular, could have an enormous impact. In Chapter 5, Jennifer Shaw uses first-hand accounts and archival material to explore the ways that Jewish Canadian women and girls participated in the war effort and experienced the war years. She discusses the ways that their responses to the war were in accord with, or diverged from, the principles and strictures of their faith. The ties of family and faith that they shared with the millions of Jews who were suffering in the Holocaust make their experiences especially pertinent and moving.

The other two chapters in Part 2 both tackle the subject of consumption, a complex and central element of Canadian women's household responsibilities. In Chapter 7, Joseph Tohill explores the role played by the thousands of women who worked and volunteered for the Consumer Branch of the Wartime Prices and Trade Board – which was conceived, organized, and run entirely by women – in support of the government's anti-inflation program during and immediately after the war. Tohill argues that, despite the popularity of images of Rosie the Riveter or uniformed CWACs, the image of Mrs. Consumer best embodies the quotidian role that women played in Canada's war. In Chapter 6, Graham Broad examines consumption from another angle. Whereas most accounts emphasize rationing, shortages, and other aspects of home front austerity, Broad shows a more complex reality in which patriotic consumption was part of women's perceived duty, and contends that interpretations of what this entailed were not monolithic. In the face of various government "austerity measures" and advertisers' competing messages about consumerism, women found opportunities to exercise sovereignty as consumers and homemakers. Throughout this part of the book, the authors portray women on the home front as engaged with the war effort in both public and private spaces.

Part 3 moves overseas but not to the armed forces. Canadian and Newfoundland women carried out important humanitarian work during the war, but their efforts are often excluded from the historiography. In Chapter 8, Marlene Epp examines Canadian Mennonite women whose pacifist beliefs put them at odds with most of their fellow citizens, arguing that their overseas relief work enabled them to express their faith through service to others. At the same time, it gave them a unique opportunity for adventure and travel. Chapter 9, written by Sarah Glassford, discusses the emotional labour and resilience of the Canadian Red Cross Corps, whose overseas contingent worked closer to the battlefields than most volunteers. Charged, in part, with re-creating a sense of home and family for enlisted men, these young women endured the strains of service by relying heavily upon the emotional bonds they created on the edges of the conflict.

The fourth and final part of *Making the Best of It* offers new perspectives on women in nursing, the military, and paid war work. These are the areas to which previous scholarship has paid the most attention, but the authors here take fresh approaches and offer important new insights. In Chapter 10, Heidi Coombs examines the neglected topic of wartime nursing in the Grenfell Mission hospitals in Labrador and northern parts of the island of Newfoundland. She shows that isolation and labour shortages gave these civilian nurses a great deal of autonomy – a situation that offers interesting parallels to the military nursing context studied elsewhere by Cynthia Toman.

Death itself is given surprisingly little space in Canadian writing about the Second World War. Sarah Hogenbirk makes it her subject in Chapter 11, placing Canada's female war dead within the charged narratives of danger and safety that surrounded women in the armed forces. She explores the physical risks that servicewomen faced during the war and then recounts the stories of those who died, the means by which they were mourned, and the ways their deaths have and have not been integrated into Canadian history. Sarah Van Vugt carries this interest in peril into Chapter 12, looking at the narratives of danger and safety regarding women in industrial workplaces. Her analysis of the visual discourse around women war workers, beauty, and danger highlights a prevailing belief that women's bodies required both care and containment in these traditionally male-gendered spaces.

The experiences of women and girls during the Second World War were diverse in and of themselves and were always mediated by other identities. Nonetheless, certain themes appear in the chapters that follow. Among them are excitement in taking on new roles and a sincere pride in seeing one's ordinary work (shopping, cooking) gain new significance. Restrictions on the opportunities presented by the war are also apparent: governmental and military policies combined with societal attitudes to limit the duration and extent of changes, while simultaneously encouraging traditional perceptions of women's abilities and value to society. Women's emotional responses and emotional labour are another recurring theme in this collection, underlining the fact that public participation or non-participation in the war was undergirded by deeply personal sentiments and states of mind. Perhaps the most resounding theme, however, is the value of relationships and collectivities. The extraordinary labours, emotions, and expectations of wartime were achievable and bearable thanks to the presence of supportive communities of many varieties, and the already terrible strains and griefs of war were heightened by isolation, discord, and disconnection from or within those groups.

This observation about the communal orientation of the war experience is by no means original. On 14 July 1940, Prime Minister Winston Churchill described the unfolding conflict as "a war of peoples" rather than of leaders or individuals. As he explained to his listeners on the BBC Radio network, the fate of Britain hinged upon a pulling together of the British Commonwealth and its Allies and well-wishers. Millions of women and girls in Newfoundland and Canada were among the "vast numbers ... in every land" whom Churchill predicted would "render faithful service in this war, but whose names will never be known." It is true that many of their names are unknown to us, and as Churchill foresaw, countless individual deeds were not recorded.[54] But with this volume, we strive to bring to light and better understand, even a little, their collective experiences.

Notes

1 Sue Ward, *One Gal's Army* (Prince George, BC: Caitlin Press, 1996), 38.

2 As a colony and dominion of Britain, the island of Newfoundland and mainland Labrador were officially known simply as Newfoundland. The two components joined Canada under that name in 1949. In 2001, the Canadian Constitution was amended to change the province's name to Newfoundland and Labrador. In this collection, we use the period-appropriate term "Newfoundland" to refer to the entire dominion/province in the 1930s and 1940s and "Labrador" to refer specifically to the mainland portion. "Newfoundland and Labrador" is used here only in connection with the period since 2001.

3 J.L. Granatstein and Peter Neary, eds., *The Good Fight: Canadians and World War II* (Toronto: Copp Clark, 1995). For a similar American argument, see Studs Terkel, *The Good War: An Oral History of World War Two* (New York: Pantheon Books, 1984); and Michael C.C. Adams, *The Best War Ever: America and World War II*, 2nd ed. (Baltimore: Johns Hopkins University Press, 2015).

4 Examples include Jeffrey A. Keshen, *Saints, Sinners, and Soldiers: Canada's Second World War* (Vancouver: UBC Press, 2004); Patricia Roy, J.L. Granatstein, Masako Lino, and Hiroko Takamura, eds., *Mutual Hostages: Canadians and Japanese during the Second World War* (Toronto: University of Toronto Press, 1992); Robert Nelson and Christopher Waters, "The Allied Bombing of German Cities during the Second World War from a Canadian Perspective," *Journal of the History of International Law* 14 (2012): 87–122; and Brian McKenna, dir., *The Valour and the Horror: Death by Moonlight: Bomber Command* (Montreal: National Film Board of Canada, 1992).

5 Tarah Brookfield and Sarah Glassford, "Home Fronts and Frontlines: A Gendered History of War and Peace," in *Reading Canadian Women's and Gender History*, ed. Nancy Janovicek and Carmen Nielson (Toronto: University of Toronto Press, 2019), 156.

6 Heather Conn, "Mary Greyeyes Reid," *The Canadian Encyclopedia* (Toronto: Historica Canada, 2017), https://www.thecanadianencyclopedia.ca/en/article/mary-greyeyes/.

7 Ellen Antler, "Women's Work in Newfoundland Fishing Families," *Atlantis* 2, 2 (1977): 106–13.

8 For a fuller discussion, including a bibliography of scholarship on women in the First World War, see Sarah Glassford and Amy Shaw, eds., *A Sisterhood of Suffering and Service: Women and Girls in Canada and Newfoundland during the First World War* (Vancouver: UBC Press, 2012).

9 Cynthia Comacchio, *The Dominion of Youth: Adolescence and the Making of Modern Canada, 1920 to 1950* (Waterloo: Wilfrid Laurier University Press, 2006), 46, 100–1, 107, 118.

10 Jane Nicholas, *The Modern Girl: Feminine Modernities, the Body, and Commodities in the 1920s* (Toronto: University of Toronto Press, 2015), 5–6.

11 Comacchio, *The Dominion of Youth,* 137. Half of all working women were under twenty-five years of age, and their jobs tended to be transitional and low-paid.

12 Keshen, *Saints, Sinners, and Soldiers,* Chapters 2–4 (forms of state intervention); Matthew Evenden, *Allied Power: Mobilizing Hydro-Electricity during Canada's Second World War* (Toronto: University of Toronto Press, 2015); R.D. Cuff and J.L. Granatstein, *Ties That Bind: Canadian-American Relations in Wartime, from the Great War to the Cold War,* 2nd ed. (Toronto: Hakkert, 1977); J.L. Granatstein, *How Britain's Weakness Forced Canada into the Arms of the United States* (Toronto: University of Toronto Press, 1989); Barbara Ladouceur and Phyllis Spence, eds., *Blackouts to Bright Lights: Canadian War Bride Stories* (Vancouver: Ronsdale Press, 1995).

13 David J. Bercuson and J.L. Granatstein, *Dictionary of Canadian Military History* (Don Mills, ON: Oxford University Press, 1992), 228–29.

14 Donald F. Davis and Barbara Lorenzkowski, "A Platform for Gender Tensions: Women Working and Riding on Canadian Urban Public Transit in the 1940s," *Canadian Historical Review* 79, 3 (1998): 440–46.

15 Nicholas, *The Modern Girl,* 10.

16 Former member, RCAF (WD), translated from French and quoted in Carolyn Gossage, ed., *Greatcoats and Glamour Boots: Canadian Women and War (1939–1945),* rev. ed. (Toronto: Dundurn, 2001), 242.

17 On Newfoundland's loss of self-government, see Chapter 7, "Collapse: 1932–3," in Patrick O'Flaherty, *Lost Country: The Rise and Fall of Newfoundland, 1843–1933* (St. John's: Long Beach Press, 2005), 376–409.

18 John N. Cardoulis, *A Friendly Invasion: The American Military in Newfoundland, 1940–1990* (St. John's: Breakwater Books, 1990), 14; John N. Cardoulis, *A Friendly Invasion II: A Personal Touch* (St. John's: Creative, 1993), 14, photo on page 41; Jenny Higgins, "Canadian Presence," Heritage Newfoundland and Labrador, 2006, https://www.heritage.nf.ca/articles/politics/canadian-presence.php.

19 Cynthia Toman, *An Officer and a Lady: Canadian Military Nursing and the Second World War* (Vancouver: UBC Press, 2007), 12, 103–6.

20 Cynthia Toman, *Sister Soldiers of the Great War: The Nurses of the Canadian Army Medical Corps* (Vancouver: UBC Press, 2016); Jean Bruce, *Back the Attack! Canadian Women during the Second World War – At Home and Abroad* (Toronto: Macmillan of Canada, 1985), 21; Barbara Green, *Girls in Khaki: A History of the ATS in the Second World War* (Stroud, UK: History Press, 2012).

21 Ruth Roach Pierson, *"They're Still Women After All": The Second World War and Canadian Womanhood* (Toronto: McClelland and Stewart, 1986), 97–100; Bruce, *Back the Attack!* 21–22. See also Susan Wade, "Joan Kennedy and the British Columbia Women's Service Corps," in *Not Just Pin Money: Selected Essays on the History of Women's Work in British Columbia,* ed. Barbara K. Latham and Roberta J. Pazdro (Victoria, BC: Camosun College, 1984), 407–28.

22 Pierson, *"They're Still Women,"* 101–2.

23 On female enlistment in Britain, the United States, Australia, and New Zealand, see, for example, Giles Whittell, *Spitfire Women of World War II* (London: HarperPress, 2007); Beryl E. Escott, *Our Wartime Days: The WAAF in World War II* (Stroud, UK: Sutton Publishing, 2009); Olga Gruhzit-Hoyt, *They Also Served: American Women in World War II*

(Secaucus, NJ: Birch Lane Press, 1995); Jeanne Holm and Judith Bellafaire, *In Defense of a Nation: Servicewomen in World War II* (Washington, DC: Military Women's Press, 1998); Brenda L. Moore, *To Serve My Country, to Serve My Race: The Story of the Only African American WACs Stationed Overseas during World War II* (New York: New York University Press, 1996); Ann Howard, *You'll Be Sorry! How World War II Changed Women's Lives,* rev. ed. (Newport, New South Wales: Big Sky, 2016); and Jim Sullivan, *Doing Our Bit: New Zealand Women Tell Their Stories of World War Two* (Auckland, NZ: HarperCollins, 2002).

24 J.L. Granatstein and J.M. Hitsman, *Broken Promises: A History of Conscription in Canada* (Toronto: Oxford University Press, 1977), 144, 190, 133, emphasis added.

25 Peter Neary, "The History of Newfoundland and Labrador during the Second World War," Dispatches: Backgrounders in Canadian Military History, Canadian War Museum, https://www.warmuseum.ca/learn/dispatches/the-history-of-newfoundland-and-labrador-during-the-second-world-war/#tabs.

26 Lisa Banister, ed., *Equal to the Challenge: An Anthology of Women's Experiences during World War II* (Ottawa: Department of National Defence, 2001), xiii–xiv; Pierson, *"They're Still Women,"* 95; Bruce, *Back the Attack!* 38, 75.

27 Banister, *Equal to the Challenge,* xv–xvi; Pierson, *"They're Still Women,"* 95; Bruce, *Back the Attack!* 94.

28 See, for instance, Sarah Glassford, *Mobilizing Mercy: A History of the Canadian Red Cross* (Montreal and Kingston: McGill-Queen's University Press, 2017), Chapter 5; *Imperial Order Daughters of the Empire: Golden Jubilee, 1900–1950* (Toronto: Imperial Order Daughters of the Empire, 1950), 65–90; Ian Mosby, *Food Will Win the War: The Politics, Culture, and Science of Food on Canada's Home Front* (Vancouver: UBC Press, 2014), Chapters 2–4; Linda McGuire Ambrose, *For Home and Country: The Centennial History of the Women's Institutes in Ontario* (Guelph: Federated Women's Institutes of Ontario, 1996), Chapter 6; and Jennifer Flight, "'We Are All in the Front Line This Time': The Patriotic Association of the Women of Newfoundland during the Second World War" (Master's research report, Memorial University of Newfoundland, 2007).

29 "Women's Patriotic Association," *Newfoundland Quarterly* 39, 2 (1939): 17–19. During a tour in early October 1939, Lady Walwyn organized WPA branches at Corner Brook, Humbermouth, Curling, Deer Lake, Grand Falls, Bishop's Falls, Badger, Botwood, and Buchans. "North East West South," *Twillingate Sun,* 21 October 1939, 4.

30 Cardoulis, *A Friendly Invasion II,* 119–22.

31 Keshen, *Saints, Sinners, and Soldiers,* 146.

32 Mosby, *Food Will Win the War,* 98–99.

33 Neary, "The History of Newfoundland and Labrador."

34 Comacchio, *The Dominion of Youth,* 37, 129–30; Katrina Srigley, "Clothing Stories: Consumption, Identity, and Desire in Depression-Era Toronto," *Journal of Women's History* 19, 1 (2007): 82–104; Linda Kealey, "Outport 'Girls in Service': Newfoundland in the 1920s and 1930s," *Acadiensis* 43, 2 (2014): 79–98.

35 See, for instance, Sarah Glassford, "Practical Patriotism: How the Canadian Junior Red Cross and Its Child Members Met the Challenge of the Second World War," *Journal of the History of Childhood and Youth* 7, 2 (2014): 219–42; Christine Hamelin, "A Sense of Purpose: Ottawa Students and the Second World War," *Canadian Military History* 6, 1 (1997): 34–41; Keshen, *Saints, Sinners, and Soldiers,* 202–4; Tamara Myers and Mary Anne Poutanen, "Cadets, Curfews, and Compulsory Schooling: Mobilizing Anglophone Children in WWII Montreal," *Histoire sociale/Social History* 38, 76 (2005): 367–98; and Mary Elizabeth Nowlan, "Junior Red Cross Knitting in Winnipeg School Division No. 1 during and Immediately after World War II (1939–1946)" (Master's thesis, University of Manitoba, 1996).

36 Comacchio, *The Dominion of Youth,* 156.
37 Keshen, *Saints, Sinners, and Soldiers,* 7; see also Myers and Poutanen, "Cadets, Curfews, and Compulsory Schooling."
38 Denyse Baillargeon, *A Brief History of Women in Quebec* (Waterloo: Wilfrid Laurier University Press, 2014), 5.
39 Joy Kogawa, *Obasan* (Markham, ON: Penguin Books, 1985); Joy Kogawa, *Itsuka* (Toronto: Penguin Books, 1993); Pamela Sugiman, "'A Million Hearts from Here': Japanese Canadian Mothers and Daughters and the Lessons of War," *Journal of American Ethnic History* 26, 4 (2007): 50–68; Pamela Sugiman, "'Days You Remember': Japanese Canadian Women and the Violence of Internment," in *Not Born a Refugee Woman: Contesting Identities, Rethinking Practices,* ed. Maroussia Hajdukowski, Nazilla Khanlou, and Helene Moussa (New York: Berghahn Books, 2008), 113–34; Pamela Sugiman, "'Life Is Sweet': Vulnerability and Composure in the Wartime Narratives of Japanese-Canadians," *Journal of Canadian Studies* 43, 1 (2009): 186–219; Pamela Sugiman, "'These Feelings That Fill My Heart': Japanese Canadian Women's Memories of Internment," *Oral History* 34, 2 (2006): 69–84.
40 Much of the following historiographical discussion is inspired and informed by the Second World War sections in Brookfield and Glassford, "Home Fronts and Frontlines."
41 Pierson, *"They're Still Women,"* 215.
42 Ibid., 9–11.
43 Tina Davidson, "'A Woman's Right to Charm and Beauty': Maintaining the Feminine Ideal in the Canadian Women's Army Corps," *Atlantis* 26, 1 (2001): 45–54; Helen Smith and Pamela Wakewich, "'Beauty and the Helldivers': Representing Women's Work and Identities in a Warplant Newspaper," *Labour/Le travail* 44 (Fall 1999): 71–107; Helen Smith and Pamela Wakewich, "Regulating Body Boundaries and Health during the Second World War: Nationalist Discourse, Media Representations, and the Experiences of Canadian Women War Workers," *Gender and History* 24, 1 (2012): 56–73; Jennifer A. Stephen, "Balancing Equality for the Post-War Woman: Demobilising Canada's Women Workers after World War Two," *Atlantis* 32, 1 (2007): 122–32; Jennifer A. Stephen, *Pick One Intelligent Girl: Employability, Domesticity, and the Gendering of Canada's Welfare State, 1939–1947* (Toronto: University of Toronto Press, 2007).
44 Dionne Brand, "'We Weren't Allowed to Go into Factory Work until Hitler Started the War': The 1920s to the 1940s," in *We're Rooted Here and They Can't Pull Us Up: Essays in African Canadian Women's History,* ed. Peggy Bristow et al. (Toronto: University of Toronto Press, 1994), 171–91. For Japanese Canadians, see, for example, Sugiman, "'A Million Hearts from Here'"; Sugiman, "'Days You Remember'"; and Sugiman, "'Life Is Sweet.'"
45 Toman, *An Officer and a Lady,* 12.
46 Keshen, *Saints, Sinners, and Soldiers,* 145–46.
47 Brookfield and Glassford, "Home Fronts and Frontlines," 153.
48 Bruce, *Back the Attack!* vii, ix; Ruth Roach Pearson [sic], "Canadian War Museum, 'Women and War,'" *Material Culture Review* 22 (Fall 1985): 2, 19, https://journals.lib.unb.ca/index.php/MCR/article/view/17255/22740.
49 Brett Bundale, "Halifax Unveils Monument to Female Second World War Volunteers," *Toronto Globe and Mail,* 16 November 2017, https://www.theglobeandmail.com/news/national/halifax-unveils-monument-to-female-second-world-war-volunteers/article36999275/.
50 "World War Women," Canadian War Museum, https://www.warmuseum.ca/event/world-war-women-2/.

51 Kelly Saxberg, dir., *Rosies of the North* (Montreal: National Film Board of Canada, 1999); Michael MacLennan and Adrienne Mitchell, *Bomb Girls* (Toronto: Global Television and Shaw Media, 2012–13). A two-hour TV movie, *Bomb Girls: Facing the Enemy* (Toronto: Global Television and Shaw Media, 2014) finished the series.

52 Bruce, *Back the Attack!* ix.

53 For the Canadian Red Cross Corps, see Frances Martin Day, Phyllis Spence, and Barbara Ladouceur, eds., *Women Overseas: Memoirs of the Canadian Red Cross Corps* (Vancouver: Ronsdale Press, 1998); and Lois MacDonald Cooper, *Wartime Letters Home* (Ottawa: Borealis Press, 2005). During the 1990s, the corps enshrined its members' privately collected archive in the Canadian Red Cross national office's library and archive for long-term safekeeping. It also donated corps uniforms to several Canadian museums. An earlier effort was Miriam C. Mitchell and Florence C. Deacon, comps., *641: A Story of the Canadian Red Cross Corps, Overseas* (St. Catharines, ON: Canadian Red Cross Corps, 1978).

54 Winston Churchill, "War of the Unknown Warriors," BBC Radio broadcast, London, 14 July 1940, transcribed by the International Churchill Society, https://winstonchurchill.org/resources/speeches/1940-the-finest-hour/war-of-the-unknown-warriors/.

Part 1
Women, Children, and the War

For my part, all I knew was that something was wrong and dangerous in the world. It had something to do with airplanes.

– Joy Kogawa, interned Japanese Canadian, age six in 1941[1]

Age is a potent factor in determining the parameters of historical experience. Not only does it constrain or enable a person's participation in certain activities, but it also influences the frameworks in which those experiences take place and the contextual information and emotional maturity available to help interpret them. A Victory Loan appeal or the departure of a family member for overseas service, for instance, would hold different emotional and practical implications for a six-year-old, a sixteen-year-old, a thirty-six-year-old, and a sixty-year-old. However, war can affect communities in ways that defy age, creating shared intergenerational experiences. Future novelist Joy Kogawa was too young to comprehend the full meaning of Canada's declaration of war against Japan in December 1940, but she would soon find herself interned alongside her parents, her brother, and other members of British Columbia's Japanese Canadian population. Her youth and status as a British subject born in Canada were no shield against racism and wartime hysteria. Children of German and Italian ancestry, as well as those from pacifist families, faced less dramatic but equally undeserved harassment thanks to adult actions and the accident of their birth.

Gender both did and did not shape the wartime lives of young people in Canada and Newfoundland. In Junior Red Cross branches, for instance, boys and girls jointly collected scrap metal and planned fundraising concerts, but the girls knitted quilt squares for bombed-out British children, whereas the boys fashioned wooden arm splints for the Canadian Army Medical Corps.[2] Older teens, both male and (after 1941) female, might join the forces, and enthusiasm to enlist knew no gendered boundaries: both adolescent boys and girls tried to enlist underage and sometimes succeeded.[3] Yet, only the boys might face combat.

Among girls, other factors mattered, too. Urban girls might shoulder new childcare responsibilities for younger siblings as their mothers took on war-related work or might find themselves in daycare rather than at home, if they were very young. Rural girls might be required to do "outside" farm work that would normally be the preserve of their brothers, fathers, or hired men. Girls in port cities such as Halifax and St. John's were surrounded by members of the Allied navies; girls on the Prairies or in other rural areas that hosted air training bases came into contact with Allied airmen at Sunday dinners or dances.

War charities and governments considered young people fair game as a source of labour, money, and symbolic power, as they drafted appeals and crafted propaganda to mobilize the populations of Canada and Newfoundland, but again, age mattered: primary school children and adolescents brought very different levels of awareness and ability to the table.[4] Here, too, other affiliations mattered. Adult concerns over juvenile delinquency, sexual immorality, and participation in the war shaped the familial and/or community support that young people did or did not receive for their war-related activities.

In this section, Barbara Lorenzkowski offers a child's-eye view of wartime Saint John, New Brunswick, and Halifax, Nova Scotia, while Claire Halstead explores the relationships between Canadian girls and British "war guest" children. Lisa Pasolli examines the debate over wartime day nurseries, and Lisa Moore takes us into the private girls' schools of Quebec. Collectively, they enrich our understanding of the ways in which gender and age intersected with each other and with other identities to shape wartime experience. At the same time, they underscore the complex dynamic between agency and powerlessness in the children and youth of Canada and Newfoundland, and how "children" as an abstract concept could also affect the options open to adult women.

Notes

1 Joy Kogawa and Timothy Nakayama, [untitled], in *Too Young to Fight: Memories from Our Youth during World War II*, comp. Priscilla Galloway (Toronto: Stoddart, 1999), 142.

2 Sarah Glassford, "Practical Patriotism: How the Canadian Junior Red Cross and Its Child Members Met the Challenge of the Second World War," *Journal of the History of Childhood and Youth* 7, 2 (2014): 234–35.

3 Cynthia Comacchio, "'To Hold on High the Torch of Liberty': Canadian Youth and the Second World War," in *Canada and the Second World War: Essays in Honour of Terry Copp*, ed. Geoffrey Hayes, Mike Bechthold, and Matt Symes (Waterloo: Wilfrid Laurier University Press, 2012), 37.

4 For instance, Ontario's war finance committee enlisted youth as patriotic fundraisers by issuing two age-appropriate dramas – *Blue Boots* and *The War Wolf's Waterloo* – for students to perform for their parents. *Blue Boots,* for Grades 1 to 4, emphasized cheerfulness in the face of war weariness. *The War Wolf's Waterloo,* for Grades 5 to 8, used the Three Little Pigs nursery rhyme as a metaphor for the strength of a future built on a foundation of Victory Bond investments and encouraged older youth to buy bonds themselves, to help win the war. *Sixth Victory Loan – Two Plays for Schools* (Toronto: National War Finance Committee, Ontario Public Relations Section, 1945), S. Glassford personal collection.

1

The Small Spaces of Childhood

Learning How to Feel in Atlantic Canada, 1939–45

Barbara Lorenzkowski

When Britain declared war on Germany on 3 September 1939, normally restrained church congregants in Saint John greeted the news with tears. For adults, it brought back the suffering of the First World War, which was still within living memory. As Margaret Adams recalled, "All the older people were crying. I could see them all sitting there; they all had their handkerchiefs out. Mum had her handkerchief out. I was thirteen and I thought, 'This is serious, very serious.' And I didn't know what war was all about."[1] Having lived through one global conflict, adults could fathom the cost of a second. It was a frame of reference that children and youth did not yet possess. For many children in Atlantic Canada, even those in the heavily militarized port cities of Saint John, New Brunswick, and Halifax, Nova Scotia, the war would remain an abstract concept, a hum in the background, far removed from the immediacy of their daily lives. "I was so used to war," remembered Dorothy Dearborn. "It didn't mean anything to me. I was really untouched by it."[2] "I know the war was just the word 'war,'" Vera Donaldson, also from Saint John, mused. "I never really paid attention that much to the war. I knew I was safe. And I never really thought too much about it."[3] Yet, for others, the global conflict would become intimately bound together with the rhythms of their childhood.

To children, the war was at its most tangible when it entered their local life-worlds. As historian Nicholas Stargardt observes, "Children established their own chronologies of the war through key events; the moment when *their* war became real."[4] Sheltered from the European battle front by the wide expanses of the Atlantic Ocean, Canadian children did not experience the collapse of the "secure world" of childhood, unlike their counterparts in Europe – Polish children suffering under German occupation, children with disabilities starving in euthanasia facilities, Jewish children dying in the ghettos and concentration camps of Eastern Europe.[5] Spared such moments of rupture, girls in Atlantic Canada learned about the war by navigating the currents of emotional expression in their families and communities. When war refashioned the urban landscape, when parents took in boarders or befriended servicemen, when neighbourhood boys and uncles died or returned home wounded in body and spirit, or when teenaged girls danced with enlisted men, the war registered sharply on the minds of the young. Girls took their emotional cues from their families, neighbours, and peers, whose behaviour they observed with the matter-of-fact stance of the young who were still deciphering the rules and conventions of the adult world. Their knowledge about war was gleaned from the "structure of feelings" of their communities.[6]

This chapter explores the childhood memories of sixteen women who grew up in Halifax and Saint John during the war, as conveyed in a series of oral history interviews conducted in 2009 and 2010.[7] To recruit interview partners, we approached local newspapers that agreed to publish short articles on the project, including a request for interviewees. The response was immediate and generous; within ten days, around thirty people came forward in each location. "War embodies history," as the oral historian Alessandro Portelli notes. "Having been in the war is the most immediately tangible claim for having been in history."[8] Indeed, our narrators seemed emboldened by the significance attached to war tales as a recognized genre of storytelling, their childhood memories intimately entwined with the "national" story of the war. The interviews ranged between one to three hours, were evenly divided between men and women, and spoke to a broad range of social backgrounds and place-based experiences.

My concern in this study is with the emotional texture of wartime memories and the emotional geographies of childhood and youth.[9] How did girls make sense of the Second World War? How did they read the emotional states of an adult world that told of fear, conflict, joy, pain, grief, loss, and elation? Which emotional norms did adults seek to impart? How did teenagers navigate the urban environment of Atlantic Canadian port cities, where the easy interaction between young women and servicemen prompted anxious public conversations about morality, respectability, and the dangers of the streets? How, in short, did girls learn to think and feel about the war?

What historians of emotions call "emotional regimes," the cultural codes of expression created by society and government, shaped the wartime subjectivities of girls in Atlantic Canada, much as it did in Great Britain.[10] Encouraged by their teacher to describe their experiences during the heavy bombing of British cities between 1940 and 1945, schoolgirls from Hull, England, referred to their calm and collected demeanour in the face of danger, drawing on cultural notions of cheerfulness and fortitude.[11] Yet, despite the power and ubiquity of such normative emotional scripts that sought to instill feelings of patriotism in school-aged children and mobilize youngsters for the war effort, emotional norms did not necessarily translate into practice.[12] We might well think of children as a social subculture that, in the words of historian Ute Frevert, "constructed their own universe of feeling," often in accordance with, sometimes in defiance of, the adult world.[13] Whether or not their war became real depended on the social and cultural worlds in which they were embedded.

This study conceives of knowledge as the product of social interactions and seeks to render legible a history written in invisible ink – of ephemeral emotions, fleeting gestures, telling silences, and moments of heightened feeling. I am interested in the ways children made sense of the war by registering the nuances of emotional expression in their families and social networks, engaging in emotional practices, and learning about emotional norms. Though mindful that the emotions evoked by narrators are refracted in the mirror of memory, I seek to explore the ways that girls in Atlantic Canada learned about the wartime world through affect. To this end, the scale of analysis has been recalibrated from emotional regimes, which are often associated with the nation-state, to place-based emotional practices and experiences. The conflict loomed large in children's lives if the emotional culture of the family home was aligned with the values of the wartime state and if the emotional conventions of their local street lent support to the war effort. Indeed, it was precisely because girls grew up in carefully circumscribed social worlds, where they spent long hours in the company of their mothers and families, that they learned how to read and speak the language of emotions, their sense of empathy honed in extended social interactions.

In an influential essay, historian Barbara Rosenwein questions the existence of a single set of emotional norms and rules, proposing instead the notion of "emotional communities," suggesting that individuals moved daily through multiple emotional communities, each with their distinct "systems of feelings," "affective bonds," and "modes of emotional expression."[14] Accordingly, this chapter follows my narrators through the multiple, often overlapping emotional communities of their childhood and youth – the home, the street, and the city at large. Young girls would remember the war in a series of vivid memory-sounds that captured the sound of air-raid sirens and the solemnity of radio broadcasts. Girls of middle childhood, discouraged from interacting with servicemen outside the family home, encountered sailors, soldiers, and airmen at their Sunday dinner table, young men who liked to make music, enjoy a home-cooked meal, and find a momentary reprieve from the war. As girls befriended these men and listened to the tales of the Battle of the Atlantic, they read signs of distress more astutely than their visitors might have realized. Whereas children were allowed to roam as long as they respected the rules of their parents and guardians, most girls stayed within a world that was bounded by a handful of streets encompassing their home, school, and play-spaces. Embedded in the emotional community of their local streets, they were closely attuned to the rhythms of neighbourhood life and noted any signs of emotional disturbance. Finally, this chapter traces the exploits of two teenaged girls – Margaret Adams in Saint John and Susan McNeill in Halifax – to explore the creative tensions between public concerns over the dangers of the street and young women's negotiations of public space in the wartime city.

Nodal Points of Conflict

As port cities, Halifax and Saint John had always been nodal points of trade and migration, intimately connected to the networks of the Atlantic world. In wartime, they would become nodal points of conflict. For six years, Halifax was the most important Allied naval base in North America.[15] Merchant ships crowded into the Bedford Basin, the city's natural harbour that extended deep inland, to assemble in convoys and carry goods and supplies across the North Atlantic. The orchestrated departures of large convoys occurred on average every four days.[16] Halifax was also an embarkation point for massive troop movements; half a million Canadian servicemen and -women passed through the city on their way overseas. The shipyards worked around the clock, repairing and outfitting over seven thousand vessels during the war, taxing repair facilities "far beyond their capacity," while the city gave much of its land resources over to the war effort.[17] Halifax was home to six military headquarters, including the North West Atlantic (Navy) and District No. 6 (Army), as well as a surging wartime population: its numbers increased from around 66,000 in 1939 to 95,459 in early 1944, putting immense pressure on the local infrastructure.[18] "The Halifax area is a war zone, and should be treated as such," wrote an exasperated D.B. Carwell, controller of ship repairs and salvage, to Minister of Munitions and Supply C.D. Howe in May 1943. "Good food is difficult to procure, sleeping space is not available for workers to rest, transportation facilities are inadequate, and, in the event of an air raid, panic conditions would surely follow."[19]

Situated at the mouth of the Saint John River, on the north shore of the Bay of Fundy, Saint John was an important ship repair and commercial loading port.[20] Although the harbour was ice-free, it was small and too narrow to provide much shelter for ships at anchor. The approach area to the harbour was shallow; large ships had to navigate a dredged channel. The high tides at the Bay of Fundy, which rose to twenty-five feet in the spring, further precluded the harbour's use as a convoy assembly port. Saint John's importance in the Battle of the Atlantic lay in its extensive dry-dock facilities that handled repairs of armed merchant cruisers and the smaller warships of the Royal Canadian Navy. The city also served as an important loading port for war equipment destined for Britain and Europe and as a base for large concentrations of fortress troops.[21] As skilled dockyard workers and their families flocked to Saint John, alongside family dependents of merchant mariners and young Maritime women in search of clerical and domestic work, the population increased by an estimated five thousand.[22] The wartime boom helped revive "the city's depression-ravaged economy," but crowding, as in Halifax, exacerbated the "indescribable slum conditions of long standing."[23] As an observer remarked in 1944, "There is more drunkenness, more drifting apart of families, more licence, more problems of sexual behaviour, but less malnutrition and the wretched domestic concomitants of poverty."[24]

As many interviewees lived within earshot and sightline of the water, the harbour anchored some of their most vivid wartime memories. Yet, as war remade the urban landscape, its sounds and sights also travelled to family homes across Halifax and Saint John. "We are fighting a total war," stated the Halifax director of civil defence, O.R. Crowell, as he explained the importance of readying residents for a potential air raid or German submarine attack.[25] Upon the wailing of air-raid sirens, which rang for about five minutes above the din of the city, all lights in Halifax were to be immediately extinguished or covered. Ships in the harbour and Bedford Basin were to dim their lights, servicemen to extinguish their cigarettes, cars to pull over to the curb and douse their lights, and private households to pull the heavy blackout drapes, switch off the lights, and wait by the soft glow of a candle until the steady note of the air-raid sirens sounded again for two minutes.[26] More often than not, efforts to dim the glare were honoured only in the breach. Yet, if young naval ratings and members of the forces dismissed the blackout exercises as playing at war, Halifax youngsters greeted the ringing of sirens with both apprehension and quiet fascination.

The Home

Children's lives revolved around the family home, in which parents set the emotional tone. To young girls, the sounding of air-raid sirens and the dimming of lights made the war tangible, even in the privacy of home. Mothers quickly drew the black drapes as girls ran to turn off the lights in the house and then gathered around a small light in the living room or kitchen until the all clear.[27] Men who were too old to sign up or who worked for essential services volunteered as wardens. Although they received advance notice of air-raid practices, this did not lessen their children's anxiety. "We knew that when the sirens started, it wasn't a real air raid," Jeanna Hill recalled, whose father worked as a warden. But when her sister "heard the sirens, she was terrified."[28] For June Rogers, "the worst was the air-raid sirens going off, and it was always after dark ... They're embedded in my mind, that siren going off. And you could hear it so loud." Just five years old in 1943, June Rogers feared for her father's safety during blackout exercises but still looked on in wonder when simulated air-raid attacks occurred. As formations of fighters and bombers roared over the city, and searchlights pierced the night sky, "I can remember standing out on the front step and watching them crisscrossing *all* over the sky, and they were so big and so bright, and it was just unbelievable to see."[29] The shrill sirens breached the privacy of homes, whereas the glare of searchlights provided amusement to girls "lying in bed and seeing the searchlights out the window practising catching the aircraft."[30]

The scripts for air-raid exercises were rigidly gendered. Mothers were the keepers of the home and girls their ready helpers, whereas fathers and male neighbours patrolled local streets to defend their kin from threats. It is telling what girls in Halifax and Saint John did not do during blackout exercises. Their brothers were recruited as firewatchers at the age of thirteen, issued a steel helmet and a gas mask, and told to report lighting infractions.[31] In Saint John, senior high school students were trained as night watchers, taking turns manning the Air Raid Precautions operation room from 6:00 p.m. to 9:00 a.m. Watching over the nighttime city, boys revelled in the splendour of their surroundings. The operation room was on the second floor of the Admiral Beatty Hotel, where boys enjoyed "the novelty of living in a first-class hotel room for one night" and an ample breakfast, "the best in the house," in the morning.[32] As girls voiced anxiety, boys expressed excitement. As girls were cast as observers, boys joined the civil defence effort.

Technology helped collapse time and space, as radio broadcasts carried the voice of Winston Churchill into Canadian homes, and BBC announcers opened the news with the solemn declaration "This is London calling."[33] What resonates in narrators' memory is the aural texture of radio broadcasts and the emotive act of listening to the news. Many interview partners remembered the hush that descended on Halifax and Saint John homes at 6:00 p.m., when families gathered around the radio. "You would hear Big Ben," Elizabeth Beatteay recalled, "and then the voice would say, 'London calling,' and somehow, I rather well realized that that was a very serious thing."[34] As adults listened to the news in strained silence, children "had to sit down and be quiet."[35] "My grandmother had a little radio in her kitchen," Susan McNeill recalled of her extended Halifax family, "and every night ... they would announce the missing and killed in action. And *faithfully* everybody – all I remember is them *all* around the kitchen table with this radio, and we kids were *not* allowed to open our mouth until that was over." Growing up in a large, protective family, she noted the deep concern of her grandmother but could not envisage any harm befalling her beloved uncles. "I never thought I'd lose anybody in it," she stated.[36]

Other girls listened uneasily to BBC evening broadcasts that incorporated sound bites into their programming. "You would hear Hitler," Nancy Prowse recalled, "and we'd be sitting around listening." The rhythmic thudding of military boots on pavement made her imagine the advance of the German army. "I used to have nightmares," she confided.[37] "During the war fear was judged to be more normal, though no less undesirable," historians Peter Stearns and Timothy Haggerty observe in their study on expert advice on childhood fears. "Psychiatrists urged wartime parents to be alert for children's anxieties and to present a calm exterior, lest they do permanent damage to their child's character."[38] But fear was not so easily contained. In Halifax, Beatrice Risser had a similar visceral reaction. "I remember my father listening to the radio – six o'clock, he listened to the news. And I hated that; I hated to listen to that." The voices on the radio, which told of German aggression, young men wounded, and lives lost, breached what Risser described as "this safe little world" of her childhood.[39] The radio synchronized family time and historical time by weaving distant, threatening events into the rhythms of everyday life, creating a troubling dissonance that young Beatrice Risser passionately resented.

If war easily crossed the threshold of private homes in the ringing of air-raid sirens and the sonorous announcements of BBC broadcasters, families carefully monitored and mediated their daughters' interaction with sailors, soldiers, and airmen. "We weren't really encouraged to speak to servicemen unless it was in our home," Barbara Whyte explained. "But the ordinary servicemen out and about on the streets, we weren't encouraged to speak to them, because you never knew. My father was so protective of us."[40] It was in the home, under the watchful eyes of their parents, that girls encountered enlisted men, whose easy conversation and playful banter belied the emotional and physical strain of the war.[41] In Halifax, Barbara Whyte's family offered room and board to a sailor who was prey to violent seasickness. Working on a corvette, an anti-submarine warship that flanked convoys on their North Atlantic runs, he faced the gales and vicious waves of the Atlantic Ocean. Fast and nimble, the sixty-metre vessels had never been intended for Atlantic crossings but were comparatively cheap to manufacture and would become the backbone of the Canadian navy.[42] Thinking of the boarder at the family dinner table, Barbara Whyte remembered,

> That poor man, he was so seasick on these corvettes that by the time the ship was out at sea for a few weeks and then came back into port ... you could see the weight he'd lost. He was just so sick! And for whatever length of time he was in port, my mother would try and feed him, and get some weight back on him before he had to go back out to sea. But as a kid, I can remember how skinny he was when he came in.[43]

Families fed more than their own boarders. Living for weeks in tight quarters at sea, naval ratings gladly accepted invitations to Sunday dinners when they were in port. In Saint John, Beryl Biefer's family hosted "any number of people, from captains of one ship down to the lowest rating ... There was quite a big dry dock here in Saint John at that time, and some of the ships were in dry dock for quite a little while, and then you got to know them quite well." In late May 1941, a group of young men who worked as stewards on converted ocean liners joined the Biefer family after church. Engaged in animated conversation, no one paid attention to the radio broadcast, save for twelve-year-old Beryl and a dinner guest: "And the news suddenly came ... of the sinking of the battleship *Hood*, which was a big ship. And these people were sailors on the Atlantic. [If] the *Hood* couldn't survive, they wouldn't either ... So no one else heard this, but he and I, and I just happened to notice – his face just drained of colour."[44]

Many sailors made light of the dangers they faced, particularly in the presence of children, but could not conceal the strain of repeated North Atlantic crossings or their shock upon learning about the HMS *Hood*, a battleship and convoy escort that the Canadian and British publics had perceived to be invincible. Fleeting as they were, these embodied feelings – the wariness of crossing the Atlantic and the fear engendered by likelihood of German submarine attacks – spoke to an intensity of emotional experience that registered with children. As historian Rob Boddice observes, "The history of emotions cannot be reduced to cultural constructs and textual analysis because emotional experience is always translated by and through the body."[45]

Whereas the Saint John Women's Institute warned of the moral danger posed by servicemen in port, childhood memories speak of young men who were keen to share stories of their own families back home and, for a moment, to delve into the comforting normalcy of family life.[46] Fathers befriended enlisted men in casual encounters on city streets, taking them out for weekend drives; mothers invited the young men over for Sunday dinner at the close of church services. Some visited whenever they were in port and would become lifelong friends. Girls thought of them as older brothers or mischievous young uncles, who raided the pantry, teased the children, and came bearing presents. As Elizabeth Beatteay remembered, two servicemen "used to come down to school and meet me after school, and I got escorted home, and I was so proud. They were like big brothers that I never had." Her father liked to take her to the gate at the Saint John dry docks, where he called out to the sailors coming off the ships, "'We're going out for a drive. Would you like to come and have a meal with us?' He seemed to be very good at picking up nice boys. Nice boys, we always had very nice visitors." One Sunday afternoon, Elizabeth and her father picked up a sailor, Jackie Watts, at the dry dock, who would stay in touch with the family for years afterward: "One time, their ship was in the dry dock for several weeks ... He came to stay with us, and he brought me a doll, which I called Jackie's doll, and which I was very proud of, and I had it for a long time."[47]

In Halifax, the father of Marjorie Ferguson, a streetcar driver, also brought home servicemen for a meal and a drive. "Three became members of our family," Marjorie recalled:

> They were stokers. And any time they were in port, they came home. We fed them and took them around ... I remember one special day. Mum had baked all day. My mother was a great cook. She had a week's food there, cookies, pies, commodores, cakes, and squares. They were cooling on the racks in the kitchen, and I was babysitting my sister when Doug and Johnny blew in, just back from another Murmansk run, smelled the baking and said, "We've talked about nothing else, and thought about your mother's cooking the whole time we were away. And the thought kept us going." They then proceeded to pour some milk – something else not available on the ships – and proceeded to eat their way through all the food. I didn't know if my mother would kill me or not, but she was glad they enjoyed it.

"They were like my father's brothers," Marjorie said. "Torment ya, and tease ya, and carry on. Just do the same thing a family member would do. We were always glad to see them come and always sorry to see them go."[48] The young visitors had slipped into the emotional communities of Halifax and Saint John households. As occasional visits turned into friendship, they were adopted into kinship networks. They were considered family, some marrying local girls, others staying in touch by writing regularly or coming to visit later in life, now men in their fifties, with spouses and children of their own.[49]

Such childhood recollections afford not only intimate glances into the dynamics of family life, but also bring to the fore gendered ways of remembering and storytelling. Women's memories evoke the webs of relationships in which narrators were embedded. They are attuned to the rhythms of domestic life, to kinship networks and emotional ties, and they feature a large cast of characters: parents and grandparents; siblings and friends; aunts, uncles, and cousins; neighbours, boarders, and visitors. The sensibility of women's stories is communal, not individualistic, reflecting a narrative stance that in itself is socially conditioned.[50] For young children, and young girls in particular, the story of the war could be told only as a family story.

The Street

For children in wartime Atlantic Canada, the local street was "an open book, superbly illustrated, thoroughly familiar, yet inexhaustible," to borrow Bernard Rudofsky's evocative phrase.[51] Girls knew the small spaces of their childhood intimately. As they spent hours on the street, turned alleys and sidewalks into

Figure 1.1

During the war, Marjorie Ferguson's father (far right) befriended servicemen and invited them over for home-cooked meals and drives in the country. For teenaged Marjorie (second from left), the young men became like uncles. | Courtesy of the Family Album of Marjorie Ferguson.

play-spaces, or ran errands for their mothers, their interactions with the neighbourhood were "more intimate, fluid and intense" than those of most adults, as the human geographer Robin Moore observes of late-twentieth-century children.[52] To listen to the "spatial stories" of my narrators is to be reminded of the ease with which the rhythms of the city intersected with that of the home.[53] The streets in their immediate neighbourhoods represented an extension of the family home, a space deeply felt and known and peopled with familiar faces.

Growing up close to the waterfront, just a few blocks north of the imposing Royal Canadian Naval Base Stadacona, girls in the North End of Halifax fell asleep to the sounds of riveting guns in the nearby shipyards and were lured out by the tunes of navy bands that turned the streets into parade squares. "They would march all over the streets, and the kids would all follow!" Marjorie Ferguson smiled. Her childhood world was intimate in scale. Each morning, she met up with her friends on the way to school in the fluid grouping that saw children walking from Fuller Terrace to nearby Bloomfield elementary school, their laughter, teasing, talking, or companionable silence a counterpoint to regimented classroom routines. Four times a day, they crossed the familiar streets – home for lunch and back to school again. "*Every house* from your house to school, everybody knew you and you knew them," Marjorie recalled. She played in the alleys near her home, started working in a neighbourhood store at age eleven, barely tall enough to read the scale on the counter, and watched the wartime transformation of her neighbourhood through the prism of familial relationships. "My three uncles and my grandfather all worked at the shipyard. And they worked; that shipyard worked twenty-four hours a day," she remembered. "And the women were the glue that kept everything going." They comforted distraught family members and neighbours, whose boys they had watched growing up on the local streets. "On my block, twenty-seven boys went to war. Only one boy didn't return," said Marjorie. "He died at Dieppe. And we were all sad. I remember when a mother received a letter, we kids would run, carry the news to the other mothers."[54] As walkers in the city, girls possessed a keen ear for any dissonant notes that told of emotional distress.

Each neighbourhood had a rhythm of its own that helped children navigate the social world of the city. In the North End, the arrival of bike messengers sent ripples of anxiety through the streets. Carrying a black-edged telegram, "a boy on a bike would pedal that bike up your street, and you always hoped he wouldn't stop at your door ... They all just stood where they were, waiting for it to go by, and *hoping* it wouldn't be at their house," Susan McNeill said. One day, when a messenger stopped at her grandmother's home, they learned that Billy, one of twelve children in the close-knit family, had been killed on D-Day. Only a few years earlier, he had bid his niece a lighthearted goodbye at Pier 21, promising to capture Hitler for her. "And he's the one that didn't come back," she added. "That's how you learned. That's how you learned. That's how you learned. Just this little boy." Across a temporal divide of six decades, the cadences of grief echo the pain that swept through the family.[55]

The war blurred the boundary between private and public spaces as communities of dockyard workers and their families sprang up in Halifax. The family of Beatrice Risser moved to Chester Avenue in May 1942, living in one of thousands of small bungalows that the federal government built for civilian employees in the Halifax area: "Just a short street it was, but we knew everybody on the block."[56] Thirteen-year-old Beatrice quickly became acquainted with the other families, who had traded their rural or small-town homes in Nova Scotia, New Brunswick, and Newfoundland for well-paying jobs at the dockyards. The easy back-and-forth between neighbours' homes helped create bonds of community, as did a shared love for music. "We *always* had a party on the weekend," Beatrice recalled, with furniture being cleared to the back of the room and guests taking out their accordion, guitar, and mouth organ or sitting down at the piano:

> These little houses, but everybody was dancing and having a good time. And you'd have lots of food, and people were on the stairs and everywhere. Packed, you know. And it was grown-ups and children; everybody was together ... Our house was like Grand Central Station ... because there was always people coming and going, playing cards, and friends dropping by.

The six-room house brimmed with the voices of guests, friends, and family members, with Beatrice's mother, "a little short stubby woman," twirling on the makeshift dance floor alongside her guests. "She *loved* to dance. She loved parties. She loved people. She loved card games." The free-and-easy weekend nights quickly shifted to the more circumscribed workaday world, especially for girls. Come Monday, Beatrice's mother assumed her weekly round of household chores once more, washing and ironing, cooking and cleaning, knitting, and shopping for groceries. As the oldest daughter, Beatrice had to help: clean the house, scrub the floors, and mind her little sisters. Whereas her brothers explored the neighbourhood on their bicycles, she was given a watch. "I resented that," she stated. "My brothers had bicycles, and I wasn't allowed to have one, because I was a girl ... I got a watch, meaning to say, 'You have to be here on time.'"[57] The boys were allowed to roam, but the girls were tethered to the home by household chores and babysitting duties.

Their movements in the city more tightly circumscribed than those of their brothers, girls of middle childhood encountered the war in their immediate neighbourhoods. It was in the "emotional communities" of the streets – be it a residential street, a working-class neighbourhood, or a housing subdivision – that they witnessed the war, heard the rhetoric of sacrifice, and had their first brush with grief. As their life-worlds revolved around the war effort, it is little wonder that Marjorie Ferguson, Beatrice Risser, and Susan McNeill remembered these years as a time of emotional intensity. Their male kinfolk and neighbours worked on the dockyards or enlisted in the services, as did close to 47 percent of men and women between the ages of eighteen and thirty-five in Nova Scotia and New Brunswick.[58] Meanwhile, their mothers and grandmothers were knitting together the bonds of community through the endlessly repeated acts of women's unpaid labour: cooking, childbirth and child rearing, volunteer work, and the emotional labour of offering comfort to bereaved family members, friends, and neighbours. To bear witness to their communities' investment in the war effort and observe the devastating cost of war constituted both an emotional formation and a source of knowledge about the meaning of war.

The City

The extent to which teenaged girls engaged with the wartime city depended on a range of factors. As historian Penny Summerfield holds in her oral history of British women during the Second World War, stories of wartime lives "fitted snugly" into the context of "familial relationships." Daughters who grew up in close-knit families that embraced the war effort and had a strong sense of agency and purpose describe the period as emotionally rich and exhilarating. Their values were aligned with those of the wartime state, while the city provided opportunities for both work and leisure.[59] Two narrators, Margaret Adams from Saint John and Susan McNeill from Halifax, shared vivid stories of coming of age in a city at war. Born two years apart, in 1926 and 1928, they were old enough to participate in civil defence efforts, to begin working, and to socialize with young servicemen, who were barely older than they. Both described their younger selves as outgoing and gregarious, skilled in navigating their large social networks, and both recalled larger-than-life maternal figures, a mother and grandmother, respectively, who kept their families together and dispensed emotional support and guidance. The strictures of their families sat easily on the two young women, who felt no need to contest family edicts or curfews. Their families allowed for adolescent agency, and their rules, in any case, seemed sensible enough. Neither Margaret nor Susan had to shoulder the burdens of babysitting and heavy housework, which were so often assigned to the eldest daughters of working-class families. Though Margaret was responsible for some household chores, she always had time to go to the beach, play with friends, or roam the countryside. It fell to her five older siblings to assist their mother with the family laundry business and mind the little ones. Susan McNeill lived with her grandparents for extended periods, where she was the youngest resident and thus unencumbered by onerous duties.

Growing up in the outskirts of Saint John, on a farm in Red Head overlooking the Bay of Fundy, Margaret Adams saw merchant cruisers and warships approaching the city. She was raised in a family of nine children, five of them born in Denmark, the other four in Canada. Her father was a quiet and understated man who worked as a landscape gardener during the week and tended to the family farm on the weekends. Her mother, Nina, a charismatic and energetic woman, raised the children, cooked, knitted and sewed the family's clothes, and ran a home laundry business in a farmhouse without running water for over a decade. "She was full of fun," Margaret said. "She was a wonderful cook, and she didn't mind some of the mischief we got into. And she told us some stories, you know, crazy stories ... She was good at everything." Nina drove the car; she carved up a whole pig, wielding the butcher knife while regaling her children with stories; and she handled the family money and affairs, her husband acquiescing amiably. "Whatever you think, Nina," he would say. Living near the water, Margaret had a close-up view of the transformation of the urban landscape. The war spilled over into her home whenever the Canadian army conducted training exercises on the farm. Afterward, soldiers would warm up in the kitchen, grateful for a cup of hot tea and a slice of freshly baked bread with jam.

On the farm, Margaret's father grew currants, raspberries, and strawberries, potatoes, turnips, and carrots, as well as leeks, Brussels sprouts, kale, and cabbage, the greens popular among Scandinavian ships coming into port:

> That's how we got to know all these Scandinavian sea captains. And they came to our house during the war. They wanted to go to a home where there were some children, and so they came out and talked to us in Danish, which we understood, and then we answered in English. And they would sit around and talk to us. And they were the nicest people ... And my mother being a real good cook, she'd cook all the Scandinavian meals for them.[60]

On Sunday afternoons, five or six cars might be parked in the yard as Margaret's mother served open-faced sandwiches, jelly roll sheets, and hot milk cake to the guests. Fond of opera arias and Viennese waltzes, one Danish captain "brought his record player and his records out to our house, and he brought his violin, and he played along with the violin. And we would dance to all this music." Exiled from Denmark, which fell to the Nazis on 9 April 1940, and cut off from their families and children, the visitors longed for a chance to speak their mother tongue and find a sympathetic ear. "And so few of them," Margaret said, "ever got back to their homeland. They were lost at sea." As the children sat in the kitchen, "ears just flapping to hear all these stories," Captain Breivick from Norway, a short and plump man, wearing a bowler hat and fond of smoking cigars, told stories of chasing German U-boats in the St. Lawrence. "He said, 'Ram the bastards!' He was very expressive. And he looked just like Winston Churchill," Margaret laughed. "He rammed this U-boat and sank it." He, too, was lost at sea: "We got word that he got within sight of Ireland, and he was hit broadside with a torpedo, and they had a load of TNT. The whole ship blew up to smithereens, and they all went down. So there was another one that we lost. And it affected our whole family." One of the Danish sea captains drove to the farm after receiving a Red Cross communiqué about his son: "He came out to our house and he said, 'Oh, I received sad, sad news.' And he said, 'Through the Red Cross, they informed me that my son was captured by the Nazis because he was working with the underground in Denmark ... I can't imagine it.'" The father's grief was palpable. He, too, would die shortly afterward, his ship hit by a German submarine.

A storyteller like her mother, Margaret produced a fluid and richly textured narrative, grounded in the perspective of a teenaged girl ensconced in a large and loving family. Her three older brothers and two older sisters all enlisted in the service and left for overseas. With that, the hierarchy of relationships, which had afforded Margaret, the sixth of nine children, much time for carefree exploits, was upended. Now the oldest child in the home, she became her mother's companion and confidante. They pinned an oversized map of Europe to the kitchen wall, using it to keep track of the advances of the Allied forces and the location of family members. When Margaret turned nineteen and wanted to work, her mother asked her to reconsider: "My mother said, 'No, I wish you would stay home.' She said, 'No, I don't think I could let you go to work yet.'" When Margaret persisted in her pleading, her mother added, "Well, I want you to stay home until we get all these kids back home again." Whereas Nina relied on Margaret's help in the household, she counted on her daughter's emotional support even more. The young adult daughter, who went out for dances in the evenings and came home with stories, brought a sense of normalcy to family routines.

In discussing the social dances with soldiers stationed nearby, Margaret noted that the young women from Red Head were carefully chaperoned:

> The army would send a bus for all the girls from Red Head, and we went out there to the dances ... And we got to know all the soldiers out there, and it was a lot of fun. Our former schoolteacher would go as the chaperone, and the rules were: You were not to leave the hall. There's no smoking, and there's no drinking. You stayed in the hall, and that was it. And if you didn't, you didn't go again.

At school, girls taught each other the latest dance steps, practising their jitterbugging and jiving: "It wasn't fox trots and waltzes anymore." Soldiers from Mispec joined dances in the Red Head community hall, and the army base on nearby Partridge Island sent a boat to ferry the village's young women to dances there. "And so we went," said Margaret. "We had a great time."[61] At age fifteen, she defied the gendered prescriptions that made civil defence an exclusive male preserve by becoming an assistant to the air-raid warden. In the evenings, she cycled or walked down Red Head Road to enforce lighting regulations during blackout exercises. As an aircraft observer, she learned to identify the silhouettes of planes and to predict their flight paths. In the small community of Red Head, where most young men had already enlisted, she was one of the few young adults. She recounted her contributions to civil defence in the same matter-of-fact tone in which she described rolling bandages and knitting scarves. Taught to be self-reliant from a young age and accustomed to roaming along the brook and through the countryside, she was a child of the outdoors, her work in civil defence yet another iteration of her family's commitment to the war effort.

In Halifax, Susan McNeill grew up in a similarly close-knit family, though in a decidedly more urban setting. At the cusp of adolescence when Britain declared war on Germany in September 1939, she remembered the newspaper boy coming down north Barrington Street, shouting, "Extra! Extra! Read all about it!" But, she added, "It didn't frighten me. I just didn't understand what it all meant."[62] Her father joined the navy in 1939, whereas her mother stayed with the two children in the North End. "She was just a mother," Susan said. "She stayed home and she looked after us. When we opened the front door, the first thing we said was 'Mum,' because we *knew* she would be there." In fact, Susan's grandmother was the formative influence in her childhood and youth. Like many Newfoundland girls who left their small outport communities to enter domestic service, the grandmother had come to Halifax as a teenager, following an older sister to the city.[63] She married at the age of fifteen, her husband only two years older than she, and was at the heart of a big and "very, very close" family – twelve children, many with families of their own – that would weave in and out of the home, a modest two-storey wooden structure on Barrington Street. Having attended school only briefly, she signed banking documents with an "X" but eventually learned how to read the newspaper. What she lacked in formal education, she possessed in the wisdom of a life richly lived. "She raised all those people," Susan said. "The boys and girls, they would've done anything for her." Having a more blustery temper, her grandfather insisted on rules and decorum in the home. "He was this little guy that everybody listened to, but it was Granny who ran the show," Susan laughed. "Granny was the one." The grandmother kept a close eye on her unmarried daughters and granddaughters, monitoring their whereabouts and intervening, whenever she deemed it necessary, with the authority of a matriarch.

The wartime influx of service personnel transformed the streets of Halifax, which Susan McNeill remembered as being "chock full of sailors." The naval complement alone increased from 500 in peacetime to nearly 17,000; in all, almost 100,000 military personnel worked in Halifax by 1945.[64] Many contemporary observers believed that the young enlisted men threatened public order and propriety, commenting on the "thundering herds" of drunken sailors, soldiers, and airmen roaming the downtown core at night.[65] Families, in turn, watched over their daughters' interactions with servicemen, acted as chaperones at local dance halls, and insisted on evening curfews. Yet, once the men were drawn into familial networks, their presence rendered familiar and welcome, young women such as Susan McNeill were permitted to embrace the opportunities for dating and leisure the wartime city afforded.

Susan's family owned a summer cottage on McNabs Island in Halifax Harbour, as did her grandparents, an aunt, and close friends. Each year, between early May and mid-October, family members moved to the island for weekend visits and extended stays. Each morning, harbour craft and duty boats carried fathers, school-aged children, and adolescents to their school or jobs in the city – it was a quick thirty-minute ride up the harbour – and home again in the evening. To teenaged Susan, the routine of this daily commute seemed unremarkable, the harbour's sights and sounds so mundane that they hardly deserved mention. More meaningful was the destination: the community of "summer people" whose young folks socialized each weekend, and many an evening, with the servicemen who were stationed on the island. It was here that she watched the latest movies, hung out with "a bunch of army guys," and learned how to dance with "the boys." The convoys slipping in and out of the harbour, the gate vessels opening and closing the net, and the batteries firing their practice ranges all provided no more than a background to the whirlwind of socializing that truly mattered to the teenagers. In the most militarized city in Canada, Susan was, literally so, at home in the harbour.

To her, McNabs Island represented an enchanted land of childhood, where she dug clams, searched for birds' nests, and enjoyed the sandy beaches and clear water, as well as a place of rich social interactions. Strategically located at the entrance to the harbour, the island – five kilometres long by one-and-a-half kilometres wide – was home to several fortifications, including Fort Hugonins, a naval establishment, and Fort McNab, an army establishment. Each Saturday, the soldiers on the island would come down to the summer cottages to dance and play music in what was very much a family entertainment. "Now, my mother had sisters who could *really* dance. And I had a girlfriend, her *mum* could really dance. So that's what they did. When they danced, they danced with us and they taught us. So we learned from our family. We learned how to dance," Susan recalled. Seven girls from the island married soldiers who were stationed at Fort McNab. As Susan came of age, she began dating a Montreal sailor from Fort Hugonins. Her grandmother, always keen to know, "Well now, who's that young man?" had her daughters inquire into his family background, which quickly ended the relationship. "'You tell Susie she can't go out with him any more,'" her daughters reported back. "They had found out he was married. So everybody squealed on everybody," Susan laughed. Far from resenting her grandmother's intervention, she felt safe and protected in her close-knit social world that allowed for freedom within carefully delineated rules.

Gainful employment marked the end of her childhood. At age sixteen, she started working as a secretary for the air force, contributing half her earnings to the household. Her easy interactions with servicemen continued, many of them hardly older than she. She attended dances at the North End Canteen every Tuesday, Thursday, and Saturday, revelling in both the band music and the company. If mothers and grandmothers went to the canteen as volunteers, preparing sandwiches and coffee for the naval ratings, Susan and her girlfriend went to meet up with "cute boys." At eleven o'clock at night, the Shore Patrol drove the young women home. At other times, a serviceman might walk Susan home after a movie. "I had to be home by midnight, no matter *what,*" she recalled. The two would sit on the stoop of her grandmother's home, talking into the wee hours of the night. In Susan's recollections, the city was an exhilarating place, a site of music, dances, movies, laughter, and conversation, with only the occasional reminder of the bitterness of war. Watching a movie with a young sailor from Ottawa, she saw him jolt at each sudden noise and throw up his arms in a protective gesture. "I always remembered that," she said, the violence of the battlefield and the fear of sudden injury or death embodied in a single gesture.[66]

The language of gestures rendered legible the "intensity of emotional experience" that broke through societal conventions of emotional restraint.[67] When words failed, gestures spoke eloquently. My interview partners did not experience the "*feeling* of interminable waiting, the need for consolation, or the state of mourning" that was so familiar to women awaiting word from husbands, fiancés, or sons who were fighting overseas, which historian Michael Roper so movingly captures in his study of British soldiers during the First World War.[68] Yet, even as children and teenagers, they took note of the immense relief and elation with which women greeted the return of their loved ones. In Saint John, Cornelia MacDonald could see Union Station from her home on Paradise Row. Waiting at the train station, one of her teachers, her hair sternly gathered into a bun, suddenly abandoned all reserve. "When she saw her husband, she jumped, her arms around his shoulders, his arms around her waist," Cornelia remembered, laughing at the seeming incongruity of a teacher, the embodiment of propriety, overtaken by emotion.[69] Working at an air force office on the corner of South and Barrington Streets in Halifax, her desk beside the window, Susan McNeill witnessed the return of the troops up close: "We pulled the windows open and then waved to them as they'd go by, just truckload after truckload after truckload." Her office supervisor, a young woman of twenty-three, was engaged to an airman, with whom she had exchanged letters throughout the war. "Her desk faced the door," Susan recalled. "All of a sudden, we heard her make this sound. And we all looked up, and [she had] the funniest look on her face. It was him. He was standing in the doorway. Well, she nearly jumped over the top of the desk and ran out into the hall."[70] Within three weeks, the couple married, their wedding attended by Susan and the other three women in the office. As emotionally charged memories, written in gesture and inflection, stories about the end of the war consolidated in vivid narrative vignettes.

If tales of young love and family reunions lent themselves to storytelling, with narrative templates circulating in popular culture and public conversations, memories of loved ones returning home, hurt and damaged, proved difficult to share. They did not fit the jubilant atmosphere that accompanied the arrival of troop ships in Halifax or the happy "bedlam" that Cornelia MacDonald recalled emanating from Union Station in Saint John. Beatrice Risser's family went down to Pier 21 to meet her uncle, who had enlisted the moment he turned eighteen. "He was always happy, and he played the mouth organ, and he was always around our place," Beatrice said, but she struggled to recognize him in the worn-out man whom they greeted at the pier:

> I remember, he was *so* – it didn't look like Uncle Marvin. He looked so worn and distressed, you know? But he had been through so much and seen so much that it wasn't actually him that we saw. So that was kind of upsetting. Oh, this doesn't look like Uncle Marvin, because he was always so gay and happy. But he wasn't happy that day, because he had been through so much.[71]

The searching tone of this recollection echoes the trepidation and unease that Beatrice felt when sensing her uncle's emotional scars. In Halifax, Susan McNeill's family was similarly stricken when her uncle George returned from combat, wounded in both body and spirit. He had lost an eye, suffered from nightmares, and drank heavily for a year. Although the First World War had bequeathed Canadians a language in which to clothe their observations – "They called it shell shock back then," Susan observed – her family helplessly watched the young man's suffering. Her vivacious aunts, who had kept an eye out for their younger cousin Susan during the war, "just wished he wouldn't drink." Even Granny, the family matriarch, was at a loss, sitting at George's bedside at night and watching him trying to drown his nightmares during the day. "He had a whole rough year. He used to wake up in the night, and he would be hollering. I can remember Granny going in. And he drank; he drank for a year."[72] Families were unprepared for the shock of encountering men who had been profoundly altered by combat. Hesitantly, and with increasing worry, they tried to bridge the emotional distance. Wordless gestures – a mother guarding her son's tortured sleep – took the place of conversation, and an uneasy silence filled the house as he sank into despair before slowly reclaiming a semblance of normalcy in his life.

If neither Margaret Adams nor Susan McNeill had grasped the meaning of war on 3 September 1939, the subsequent six years offered an emotional education that was complex, difficult, and exhilarating all at once, consisting of civil defence work and social dances, late-night conversations with visiting sailors, and wartime stories, both colourful and achingly sad, told at the kitchen table. Navigating the dense social network of their families and ensconced in the company of other women – mothers, grandmothers, neighbours, and aunts – from whom they took their emotional cues, they would remember the war as a time of emotional intensity. Their youth sheltered them from the incessant worry of their elders, whose fear they registered but did not share, though they both felt the sharp pain of grief.

This chapter has employed a spatial lens in examining the childhood memories of sixteen women who grew up in Halifax and Saint John during the Second World War, showing that they encountered the war in the small spaces of their childhood. They were embedded in local life-worlds, their sense of belonging anchored in place and bound up with families and friends. The social spaces that they inhabited every day; the daily rhythms of walking and playing on neighbourhood streets; the language of feeling they encountered in gestures, facial expressions, and tone of voice possessed a deep emotional resonance. By contrast, the mobilization of children and youth for the war effort and the circulation of wartime news through children's magazines and newsreels hover at the periphery of memory. It was in practices of daily life that children made sense of the war. If we are to understand how it reverberated in the lives of Canadian girls, we must revisit their homes, walk their streets, and delve into the webs of relationships that constituted their world.

To assert that girls in Atlantic Canada learned to think and feel about the war by observing the emotional expression in their social networks seems to hearken back to an attitude of earlier centuries that cast sympathy, compassion, and empathy as female virtues. "As a general rule," writes historian Ute Frevert, "women were perceived as the sensitive sex while men owned a 'creative mind' that privileged reason and a capacity to dissect, reflect, and abstract."[73] While the dichotomy of thinking and feeling, of cognition and affect, is deeply rooted in Western culture and society – one gendered as male, the other as female – this study has sought to demonstrate how emotions were shaped by social interactions.[74] If the narrators acquired fluency in the language of feelings, noting any disturbances on their street and vividly recalling moments of emotional intensity, it was because their lifeworlds were circumscribed by parental edicts, household chores, and family responsibilities. As their lives unfolded in spaces that were narrow in range but deep in experience, they had ample opportunity to observe the emotional practices of family and friends, and to learn about emotional norms. Girls spent long hours in the school of emotion that was the home and the local street, in the process becoming attuned to the telling silence and fleeting gesture that spoke of fear, pain, elation, or grief. Theirs was a gendered experience, but it was also intertwined with the emotional culture of the home and the neighbourhood. The more closely the small spaces of childhood were aligned with the values of the wartime state, and the louder the steady beat of war that underwrote the rhythms of childhood, the deeper the traces war would leave in memory.

Notes

1 Astrid Margaret Adams, interview by Kristin Biefer, 26 August 2010, Saint John, New Brunswick.

2 Dorothy Dearborn, 20 August 2010, interview by Kristin Biefer, Saint John.

3 Vera Donaldson, interview by Kristin Biefer, 18 August 2010, Saint John. In a similar vein, another interview partner recalled that the war "didn't mean a great deal, you know ... Nothing stands out. It was just day to day." Mary Whitehill (pseud.), interview by Kristin Biefer, 27 August 2010, Saint John.

4 Nicholas Stargardt, *Witnesses of War: Children's Lives under the Nazis* (New York: Vintage Books, 2007), 12 (emphasis in original).

5 Ibid.

6 Raymond Williams, *Marxism and Literature* (Oxford: Oxford University Press, 1977), 130–32.

7 Interviews in Halifax, Dartmouth, Antigonish, and Lunenburg were conducted by the author in 2009. Interviews in Saint John were conducted in 2010 by my research assistant Kristin Biefer, who had recently completed her Master's degree in history at Concordia University. I would like to acknowledge her superb work.

8 Alessandro Portelli, *The Battle of Valle Giulia: Oral History and the Art of Dialogue* (Madison: University of Wisconsin Press, 1997), 7.

9 Stephanie Olsen, ed., *Childhood, Youth and Emotions in Modern History: National, Colonial and Global Perspectives* (New York: Palgrave Macmillan, 2015), offers an excellent introduction to the history of emotions as it concerns the "emotional formation" and emotional experiences of children and youth. See also Rob Boddice, "The Affective Turn: Historicizing the Emotions," in *Psychology and History: Interdisciplinary Explorations*, ed. Cristian Tileaga and Jovan Byford (New York: Cambridge University Press, 2014), 147–65; Susan J. Matt, "Recovering the Invisible: Methods for the Historical Study of the Emotions," in *Doing Emotions History*, ed. Susan J. Matt and Peter N. Stearns (Urbana: University of Illinois Press, 2014), 41–53; Peter Stearns, "Girls, Boys and Emotions: Redefinitions and Historical Change," *Journal of American History* 80, 1 (June 1993): 36–74; and Jan Plamper, *The History of Emotions: An Introduction*, trans. Keith Tribe (New York: Oxford University Press, 2015).

10 In a pioneering work that spans the disciplines of psychology, history, and anthropology, William Reddy develops the term "emotional regimes" to describe collective efforts to construe certain emotional codes as desirable. William Reddy, *The Navigation of Feeling: A Framework for the History of Emotions* (New York: Cambridge University Press, 2001), 47. See also the concept of "emotional standards," as developed in Peter N. Stearns and Carol Z. Stearns, "Emotionology: Clarifying the History of Emotions and Emotional Standards," *American Historical Review* 90, 4 (1985): 813–36.

11 James Greenhalgh, "'Till We Hear the Last All Clear': Gender and the Presentation of Self in Young Girls' Writing about the Bombing of Hull during the Second World War," *Gender and History* 26, 1 (April 2014): 167–83. See also Amy Helen Bell, *London Was Ours: Diaries and Memoirs of the London Blitz* (London: I.B. Tauris, 2008).

12 Studies of children's lives on the North American home front that are framed around wartime mobilization, civil defence, and the inculcation of patriotism include Lisa L. Ossian, "Fragilities and Failures, Promises and Patriotism: Elements of Second World War English and American Girlhood, 1939–1945," in *Girlhood: A Global History*, ed. Jennifer Helgren and Colleen A. Vasconcellos (New Brunswick, NJ: Rutgers University Press, 2010), 162–78; Tamara Myers and Mary Anne Poutanen, "Cadets, Curfews, and Compulsory Schooling: Mobilizing Anglophone Children in WWII Montreal," *Histoire sociale/Social History* 38, 76 (2005): 367–98; and Jeffrey A. Keshen, "The Children's War: 'Youth Run Wild,'" in Jeffrey A. Keshen, *Saints, Sinners, and Soldiers: Canada's Second World War* (Vancouver: UBC Press, 2004), 194–227. For works that foreground the lived experience of wartime, see William Tuttle Jr., *"Daddy's Gone to War": The Second World War in the Lives of America's Children* (New York: Oxford University Press, 1993); Barbara Lorenzkowski, "The Children's War," in *Occupied St. John's: A Social History of a City at War, 1939–1945*, ed. Steven High (Montreal and Kingston: McGill-Queen's University Press, 2010), 113–50; and Anna Sheftel and Stacey Zembrzycki, "'We Started Over Again, We Were Young': Postwar Social Worlds of Child Holocaust Survivors in Montreal," *Urban History Review/Revue d'Histoire Urbaine* 39, 1 (Fall 2010): 20–39.

13 Ute Frevert, *Emotions in History – Lost and Found* (Budapest: Central European University Press, 2011), 206. For an exquisite case study to this effect, see Neil Sutherland, "Children in the Culture of Childhood," in Neil Sutherland, *Growing Up: Childhood in English Canada from the Great War to the Age of Television* (Toronto: University of Toronto Press, 1997), 220–53.

14 Barbara Rosenwein, "Worrying about Emotions in History," *American Historical Review* 107, 3 (2002): 842.

15 Jay White, "Conscripted City: Halifax and the Second World War" (PhD thesis, McMaster University, 1994), provides the most comprehensive treatment of the city's

transformation during the war years. Other studies with a more popular bent include Stephen Kimber, *Sailors, Slackers and Blind Pigs: Halifax at War* (Toronto: Anchor Canada, 2002); and William D. Naftel, *Halifax at War: Searchlights, Squadrons and Submarines, 1939–1945* (Halifax: Formac, 2008).

16 Library and Archives Canada (LAC), RG 24, vol. 11696, file D.H. 1003-7-3, vol. 1, "Convoy Schedules – Monthly Schedules of Arrivals and Sailings to CAN. for RCMP from 26/3/32."

17 In the words of an American investigator, quoted in Ernest R. Forbes, "Consolidating Disparity: The Maritimes and the Industrialization of Canada during the Second World War," *Acadiensis* 15, 2 (Spring 1986): 18.

18 Ibid., 15. For detailed results of the 1944 population survey, see LAC, RG 19, vol. 9, file H-13, 1942–1944, E.L. Cousins to the Honourable C.D. Howe, Minister of Munitions and Supply, Ottawa, "Census Returns – Halifax, Dartmouth," 17 July 1944, 1.

19 LAC, RG 19, vol. 9, file H-13, 1942–1944, D.B. Carwell, Controller of Ship Repairs and Salvage, to the Honourable C.D. Howe, Minister of Munitions and Supply, Ottawa, 8 May 1943.

20 Roger Sarty and Doug Knight, *Saint John Fortifications, 1630–1956*, New Brunswick Military Heritage Series 1 (Fredericton: Goose Lane, 2011), 75 and 89.

21 Gilbert Norman Tucker, *The Naval Service of Canada – Its Official History*, vol. 2, *Activities on Shore during the Second World War* (Ottawa: King's Printer, 1952), 152–58; B.S. Kierstead, *The Economic Effects of the War on the Maritime Provinces of Canada* (Halifax, 1944), 203, typescript, Dalhousie University, Halifax, https://dalspace.library.dal.ca/handle/10222/11030. See also Marc Milner and Glenn Leonard, *New Brunswick and the Navy: Four Hundred Years*, New Brunswick Military Heritage Series 16 (Fredericton: Goose Lane and the New Brunswick Military Heritage Project, 2010), 69–70.

22 Kierstead, *The Economic Effects of the War*, 203. See also Bonnie Huskins and Michael Boudreau, "Irresponsibility, Obligation, and the 'Manly Modern': Tensions in Working-Class Masculinities in Postwar Saint John, New Brunswick," *Labour/Le travail* 78 (Fall 2016): 165–96.

23 Kierstead, *The Economic Effects of the War*, 212. According to Carmen Miller, the population of Saint John rose from 70,927 in 1941 to 78,337 in 1951. See Carmen Miller, "The 1940s: War and Rehabilitation," in *The Atlantic Provinces in Confederation*, ed. E.R. Forbes and D.A. Muise (Toronto: University of Toronto Press, 1993), 314.

24 Kierstead, *The Economic Effects of the War*, 211.

25 Halifax Regional Municipality, City of Halifax fonds, RG 25, 102 Series 36c, "Halifax (N.S.), Director of Civil Defence, 1942–1945, C. 11 Correspondence re.: Army, 1942–1945," 9 January 1943.

26 Ibid., C. 27 Misc. re. Civil Defence, 1941–42; C. 19, "Blackouts, 1942."

27 Barbara Whyte, interview by author, 3 August 2009, Halifax.

28 Jeanna Hill, interview by author, 18 August 2009, Halifax.

29 June Rogers, interview by author, 10 August 2009, Antigonish, Nova Scotia (emphasis in original).

30 Shirley Hill, interview by author, 17 August 2009, Halifax.

31 As Frederick Allen, a narrator from Halifax, recounts, "We were trained to extinguish incendiary bombs! ... You had your helmet hanging up and your gas mask and your kit hanging up in the back porch, and ... we'd be training every week." Frederick Allen, interview by author, 29 July 2009, Halifax.

32 "Saint John High Boys 'Doing Bit': Go on Night Duty at A.R.P. Operational Room," *Saint John Evening Telegram*, 25 November 1941, 9 and 14.

33 Eva McKay (pseud.), interview by Kristin Biefer, 27 August 2010, Saint John; Beryl Biefer, interview by Kristin Biefer, 31 July 2010, Saint John.

34 Elizabeth Beatteay, interview by Kristin Biefer, 12 August 2010, Saint John.
35 June Rogers, interview by author, 10 August 2009, Antigonish.
36 Susan McNeill (pseud.), interview by author, 27 July 2009, Dartmouth, Nova Scotia (emphasis in original).
37 Nancy Prowse, interview by Kristin Biefer, 12 August 2010, Saint John.
38 Peter N. Stearns and Timothy Haggerty, "The Role of Fear: Transitions in American Emotional Standards for Children, 1850–1950," *American Historical Review* 96, 1 (February 1991): 84.
39 Beatrice Risser, interview by author, 8 August 2009, Lunenburg, Nova Scotia.
40 Barbara Whyte, interview by author, 3 August 2009, Halifax.
41 Many families also agreed to take in boarders to help ease the housing shortage. According to the 1941 census, 14 percent of Halifax households kept boarders, and 17 percent had entire families boarding with them. Nova Scotia Archives, MG 23, vol. 37, no. 8, *Halifax Housing Atlas* (Ottawa, 1944), 2. See also LAC, RG 19, vol. 715, file 203-C, J.L. Ilsley to Angus L. Macdonald, Minister of National Defence for Naval Service, Ottawa, "Secret," 13 September 1943.
42 Tim Cook, *The Necessary War: Canadians Fighting the Second World War, 1939–1943*, vol. 1 (Toronto: Allen Lane, 2014).
43 Barbara Whyte, interview by author, 3 August 2009, Halifax.
44 Beryl Biefer, interview by Kristin Biefer, 31 July 2010, Saint John.
45 Boddice, "The Affective Turn," 157.
46 "Favors Enacting City Curfew Law on 3-Month Trial: Common Council; As Committee Recommends Action following Discussion at City Hall; Would Become Effective Feb. 15," *Saint John Evening Telegram*, 6 February 1943, 8.
47 Elizabeth Beatteay, interview by Kristin Biefer, 12 August 2010, Saint John.
48 Marjorie Ferguson, interview by author, 28 July 2009, Halifax.
49 Ibid.; Elizabeth Beatteay, interview by Kristin Biefer, 12 August 2010, Saint John.
50 Sutherland, *Growing Up*, 6.
51 Quoted in Colin Ward, *The Child in the City* (London: Bedford Square Press, 1990), 13.
52 Robin C. Moore, *Childhood's Domain: Play and Place in Child Development* (London: Croom Helm, 1986), 57.
53 As the French philosopher Michel de Certeau suggests, "space is a practiced place." See his essays "Walking in the City" and "Spatial Stories" in Michel de Certeau, *The Practice of Everyday Life* (London: University of California Press, 1988), 91–110 and 115–31, in particular 117. Historians have been drawn to studying what the sociologist Kim Rasmussen once called "spaces for children" – institutional settings such as schools or orphanages that were designed by authorities for children. More rarely have historians turned to "children's spaces," such as the street, which children could appropriate as social actors in their own right. For notable examples of the latter, see David Nasaw, *Children of the City at Work and at Play* (New York: Anchor Books, 1985); Anna Davin, *Growing Up Poor: Home, School and Street in London, 1870–1914* (London: Rivers Oram Press, 1996); Simon Sleight, *Young People and the Shaping of Public Space in Melbourne, 1870–1914* (Farnham, UK: Ashgate, 2013); and Pamela Riney-Kehrberg, *The Nature of Childhood: An Environmental History of Growing Up in America since 1865* (Lawrence: University of Kansas Press, 2014).
54 Marjorie Ferguson, interview by author, 28 July 2009, Halifax (emphasis in original).
55 Susan McNeill (pseud.), interview by author, 27 July 2009, Dartmouth (emphasis in original).
56 Beatrice Risser, interview by author, 8 August 2009, Lunenburg; White, "Conscripted City," 19.

57 Beatrice Risser, interview by author, 8 August 2009, Lunenburg (emphasis in original).
58 Miller, "The 1940s: War and Rehabilitation," 308–9.
59 Penny Summerfield, *Reconstructing Women's Wartime Lives: Discourse and Subjectivity in Oral Histories of the Second World War* (Manchester: Manchester University Press, 1998), 44, 52–53. Feminist scholars who have explored the intersection of culture, gender, and memory also include Carolyn Steedman, *Landscape for a Good Woman: A Story of Two Lives* (New Brunswick, NJ: Rutgers University Press, 1987); Penny Summerfield, "Culture and Composure: Creating Narratives of the Gendered Self in Oral History Interviews," *Cultural and Social History* 1, 1 (2004): 65–93; Pamela Sugiman, "Memories of Internment: Narrating Japanese Canadian Women's Life Stories," *Canadian Journal of Sociology* 29, 3 (Summer 2004): 359–88; and Pamela Sugiman, "'These Feelings That Fill My Heart': Japanese Canadian Women's Memories of Internment," *Oral History* 34, 2 (2006): 69–84.
60 Astrid Margaret Adams, interview by Kristin Biefer, 26 August 2010, Saint John.
61 Ibid.
62 Susan McNeill (pseud.), interview by author, 27 July 2009, Dartmouth.
63 Ibid. (emphasis in original). For a point of comparison, see Linda Kealey, "Outport 'Girls in Service': Newfoundland in the 1920s and 1930s," *Acadiensis* 43, 2 (2014): 79–98.
64 Susan McNeill (pseud.), interview by author, 27 July 2009, Dartmouth; White, "Conscripted City," 18; Miller, "The 1940s: War and Rehabilitation," 316.
65 Nova Scotia Archives, Accession no. 1992–304 489 A, H.B. Jefferson Journal 12 July 1942. As the censor for Atlantic Canada, H. Bruce Jefferson noted in his journal on 4 October 1942, "there have been a number of genuine cases of girls molested or chased by them [servicemen]." Similarly, Saint John expressed a flurry of public anxiety over young women laughing and bantering with servicemen on the city streets in the evenings. See "Sees Opportunity to Help Youth of City: Juvenile Delinquency Is Subject of Informative Address," *Saint John Evening Telegram,* 28 September 1942, 9 and 11; and "Favors Enacting City Curfew Law on 3-Month Trial," *Saint John Evening Telegram,* 8.
66 Susan McNeill (pseud.), interview by author, 27 July 2009, Dartmouth (emphasis in original).
67 Michael Roper, "Slipping Out of View: Subjectivity and Emotion in Gender History," *History Workshop Journal* 59 (Spring 2005): 62.
68 Ibid. (emphasis in original). See also Michael Roper, *The Secret Battle: Emotional Survival in the Great War* (Manchester: Manchester University Press, 2009).
69 Cornelia MacDonald (pseud.), interview by Kristin Biefer, 27 August 2010, Saint John.
70 Susan McNeill (pseud.), interview by author, 27 July 2009, Dartmouth.
71 Beatrice Risser, interview by author, 8 August 2009, Lunenburg (emphasis in original).
72 Susan McNeill (pseud.), interview by author, 27 July 2009, Dartmouth. See also Desmond Morton, *Winning the Second Battle: Canadian Veterans and the Return to Civilian Life, 1915–1930* (Toronto: University of Toronto Press, 1987).
73 Frevert, *Emotions in History,* 105, 149.
74 As the anthropologist Michelle Z. Rosaldo suggests, "what individuals can think and feel is overwhelmingly a product of socially organized modes of action and of talk." Quoted in Reddy, *The Navigation of Feeling,* 35, 38.

2

Fostering Friendships

Canadian Girlhood and the Evacuation of British Children to Canada

Claire L. Halstead

> *We are going to a holiday camp after this – Pam and I, called camp Occouto about 50 girls I think on a lake, and sailing, bathing, canoeing, and all that sort of thing happens. I don't know much about it but a lot of Canadian girls go and everyone enjoys themselves.*
>
> – Veronica Owen, 21 July 1940[1]

Just twenty-six days before composing this letter to her parents, fifteen-year-old Veronica Owen had boarded the *Duchess of Atholl,* waved goodbye to England, and embarked on her voyage to Canada. Veronica and twenty-seven of her classmates from Sherborne School, an independent girls' school in Dorset, were being evacuated to protect them from the dangers of the Second World War. After arriving in Montreal, they travelled to Ontario's cottage country for a period of recuperation and a brief rural respite before starting school in Toronto. For the newcomers, this time became both a crucial introduction to the differences in Canadian life and an opportunity to meet Canadian girls. Veronica's letter not only portrays her sense of unfamiliarity with the Canadian tradition of summer camp, but also reflects her trust in the judgment of her Canadian peers. Like many other evacuees, she looked to Canadian youth to help her navigate this part of her childhood.

The evacuation of British children to Canada began as a civilian protection scheme and temporary child migration program. Employing the lens of gender, this chapter explores how the experience also became an opportunity to build and strengthen transnational relationships and suggests that evacuation was rooted in the concept of friendship. This meant that hosting and befriending evacuee girls became a practical way for Canadian women and girls to contribute to the war effort. In exchange, evacuees came to serve as didactic symbols of the war. Their experiences of relocation were shaped by their interactions with Canadian children, and equally, their presence in homes, schools, and communities became a significant part of Canadian children's wartime experiences and childhoods. Although Canadian and evacuee boys probably shared many of these experiences, and there were many mixed-gender foster-sibling dynamics, friendships, and romantic relationships as well, this chapter concentrates exclusively on girls. It explores the intersection of Canadian and evacuee girlhood and argues that the unprecedented circumstances of relocation enabled girls to establish a non-biological sisterhood in foster homes and communities, and through friendships at school. In a world divided by bitter enmity, the concept and rhetoric of friendship marked Canadian and British discussions of evacuation. Yet, it was not always easy to create these friendships, as cultural tensions, personality conflicts, and severe homesickness complicated the mixing of Canadian and British children. Nonetheless, friendships did blossom, sometimes enduring long after hostilities ended.

British social memory of the war is dominated by narratives of urban children who were sent to the safety of the countryside; the experience of those who were transferred to the dominions is less often discussed.[2] The limited literature that does focus on overseas evacuation concentrates on the experiences of the children themselves, often relying solely on post-war oral accounts.[3] Yet, we cannot fully understand the subject without considering the host society and its interaction with and reception of evacuees. Overseas evacuation was an unprecedented child migration scheme. Unlike the British Home children, who were traditionally orphans or paupers brought to Canada permanently for a "better life" (although often abused and maltreated), evacuees were supposed to stay only for the duration of the war. Rather than an immigration scheme, evacuation was a "child-caring" program in which Canadians offered a haven to Britain's children. Upon arrival, they were not institutionalized or used as farm labour – unlike the Home children – but instead were publicly prized and feted as "war guests."[4] They were placed with families and integrated into society, where they interacted with Canadian children in homes, schools, churches, sports teams, and neighbourhoods. Whereas literature on Canadian children in the war has concentrated on delinquency or portrayed them as witnesses to war, friendship provides a new understanding of their wartime experience and their agency.[5]

At the outbreak of war in 1939, over a million British children were sent to the countryside, relocated from urban areas that were deemed at risk of aerial bombardment. Their plight came to the attention of Canadians who wanted to extend a hand of friendship by providing safe homes for them.[6] However, both the British and Canadian governments were hesitant to organize a large-scale evacuation plan, as the lack of any immediate bombings during what became known as the Phoney War led many children to return home. The fall of France and the Low Countries in mid 1940 subsequently reignited fears, and once again, British children were transported to "safe zones" across the country. The German advance drastically escalated the anxieties of British parents: if an invasion were next, the British Isles could no longer guarantee the safety of their children. Young people, such as Veronica Owen, whose parents could afford the £15 transport fee, began to arrive in Canada as privately sponsored evacuees in 1940. At just the right time, a Canadian grassroots movement reissued a call for Canada to create an evacuation scheme. The British government came under similar public pressure to facilitate a program that would enable children from all social classes to be sent overseas. The product was the Children's Overseas Reception Board (CORB). During the summer of 1940, Canada received nearly 4,000 British children, of which 1,532 were CORB evacuees. The number was far fewer than the 10,000 whom Canada had pledged to accept, but the program was halted in September 1940 after the ship *City of Benares* was torpedoed while carrying evacuee children. Over seventy-seven perished.[7]

From the very beginning, overseas evacuation was rooted in the concept of friendship. Both private and CORB evacuation depended upon the goodwill of individual Canadians, and some independent schools, to care for the children. The task was great: they had to clothe, feed, and house evacuees at their own expense and guide, discipline, and love them as if they were their own. Many Canadians who hosted children were inspired by personal connections, or friendships, with evacuee families. For instance, Julie Kemp travelled to Vancouver to stay with friends of her parents.[8] Some connections were forged through business and professional relationships: the children of Ford Motor Company employees went to their counterparts in Windsor, Ontario, and the University of Toronto facilitated the movement of children of faculty members at various British universities.[9] Other hosting arrangements were the result of friends and family immigrating to Canada in the preceding years. Of the 1,532 CORB children, 644 went to homes that had been "nominated" by their parents because of family and friendship connections.[10]

British parents displayed a great deal of confidence in these connections and entrusted these individuals with the care of their children, in a different country, across an ocean, for an indefinite period. For some upper-class parents, this would not have differed drastically from the tradition of sending their children to boarding school, albeit such schools were at least within Britain. For upper-class children, evacuation provided a similar familial separation, just in a wartime and different geographical context. Whereas many private evacuees came from upper- and upper-middle-class families, CORB mandated that most of its children must be from working- or middle-class homes. Though CORB rejected pauper, orphaned, and "unsuitable" children, its mandate repudiated the impression that only rich children would be saved. In practical terms, it also meant that relocation would be an unexpected separation and experience for the clear majority of its evacuees. British parents often used the concept of friendship as a way to explain the situation to their children. The father of eight-year-old Patricia Cave and six-year-old Colin Cave expressed this sentiment in his goodbye letter of July 1940: "My darling Paddy and Colin, I do hope you will have a good time on the way to Toronto and while you are there. You are going on a visit to friends and will have lots of fun, and new experiences."[11] That Paddy and Colin were actually going to stay with friends of their parents' friends was of little consequence.

When personal connections were absent, the concept of friendship was still utilized, though presented as a bond that existed across the British Empire. Children could be reassured about their "adventure" because they were destined for Canada, Britain's sovereign sister. This in turn inspired both Britons and Canadians to frame overseas evacuation as something more significant than a mere child protection scheme: it was a friendship-building program that would strengthen ties between the empire and the dominions. On 28 August 1940, the *Halifax Chronicle* outlined the overarching value of evacuation: "The children at an impressionable age would form associations and friendship which would strengthen the ties of the British commonwealth of nations. Their outlook would be broadened and those that returned would be imbued with new ideas and impressed with wider horizons. Those who remained would contribute to the prosperity and greatness [of the Commonwealth]."[12]

Similar sentiment was expressed in Britain, as the House of Commons debated the merits of overseas evacuation. Sir Albert Braithwaite, a Conservative representative for Buckrose, argued that a lasting benefit of the evacuation would be to "build up strong ties of friendship which w[ould] be invaluable in the future." Braithwaite envisioned that the children would "go out as little ambassadors from this country, promoting goodwill and fellowship and making substantial contribution to the feelings that others have for us." Upon returning home, they would "bring to our own island here a knowledge of life overseas which should be of great value in our Empire-building after the war."[13] Evacuation relied on existing ties of friendship but would equally forge new bonds that would serve the British Empire in future.

Evacuation, by virtue of being a childcare program, largely depended on women's efforts. Once the children arrived in Canada, they were conveyed to their pre-arranged foster families or, if unnominated, were matched by Canadian authorities with appropriate families.[14] The exceptions were students from independent schools, who often remained with their school groups and joined Canadian private schools. Veronica Owen and the other Sherborne girls, for instance, were welcomed by Branksome Hall in Toronto.[15] As was traditional at the time, women oversaw the day-to-day care of evacuees and managed their households and family units with the addition of these young guests. Becoming a foster mother constituted a valuable gendered contribution to the war and, like the consumption-related efforts discussed in Chapter 6 of this volume, should be seen as yet another of women's many forms of home front work.[16] Canadian women could use mothering to help win the war; knowing that their children were safe in Canada would, so the argument went, help British parents to focus on defeating the Axis powers.[17] Many foster mothers wrote to the mothers of evacuees, sharing both daily news and major milestones as a way to ensure that the latter would not miss out on their offspring's childhoods, even if separated by an ocean. This practice often led to new, deep friendships between writers and recipients.[18]

Canadian girls had a similarly important role to play in evacuation; being welcoming and friendly toward the newcomers was part of their duty and contribution to the war effort. After all, the British girls were referred to publicly as Canada's "war guests" or "guest children" – hospitable terms that implied they should be treated as guests of the imperial family, not as foreign visitors or war refugees. Doing so was supposed to benefit not only the evacuees but also Canadian children. In 1943, Dr. Karl Bernhardt, a child psychologist at the University of Toronto Institute of Child Study, presented a series of CBC broadcasts called *Youth on Parade*. In his first episode, Bernhardt used evacuees as a point of comparison, reminding listeners that they had "been bombed, wounded, killed, evacuated, bereaved and made homeless" and that Canadian children "should be aware of the war," as "they need to know what we are fighting for." Children needed to feel that they had a part to play, because doing so would provide a "valuable education" and would prepare them "for the big job the[y] will have in a few years when they shoulder the important job of reconstruction."[19] Evacuees therefore became didactic symbols of the war who would remind Canadian children of the conflict but would also teach them about Britain in order to strengthen ties across the empire. They were routinely called on to act as representatives of Britain, whether by telling stories of the bombings or singing a patriotic song, like Patricia Silver, who attended a Masonic International night with friends of her foster father to sing songs such as "There'll Always Be an England."[20] In October 1941, Jean Ingham from Sherborne wrote to her parents to tell them that she and the ninety-four other English girls at Branksome Hall had performed the play *1066 and All That* for their Canadian colleagues and friends in aid of the Red Cross Prisoners of War fund.[21]

The influx of British youth meant that, when school started in September 1940, many Canadian children noticed unfamiliar faces in their classrooms. This was the opportunity for them to make friendly overtures, as school became a space where evacuees interacted with them. The British students had to acclimatize to Canadian subjects, and Canadian girls often helped by explaining differences. Patricia Cave wrote home, "there is arithmetic and geography. In Canada geography is called natural science. Funny name."[22] Some evacuees made fast friends with Canadian girls and recorded their progress in letters to their parents. On 9 October 1940, just a month after starting school, Patricia Cave told her parents, "I have made a lot of friends. I am learning dancing."[23] Canadian girls often guided evacuee girls through this transition and did so by teaching Canadian terms and phrases. Veronica Owen explained to her parents, "Canadians call some things quite different." As examples, she listed "wireless = radio, cinema = movies, biscuits = cookies ... trams = streetcars, garden = backyard." She added that Canadian girls were "trying to teach us to say OK properly because we mustn't say it unless with the right accent as it doesn't mean much."[24]

Canadian children were keenly aware of their visitors, not only for their presence but also because newspapers were replete with stories about evacuees throughout the latter half of 1940. Nor could the evacuees hide their Britishness or their role as guests. Their clothes were an immediate identifier, their accents a secondary confirmation. Some found that they were not immune from teasing, as their dress, accents, and vocabulary were noticeably different. Even in the official climate of hospitality, the regular law of the playground could rear its head. Evacuees brought new interest and entertainment to their classrooms. Masie Goat was stopped on the street in Sackville, New Brunswick, and asked for the time, just so people could hear her accent.[25] In some instances, the evacuees' public image as war guests helped establish friendships in school. Margaret Beal's "high profile" identity generated numerous dinner invitations from schoolmates.[26] Before she had spent two months in Stratford, Ontario, Mary Hume had made many friends. Signalling their blossoming attachment, Mary's new friend Marjorie Bradley wrote in her autograph book on 11 November 1940, "Dear Mary – Remember the 'Miss' who scribbled in this." Mary's friend Audrey Goldner added, "My pen is bad, My ink is pale, My love for you will never fail, As long as a monkey has a tail. Your school chum." Mary Hume formed a particularly close friendship with Marjorie Hollenbeck. When the relationship between Mary and her great-aunt (her original host) deteriorated, Mary went to live with Marjorie and her family for the remainder of the war.[27] The move enabled Mary to leave an unhappy household but still maintain her friendship circle.

The arrival of evacuees was often mentioned in school yearbooks, with Canadian youth using the books as a creative outlet to share their perceptions of their new peers. The 1941 issue of *Techalogue*, the Saskatoon Technical High School yearbook, formally welcomed the "guest students who ha[d] come from England because of the war" and remarked that "they have joined in many activities, and are indeed a credit to our school. Tech. is richer because of their presence in our classes."[28] The 1941 *Branksome Hall Slogan* began with a note from the editors that proclaimed 1940 would be remembered as "the year we had 43 girls from Sherborne school in England who became loyal 'Branksomites' and who taught us just why Winston Churchill could say with conviction: we shall not flag nor fail." The additional forty-five English girls who subsequently arrived at the school showed that "courage and loyalty belong to all girls ... in Great Britain," the editors claimed, adding that their presence "was of such value" that every girl who attended the school that year "may consider herself fortunate indeed."[29] With a similar sentiment and reflection of new friendship, Julia Cowgill, an evacuee from St. Hilda's School, recorded her perceptions of Alma College, a girls' boarding school in St. Thomas, Ontario. Writing in the 1941 student yearbook, the *Almafilian,* she recounted that she had been "completely baffled" by the school's classrooms and timetable. Furthermore, she and the other nineteen St. Hilda's girls felt bewildered at the "first night's party." They "crowded into a little group in the corner and stared with dilated pupils at the large crowd of chattering, laughing Canadians." But now, she continued, "we no longer crowd together ... We mix with everyone else and contribute our rather generous share to the general hubub [sic]."[30]

Evacuees also had to accustom themselves to the non-academic parts of Canadian life, and here, too, they interacted and formed friendships with Canadian girls. Sheila Westcott recalled that she spent her "first winter ... learning to adapt to the life and the snow." She made friends at school and was often invited to the homes of classmates.[31] Patricia Cave used winter activities to forge friendships, and in 1941 she routinely reported to her parents that she had gone tobogganing with her friends Helen and Robin.[32] In the summer, some fortunate evacuees returned to summer camp, where they explored the unique landscape and met other Canadian girls. Extracurricular activities, such as participation in the Girl Guides, also enabled evacuees to interact with Canadians. Given that the Girl Guides was an empire-wide organization with roots in Britain, this served as a point of commonality for everyone.[33] Some activities were small-scale, such as Elizabeth Paish collecting orders for a Guides doughnut drive.[34] In other instances, they were large events, as when Elizabeth attended a 1943 Guides rally in Ottawa, where they listened to Lady Baden-Powell's speech on the wireless.[35] Sharing experiences, evacuees participated in the war effort alongside Canadian children. June Jolly, for instance, made candy to sell and filled "ditty bags" for sailors.[36] Wartime offered a space and a common interest whereby the girls could come together and fight the same fight.

This service of being a friend to evacuees was clearly visible in the neighbourhood block, a space that lay beyond adult influence. For Margaret Starr, the walk home from W.H. Ballard Public School in Hamilton, Ontario, though brief, gave her coveted extra time with Eva Stevenson, who came from Stoctford, Lancashire.[37] Sometimes, foster mothers caught glimpses of how the children were interacting, duly providing a progress report to parents in Britain. In October 1940, Patricia Silver's foster mother described Patricia's walk home from school:

> I just wish you could see the kids coming home from school. Pat is in the centre, one kid on each side of her with their arms around her, and the others in front and behind seemingly acting as a body guard, and when they have safely delivered her at the house, they just scatter and act as if they are satisfied that they have delivered her safely home.[38]

The foster mother later followed up: "I only wish it were possible for you to see the love and affection that is being bestowed on our Pat by everybody, she has made more true friends, in the few weeks she has been with us, than she would have made in 2 lifetimes in old England."[39]

Friendships and interactions between the girls were not always easy, especially as the arrival of evacuees was more of an overnight flood than a gentle trickle. There was an initial reaction, and though some Canadian girls willingly embraced the duty to be nice and hospitable, others resented the attention and glowing praise being lavished on the visitors. Markers of cultural differences sometimes prompted Canadian youth to make fun of evacuees. In some cases, the arrival of a British girl disrupted the dynamic of a family and led to jealousy. Sheila Westcott had to navigate a rocky start to her relationship with her foster sister Joan. Sheila recalled,

> I was homesick after the first novelty of being there wore off. I felt a complete outsider and my clothes, accent and manner were all wrong. Joan, I felt, did not like me and often made comments to my detriment. However at times we got on really well and sometimes stood shoulder to shoulder against those who were nasty to us and the family. Perhaps sisters behave like that and also Joan had been the only girl and baby of the family so she probably did not like and [sic] outsider coming in and having to share with me.[40]

Eventually, Joan and her friends adopted Sheila as their own and took her around Westmount, showing her schools, churches, and shops, and introducing her to the novelties of drugstores, ice cream sundaes, and milkshakes.[41] Thirteen-year-old Margaret Burt Hamilton had a similar experience in North Toronto with the Carter family, whose daughter Mary was in high school. Although Mary introduced her to skiing and skating, she recounted, "They pulled my leg a lot, as did my schoolmates who had fun imitating my broad Yorkshire accent. Bit by bit I felt more comfortable and they really were very kind to me. In a way they were overly protective of me."[42] Some friendships were not immediate, as girls took time to warm up to each other. This can be attributed to the almost flippant nature of children, as they either completely overlook differences or home in on them and use them to isolate other children. Additionally, all the usual differences and dynamics of personality would have been at play; some evacuees would be easier or more difficult to like, and some Canadians would be kinder or meaner for the same reasons.

The vast majority of female evacuees remained in Canada until the end of the war. The exception were those who returned to Britain to enlist, such as Veronica Owen and Dorothy Slee. Veronica gained her parents' permission to return from Canada in 1942 so she could join the Women's Royal Naval Service, and Dorothy enlisted in the RCAF (Women's Division).[43] Many who stayed in Canada developed close friendships with local girls. In part, these friendships were grounded in the relative stability of foster home placements: 56 percent of CORB evacuees remained in one home throughout the war.[44] This differs from domestic evacuation, in which children moved around more often, undermining their chances of settling into a home, let alone forming a friend group.

Another way for historians to access the theme of friendship is to explore the connections that evacuees maintained after returning to Britain. When Maureen Burke left London, Ontario, all of her classmates came to the train station to see her off – unlike her uncle, who was "too upset."[45] As a tribute to the bonds they had created, many Canadian girls showered their departing friends with gifts. When Sheila Westcott left Montreal in 1944, she was given a book on the St. Lawrence River that was signed by all her friends, some jewellery, clothes, makeup, and an assortment of souvenirs.[46] Also important were tokens of remembrance. Catherine Anderson received a gold Guide pin from her Girl Guide group, and her class gave her a silver bracelet with an enamel maple leaf.[47]

Mary Hume made meaningful friendships during her time in Stratford, Ontario, and the signatures in her autograph book provide a rare insight into how Canadian youth expressed their feelings when parting from evacuees. Some notes were humorously lighthearted: one person wrote, "I hope you never feel the colour of this page." The page, of course, was blue. Reflecting the importance of Mary's friendship to her Canadian peers and a fear that she might forget them, the notes emphasized her need to *remember*, both them and her time in Canada. On 26 July 1945, Mary's friend Isobel Walker wrote, "Dear Mary, In your woodbox of remembrance, Place a chip for me." Her friend Joan Bowers wrote, "Dear Mary: I write here not for beauty, I write here not for fame, I write to be remembered, and here I sign my name." Shirley Brown wrote, "Remember the good old school days When you and I were young We used to sit together And chew each others [sic] gum Yours till Iskimos [sic] wear straw hats." Shirley signed "12B," indicating the class they shared together.[48]

The departure from Canada marked the start of reintegration into British civilian life. Re-establishing themselves could be tricky for evacuees, given not only the time apart, but also changing family dynamics due to deaths, births of new siblings, and relocations due to bombings while they had been in Canada. Exacerbating this was the fact that during their four to five years away, they had grown up. Many left Britain with their hair in girlish braids but returned home sporting adult hairstyles. For some, the change was so dramatic that their parents did not initially recognize them, a shocking and painful experience, as was the case for Pam Mace.[49] Mary Hume's mother failed to recognize her because of her makeup.[50] Of course, the cessation of hostilities brought similar reunions between families and servicemen who had been changed by war, but the fact that evacuees had become young adults during their time in Canada left many parents with a lifelong sense of having missed their childhood.

The changes were more than cosmetic: evacuees, especially teenagers, returned to Britain embodying the traits of Canadian girlhood. Now they wore adult clothing, short hair, cosmetics, and even nail polish (for which one evacuee was immediately scolded by her father, who demanded she remove it at once). Such displays clashed with parents' more conservative perceptions of girlhood and were out of place in a country that was subject to more stringent rationing and deprivation than Canada. Upon their return, evacuees had to reintegrate into British society, coping with challenges that mirrored those of overseas. Their Canadian clothing, changed accents, and norms of behaviour stood out. Sheila Westcott recalled, "It was hard for me to settle and I suppose hard for my parents as I was an alien creature ... I was more outspoken, 'louder' than my family liked. I had a Canadian accent and a lot of strange ideas."[51] Ultimately, this made it difficult to rekindle or form new friendships with their British peers, despite the best efforts of their relatives. Soon after Sheila returned, her great-aunt arranged for her to have tea with her granddaughter, who was about Sheila's age, so they could make friends. But Sheila found herself bewildered as she, wearing one of her Canadian dresses and high heels, sat beside the girl in her grey school uniform: the two had "nothing in common." Sheila tried to reconnect with her two best friends, but she "could not relate to them and [they] had grown too far apart."[52] The fact that newly returned evacuees were sometimes censured as "bomb dodgers" did not help. In Canada, they had been welcomed by a newspaper and grassroots campaign, but nothing similar greeted them upon their return to Britain, where their war guest identity could be scathingly replaced with that of bomb dodger. Their attempts to reintegrate often left them with lasting struggles and even prompted many to permanently immigrate to Canada.

In this context, it is unsurprising that many evacuees held on to their Canadian friendships, as was the case for Anne Gibbon, who befriended Jacqui Krech, a native of Windsor, Ontario. Anne and Jacqui kept in touch as pen pals for many years. As is not uncommon with childhood friends, they eventually lost touch, though Jacqui still has a picture that Anne sent to her of Anne on holiday in 1947. The photo shows two girls sitting on a rugged stone wall, with the sea in the background. Jacqui so cherished it that she "cut the sides off the photo so it would fit in [her] wallet."[53] Many of these friendships lasted well into the post-war period, and some, like that between Anne Wasylyk Koivu and Pat Mortimer, who now lives in the Netherlands, still thrive today.[54] For some evacuees, such as Mary Hume, friendships even contributed to the decision to move permanently to Canada.[55]

Even when the friends lost contact over the years, evacuees' presence became a fundamental part of Canadian children's memories of both the war and their childhood. Anne Wasylyk Koivu attended Alma College during the war, and in 2017, she immediately recalled the British girls who had joined the school. According to Anne, "all of us interacted with the girls from England and treated them no different than any of the other girls. We all wore the same uniforms so the only thing different was their accents ... We competed against each other as we represented different houses at Alma."[56] Budge Wilson, who grew up in Halifax during the war, included the evacuees in her childhood memories: "My own school seemed to be full of them. They became a crucial element in my journey through and out of childhood." Budge recalled that Canadian children had a "love-hate relationship" with evacuees: their advanced skills in academics and formidable pluck made them almost "too admirable." They made Canadian children "feel like spoiled brats" and had enviable first-hand experience with the war. "But we also loved the guests and respected them," Budge continued, "we copied a number of their British expressions ... I remember looking in vain in our stores for one of those little belted coats. We listened to their stories of air raids and the whistling bombs, and felt a grudging admiration."[57] Even as the British girls worked to fit in, their Canadian counterparts were fascinated by their difference. The mixing of these children and their navigation through a wartime childhood was complex and at the end of the day, was something that each girl had to figure out for herself.

Evacuees had an impact on Canadian society that was disproportionate to their numbers. It is no exaggeration to say that Canadians who grew up during this period still recall "those British kids," who appeared on their doorsteps and in their classrooms in 1940. In part, this arose from the widespread public attention they received, but it also speaks to the interactions between the children themselves. Whether they liked it or not, Canadian children had to cope with these young guests in their homes, schools, and activities, and the evacuees had to acclimatize to a new way of life. The natural landscape and social spaces in Canada provided unique opportunities to build friendships.

Although treating evacuees hospitably was cast as a contribution to the war effort, children do not always listen to their parents and teachers, especially over the stretch of years. One should not overstate the friendships that blossomed between these girls. However, Canadian girls played a crucial role in guiding the evacuees through their time away from home and in teaching them Canadian terms and customs. They also decided how to form their perceptions of evacuees, which they would record in yearbooks and other sources for posterity. They introduced evacuees to a version of girlhood that was generally more liberal than that of Britain, especially for upper- and upper-middle-class Britons. Evacuation not only "saved" children from danger, it also gave them a set of cultural experiences that distinguished them from their British peers and made reintegration difficult. Little wonder, then, that many of the friendships forged during the war survived for years afterward and continue today. Similarly, many Canadian foster mothers also maintained contact and friendships with British mothers long after the war.

Never just a child-saving program, evacuation was rooted in the concept of friendship between individuals and nations. As CORB children were also sent to Australia, New Zealand, and South Africa, their relocation was a larger exercise in strengthening imperial friendships. When British girls began to depart from Branksome Hall, Principal Edith Read gave each one a farewell letter. She thanked the girls for helping to give the school "the most interesting four years in [its] history" and shared her opinion of the experience:

> I believe that by living and working together you from Britain and our girls of Canada gained something which is invaluable not only for ourselves but for our empire. I believe also that all those who took part in this exercise feel that they have a responsibility to play a part in some special way to help strengthen the ties which exist between Canada and Great Britain.[58]

She then suggested that the students should have a "grand reunion" in London and thanked the evacuees for their "patience with us and our strange Canadian ways ... and for the splendid contribution you made not only to our school but to Canada – we shall always be in your debt."[59] As early proponents argued, evacuation had forged new friendships between Canadian and British girls and established lasting connections across the empire. These children established powerful personal ties of affection and friendship within an empire whose economic and geopolitical bonds were on the verge of dramatically loosening in the post-war world.

Notes

1 Imperial War Museum (IWM), London, Private Papers of Miss V.M.H. Owen, Documents 134, Veronica Owen to her parents, 21 July 1940.

2 John Welshman, *Churchill's Children* (Oxford: Oxford University Press, 2010); Martin Parsons and Penny Starns, "Against Their Will," in *Children and War: A Historical Anthology*, ed. James Marten (New York: New York University Press, 2002), 266–67; Martin Parsons, *"I'll Take That One": Dispelling the Myths of Civilian Evacuation, 1939–45* (Peterborough, UK: Beckett Karlson, 1998).

3 Geoffrey Bilson, *The Guest Children: The Story of the British Child Evacuees Sent to Canada during World War II* (Saskatoon: Fifth House, 1988). Sole reliance on oral history and memoirs is problematic because it fuels an adult-retrospective view of evacuation and neglects to consider the ways in which evacuees themselves, as children, perceived their experience.

4 Claire L. Halstead, "From Lion to Leaf: The Evacuation of British Children to Canada during the Second World War" (PhD diss., University of Western Ontario, 2015), 244–302, Electronic Thesis and Dissertation Repository, 3329, https://ir.lib.uwo.ca/etd/3329.

5 For example, see Christabelle Sethna, "Wait till Your Father Gets Home: Absent Fathers, Working Mothers and Delinquent Daughters in Ontario during World War II," in *Papers in Post-Confederation Family History*, ed. Lori Chambers and Edgar Montigny (Toronto: Canadian Scholars, 1998), 19–37; Jeffrey A. Keshen, "The Children's War: 'Youth Run Wild,'" in Jeffrey A. Keshen, *Saints, Sinners, and Soldiers: Canada's Second World War* (Vancouver: UBC Press, 2004), 194–227; Cynthia Comacchio, "'To Hold on High the Torch of Liberty': Canadian Youth and the Second World War," in *Canada and the Second World War: Essays in Honour of Terry Copp*, ed. Geoffrey Hayes, Mike Bechthold, and Matt Symes (Waterloo: Wilfrid Laurier University Press, 2012), 33–65.

6 "Our Duty to British Children," *Toronto Globe and Mail*, 8 July 1939.

7 "'Like Hitler' to Torpedo Children," *Halifax Chronicle*, 2 September 1940.

8 IWM, Private Papers of Miss J.M. Kemp, Document 8139.

9 University of Toronto Archives (UOTA), University of Toronto, Women's War Service Committee B1972-0004/001 (07); Canadian Museum of Immigration at Pier 21 (CMI), Halifax, British Evacuee Child Collection, Audrey Scholes nee Buxton. Audrey Buxton went with her sister to Canada under the auspices of the English Electric Company.

10 Halstead, "From Lion to Leaf," 430.

11 IWM, Private Papers of Mrs. P. Cave, Document 10034.

12 "Value of Evacuating Children from England Is Stressed," *Halifax Chronicle*, 28 August 1940.

13 Britain, House of Commons, *Hansard*, 5th series, vol. 362, 6 June 1940.

14 Canadian child welfare and Children's Aid Society officials ensured that the process was complex and carefully executed.

15 "Adaptability and Ingenuity: 103 Years of Growth, Change and Challenge," Branksome Hall Archives, 2005 and 2016, http://www.branksome.on.ca/Alumnae/Documents/READ-Archives.pdf.

16 See Magda Fahrni, *Household Politics: Montreal Families and Postwar Reconstruction* (Toronto: University of Toronto Press, 2005); and Ruth Roach Pierson, *"They're Still Women After All": The Second World War and Canadian Womanhood* (Toronto: McClelland and Stewart, 1986).
17 "Canada Equal to the Task," *Toronto Globe and Mail,* 13 July 1939. Many parents talked about this in their letters.
18 Julie Kemp's mother and foster mother, for instance, established a deep friendship. IWM, Private Papers of Miss J.M. Kemp, Documents 8139.
19 UOTA, Karl Bernhardt fonds, MS Coll 368.
20 IWM, Private Papers of Miss P.M. Silver, Document 15995.
21 IWM, Private Papers of Miss J. Ingham, Document 15368.
22 IWM, Private Papers of Mrs. P. Cave, Document 10034.
23 Ibid.
24 IWM, Private Papers of Miss V.M.H. Owen, Document 134.
25 Canadian Museum of Immigration at Pier 21 (CMI), Halifax, British Evacuee Child Collection, Masie Lugar nee Goat and R. Stanley Goat.
26 CMI, British Evacuee Child Collection, Margaret Smolensky nee Beal.
27 Author's British child evacuee collection, "Mary Richardson nee Hume."
28 Saskatoon Technical High School, *Techalogue,* 1941, Saskatoon Public Library.
29 *The Branksome Slogan,* 1941, https://archive.org/stream/theslogan1941bran#page/18/mode/2up.
30 Elgin County Archives, Alma College fonds, *Almafilian,* 1941.
31 IWM, Private Papers of Mrs. S.H. Cooley, Document 1750.
32 IWM, Private Papers of Mrs. P. Cave, Document 10034.
33 For more on the Girl Guides, see Kristine Alexander, "The Girl Guide Movement and Imperial Internationalism during the 1920s and 1930s," *Journal of the History of Childhood and Youth* 2, 1 (Winter 2009): 37–63.
34 IWM, Private Papers of Anthony Paish, Document 3284.
35 Ibid.
36 June Jolly, "A British Child Guest Remembers," *Walkerville Times,* http://www.walkervilletimes.com/29/british-child.html.
37 Author's British child evacuee collection, "Margaret Vance."
38 IWM, Private Papers of Miss P.M. Silver, Document 15995.
39 Ibid.
40 IWM, Private Papers of Mrs. S.H. Cooley, Document 1750.
41 Ibid.
42 CMI, British Evacuee Child Collection, "Margaret Burt Hamilton."
43 IWM, Private Papers of Miss V.M.H Owen, Document 134. Author's British child evacuee database.
44 Author's British child evacuee database.
45 Author's British child evacuee collection, "Maureen Burke."
46 IWM, Private Papers of Mrs. S.H. Cooley, Document 1750.
47 Author's British child evacuee collection, "Catherine Anderson."
48 Author's British child evacuee collection, "Mary Richardson nee Hume."
49 Author's British child evacuee collection, "Pam Mace nee Bland."
50 Author's British child evacuee collection, "Mary Richardson nee Hume."
51 IWM, Private Papers of Mrs. S.H. Cooley, Document 1750.
52 Ibid.
53 Jacqui Krech, Private collection.
54 Anne Wasylyk Koivu, Private collection.

55 Author's British child evacuee collection, "Mary Richardson nee Hume."
56 Anne Wasylyk Koivu, Private collection.
57 Budge Wilson, "To Live in Halifax, Nova Scotia, Is to Be Aware of the Shadow of War – Even in Peacetime," in *Too Young to Fight: Memories from Our Youth during World War II,* comp. Priscilla Galloway (Toronto: Stoddart, 1999), 179–80.
58 IWM, Private Papers of Miss V.M.H. Owen, Document 134.
59 Ibid.

3

Casualties of War

Children, Mothers, and Wartime Day Nurseries

Lisa Pasolli

When the Dominion-Provincial Wartime Day Nurseries Agreement (WDNA) was being negotiated through the summer of 1942, federal officials consulted experts on the implementation of this unprecedented social experiment of publicly funded childcare. One natural choice was Dr. William E. Blatz, director of the University of Toronto Institute of Child Study and a renowned child psychologist who was known for his work with the Dionne quintuplets. Blatz was closely involved with the WDNA-sponsored nurseries throughout the war, especially in designing training programs for their staff. In 1946, amid the end-of-war plans to wind down the day nurseries, Blatz was asked whether he thought they should continue to operate. If they did, he said, they should be professionally staffed and focused on education and moral training rather than custodial care. As he told a crowd in Winnipeg, nursery schools should *not* "be operated for the purpose of keeping children off the streets or so that mothers may work."[1]

Is daycare intended for mothers, or is it for children? This question has been at the heart of childcare debates in Canada for as long as such services have existed, but it took on new urgency with the introduction of the WDNA, and its accompanying federal funding, in 1942. Blatz clearly thought that the interests of children should take precedence; more to the point, he felt that nursery school services were best reserved for middle-class children and should run only as a part-day supplement to parental care in the home. In this, he differed sharply from those who saw mothers' wartime wage earning as a new frontier in economic and social rights for women and who dared to suggest that working mothers were *entitled* to day nursery services. Blatz's proposals and the nascent women's rights rhetoric were both relatively new framings of daycare that gained traction because of the WDNA. Neither, however, managed to displace the much more familiar assumption that day nurseries were for poor children who risked being neglected by their pitiable working mothers. This entrenched charitable rationale was a product of the "deeply ingrained preference for 'mother care'" and the corresponding assumption that working mothers were a "social problem" who threatened to betray their children's best interests.[2] The remarkable experiment that was the WDNA did not convince Canadians and their governments that public childcare could mutually protect and advance women's *and* children's interests together, and thus it is little surprise that such programs remained difficult to justify long after the war had ended.

The WDNA was introduced in July 1942 and overseen by the National Selective Service Women's Division (NSSWD). It provided for the daytime care of the young children of women who worked in "essential" war industries. Under the WDNA, the federal government offered to share the costs, on a fifty–fifty basis, with any province that considered daycare necessary to facilitate mothers' entry into the wartime labour force. The first WDNA day nursery was established in October 1942 in Toronto; eventually, Ontario supplied funding for twenty-eight more, as well as several dozen school-based programs that provided lunchtime and after-school care.[3] Quebec, where six WDNA nurseries were founded, was the only other province to sign on to the agreement. The remaining provinces did not take advantage of the federal funds, although several, such as British Columbia and Alberta, faced pressure from social agencies that working mothers were in dire need of childcare services.[4] All told, more than 6,500 children received care in these programs between 1942 and 1946, when the WDNA was cancelled. It remains the only example in Canadian history of direct federal funding to childcare centres.

Historical analysis of the WDNA generally falls into two groups. The first sees the experiment as a women's story. This body of literature examines the WDNA for what it reveals about women's social rights in the Canadian welfare state. More specifically, it tends to perceive the cancellation of the WDNA as part of a long history of "rights withheld" from female workers.[5] Federal officials made it clear in 1945–46 that they saw mothers' employment as nothing more than a temporary wartime measure and that working motherhood was not a normal situation that merited public support.[6] As feminist scholars of social policy have argued, the withdrawal of childcare services was symptomatic of the government's refusal to see women, and especially mothers, as entitled to the rights of post-war "worker-citizenship."[7] Instead, work-based rights were reserved for male breadwinners, and women's entitlements to social services were conditional upon their roles as dependent wives and mothers, and were offered on a more tenuous and partial basis than those of male workers. In the bourgeoning welfare state, this gendered logic was reflected and reinforced not only through the absence of childcare services, but also through tax amendments that encouraged women to leave the workforce, discriminatory unemployment insurance provisions, and perhaps most clearly, family allowances, which were meant in part to nudge women back into their homes.[8] In this formula, childcare was a threat to gender norms, not a legitimate public service for women.[9]

A second body of work assesses the WDNA as part of the history of childhood, especially of early childhood education and care. In this vein, historians have given special attention to the WDNA as a watershed moment because it shifted Canadian attitudes toward services for children under six. Prior to the war, day nurseries were seen as custodial care services, run by charitable groups of reform-minded women. The WDNA presented an opportunity for those in the increasingly professionalized fields of nursery education and child development to make their mark. The role of Blatz and the University of Toronto Institute of Child Study in staff training and program development, for example, sent the message that nurseries were more than simply a stop-gap measure for desperate families. Instead, they could provide essential supports for children's emotional, psychological, physical, and educational development. They could be, in other words, a "normal support for families," including middle-class families.[10] In this scholarly framing, the WDNA was significant because it led to important developments such as the post-war kindergarten and pre-school education movement.[11]

This chapter draws on both these bodies of literature but seeks to move away from the tendency to consider the WDNA as either "for mothers" or "for children." For the simple reason that mothers were and still are primarily responsible for the care of their children, the interests of each did not exist in isolation from the other. The starting point for this chapter is that the relative importance of children's and mothers' interests, whether one set of interests should trump the other, or whether and how they could be mutually protected, was a deeply contested issue during the war. Indeed, it has been a central dilemma of social policy making in the twentieth century, a point perhaps best demonstrated by Sonya Michel in her remarkable history of American childcare policy, *Children's Interests/Mothers' Rights*.[12] The WDNA must be perceived as a key part of the long history of entanglements of mothers' and children's rights in Canada. Crucial insights about this issue have been gleaned from scholarship on early-twentieth-century mothers' allowances and pension programs in both Canada and the United States. As Linda Gordon suggests, state support for impoverished mothers "seemed a move towards inaugurating a mutual *right* between children and mothers," although these rights were based on the relatively narrow maternalist notion that "it was bad for children to lose their mothers and bad for women to lose their children."[13] But though mothers' allowances were intended to keep mothers in the home and children out of institutions, this maternalist premise was not borne out in reality. Welfare officials, worried about chronic dependency and the lack of a work ethic in poor families, subjected mothers to constant surveillance and kept allowance rates low, forcing women into marginal work and standards of morality that only curtailed their freedoms. The "perverse" result, as Gordon and others point out, was that neither mothers nor children were well served by allowances, despite the promise that both would have their rights protected.[14]

The WDNA was similarly ensnared in the debates about whose interests were really being served, a question made all the more urgent by unprecedented federal funding. Officials in Ottawa clearly viewed the WDNA solely as an emergency measure, but others who had a stake in childcare services – social agencies and private welfare organizations, women's groups, child development professionals, and others – all had their own views of what was best for children and their mothers, as well as the kinds of services that mothers and children needed and those to which they were entitled. This chapter will examine the competing beliefs about daycare during and immediately after the war and will show that discourses about what was best for children – middle-class children and especially those who were, along with their poor and marginalized working mothers, believed to need welfare intervention – shaped much of the programming and policy decisions around day nursery services. As those who are interested in recent policy developments have asserted, the continuing absence of a comprehensive childcare strategy in Canada has its roots in these mid-twentieth-century assumptions that working mothers could not be trusted to act in their children's best interests.

By the time the Second World War began, day nurseries (sometimes called crèches) had a long history in Canada. Most cities had at least one, and in nearly all cases they were operated by charitably oriented women reformers who saw their mission as "sav[ing] children from neglect caused by the mother's enforced daily absence from the home."[15] With the beginning of war, most of these nurseries faced unprecedented demand on their services. In Toronto, Hamilton, Montreal, and Oshawa, employment of all kinds quickly escalated, and for many families nurseries were the only option for safe and reliable care. The West End Crèche in Toronto, for example, reported turning away 450 "urgent requests" in 1940–41. Though part of the soaring demand could be attributed to mothers' wartime factory work, the West End Crèche clientele was greatly dominated by "young married people having one child and living in two rooms in a crowded manufacturing district on less than $22.00 a week," most of them "foreign-born" or newly immigrated to Canada.[16] After years of depression and hardship, these families were taking advantage of the new wartime employment to finally earn a decent standard of living through two incomes. For mothers, such opportunities rose from improved prospects in traditionally female jobs, most of them in the domestic field but also including shops and stores, cafes, laundries, and cleaning.[17] The operators of the West End Crèche believed that these women accepted paid employment due to financial desperation and viewed their circumstances with pity and suspicion. As the 1941 annual report explained, the purpose of the crèche was thus to prevent children from becoming "casualties in the battle of living."[18] A cross-country survey by the Canadian Welfare Council in the spring of 1942 revealed that dozens of day nurseries and welfare agencies also saw this as their essential objective: to keep children off the streets, provide them with the supervision, nutrition, and health care services they were not getting in their overcrowded homes, "Canadianize" immigrant children, and furnish them with the nurture they (supposedly) were not receiving from their overworked parents.[19]

When Order-in-Council PC 6242 established the WDNA on 20 July 1942, the landscape of day nursery services changed dramatically. Responsibility for the WDNA fell to Fraudena Eaton, the director of the NSSWD. Eaton's focus throughout the summer and fall of 1942 was registering and recruiting unmarried, childless women for war work, which often meant relocating them from the Prairies and the Maritimes to industry-heavy areas in Ontario and Quebec to prevent "employers building up huge staffs of married women with children."[20] Eventually, though, the employment of mothers became necessary. In late July and early August 1942, Eaton finalized WDNA agreements with Ontario and Quebec, the provinces that most clearly demonstrated industrial labour needs, and in October, Margaret Grier was appointed under Eaton to administer the WDNA. Both Eaton and Grier were insistent that the sole purpose of the nurseries was to mobilize vital wartime labour, *not* to serve "mothers [who] must work by reason of domestic circumstances."[21] Accordingly, the agreement included a provision, clause 11, that reserved 75 percent of WDNA-supported nurseries for mothers whose work was "essential" to the war effort, which included the obvious things, such as labour in munitions factories, as well as laundries, canneries, and garment factories fulfilling war orders.[22] The remaining 25 percent of spaces could be used by mothers doing non-essential jobs, a concession that Eaton offered only after getting pushback from overburdened nurseries and social welfare agencies.

Part of Eaton's challenge in tapping into the labour reserve of mothers was the fact that day nurseries were held in low esteem by much of the Canadian public. Long stamped with the stigma of charity, they were assumed to offer second-rate care to impoverished children.[23] They were viewed as not much more than custodial services that lacked stimulation and nurturing, and many Canadians worried that offering more of the same was a troubling prospect for a nation that needed to build up a generation of vigorous and productive post-war citizens. To assuage such concerns, Eaton and Grier launched a series of public relations campaigns meant to normalize nursery care. Happy, healthy, safe, and rosy-cheeked children were the stars of these campaigns; their worry-free mothers and the well-trained staff played supporting roles. For example,

Figure 3.1

Originally captioned "Mrs. Jack Wright reads her two sons Ralph and David a bedtime story," this photo is part of a series produced by the National Film Board. The series showed Ralph and David at their local nursery while their mother worked at a factory; this image was meant to reassure mothers that they would still have time to nurture their children. September 1943. | Library and Archives Canada, National Film Board of Canada, Photothèque, 3196969.

Mrs. Jack Wright and her two sons were featured in a photo series of September 1943 that showed the boys under the nurturing care of nursery workers and spending quality time with their mother on weekends and evenings.[24] Eaton and her colleagues also collaborated with the National Film Board to produce the documentary *Before They Are Six*.[25] In this short film, scenes of unsupervised delinquent boys fighting in the streets contrast with happy children inside the nurseries. To avoid "making casualties" of the children of war workers, the narrator explains, trained staff and public health nurses carefully oversee a day filled with crafts, playtime, healthy meals, naptime, and training in cleanliness and manners.[26]

Eaton hoped that *Before They Are Six* would enhance the WDNA program, especially in Quebec, where it was slow to get off the ground despite evidence that nurseries were badly needed.[27] In Montreal, NSSWD officials received reports that "many children of munition workers are badly cared for, left with older children or with neighbours," yet only six nurseries had been established by late 1943, and even those struggled with attendance.[28] There were several reasons for this lacklustre take-up, some of which had to do with a dearth of suitable spaces for nurseries in crowded neighbourhoods and with sectarian divisions between Protestant, Catholic, and Jewish social agencies.[29] The shortage of suitable personnel was another concern.[30] Deeply held suspicion of the very principle of day nurseries, though, was perhaps the central impediment to the success of the WDNA in Quebec. Local welfare officials reported that in factories that employed hundreds of women, offers to provide information about nursery services had generated "no response." Instead, mothers almost always indicated that they had made "satisfact[o]ry private arrangements."[31] Whether this was indeed the case or whether mothers were reluctant to admit needing help was unclear. Nevertheless, the strong current of public feeling against day nurseries was undeniable in Quebec. Reports of scandal in "faulty private nurseries" in Montreal did not help, nor did frequent statements from clergymen that nurseries posed a threat to family life.[32] The dominant attitude in Quebec was that nurseries worked against both women's and children's interests. Care from the extended family was almost always preferred to a government-sponsored day nursery – but ideally, a mother would have no need to go to work.[33]

While the program struggled in Quebec, Eaton and Grier faced a problem of another kind in Ontario – pressure to expand the number of spaces in the WDNA nurseries that were available to mothers who did "non-essential" work. By the spring of 1943, a campaign that targeted clause 11 of the WDNA was well under way, led by the Toronto Welfare Council, with support from the Toronto Board of Education and others. Campaigners insisted that the nurseries served an important social welfare function for children, regardless of the kinds of work their mothers performed.[34] This made Eaton and her colleagues uneasy; they had never intended that the nursery program would become enmeshed in child welfare and family poverty issues.[35] Nevertheless, Eaton reluctantly called a series of meetings to consider the expansion of the nurseries' mandate. The NSSWD remained firm on its 75 and 25 percent policy through 1943 but, due to public pressure and especially the insistence of social agencies, was forced to amend clause 11 in both Ontario and Quebec during the spring of 1944, opening nurseries to mothers who held a wider range of jobs. The clause 11 battle was an important symbol of the disconnect between federal officials and on-the-ground nursery and welfare services, with respect to the meaning and purpose of nurseries. This disconnect would become even more apparent as peace approached.

Whereas the welfare-based vision of day nurseries made Eaton and Labour Department officials nervous, no doubt they would have been even more unsettled by the idea that the WDNA was creating a precedent for working women's *rights* to childcare. Especially with the war's end looming, a small but determined chorus of voices started to question whether women should be expected to give up their jobs and their access to reliable, publicly funded childcare. For the most part, this kind of rhetoric came from female federal politicians on the left. The most outspoken was Unity/Labour Progressive MP Dorise Nielsen, who declared that the "emancipation of women as wage earners has come to stay" and that thanks to their wartime experiences the women of Canada resented the assumption that "the only place fit for them is in the home."[36] Grace MacInnis, Dorothy Steeves, and Laura Jamieson, all of whom were CCF members from British Columbia, expressed similar views, making the case that nurseries should be included in a package of rights for working women that encompassed equal wages and fair working conditions.[37] And, as Susan Prentice shows, communist women in Toronto (and their allies) who fought for the continuation of nurseries were offering, in "a preliminary way," a rights-based notion of childcare that broke its "long association ... with charity and the 'deserving poor.'"[38]

These kinds of discourses planted important seeds that allowed the feminist argument for daycare to flourish in the post-war years. But the working-women-centred demands for nurseries advanced by Nielsen and others were no match for the powerful, widespread view that mothers were simply temporary members of the labour force. Moreover, the administration of the WDNA reflected the assumption that working mothers could not be trusted to act in their children's best interests. As Eaton explained to a concerned women's group, local NSS offices carefully "counselled married women with children as they seek employment." She added, "unless our officer is satisfied that ... care for the children has been arranged," the mother would be persuaded to "give up the idea of employment."[39] In Ontario, the Children's Aid Society (CAS) was sometimes brought in to add another level of surveillance to mothers' decisions to take paid labour. At Algoma Steel in Sault Ste. Marie, for example, plant managers co-operated closely with the NSSWD and CAS to develop procedures for hiring mothers. "If a female applicant to the Corporation were married, all statistical information was taken either at the plant or by Selective Service," the CAS *Bulletin* explained. "She was then referred to the [Children's Aid] Society ... together with a request that an investigation be conducted and a recommendation be made to Selective Service as to the advisability of the Corporation employing the applicant." The benefits to the community of such a policy were "fewer broken homes," "less juvenile delinquency," and "less general child neglect."[40] It was certainly true, as Jeffrey Keshen argues, that "even while the war raged, it was clear that many viewed the widespread phenomenon of working mothers as too high a price to pay for victory."[41]

This inherent suspicion of working motherhood was the context in which debates about the post-war fate of the day nurseries unfolded. Eaton and her superiors in the Labour Department were clear: when hostilities ceased, the nurseries would be shut down.[42] Those who operated and supported the nurseries, however, recognized that working motherhood was not just a "fad."[43] Facing the loss of public funding, campaigns emerged to keep the nurseries open after the war. The arguments centred on the familiar rhetoric of avoiding the "hazards of unsupervised children, particularly in crowded districts."[44] In Montreal, for example, a group of mothers petitioned Ottawa for continued funding for their nursery, saying that otherwise their children would be "dans d'autres institutions ou laissés sur la rue."[45] This protest was half-hearted, though, compared to the campaign that emerged in Toronto. As Susan Prentice shows, a "broad coalition" of individuals and groups came together as the Day Nurseries and Day Care Parents' Association, launching petitions, rallies, and letter-writing campaigns to the federal and provincial governments. Prentice suggests that this coalition should be considered the first childcare movement in Canada, but there was nothing new about its strategy. The language of juvenile delinquency, Prentice argues, brought together a range of interests in the common cause of day nurseries, including the unlikely allies of right-wing women, CCF supporters, and members of the Communist Party. In the immediate post-war years, the language of delinquency gave nursery supporters a sense of "urgency and moral righteousness" that "deflected conservative criticism" about the breakdown of family life.[46] This strategy was a success, in the sense that the Ontario government passed the Day Nurseries Act in April 1946, which kept many of the province's nurseries open through a fifty–fifty cost-sharing arrangement between the provincial and municipal governments.[47]

A growing nursery school movement was also fighting for day nurseries to occupy a more permanent place on the roster of post-war social services. For a fledgling cohort of early childhood education and development professionals, the WDNA represented an opportunity to establish a more solid foothold in nursery services. Dr. William Blatz was at the centre of this education-based endeavour. As mentioned, he had been brought in during the early planning stages of the WDNA to consult on the training of nursery staff and volunteers, as well as curriculum and programming (he had also been invited to England to offer the same services to its nursery programs).[48] In 1942, the Institute of Child Study began to offer intensive training courses in "child study and nursery education" whose graduates became the major provider of WDNA nursery personnel.[49] Blatz hoped to see these professionalized education initiatives preserved after the war, and as we have seen, he sought to distance nursery education from the undesirable elements of poor working mothers. He was not alone in prioritizing children over mothers. The Canadian Welfare Council suggested that "existing circumstances present possibilities whereby day nurseries may move away from the function they have performed hitherto as largely charitable institutions toward a broader field as educational agencies with specialized services supported by public funds and supplemented by fees from parents."[50] Many who worked in the day nursery field felt that the expansion of nurseries in Britain should inspire a similar pattern in Canada. "Surely," the director of the West End Crèche urged in 1946, "it is just as important for us ... to have our future citizens develop at an early age those characteristics so urgently needed of tolerance, co-operation, responsibility and initiative. Let us also, therefore, work towards the goal of nursery school education for all."[51]

For the mothers who had used day nurseries during the war, all these reasons – social welfare, juvenile delinquency, educational benefits for children, and more – were grounds to sustain public funding in childcare services. It is perhaps not surprising that these mothers viewed their own interests and those of their children as one and the same: the economic security of a job would enable them to provide for their children, and they deserved the peace of mind of knowing that the children were well cared for during the day. Keeping the nurseries open, as one woman explained to Minister of Labour Humphrey Mitchell, "would be a very great thing to me and many more mothers."[52] Another stated that the nurseries were "simply a god send," as her husband's low earnings forced her to work "to make both ends meet." Her only other option was the undesirable one of accepting charity.[53] When mothers wrote to Mitchell, though, it was more common for them to emphasize how and why their *children* needed the nurseries, perhaps in recognition of which argument would be most persuasive. Dozens of mothers noted that their children had been kept "safe from the streets," voiced relief in not having to rely on strangers to look after them, and expressed gratitude that they had been given a head start in their educational development.[54] Jean Grant's entreaty to Mitchell was typical. A "sole support" mother of four-year-old twins, she explained that

> we live in two rooms, cook on a two-plate grill and share the bathroom in the house. If the children were home all day, we could no longer continue to live there, landlords not being partial to children. The street is also not a very safe nor satisfactory playground. If you could only see the benefit to the children – how much better their physical condition is, how much better behaved they are.

Pressing her point, she asked, "Can you think of any better memorial to the boys who died overseas than that the small children should have a chance in life – the best chance of all – to be properly fed, properly looked after free from the fear of want. It does seem that a living memorial is a thousand times better than a marble one."[55]

As a whole, then, the advocacy for day nurseries at the end of the war – from mothers, education professionals, and social welfare groups – clearly prioritized the interests of children over the working rights of women. This child-focused framework aligned with other federal government initiatives in the post-war period, most notably family allowances. As Dominique Marshall demonstrates, the family allowance program, introduced in 1944 as Canada's first universal welfare offering, was perhaps the clearest end-of-war example of a policy initiative that was packaged in the rhetoric of children's rights.[56] In many ways, this rhetoric mirrored the education- and development-based rationales for day nurseries. Indeed, the first pamphlet to advertise family allowances was titled *The Children's Charter,* and "provincial and federal politicians alike invoked the rights of youngsters to a 'minimum of welfare' and to a 'minimum of education.'"[57] However, a closer look at the administration of family allowances also reveals the perils of prioritizing children's interests over mothers' rights. Like the moralistic mothers' allowance administration from earlier in the century, which undercut women's ability to provide for their children, the parameters of family allowance eligibility could, paradoxically, subvert a family's economic security.[58] Of course, this problem was not unique to family allowances. Linda Gordon argues that the "putting-children-first strategy has yielded poor results" in the realms of custody, illegitimacy, family violence, immigration, and welfare policy. Failing to provide material support to mothers, using threats of discipline that diminished their effectiveness as parents, undercutting parents' claims to support because of children's unique deservedness – all these things, Gordon asserts, have historically made it difficult to help children.[59]

When childcare debates focus on the "interests of children," they can similarly backfire. As Prentice's study of post-war Ontario reveals, the child-focused angle can easily be co-opted by conservative interests who insist that children are best served by their own mothers in their own homes. Moreover, the maternalist influence in childcare debates can also "[subsume] women's rights to children's rights," making it difficult, as Alvin Finkel shows, "for women to proclaim a right to economic independence as citizens."[60] Childcare policy as it unfolded in Canada during the 1950s and beyond gave way to both these patterns. The childcare landscape was dominated by concern for children's welfare, education, poverty, and development, which resulted in a strained balance between targeted childcare subsidies for "needy" families and an ongoing insistence that "normal" families did not need childcare. The feminist argument for childcare – that it is an essential component of women's economic and social rights – has never been able to dislodge the power of child-centred rhetoric, and indeed childcare policy making has been "driven apart" from efforts to improve women's employment equality.[61] The consequence has been a dismal record in childcare services for both children and mothers.[62]

Many advocates insist that the creation of a national, universal, and comprehensive childcare program is the only way in which the interests, needs, and rights of both children and mothers can reliably be met. As the sole example of direct federal funding to childcare in Canadian history, the WDNA seemed to offer the possibility that mothers' rights and children's interests could be mutually fulfilled. Somewhat ironically, however, the experience of wartime women's work and this remarkable social policy experiment simply reinforced the disconnect between women's and children's rights in the Canadian state. Children remained the prevailing concern before, during, and after the Second World War, which meant that the WDNA was not built on a foundation of mothers' and children's mutual rights. Thus, it was easy to tear down the program in 1946 and replace it with targeted, partial, and limited childcare services while espousing children's right to be cared for by their own mothers. The history of the WDNA, then, is yet another example of the uneasy relationship between mothers and children in Canadian policy making, with the result that neither group has been served very effectively.

Notes

1 "Objective of Nursery Schools Explained by Dr. W.E. Blatz," *Winnipeg Free Press*, 6 April 1946, 7, quoted in Bob Hummelt, "Trouble on the Home Front: Perspectives on Working Mothers in Winnipeg, 1939–1945" (Master's thesis, University of Manitoba, 2001), 125.

2 Sonya Michel, *Children's Interests/Mothers' Rights: The Shaping of America's Child Care Policy* (New Haven: Yale University Press, 1999), 3.

3 The first Toronto WDNA nursery was an existing day nursery, whose services were expanded because of the new sources of funding. This chapter focuses solely on day

nursery programs for children under the age of six; the school-age programs deserve separate treatment.

4 Lisa Pasolli, "'I Ask You, Mr. Mitchell, Is the Emergency Over?': Debating Day Nurseries in the Second World War," *Canadian Historical Review* 96, 1 (March 2015): 21–26; Tom Langford, *Alberta's Day Care Controversy: From 1908 to 2009 and Beyond* (Edmonton: Athabasca University Press, 2011), 19–37.

5 Michel, *Children's Interests/Mothers' Rights,* 3.

6 Ruth Roach Pierson, *"They're Still Women After All": The Second World War and Canadian Womanhood* (Toronto: McClelland and Stewart, 1986), 56–60.

7 See, for example, Annis May Timpson, *Driven Apart: Women's Employment Equality and Child Care in Canadian Public Policy* (Vancouver: UBC Press, 2001), especially Chapter 2.

8 Alvin Finkel, *Social Policy and Practice in Canada: A History* (Waterloo: Wilfrid Laurier University Press, 2006), 131–32. See also James Struthers, "Family Allowances, Old Age Security, and the Construction of Entitlement in the Canadian Welfare State, 1943–1951," in *The Veterans Charter and Post-World War II Canada,* ed. Peter M. Neary and J.L. Granatstein (Montreal and Kingston: McGill-Queen's University Press, 1997), 179–204; and Nancy Christie, *Engendering the State: Family, Work, and Welfare in Canada* (Toronto: University of Toronto Press, 2000).

9 For a more detailed discussion, see Lisa Pasolli, *Working Mothers and the Child Care Dilemma: A History of British Columbia's Social Policy* (Vancouver: UBC Press, 2017).

10 Larry Prochner, "A History of Early Education and Child Care in Canada, 1820–1966," in *Early Childhood Care and Education in Canada,* ed. Larry Prochner and Nina Howe (Vancouver: UBC Press, 2000), 54.

11 See Larry Prochner, "'Share Their Care Mrs. Warworker': Wartime Day Nurseries in Ontario and Quebec, 1942–1945," *Canadian Journal of Research in Early Childhood Education* 5, 1 (1996): 115–26; Larry Prochner and Nina Howe, "The Wartime Child Care Centres in Canada and Great Britain: The 60th Anniversary," *Canadian Children* 26, 2 (Fall 2001): 20–27; and Donna Varga, *Constructing the Child: A History of Canadian Day Care* (Toronto: James Lorimer, 1997).

12 Michel, *Children's Interests/Mothers' Rights.* See also, for example, Linda Gordon, *Pitied but Not Entitled: Single Mothers and the History of Welfare* (Cambridge, MA: Harvard University Press, 1998); and Seth Koven and Sonya Michel, eds., *Mothers of a New World: Maternalist Politics and the Origins of Welfare States* (New York: Routledge, 1993).

13 Linda Gordon, "The Perils of Innocence, or What's Wrong with Putting Children First," *Journal of the History of Childhood and Youth* 1, 3 (Fall 2008): 342 (emphasis in original).

14 Ibid., 333; Margaret Hillyard Little, *No Car, No Radio, No Liquor Permit: The Moral Regulation of Single Mothers in Ontario, 1920–1997* (Don Mills, ON: Oxford University Press, 1998).

15 Library and Archives Canada (LAC), Canadian Council on Social Development fonds, MG 28 I10, vol. 41, file 180; Margaret S. Gould, *The Day Nursery in the Programme of Child Care* (Toronto: Canadian Welfare Council and Child Welfare Council of Toronto, 1933), 1.

16 Archives of Ontario (AO), West End Crèche Child and Family Clinic fonds, F 4336, Annual Reports F 4336-3-0-21, B434186, *Thirty-Third Annual Report of the West End Crèche* (1 October 1940 to 30 September 1941), 6.

17 Pasolli, "'I Ask You, Mr. Mitchell,'" 10–11.

18 *Thirty-Third Annual Report of the West End Crèche,* 6.

19 LAC, MG 28 I10, vol. 49, file 448c, Canadian Welfare Council, "Summary of General Comments re Day Nursery Care Based on Information Received by the Canadian Welfare Council," c. spring 1942; Wendy J. Atkin, "Playing Together as Canadians: Historical

Lessons from the West End Crèche," in *Changing Child Care: Five Decades of Child Care Advocacy and Policy in Canada*, ed. Susan Prentice (Halifax: Fernwood, 2001), 27–38.

20 Quoted in Pierson, *"They're Still Women,"* 24.

21 LAC, Department of Labour fonds, RG 27, vol. 609, file 6–52–1, pt. 1, "Day Care of Children," speech given by unnamed Department of Labour official, probably Eaton, 1 July 1943.

22 LAC, RG 27, vol. 609, file 6–52–1, pt. 1, Fraudena Eaton to George Greene, 13 June 1942.

23 Pasolli, "'I Ask You, Mr. Mitchell,'" 21–24.

24 See, for example, Figure 3.1 and LAC, National Film Board of Canada, Photothèque, 3196950, September 1943.

25 LAC, RG 27, vol. 609, file 6–52–1, pt. 1, "General Treatment for Day Nursery Film," n.d.

26 Gudrun Parker, dir., *Before They Are Six* (Ottawa: National Film Board of Canada, 1943), https://www.nfb.ca/film/before_they_are_six/.

27 LAC, RG 27, vol. 609, file 6–52–1, pt. 1, Eaton to A. MacNamara, Associate Deputy Minister of Labour, 27 January 1943.

28 LAC, RG 27, vol. 611, file 6–52–5–2, pt. 1, Miriam Chapin, Secretary, Montreal Wartime Day Nurseries Committee, to L. Austin Wright, Assistant Director, NSS, 9 April 1942.

29 LAC, RG 27, vol. 610, file 6–52–2, pt. 1, Eaton to MacNamara, 11 March 1943.

30 LAC, RG 27, vol. 611, file 6–52–5–2, pt. 1, Florence Martel, Montreal NSS, to Grier, 18 December 1943.

31 LAC, RG 27, vol. 611, file 6–52–5–2, pt. 1, D. McCallum, RCA Victor Company, to E. Lalande, Quebec Ministry of Health and Social Welfare, 3 November 1942.

32 "Public Probe Planned of Nursery Conditions," *Montreal Gazette*, 4 December 1943.

33 See also Magda Fahrni, *Household Politics: Montreal Families and Postwar Reconstruction* (Toronto: University of Toronto Press, 2005), 57–60.

34 Pierson, *"They're Still Women,"* 54–55.

35 LAC, RG 27, vol. 609, file 6–52–1, pt. 1, "Conference on the Day Care of Children," 10 June 1943.

36 Dorise Nielsen, quoted in "Day Nursery Plan Comes before House of Commons," *Victoria Daily Colonist*, 3 July 1943, 6.

37 Alvin Finkel, "Even the Little Children Cooperated: Family Strategies, Childcare Discourse, and Social Welfare Debates 1945–1975," *Labour/Le travail* 36 (1995): 107.

38 Susan Prentice, "Workers, Mothers, Reds: Toronto's Postwar Day Care Fight," *Studies in Political Economy* 30 (Autumn 1989): 137.

39 LAC, RG 27, vol. 3538, file 3–26–45, Eaton to Mrs. S.H. Simon, Provincial Council of Women of BC, 8 December 1943.

40 LAC, RG 27, vol. 609, file 6–52–1, pt. 1, "An Over-All Community Project," *The Bulletin* (Association of the Children's Aid Societies of Ontario, May 1944), 1.

41 Jeffrey Keshen, "Wartime Jitters over Juveniles: Canada's Delinquency Scare and Its Consequences, 1939–1945," in *Age of Contention: Readings in Canadian Social History, 1900–1945*, ed. Jeffrey Keshen (Toronto: Harcourt Brace, 1997), 369.

42 Pasolli, "'I Ask You, Mr. Mitchell,'" 24.

43 *Thirty-Third Annual Report of the West End Crèche*, 6.

44 LAC, MG 28 I10, vol. 50, file 448e, Day Nurseries Committee of the Welfare Council of Toronto and District, "Report of Committee on Day Care of Children," n.d.

45 LAC, RG 27, vol. 3538, file 3–26–25, "Requete aupres du gouvernement federal en faveur des garderies," [sic] October 1945.

46 Prentice, "Workers, Mothers, Reds," 120.

47 Ibid., 119.

48 Prochner and Howe, "The Wartime Child Care Centres."

49 LAC, RG 27, BAN 2002–0153–5, vol. 1, file 10, Department of Labour, "History of the Wartime Activities of the Department of Labour: Employment of Women and Day Care of Children, Part Two," n.d.

50 LAC, MG 28 I10, vol. 283, file 26, Canadian Welfare Council, "Day Care of Children in Wartime," November 1942.

51 AO, F 4336, Annual Reports F 4336–3–0–26, B434186, *The West End Crèche 38th Annual Report 1946*, 12.

52 LAC, RG 27, vol. 3538, file 3–26–45, Mrs. Mary Salomone to Humphrey Mitchell, 22 May 1946.

53 LAC, RG 27, vol. 3538, file 3–26–45, Mrs. Annie Creswell to Mitchell, 22 May 1946.

54 The many letters containing these sentiments were written in late 1945 and early 1946; they can all be found in LAC, RG 27, vol. 3538, file 3–26–45.

55 LAC, RG 27, vol. 3538, file 3–26–45, Mrs. Jean Grant to Mitchell, 23 May 1946.

56 Dominique Marshall, *The Social Origins of the Welfare State: Quebec Families, Compulsory Education, and Family Allowances, 1940–1955*, trans. Nicola Doone Danby (Waterloo: Wilfrid Laurier University Press, 2006), 78–79. For an exploration of the other political and economic rationales behind family allowances, see Raymond Blake, *From Rights to Needs: A History of Family Allowances in Canada, 1929–92* (Vancouver: UBC Press, 2009).

57 Dominique Marshall, "Reconstruction Politics, the Canadian Welfare State, and the Ambiguity of Children's Rights, 1940–1950" in *Uncertain Horizons: Canadians and Their World in 1945*, ed. Greg Donaghy (Ottawa: Canadian Committee for the History of the Second World War, 1996), 266.

58 Marshall, *The Social Origins*, 82–90.

59 Gordon, "The Perils of Innocence," 347.

60 Finkel, "Even the Little Children Cooperated," 93.

61 Timpson, *Driven Apart*.

62 See Pasolli, *Working Mothers and the Child Care Dilemma*, Chapters 4–6.

4

Civic Identities in Conflict

Montreal's Anglophone and Francophone Private School Girls

Lisa Moore

> *You are the ones to build our native land once more. / We'll need strong minds and wills, strong bodies for that task; / So work, work hard at what you do, just that we ask of you Canadians. / Rejoice, be thankful that it's not too late / To save your land, your Canada; be glad that you / Will have a hand in moulding Canada anew.*
>
> – Trish Rogers, "A Song for Canadian Youth," 1943[1]

> *J'étais en sixième lorsque la guerre fut declarée. Elevées dans un pays pacifique, nous ne pouvions soupçonner la gravité de ce qui s'annonçait. Nous ne fûmes pas longues à le réaliser. Durant bientôt six ans, nous avons prié avec foi et confiance. Une paix définitive n'est pas encore établie dans le monde mais nous gardons l'espoir de vivre un jour dans un monde meilleur et pacifié.*
>
> – Manon Latour, "Ma biographie," 1944[2]

The passages above were written by two adolescent girls attending private school in Montreal at the height of the Second World War. The first, a poem by an anglophone student, calls upon Canadian youth to prepare for their role in rebuilding and reshaping the nation in the aftermath of the conflict. The second, part of a school assignment composed by a francophone student, emphasizes the growing severity of the war and the urgent need for its end. In the first case, a direct call to action urges participation in the war effort; in the second, an appeal for peace is overshadowed by a sense of anxiety and despair. When juxtaposed, these two texts reveal an important division in the way that female adolescents from Montreal's English- and French-speaking populations understood their roles in the Second World War,[3] perceptions that echoed those of the linguistic and religious communities from which they came.

This chapter examines the wartime experiences of anglophone and francophone girls in Montreal's private school system between 1939 and 1945, illustrating how their differing reactions to the war reflected the broader social and political climate in Quebec. At the time, a significant ideological discord existed between the two linguistic communities, one that was grounded in their fundamental disagreement over Canada's participation in the war. On the one hand, the overwhelming majority of Montreal anglophones supported their nation's role in the conflict as part of the larger British imperial cause. On the other hand, though a significant number of French Canadian men did enlist in the armed forces, many also opposed federal conscription, a policy widely perceived as an encroachment on provincial autonomy.[4] Within the larger context, francophones adopted a critical view of the war, not only because it involved French Canadians in a British-led campaign, but also because it conflicted with the Catholic Church's notion of peace.[5] These divergent opinions were transmitted by parents, teachers, school administrators, community leaders, and religious authorities to Quebec's female youth, playing a major role in shaping their daily lives during the war.

Along with these normative messages from their superiors, age, gender, and class also mediated girls' participation in home front activities. This was especially true for Montreal's English-speaking private school girls, whose privileged status created unique opportunities to contribute to the war effort, while at the same time placing significant restrictions on the kinds of services they could offer. While this chapter recognizes the influence of these socializing forces, it also emphasizes the agency that girls displayed in resisting them. Historical agency is often described as the collective action of men in response to oppression, but this definition does not encompass voiceless and marginalized groups, which is especially problematic for the examination of girls.[6] Feminist scholars and historians of children and youth have redefined common perceptions of agency by examining the daily activities of women and girls. This approach allows us to view the words and actions of young women as expressions of their agency.

To present a comprehensive understanding of the city's female private school network during the Second World War, this chapter examines three schools: Miss Edgar's and Miss Cramp's School (ECS) largely served an English-speaking clientele, the École normale de filles de Notre-Dame catered exclusively to French-speaking girls, and Villa Maria admitted pupils from both communities, creating a unique environment in which students, who shared the same faith but spoke different languages, often held opposing views of the war. ECS was founded independently in 1909 by Maud Edgar and Mary Cramp, two teachers from Toronto's Havergal College who shared a dissatisfaction with the limited education provided to girls. Imagining a better education than the one offered in many private boarding schools and in the public school system, they decided to open their own school in Montreal.[7] The École normale de filles de Notre-Dame and Villa Maria were institutions led by the Congrégation Notre-Dame, a Catholic order of nuns dedicated to the education of young women. The École normale de filles de Notre-Dame (hereafter referred to as Notre-Dame) was established in 1899 as the sister school of the École normale Jacques-Cartier, an institution for young men. It belonged to a larger network of écoles normales in Quebec, which were private institutions normally led by religious congregations that provided professional teacher training separately to boys and girls.[8] Founded in 1854, Villa Maria was a convent boarding school whose prestige was such that it attracted students from across Quebec, Ontario, the Maritimes, and even the United States, accounting for its English-speaking student body during the war.[9] Despite their differences, all three schools shared one important commonality: they provided instruction to the daughters of upper-middle-class and elite families.[10] This chapter draws upon archival materials from the schools – annual reports, student assignments, yearbooks, the meeting minutes of student groups and alumnae associations – as well as oral history interviews to uncover the wartime experiences of the students who attended them.[11]

The history of the Second World War in Quebec remains understudied, which Tamara Myers and Mary Anne Poutanen attribute to the "seeming ambivalence" of Quebec historians regarding the conflict.[12] Other than the general histories of Quebec that briefly discuss the war period,[13] there is Serge Durflinger's analysis of wartime Verdun, a bilingual, working-class area of Montreal. There are also three significant historical analyses of wartime education in Quebec. The first is Tamara Myers and Mary Anne Poutanen's examination of the Protestant school system's campaign to use home front activities as a method of civic training and as a prescription for youth delinquency.[14] Another is Roderick MacLeod and Mary Anne Poutanen's chapter on the home front activities of boys and girls in Quebec Protestant public schools.[15] Finally, Anne Millar and Jeffrey Keshen compare the wartime experiences of anglophone schoolchildren in Montreal and Toronto.[16] This chapter builds upon these studies by examining private female schooling in Montreal during the war.

Unlike wartime Quebec, English Canada during the Second World War has been well studied by historians, with numerous works focusing on the adolescent population.[17] Some historians have considered the wartime experiences of Canadian youth as a whole.[18] However, most examine the home front activities of young people within the particular sociopolitical environments of their cities and provinces.[19] Others explore Canadian adolescents' involvement in youth organizations, such as the Junior Red Cross and the Girl Guides of Canada.[20] What the current body of work lacks, however, is a meaningful assessment of how Quebec's adolescent population fit within the wartime narrative. This chapter fills in some of the gaps.

Quebec's Education System

From its establishment in the mid-nineteenth century, the provincial education system in Quebec was composed of a number of denominational school boards that catered to the religious beliefs of its population. In Montreal, the two most significant school boards were the Montreal Protestant Central Board and the Montreal Catholic School Commission, which, between them, offered education to most of the city's youth, regardless of their gender or class.[21] As an alternative to the denominational public system, upper-middle-class and elite families often sent their children to one of Montreal's private schools, generally run by religious orders or by individuals. Like the denominational public schools, these institutions tended to be divided along religious and linguistic lines. However, they exclusively admitted the sons and daughters of upper-class families, a condition regulated by costly tuition fees. In addition, they were often single-sex environments,[22] which was conducive to instilling and promoting traditional gender roles. Thus, girls attending a Montreal private school received academic and moral instruction that not only reflected the broader principles of their communities but also adhered to class- and gender-based principles.

During the Second World War, the views of private school teachers and administrators often informed students' understandings of the conflict. Largely from English Protestant backgrounds, faculty and staff at the anglophone private schools of Montreal reacted to the outbreak of war in two key ways. First, they assumed the responsibility of preparing their students for what was to come. In September 1939, the headmistresses of ECS, Maud Edgar and Mary Cramp, held an emergency meeting to establish the role that teachers would play in guiding their students through the inevitable hardships of the war. "The immediate present will be settled on the battlefields, [but] the future is with those who have the charge of the boys and girls of today," they told their staff:

> We shall find our problems intensified by the nervous strain under which many of our parents and older girls will be living. We shall, perhaps, have our personal anxieties weighing on us. Yet, we must keep a brave heart and steadfast spirit, forgetting our own problems in those of others, and doing our utmost to fit the coming generation to strive for truth, honour, justice, freedom and love.[23]

Second, educators worked to inculcate students with a sense of Canadian patriotism and a love of British values.[24] This initiative was not only intended to increase student support for the war effort, but also to allow teachers to train their pupils in civic responsibility.[25] At ECS, the school calendar was punctuated by regular assemblies, when students received updates on the advances of British and Canadian troops, as well as encouragement to participate in fundraising campaigns, clothing collections, and similar activities.[26] Administrators also responded to Britain's call for help in assisting evacuated children, as discussed by Claire Halstead in Chapter 2 of this volume. The school offered lodging and educational instruction to sixteen young girls from England. This act of patriotism not only demonstrated to students the importance of contributing to the war effort, it also revealed the ways that age and social position determined the kinds of assistance that women could provide.

Members of a linguistic and religious community that largely opposed conscription and British influence over Canadian affairs, French-speaking educators were more ambivalent regarding the war effort. Many Catholics supported conservative leader Maurice Duplessis, who won the 1944 provincial election thanks to his anti-conscription and Quebec nationalist platform.[27] In educational institutions, teachers' disapproval of the war was illustrated by the decision not to involve their schools or their students in any war-related home front initiatives. At Notre-Dame, this choice was communicated via complete silence on the war effort. Home front activities were neither organized nor encouraged, and the school's annual reports made not a single mention of the conflict.[28] Both Notre-Dame and Villa Maria also decided against offering shelter and schooling to evacuated children from Britain, a choice that most French Catholic schools made during the war.[29] Although Villa Maria was bilingual, its francophone teachers outnumbered its anglophone ones. As a result, they had more control over the day-to-day operations of the school and had the final say in the decision not to implement a war effort program. In fact, they reacted similarly to educators at Notre-Dame, remaining relatively silent on the war. When the francophone teachers did discuss it, they framed it as a threat to world peace and to the preservation of French Canadian culture, demonstrating both their Catholic and nationalist values. The school's annals feature expressions of anxiety about the enduring conflict, which God alone could end. "Le monde est en guerre. De partout, il vient des demandes de paix, nous continuons d'exprimer ce désir dans l'oraison de la messe," wrote the headmistress in 1940. "Donnons-nous, Seigneur, cette paix que le monde ne peut donner, paix durable basée sur la justice et sur la charité. Si l'ordre ne reigne pas dans notre vie, il n'y a pas de paix. Sâchons qu'elle existe dans nos communautés pour que les âmes se sanctifient et les pays se pacifient."[30] Teachers also encouraged their students to pray for peace, using Catholic ceremonies such as the 40 Hours Devotion and the Feast of the Immaculate Conception as opportunities to ask God and the Virgin Mary to end the hostilities.[31] Probably fearing that the war effort would change their students' understanding of their position in society – especially as increasing numbers of Quebec women entered the paid workforce – educators at Villa Maria invited religious leaders to lecture on the importance of women's place in the home. Specifically, French-speaking students were told that their eventual roles as wives and mothers were vital to the survival of the French Catholic population in a country that was dominated by English-speaking Protestants.[32] Though dramatically different from each other, the views and teaching strategies of educators in the francophone and anglophone schools had equally important impacts on their students' understanding and experience of the war.

Students' Reflections

Using the creative outlets available to them,[33] such as yearbooks and school assignments, Montreal's privately educated adolescent girls found meaningful ways to express their views of the conflict. At ECS, students produced a yearbook entitled the *Beaver Log*. Consisting of poems, opinion pieces, records of school activities and events, as well as images and messages from the graduating class, the *Beaver Log* provides a glimpse into student life. During the war, its pages were almost entirely devoted to the conflict overseas, its content echoing the patriotic call to action put forward not only by ECS teachers but also by Montreal's wider community of English Protestant educational leaders. In 1942, the yearbook editor urged her fellow students to defend democracy by contributing to the war effort: "Today when many different 'isms' are attempting to overthrow democracy our peoples are coming to their senses and realizing what great privileges they have, and how fortunate they are to be living under democratic institutions." She continued, "It is imperative that such privileges be defended and that all democrats rally together to keep burning the torch of liberty."[34]

Poems, short fiction, and other creative expressions communicated a similar message, praising Britain's defence against the blitz and portraying Nazi Germany as the ultimate threat to freedom and democracy. Probably influenced by anti-German advertisements – such as one from Simpson's department store in the 1944 yearbook that urged students to "help lick Hitler!" – ECS students spoke openly about their contempt for the enemy.[35] In a short story published in the 1943 issue, one student referred to the Nazis as "inhuman" and "hateful Huns."[36] Examples like these are numerous across the six yearbooks published during the war, pointing to the enormous influence of teachers *and* the Canadian propaganda machine on the views of these young women. Although Villa Maria's archives contain less information about the school's anglophone girls, a few records of their wartime reflections do exist. For instance, the annals mention a school assembly in 1943, at which English-speaking students directed a play that praised the courage and sacrifice of Canadian soldiers.[37] The recollections of former students also reveal their thoughts: a 1941 alumna remembered feeling frustrated with her teachers' unwillingness to discuss the fighting overseas.[38]

Unsurprisingly, francophone girls were more critical in discussing the topic, often expressing opinions that were at odds with their English-speaking counterparts. The wartime issue that gained the most attention was conscription. At Villa Maria, the subject was raised in student autobiographies, an assignment required of all francophone graduates before they departed.[39] In an autobiography from 1941, Pauline Drolet commended her father's refusal to respond to the call of the battalion he had fought with during the First World War but worried about the threat of his impending conscription, demonstrating that students were also influenced by the beliefs and actions of their parents and were concerned about the immediate effect of the war on their families.[40] Anti-conscription sentiments became more assertive after 1942, when Prime Minister King held a referendum asking Canadians to release the Liberal government from its pledge against overseas conscription, which it had made at the beginning of the war.[41] The results revealed that 85 percent of French-speaking Quebecers opposed conscription, leading King to postpone its implementation until 1944.[42] In that year, a student from Notre-Dame penned an essay critical of the departure of young men to the European front, lamenting the "beaux régiments de jeunesse" that would now have to suffer "les divers côtés tragiques."[43] When students from Notre-Dame did praise the bravery of French Canadian men who fought overseas, it was for their defence of "la vieille France."[44]

While some expressed critical views of conscription, many students imitated their teachers by remaining silent about the war. In fact, of the twenty Villa Maria autobiographies written in 1942, not one made any mention of the war. Instead, they focused on the three-hundredth anniversary of the founding of Montreal. The girls recalled their excitement at helping to organize the festivities at their school and at attending the celebratory Mass at the Notre-Dame Basilica of Montreal.[45] Whether or not the French-speaking students at these schools intentionally disregarded the war, their writings demonstrate that celebrating Quebec's heritage was more important to them than participating in the Canadian war effort.

For students from both linguistic communities, the war could produce significant life changes and trigger emotional distress, especially when loved ones were killed in the fighting. Bereavement was a common emotion expressed by all students who lost close relatives, regardless of their position on the conflict. However, anglophone and francophone girls differed strikingly in making sense of this loss. For example, English-speaking girls framed the deaths of their fathers, brothers, uncles, and friends as noble sacrifices. This is especially observable in a poem written by eighth grade ECS student D. Millar in 1940:

> We are sad when the setting sun sinks
> Over the western rim; and yet the trail
> Of glory left behind compensates for
> The glory that is gone. So is it when
> A great soul takes its flight, and, silently,
> Slips from the present into the great Beyond.
> His memory will not fade away as mist
> (What is immortal cannot disappear);
> His work lives on and praises him in death
> As did in life his modest charm, his grace,
> His love of all that's good, noble, true.
> Willing to serve, to lend a helping hand,
> Humble, devout, courteous to all
> From farthest north to south, from east to west,
> His love remains in all our hearts today.[46]

In the francophone community, it was largely unacceptable to depict the deaths of relatives fighting overseas as patriotic sacrifices, so French-speaking students struggled with how to express the loss. Many focused on the trauma of the event and its ability to rupture family bonds. For Villa Maria's Henriette Moreau, the pain of her brother's death was still unspeakable five years after the fact. "Sh! Je ne raconterai pas encore une fois toute la douleur dans laquelle une telle perte me plongeait," she wrote, adding that her mother never fully recovered from the death of her son.[47] For another student at Notre-Dame, the mere departure of loved ones for the front signalled an intense loss. In a creative essay, she wrote, "'Ils vont partir! Ils partent! Ils sont partis!' En ces mots simples comme des coups de tambour, forts comme la fatalité, retentit l'alerte ordinaire de nos temps, se condense l'émotion commune et quand même toujours frappante sans être une surprise." Reflecting upon the emotional goodbyes that regularly occurred as family members left for the front, she continued, "Si bien que les gares, les quais, les aérodromes deviennent le théâtre incessamment active des séparations et des disparitions indéfinies."[48] What these expressions illustrate is that the young girls who lived through the war experienced profound loss in ways they never had before. What they also show is that their reactions were mediated and influenced by the views and messages of parents, teachers, and other leading members of their communities.

Student Activities

In addition to their positions on the war effort, teachers' understandings of age, gender, and class were equally influential in determining the nature of their students' wartime activities. One of the few principles shared by private school educators from both linguistic communities was the importance of preparing students to assume their roles as members of the elite. For anglophone teachers, the war created new age-based activities that could be used to reinforce traditional gender and social roles. Perhaps the most suitable project was fundraising, since it prepared students for their eventual social responsibilities. As married women of the upper class, they would likely engage in philanthropic endeavours and spend much of their time hosting social events. Fundraising was also effective in training students to shoulder civic responsibility because they could be tasked with specific objectives that would benefit the war effort.

At ECS, fundraising events were frequent occurrences, and many students responded to them with a sense of purpose and enthusiasm. Extracurricular programs were adapted to support the war effort, providing spaces where students could become acquainted with and engage in home front activities. For example, members of the Social Service Club, who regularly purchased food and clothing for underprivileged families, expanded their charitable services to working-class wives and mothers whose husbands and sons were fighting overseas.[49] In addition, new fundraising programs enabled girls to raise money while simultaneously practising their hosting skills. In 1942, to support the Queen's Canadian Fund, the older students hosted a fair for their younger classmates, where, for a nominal entrance fee, they enjoyed refreshments and games.[50] Students also tested out their abilities on more important guests, holding a variety show for teachers, parents, relatives, and alumnae, the profits of which benefitted the Red Cross. Other fundraising initiatives, such as the Victory Loan Program, fostered collaboration between students and invoked a sense of patriotic duty. "This year for the first time the school was asked to have staff and girls purchase bonds through the school," wrote one student in the *Beaver Log*. "Subscriptions came tumbling in so quickly we had our $1,000 almost at once, and we saw that the money would bring our fighters back to civilian life."[51] Other forms of collection, however, were considered inappropriate for privileged young ladies. Most private anglophone girls' schools did not encourage their students, for example, to collect scrap materials such as metal, rubber, and paper – as Canadian youth of other classes commonly did – because it was viewed as beneath their social station.[52] Clothing collection, however, was acceptable, especially because most girls donated unwanted or ill-fitting items from their own wardrobes. This was particularly true at ECS, where students regularly collected clothing for British children left homeless or orphaned by the war.[53]

Like the fundraising projects, activities that promoted domestic training and traditional female roles also consumed the time and efforts of young anglophone girls in Montreal. These included a wide variety of gender-specific tasks, such as making bandages, knitting socks for soldiers, and preparing food for military canteens. At ECS, the graduating class of 1940 established a Junior Red Cross Society, which would help younger classmates produce supplies for the war effort.[54] The Canadian Red Cross Society was a well-respected organization, and many ECS students would have been familiar with it, given that many upper-class women, and in all likelihood the girls' own mothers, were Red Cross volunteers.[55] Members of the ECS Girl Guides chapter also produced supplies for overseas, adapting their regular activities to the needs of the moment.[56] Though perceptions of appropriate gender roles limited the kinds of work that the students could do, their social positions – and by extension, their access to wealth – allowed them to make large, good-quality contributions. As the president of the ECS Junior Red Cross Society explained in the 1944 *Beaver Log*, the chapter had been particularly successful thanks to the substantial clothing donations received from fellow classmates. She remarked, "Instead of knitting just socks and sweaters for the troops, we had wool of all colours, which was made into outfits for the bombed children of England as well as for those countries we occupy."[57]

Despite adhering to the same gender- and class-based principles as anglophone educators, the sisters of Montreal's French Catholic private schools did not adapt existing extracurricular programs to the war effort and did not introduce new ones. This was probably because they felt that Canada should not have entered the fight, but it was also because their pedagogical programs already placed sufficient emphasis on feminine training. This was especially true at Villa Maria, where students were regularly graded in discipline, silence, uniform and appearance, manners, language, and punctuality. Every movement was regulated, with students obeying strict rules for eating, sitting, speaking, going upstairs, entering a room, and greeting teachers.[58] The students who attended Notre-Dame in the 1940s learned subjects that they would eventually teach to their own pupils, such as Latin, arithmetic, and geography, but they were also instructed in music, drawing, and domestic science.[59]

In addition to having well-established gender-oriented pedagogical programs, many French Catholic private schools implemented a number of courses for developing and perfecting the social skills of their students. Such courses were quite extensive at Villa Maria but less so at Notre-Dame, because its students were training to become teachers. As one Villa Maria alumna recalled, the domestic science courses of the 1940s instructed pupils on the proper etiquette for hosting and attending high society dinner parties.[60] Girls also learned how to set tables and serve guests, skills that they practised during the annual alumnae reunions.[61]

These schools also regularly contributed to charitable associations, the majority of which were affiliated with the Catholic Church. In 1942, a provincial school inspector wrote to Quebec's superintendent of public instruction, explaining that his efforts to sell war savings stamps to children at French Catholic schools failed miserably because they were already donating their money to the Oeuvre de la Sainte-Enfance, a Catholic charitable association that supported missionary work.[62] According to the inspector, teachers gave students incentives to raise funds for the Sainte-Enfance, such as exemptions from homework, which certainly had the effect of diverting donations from war-related charities.[63] Though the inspector did not name the institutions he visited, he probably would have received a similar response from the students at Notre-Dame and from their francophone counterparts at Villa Maria, given that their fundraising efforts were directed toward their schools and to Catholic charities. For example, in early 1946, French-speaking students at Villa Maria held a casino party, complete with bingo games and a wheel of fortune to raise money for their school.[64] Shortly after their classmates organized the casino party, the English-speaking students at Villa Maria began collecting funds for European children devastated by the war, an initiative like the one undertaken by girls at ECS.[65] With no direction or encouragement from faculty, they also used their weekly knitting club to make socks for soldiers. These examples illustrate the agency of students who found ways to make wartime contributions despite being a minority in a school filled with francophone girls, who probably disapproved of (or were at best indifferent to) their actions.

Although many students from both linguistic communities adopted the wartime values of their educators, the example of Villa Maria's anglophone students demonstrates that they also challenged them. Students' defiance resulted from two desires: to engage in meaningful adolescent activities and to follow their own codes of ethics and morality. For many girls, especially those from English-speaking families, home front responsibilities consumed their daily lives, diminishing their opportunities to participate in age-based rituals and pastimes. Unwilling to entirely sacrifice their adolescent years to the war, students found ways to juggle their home front activities with their regular pursuits. At ECS, the typical preoccupations of teenaged girls – field trips, sporting matches, social events, and the like – were written into the yearbooks alongside discussions of the war. Though many were technically school-sanctioned activities, their frequency and central role in student culture signified the girls' desire to maintain their social lives despite the added duties of war work. Concentrating on what had mattered most to students during the preceding year, the yearbook editorial of 1945 commented on the election of a new student council, the playoff victory of the basketball team, the ski trip, and the Gym Demonstration (a day of sports-related activities), with only a brief mention of the girls' contributions to the Red Cross.[66]

Equally important to young girls was the coming-of-age process and, with that, the desire to interact socially with boys. Although the pedagogical programs of most female private schools did include marriage preparation, unsupervised meetings with young men were vehemently discouraged and often prohibited on school grounds. However, many girls used the special conditions of wartime to circumvent these restrictions. In their yearbooks, ECS students referred to romantic relationships in poems and short stories about the war.[67] In the questionnaire that accompanied their photographs, several 1942 graduates listed their pastimes as "writing letters" to soldiers and "correspondence with Canadian Forces."[68] Students also volunteered to provide entertainment at local canteens for troops on leave, creating opportunities for interactions with young men.[69]

With no organized war effort program to dictate their daily activities, francophone girls often went about their normal routines, altered only by government-implemented measures such as rationing and air-raid drills.[70] Driven by their own moral understandings of the war, some French-speaking students did participate in home front activities, defying the values and directives of their superiors. As Villa Maria offered them no opportunities to engage in the war effort at school, several of its French-speaking students joined the Girl Guides. Although the boarding regulation limited their attendance at meetings, they spent their allotted free time during the week and on weekends with their fellow Guides, making bandages, sewing clothing for European children, and learning practical survival skills tailored to the conditions of war.[71] Other students challenged the nationalist views and anti-conscription sentiments of their superiors by supporting Canadian involvement in the war. At Notre-Dame, a few meetings of the literary circle opened and closed with the singing of "O Canada" and included discussions of the Canadian contribution to the fighting overseas.[72] Similarly, students at Villa Maria referred to soldiers as "nos braves Canadiens" and praised their efforts to defend their country.[73]

The unique conditions produced by the war also persuaded girls to reflect upon their prescribed gender and social roles. In addition to gaining the provincial vote in 1940, women in Quebec were called upon to replace men in the workforce and to assume non-combat positions in the armed forces. This prompted many female students, especially at anglophone institutions, to view their place within society in new ways. At ECS, the *Beaver Log* began to print

Figure 4.1

Members of the ECS Girl Guides chapter during the 1939–40 school year. ECS publications highlighted alumnae who were taking on active roles in the war effort, presumably to inspire girls like these. | Miss Edgar's and Miss Cramp's School Archives, HA-0007.11.002.

a "War Services" section in 1940, reporting on alumnae who were contributing to the war effort and simultaneously informing its readers of upper-class women who were challenging gender roles. This feature provided news of recent graduates who had joined the Canadian Women's Army Corps (CWAC), the Canadian Women's Auxiliary Air Force, and the Women's Royal Canadian Naval Service, as well as other wartime organizations. Learning about alumnae activities encouraged ECS girls to take on similar kinds of work that pushed the boundaries of accepted gender roles and provided alternatives (at least temporarily) to marriage and motherhood. In 1942, several alumnae visited their alma mater to share their experiences as volunteers with St. John Ambulance, which provided first aid training to individuals, as well as medical care and support to those in need.[74] A number of graduating students were so inspired by the presentation that they took a course with St. John Ambulance, preparing to offer their own volunteer services following graduation.[75]

Girls' Roles after Graduation

Once they were free from the obligations of secondary school, recent graduates could achieve much more for the war effort than they had as students. No longer subject to the restrictions of their educational institutions, they enjoyed new freedoms and opportunities. The "Old Girls" of ECS in particular took advantage of their new positions in society. For example, many graduates made direct contributions to the war effort by joining the women's divisions of the Canadian armed forces. In the 1943 issue of the *Beaver Log,* the "War Services" section listed five Old Girls who were on active duty in Canada or overseas with the CWAC, the Royal Canadian Air Force (Women's Division), or the Canadian Red Cross Corps, or who were nursing with the Royal Canadian Army Medical Corps. Two were noted as having achieved positions of high rank and responsibility.[76] Subsequent issues of the *Beaver Log* as well as issues of the *Old Girls' Log* mentioned many more former students who held positions at home and overseas in the women's armed services, the military nursing corps, and the Red Cross, as well as in voluntary organizations such as St. John Ambulance, the YWCA, and the Voluntary Aid Detachment. Other young women who married shortly after graduating managed to make remarkable contributions despite their household and parental responsibilities. Peggy Aikens Sellars, whose husband was a wing commander for the RCAF, was one example. She founded two auxiliaries at the Yorkton base, "one for officers' wives and one for airmen's wives," created an airmen's club, and launched "a kindergarten for airmen's children."[77] A number of Old Girls also took on paid jobs, such as Diana Dawes and Carol Owens, who were both hired at the Bouchard Munitions Plant north of Montreal.[78]

Wartime conditions also motivated young women to pursue higher education. In fact, by 1945, there was a notable increase in the number of female students at Montreal's anglophone and francophone universities.[79] Taking advantage of both the unique social climate and their privileged positions, private school graduates increasingly enrolled in post-secondary institutions. During the war years at ECS, many students came to view university education as a viable option following graduation and, for some, as an alternative to marriage. Graduating student J. Johnson wrote in the *Beaver Log* that further education might be "the difference between a restless, unhappy mind and one that is content and at peace with itself" because it gave a woman "a store of knowledge from which she can draw all the rest of her life." The training in critical thinking that a college education provided would also help her "to analyse the people that she encounters and the situations she meets later in life."[80] Between 1940 and 1945, the number of ECS alumnae attending university increased by 45 percent.[81] This was also the case at Villa Maria, where by the end of the war, more graduates than ever before expressed interest in continuing their education at schools such as Collège Marguerite Bourgeoys, the Institut de pédagogie familiale, and Royal Victoria College. However, the archival records of Notre-Dame do not indicate that alumnae pursued higher education, presumably because their training had been geared toward taking up teaching positions after graduation.

While some young women ventured out into the world to engage in war work and home front activities, others stayed close to home and joined the alumnae associations of their alma maters. Whether limited in their freedom of movement due to the obligations of marriage and motherhood or committed to lending a helping hand to their former schools, alumnae played an important role at private educational institutions during the war years. At ECS, the Old Girls' Association was responsible for overseeing the management and care of evacuated children from Britain.[82] It also launched fundraising activities and helped current students plan their own events. Interestingly, given the sharp linguistic divide in students' war-related pursuits, anglophone *and* francophone members of Villa Maria's alumnae association were jointly responsible for establishing a chapter of the Red Cross Society, whose meetings were held at the school on a weekly basis.[83] This initiative was significant for two reasons: it demonstrated the importance of educational status in determining a woman's ability to engage in home front activities and it also revealed a bilingual, bicultural collaboration among alumnae, around the war effort. Unsurprisingly, however, Notre-Dame graduates remained critical of the war, openly voicing their disapproval of Canada's support for Britain.[84] Although their wartime contributions varied, the alumnae of ECS, Villa Maria, and Notre-Dame clearly gained new opportunities and responsibilities as they left their schools and became adults.

When the war in Europe concluded on 8 May 1945, thousands of Quebecers celebrated – anglophone and francophone, Protestant and Catholic. However, the ways in which these communities framed the Allied victory reflected the broader values and beliefs they had maintained throughout the war. Francophone and anglophone students at private girls' schools in Montreal also reacted differently to the news of peace. The English-speaking girls at ECS and Villa Maria responded to V-E Day with general praise for the British Commonwealth in ending the conflict and by holding celebrations at their schools, though the Villa Maria students had their festivities cut short by teachers who reminded them of the immense losses that had been suffered as a result of the war.[85] Alternatively, French-speaking students at Notre-Dame and Villa Maria shared the belief that victory belonged to God, a message they communicated in their essays and assignments and one that was reinforced by the cardinal of Quebec in a province-wide radio broadcast shortly after the armistice.[86]

The female youth of the province, represented here by the students at ECS, Notre-Dame, and Villa Maria, viewed and experienced the Second World War in dissimilar and sometimes opposing ways, largely because their allegiances as Canadians were fundamentally different. For anglophone girls, being a Canadian meant playing an important role in the building and shaping of a young nation that owed its existence to Britain. For francophone girls, it meant honouring the legacy of French Canada by protecting its language, values, and traditions. The war had the considerable effect of sharpening this division: while English-speaking students were collecting clothing for the children of Britain and fundraising for the Red Cross, French-speaking students were choosing not to participate in a war effort that they perceived as a direct threat to the autonomy of their community. Despite sharing the same age, gender, citizenship, and social class, these anglophone and francophone girls developed dramatically different civic identities during the war, ones that would undoubtedly continue to clash as Quebec nationalism came to the fore during the post-war era.

Notes

1 Archives of Miss Edgar's and Miss Cramp's School (ECS Archives), Trish Rogers, "A Song for Canadian Youth," *Beaver Log*, 1943, 25.

2 "I was in the sixth grade when war was declared. Raised in a peaceful country, we could not suspect the seriousness of what was coming. We were not slow to realize it. For almost six years, we prayed with faith and trust. A definitive peace is not yet established in the world but we keep the hope of one day living in a better and peaceful world." Archives of the Congrégation de Notre-Dame de Montréal, CND Archives, Manon Latour, "Ma biographie," in "Autobiographies manuscrites," 1944, Villa Maria. In compliance with the regulations of the Archives Services of the Congrégation de Notre-Dame de Montréal, the names of the students have been changed.

3 I use the terms "female adolescent," "female youth," and "girl" interchangeably to denote students aged roughly twelve to seventeen, who were enrolled in secondary courses at private girls' schools in Montreal.

4 Sébastien Vincent argues that in the collective memory of Quebecers, the province's anti-conscription stance overshadows the fact that many French Canadian men voluntarily enlisted during the war, making up 20 percent of the total number of Canadian volunteers. For more on this subject, see Sébastien Vincent, *Laissés dans l'ombre: Les Québécois engagés volontaires de 39–45* (Montreal: VLB Éditeur, 2004).

For more on the debate surrounding conscription, see John Dickinson and Brian Young, *A Short History of Quebec*, 4th ed. (Montreal and Kingston: McGill-Queen's University Press, 2008), 295–96; and J.L. Granatstein, *Canada's War: The Politics of the Mackenzie King Government, 1939–1945* (Toronto: University of Toronto Press, 1990), 28.

5 Paul-André Linteau et al., *Quebec since 1930* (Toronto: James Lorimer, 1991), 60, 104; Susan Mann Trofimenkoff, *The Dream of Nation: A Social and Intellectual History of Quebec* (Toronto: Gage, 1982), 250–51.

6 For more on agency and youth, see Mary Jo Maynes, "Age as a Category of Historical Analysis: History, Agency and Narratives of Childhood," *Journal of the History of Childhood and Youth* 1, 1 (2008): 117.

7 For the founders and the history of ECS, see Old Girls' Association of Miss Edgar's and Miss Cramp's School, *Miss Edgar's and Miss Cramp's School: A Retrospect* (Westmount, QC: Anlo, 1984).

8 For a discussion of the Quebec écoles normales for girls, see Micheline Dumont and Nadia Fahmy-Eid, *Les couventines: L'éducation des filles au Québec dans les congrégations religieuses enseignantes, 1840–1960* (Montreal: Boréal, 1986), 97–101.

9 For the history of Villa Maria, see Lisa Moore, "Becoming a 'Villa Girl': Youth Culture and the Student Experience at a Single-Sex Private School in Montreal, 1916–1980" (Master's thesis, Concordia University, 2014); and Helen Lanthier, *Monklands Then, Villa Maria Now: The Story of a Convent School Which Grew from the Estate of Sir James Monk to a Modern, Private High School* (Montreal: Congrégation de Notre-Dame, 2004).

10 The schools were located in Westmount, an upper-class neighbourhood on the slopes of Mount Royal, just west of downtown Montreal. For the history of Westmount, see Aline Gubbay, *A View of Their Own: The Story of Westmount* (Montreal: Price-Patterson, 1998).

11 Interviews: May Vernon, telephone interview by author, 12 July 2014; Louise Simard, interview by author, 10 July 2014, Montreal. The names of the interviewees have been changed to preserve their privacy.

12 Tamara Myers and Mary Anne Poutanen, "Cadets, Curfews, and Compulsory Schooling: Mobilizing Anglophone Children in WWII Montreal," *Histoire sociale/Social History* 38, 76 (2005): 370.

13 See Chapter 8, "From Depression to Quiet Revolution," in Dickinson and Young, *A Short History of Quebec*, 271–304; also see Linteau et al., Chapter 10, "Managing the War," in *Quebec since 1930*, 99–110.

14 Myers and Poutanen, "Cadets, Curfews, and Compulsory Schooling."

15 Roderick MacLeod and Mary Anne Poutanen, Chapter 8, "Daughters of the Empire, Soldiers of the Soil: Protestant School Boards, Patriotism, and War," in Roderick MacLeod and Mary Anne Poutanen, *A Meeting of the People: School Boards and Protestant Communities in Quebec, 1801–1998* (Montreal and Kingston: McGill-Queen's University Press, 2004), 223–43.

16 Anne Millar and Jeffrey A. Keshen, "Rallying Young Canada to the Cause: Anglophone Schoolchildren in Montreal and Toronto during the Two World Wars," *History of Intellectual Culture* 9, 1 (2010–11): 1–16.

17 For general histories of Canada during the Second World War, see Brereton Greenhous and W.A.B. Douglas, *Out of the Shadows: Canada in the Second World War*, rev. ed. (Toronto: Dundurn Press, 1996); and J.L. Granatstein and Peter Neary, eds., *The Good Fight: Canadians and World War II* (Toronto: Copp Clark, 1995). Jeffrey A. Keshen also considers the wartime experiences of adolescents in "The Children's War: Youth Run Wild," in Jeffrey A. Keshen, *Saints, Sinners, and Soldiers: Canada's Second World War* (Vancouver: UBC Press, 2004), 194–227.

18 Cynthia Comacchio, *The Dominion of Youth: Adolescence and the Making of Modern Canada, 1920–1950* (Waterloo: Wilfrid Laurier University Press, 2006); Cynthia Comacchio, "'To Hold on High the Torch of Liberty': Canadian Youth in the Second World War," in *Canada and the Second World War: Essays in Honour of Terry Copp*, ed. Geoffrey Hayes, Mike Bechthold, and Matt Symes (Waterloo: Wilfrid Laurier University Press, 2012), 33–66.

19 For example, Christine Hamelin, "A Sense of Purpose: Ottawa Students and the Second World War," *Canadian Military History* 6, 1 (1997): 34–41; Charles M. Johnston, "The

Children's War: The Mobilization of Ontario Youth during the Second World War," in *Patterns of the Past: Interpreting Ontario's History,* ed. Roger Hall, William Westfall, and Laurel Sefton MacDowell (Toronto: Dundurn Press, 1988), 356–80; and Barbara Lorenzkowski, "The Children's War," in *Occupied St. John's: A Social History of a City at War, 1939–1945,* ed. Steven High (Montreal and Kingston: McGill-Queen's University Press, 2010), 113–50.

20 For the Red Cross, see Sarah Glassford, "Practical Patriotism: How the Canadian Junior Red Cross and Its Child Members Met the Challenge of the Second World War," *Journal of the History of Childhood and Youth* 7, 2 (Spring 2014): 219–42. Kristine Alexander has examined the history of the Girl Guide movement in Canada within the context of British imperialism, most notably during the interwar period. See Kristine Alexander, "Canadian Girls, Imperial Girls, Global Girls: Race, Nation and Transnationalism in the Interwar Girl Guide Movement," in *Within and without the Nation: Canadian History as Transnational History,* ed. Karen Dubinsky, Adele Perry, and Henry Yu (Toronto: University of Toronto Press, 2015), 276–92; Kristine Alexander, "Picturing Girlhood and Empire," in *Colonial Girlhood in Literature, Culture and History, 1840–1950,* ed. Kristine Moruzi and Michelle Smith (Basingstoke, UK: Palgrave Macmillan, 2014), 197–213; and Kristine Alexander, "The Girl Guide Movement and Imperial Internationalism during the 1920s and 1930s," *Journal of the History of Childhood and Youth* 2, 1 (Winter 2009): 37–63. Cynthia Comacchio discusses the wartime contributions of Canadian Girl Guides in Comacchio, *The Dominion of Youth,* 203. For more on the Girl Guides in the Second World War, see Tammy M. Proctor, *Scouting for Girls: A Century of Girl Guides and Girl Scouts* (Denver, CO: ABC-CLIO, 2009), 77–100.

21 On Montreal's Catholic school boards, see Robert Gagnon, *Histoire de la Commission des écoles catholiques de Montréal: Le développement d'un réseau d'écoles publiques en milieu urbain* (Montreal: Boréal, 1996). On the Protestant school system in Quebec, see MacLeod and Poutanen, *A Meeting of the People.*

22 Whereas many public schools also separated boys and girls in the classroom, students of both sexes shared the same facilities and common spaces.

23 ECS Archives, "Staff meeting," 18 September 1939, Miss Edgar's and Miss Cramp's School.

24 For more on school campaigns to foster patriotism and civic responsibility, see MacLeod and Poutanen, *A Meeting of the People,* 226.

25 Ibid.; also see Comacchio, *The Dominion of Youth,* 66; and Myers and Poutanen, "Cadets, Curfews, and Compulsory Schooling," 369.

26 For example, see ECS Archives, "School Calendar," *Beaver Log,* 1943, 69.

27 Granatstein, *Canada's War,* 28; Trofimenkoff, *The Dream of Nation,* 259.

28 CND Archives, "Rapport Annuel de L'École Normale de Filles de Jacques-Cartier," 1939–40, 1940–41, 1941–42, 1942–43, 1943–44, 1944–45, École normale de filles de Notre-Dame.

29 On the francophone population's disinterest in assisting evacuated children from Britain, see Keshen, *Saints, Sinners, and Soldiers,* 196.

30 "The world is at war. From everywhere, there are requests for peace, we continue to express this desire in prayer at Mass. Let us give, Lord, this peace that the world cannot give, lasting peace based on justice and charity. If order does not reign in our life, there is no peace. Let us know that it exists in our communities so that souls may sanctify themselves and nations may pacify themselves." CND Archives, "Annales manuscrites," 3 January 1940, 48, Villa Maria.

31 CND Archives, "Annales manuscrites," 1 February 1941, 71, Villa Maria.

32 CND Archives, "Annales manuscrites," 5 March 1944, 159, Villa Maria.

33 Although the students could probably avail themselves of many creative outlets, only those recorded in the school archives are discussed here.
34 ECS Archives, "Editorial," *Beaver Log,* 1942, 14–15.
35 ECS Archives, "Help Lick Hitler!" Simpson's ad, *Beaver Log,* 1944, 11.
36 ECS Archives, "Nazi Dawn," *Beaver Log,* 1943, 28, 29.
37 CND Archives, "Annales manuscrites," 12 February 1943, 128, Villa Maria.
38 May Vernon, telephone interview by author, 12 July 2014.
39 Anglophone graduating students at Villa Maria also wrote autobiographies until at least 1935. It is unclear whether the assignment was stopped in 1935 or if the autobiographies from 1936 onward are missing from the archives.
40 CND Archives, Pauline Drolet, "Ma biographie," in "Autobiographies manuscrites," 1941, Villa Maria.
41 Granatstein, *Canada's War,* 28; Dickinson and Young, *A Short History of Quebec,* 295–96.
42 This figure is from Linteau et al., *Quebec since 1930,* 104.
43 CND Archives, "Les départs," in "Travaux des étudiantes," 1944, École normale de filles de Notre-Dame.
44 CND Archives, "La vie militaire au Canada," in "Procès verbaux du Cercles d'études Notre-Dame-des-Écoles," March 1940, École normale de filles de Notre-Dame.
45 CND Archives, Lise Beauchemin, "Autobiographies manuscrites," 1942; CND Archives, "Historique de l'École normale Jacques-Cartier," 30–36, École normale de filles de Notre-Dame.
46 ECS Archives, D. Millar, "Departure," *Beaver Log,* 1940, 21.
47 "Sh! I will not explain once more all the pain into which such a loss plunged me," CND Archives, Henriette Moreau, "Autobiographies manuscrites," 1946, Villa Maria.
48 "They are going to leave! They leave! They have gone away!" In these simple words, like drumbeats, as strong as death, the everyday alarm of our times resounds, all of our emotions are condensed and we are struck again and again and are no longer surprised by it. So much so that the stations, the quays, the aerodromes become the incessant active theatres of indefinite separations and disappearances." CND Archives, "Les Départs," "Travaux des étudiantes," 1944, Villa Maria.
49 ECS Archives, "Social Service Club," *Beaver Log,* 1940, 70.
50 ECS Archives, "School Calendar," *Beaver Log,* 1942, 89.
51 ECS Archives, "Over the Top," *Beaver Log,* 1943, 66.
52 On Canadian children's participation in scrap collection, see Johnston, "The Children's War," 367. For the American context, see Robert William Kirk, "Getting in the Scrap: The Mobilization of American Children in World War II," *Journal of Popular Culture* 29, 1 (1995): 223–33.
53 ECS Archives, "Junior Red Cross," *Beaver Log,* 1943, 58.
54 Ibid., 1940, 6.
55 For more on the work of elite women with the Red Cross Society during the Second World War, see the discussion of the College Heights and Rosedale Association in Sarah Glassford, *Mobilizing Mercy: A History of the Canadian Red Cross* (Montreal and Kingston: McGill-Queen's University Press, 2017), 189–90.
56 ECS Archives, "Girl Guide Report," *Beaver Log,* 1940, 84.
57 ECS Archives, "Junior Red Cross," *Beaver Log,* 1944, 61.
58 Moore, "Becoming a 'Villa Girl,'" 70–71.
59 CND Archives, "Rapport Annuel de L'École Normale de Filles de Jacques-Cartier," 1939–40, 1940–41, 1941–42, 1942–43, 1943–44, 1944–45.
60 Louise Simard, interview by author, 10 July 2014, Montreal.

61 In their autobiographies, many Villa Maria girls mention serving at the annual reunions for alumnae.

62 Centre d'Archives du Québec et Chaudiere-Appalaches, "La Sainte-Enfance et l'effort de guerre," in *Reflets d'éducation: Un siècle de correspondance du Département de l'Instruction publique*, 9 November 1943.

63 Ibid.

64 CND Archives, "Annales manuscrites," 5 March 1946, Villa Maria.

65 CND Archives, "Annales manuscrites," 14 June 1946, Villa Maria.

66 ECS Archives, "Editorial," *Beaver Log*, 1945, 14–15.

67 ECS Archives, "Memoirs of a Canteen," *Beaver Log*, 1943, 36–37.

68 ECS Archives, "Photo questionnaire" *Beaver Log*, 1942, 66–67.

69 ECS Archives, "Canteen," *Beaver Log*, 1941, 17–18.

70 Louise Simard, interview by author, 10 July 2014, Montreal.

71 At Villa Maria, the boarding regulation required students to live in dormitories and controlled how much time they could spend away from school. CND Archives, Jeannette Dupuis, "Autobiographies manuscrites," 1947, Villa Maria.

72 CND Archives, "Procès verbaux du Cercle pédagogique," 1940, École normale de filles de Notre-Dame.

73 CND Archives, Hélène Dupuis, "Autobiographies manuscrites," 1943, Villa Maria.

74 For more on St. John Ambulance, see Christopher McCreery, *The Maple Leaf and the White Cross: A History of St. John Ambulance and the Most Venerable Order of the Hospital of St. John of Jerusalem in Canada* (Toronto: Dundurn Press, 2008).

75 ECS Archives, "Editorial," *Beaver Log*, 1942, 28.

76 ECS Archives, "War Services," *Beaver Log*, 1943, 77. In particular, Mary Cross Dover became a lieutenant-colonel, commanding the Kitchener training post for the CWAC; Helen Shanks was matron of the Rideau Military Hospital in Ottawa and gained the rank of captain; Catherine Skinner Spielman joined the Red Cross in London and became a driver; Dorothy King travelled to London to work in the Red Cross Office Administration Section; and Adèle Coleman won her commission in the Women's Division of the RCAF.

77 ECS Archives, "War Services," *Old Girls' Log*, 1942, 28.

78 ECS Archives, "War Services," *Beaver Log*, 1942, 90.

79 See Karine Hébert, "Carabines, poutchinettes, co-eds ou freschettes sont-elles des étudiantes? Les filles à l'Université de Montréal (1900–1960)," *Revue d'histoire de l'Amérique française* 57, 4 (2004): 593–625.

80 ECS Archives, J. Johnson, "Higher Education for Women," *Beaver Log*, 1940, 29.

81 ECS Archives, "Studies," *Beaver Log*, 1940, 1945.

82 ECS Archives, "The Twenty-Ninth Annual Business Meeting of the Old Girls' Association of Miss Edgar's and Miss Cramp's School Inc.," *Old Girls' Log*, 1941, 11.

83 CND Archives, "Annales manuscrites," 4 June 1940, 57, Villa Maria.

84 CND Archives, "Procès verbaux du Cercles d'études Notre-Dame-des-Écoles," March 1940, École normale de filles de Notre-Dame.

85 Louise Simard, interview by author, 10 July 2014, Montreal.

86 CND Archives, "Annales manuscrites," 13 May 1945, 183.

Part 2
Women and the War at Home

Our hearts and hands will give freely while the need lasts.

– Eleanor MacPherson, Red Cross convenor, Women's Patriotic Association of Newfoundland[1]

To modern readers, the home front voluntary, charitable, and domestic work of Canadian and Newfoundland women and girls during the Second World War can seem old-fashioned and dull. This is particularly true when it is compared to women's munitions work, military nursing, and service in the army, navy, and air force. The more traditional realms of women's war work rarely disrupted gender norms, broke little new ground for women, and were seldom novel. In fact, many of the same women and girls did the same types of work for the same reasons in both world wars. But it is for precisely these reasons that this home front involvement is worth studying. In both Canada and Newfoundland, women's traditional home front work demonstrates that, even as some women embraced new opportunities, others took refuge in familiar tasks. Thus, the war simultaneously challenged *and reinforced* traditional gender roles and expectations. Indeed, the deeply conservative gender relations of the 1950s make sense only in light of this fact.

As in the First World War, women's Second World War voluntary and domestic work raised tens of millions of dollars for war charities and Victory Loans, conserved and preserved valuable foodstuffs and household materials, and produced millions of comforts, hospital supplies, and food parcels for military personnel and war-affected civilians. This work offered meaningful, socially approved venues for women and girls to exercise their leadership skills and executive abilities, and it drew upon their talents in manifold ways. They knew they were capable of rising to the occasion and explicitly looked to their Great War predecessors' extraordinary accomplishments for inspiration when they mobilized in 1939. At the inaugural meeting of the Second World War version of the Women's Patriotic Association of Newfoundland (WPA), for instance, Lady Walwyn, wife of the governor, explained that her conversations with WPA members of the previous war had convinced her that, for Newfoundland women, "reviving the W.P.A. on active lines" was the best way "of pulling our weight." The example of the earlier generation would stimulate equal or greater achievements now, she believed, including the addition of civilian work made necessary by the Great Depression: ongoing relief for impoverished Newfoundlanders.[2]

Across Canada and Newfoundland, women responded to home front mobilization efforts. However, socio-economic class, racial/ethnic identity, and religious affiliation could each influence their participation or non-participation in voluntary war work. Women in Holyrood, Newfoundland, could not sustain their WPA branch in the face of opposition from the Catholic parish's anti-war priest. By contrast, Québécoise Madeleine Auger remembered that the priest in her community explicitly permitted women to knit on Sundays for the war effort.[3] Meanwhile, financial need steered some women toward paid employment in the war industry and away from voluntary war charity work. Racial prejudices continued to shape the opportunities for non-white women to participate in both sectors.[4]

In this section, Jennifer Shaw explores Canadian Jewish women's home front experiences, while Graham Broad and Joseph Tohill each examine aspects of women's roles as consumers in wartime. Together, they show that women's voluntary, charitable, and domestic work on the home front was economically valuable and a significant prop to civilian morale. Moreover, it was every bit as dynamic, complex, and fraught with gendered tensions as women's war work in factories, hospitals, and military spaces.

Notes

1 Centre for Newfoundland Studies, Memorial University of Newfoundland, Women's Patriotic Association, "4th Annual Report of the Patriotic Association of the Women of Newfoundland, October 1st, 1942–September 30th, 1943" (St. John's, 1943), 20, http://collections.mun.ca/cdm/ref/collection/cns2/id/29659.

2 "Women's Patriotic Association," *Newfoundland Quarterly* 39, 2 (1939): 17–18.

3 Centre for Newfoundland Studies, Memorial University of Newfoundland, Barbara Doran, "Women's War Efforts – First and Second W.W. in the Women's Patriotic Association of Newfoundland" (paper submitted for History 3813 – Linda Kealey – 12 April 1982), 12; Geneviève Auger and Raymonde Lamothe, *De la poêle à frire à la ligne de feu: La vie quotidienne des Québécoises pendant la guerre '39–'45* (Montreal: Boréal Express, 1981), 110.

4 See, for instance, Dionne Brand, "'We Weren't Allowed to Go into Factory Work until Hitler Started the War': The 1920s to the 1940s," in *We're Rooted Here and They Can't Pull Us Up: Essays in African Canadian Women's History*, ed. Peggy Bristow et al. (Toronto: University of Toronto Press, 1994), 171–91.

5

"A Token Jew Everywhere"

Canadian Jewish Women on the Home Front

Jennifer Shaw

IN HISTORIAN IRVING Abella's popular survey of Canadian Jewish history, *A Coat of Many Colours,* two photographs tantalize the reader with glimpses into Jewish Canadian women's home front experiences of the Second World War. The first shows a group of middle-aged women, gathered around several sewing machines and piles of clothes. The caption reads, "Jewish women sewing for the war effort, 1942." The second photograph, taken somewhere in the Maritimes, depicts a Passover Seder meal, with two hundred uniformed Jewish soldiers sitting at long tables in a community hall. A single woman stands at the front of the room.[1] The photographs – reproduced without any accompanying text to explain the wider context of Jewish women's wartime participation – provoke a variety of questions: Who were these women and girls? Why did they become involved in the war effort? Did they feel a special responsibility to do so because of their Jewishness? What organizations did they join? In other words, what did it mean to be a Canadian Jewish woman or girl during the Second World War?

This chapter explores these questions through the lens of the lives and experiences of a small number of Canadian Jewish women whom I interviewed in 2016. As might be expected, there were few left who could speak to their experiences in the war, so finding interview partners was a challenge. I located them by publishing an article about my research in the *Canadian Jewish News* and providing a contact number for interested people, and by giving introductory talks at Jewish seniors' residences in Toronto. Despite how few women I ultimately found, those who figure in this chapter represent a variety of experiences and backgrounds. One, Clara Halpern, grew up in Saskatchewan and is the daughter of an Orthodox rabbi who immigrated to Canada when she was two. She was a high school student during the war years. Another, Ida Holtzkener, was born in Canada, grew up working class in southwestern Ontario, attended synagogue with her family, and ended up working in an aircraft factory during the war. Another, Ruth Rischall, was born and raised in Ottawa, worked for the Postal Censorship Office, and was mostly indifferent to religion.

These women, ranging in age from eighty-eight to ninety-two, had varied experiences of home front life during the Second World War. Often, they described not only their own lives, but also those of their mothers – many of whom had left family behind in Europe. Oral history offers a clear understanding of how these women understood their own lives, their motivations for their actions, and how being Jewish shaped their experiences on the Canadian home front. Their words open a window into a time when Jewish women and girls shared many experiences with other Canadian women, but in ways deeply influenced by their Jewishness.

Oral History: A Window into Jewish Canadian Women's Lives

In "The Politics of 'Selective' Memory," Pamela Wakewich and Helen Smith discuss images of Canadian women patriotically engaging in non-traditional roles during the Second World War, such as aeronautical engineer Elsie MacGill, "Queen of the Hurricanes," and factory worker Veronica Foster, "the Bren Gun Girl."[2] They argue that the prominence of such depictions (both then and now) reinforces the idea that all women and girls experienced life on the home front in the same way, making invisible the lives of ordinary women. In *They're Still Women After All,* Ruth Roach Pierson examines the vital roles that women played, but pays little attention to how various groups of women were affected by other identifiers, such as religion or ethnicity.[3] The emergence of the concept of "intersectionality" among feminist scholars, however, makes it clear that applying a more nuanced approach to understanding how gender operates in wartime will bear fruitful results.[4] Thus far, Canadian historical research in this area is limited. Dionne Brand's exploration of the war experiences of African Canadian women, Sandra Battaglini's study of the lives of Italian Canadian women who worked in the mines in Sudbury, and Pamela Sugiman's work on Japanese Canadian women and girls who were interned as enemy aliens are groundbreaking in this field.[5] This scarcity applies even in scholarship on Jewish Canadian history, with little attention given to Canadian Jewish women's particular experiences of the war on the home front. To date, the subject has been briefly discussed in one chapter of Gerald Tulchinsky's two-part history of the Jewish people in Canada, and in roughly two sentences in his later one-volume history of Jewish life in Canada.[6] Similarly, James Walker, in examining the struggle for equality for Canadian Jewry between 1933 and 1945, devotes a single paragraph to the contributions of Jewish women on the home front. This paragraph, which deals with the sixteen Jewish enlisted men's centres that were open to all servicemen and -women regardless of race, creed, or religion, is indicative of the way in which historians have ignored and devalued Jewish women's contributions on the home front. Although the centres were organized, administered, and run by women, Walker states merely that women staffed them.[7] Given the immense academic and public knowledge about the Holocaust, as well as the gendered experience of it, this lack of attention is surprising.[8]

What little has been written on the topic tends to stress family-related responsibilities, as evidenced by Tulchinsky's understanding of Jewish Canadian women as having solely relational identities and roles: as mothers, sisters, and wives. Of course, their work in these roles was important, especially for keeping soldiers connected to their family, religion, and culture, and for maintaining morale, but Tulchinsky does not consider the variety of jobs and experiences that women had during the war, and he neglects the ways in which they were affected by the intersection of gender and religion. The methodologies of oral history, however, enable us to gain valuable insights into the wartime lives of ordinary Jewish Canadian women that have otherwise been overlooked.[9]

Collecting oral histories of women can be challenging. Due to gendered socialization, many believe that their stories are not important or "historical." Older women commonly ask, "Are you sure you want to hear this?" or state, "I really don't have a lot to tell you." For minority women, this reaction can also be an attempt to downplay the terrible events they experienced. In her work with Japanese women who were interned during the Second World War, Pamela Sugiman notes this response: most of her interview partners stressed their ordinariness and their "unspectacular lives," despite living through events that deeply and permanently affected them.[10] Producing such a nostalgic view of the past, or the "good old days," is one way that women protect themselves from painful and scarring memories. Though they were not interned, Jewish Canadian women also experienced highly traumatic events during the war years. Thus, the combined effects of socialization and the desire to gloss over negative memories were common threads in my work with elderly Jewish women, complicating my attempt to fill out the historical record. These difficulties, combined with the paucity and shallowness of the literature, underscore the imperative need to record Jewish women's recollections. The stories of their lives can give us new narratives, new insights, and a fuller and more nuanced view of Canada, its people, and its history.

Jewish Women and Girls on the Canadian Home Front

As the research of Ruth Roach Pierson, Jeff Keshen,[11] and the chapters in this collection demonstrate, women and girls experienced life on the home front and contributed to Canada's war effort in myriad ways: through paid labour, pacifism, military enlistment, volunteer work, growing Victory Gardens, or selling war bonds. We know that their input was critical. What is less understood is how other identifiers, such as religion, influenced their experiences. What was it like to be a *Jewish* woman or girl on the home front at this time?

Franklin Bialystok argues that Jews in Canada during the Second World War were "isolated, far from the horror, cognizant of the calamity, but removed by space, time, and experience from the [Holocaust] while being protected in the warm safety of North America."[12] Only one of my interviewees supported this view. Asked what it felt like to be a Jewish woman during the war years and whether she thought much about what was going on, Ida Holtzkener, who was sixteen in 1939, replied, "No, I don't think we knew what was going on ... I don't think it affected me, because I was not aware of what was going on."[13] However, she seemed to be in the minority, as most interviewees felt the effect of the war very personally. Their recollections reveal its impact on them as Jewish women.

In contrast to Ida and to Bialystok, scholars such as Rebecca Margolis show that many, if not most, in the Canadian Jewish community were very knowledgeable about the violence suffered by European Jews.[14] They might have been physically isolated from the Holocaust, but many Canadian Jews had family in Europe, such as grandparents, aunts, and uncles. For my interview partners, having family in Europe made the war years even more difficult. In the years leading up to the conflict, Helen Mlotek remembered, "My mother was very depressed because she was trying to get her mother and brother [out of Poland]."[15] Twice, the British turned them back, and when the war started in 1939, Helen and her mother lost contact with them. More than fifty members of Helen's extended family perished in the Holocaust, including her grandmother and uncle. Staying connected with family was of utmost concern to my interview partners and their families, and letter writing was the main way in which they accomplished this. Fran Parnes stated that, before the war began, "My mother would write aerograms to her family in Poland, and she always left space at the bottom of her letter for me to write to my *bubbe* and *zaidy* ... and she would be able to send those letters to Poland from Canada."[16] Although European family members were geographically distant, connections to them remained strong, and they personalized the war in ways that other women did not experience. For Jewish women, the war was not just killing millions of people, it was killing their loved ones.

Scholar Jenny Hartley argues that wartime letters took on even more significance than those written during peacetime, acting as a "life-support system" that helped to maintain lines of communication and boost morale.[17] This was undoubtedly the case for many of my interviewees, as they tried to gather information about what was happening to their loved ones. After war was declared, Fran's mother was forced to find an alternative method of getting mail to her family in Poland. Initially, she sent her letters to an American friend who forwarded them to Poland, with the replies returning by the same route. After the United States joined the war, letters instead had to be sent to Hungary via a work friend of Fran's father and were then mailed to Poland. Along with providing connection and communication, parcels mailed by Fran's family to

European relatives were quite literally life saving, as they included clothing and non-perishable food, necessities they would not have had otherwise.[18]

Staying in touch was often the responsibility of women, who were usually the main letter writers in the family. Hartley argues that women served as conduits for news, stitching together various branches of their families. For my interview partners, wartime postal restrictions added difficulty to the task, forcing women to devise intricate methods for remaining in contact with their loved ones.[19] Censorship in occupied countries meant that news became increasingly difficult to pass along as the war progressed, so Fran's family invented a code for sharing information. In writing about a death in the family, "they didn't want to say so-and-so died or was killed. They would say so-and-so went to visit Grandma so-and-so, who'd been dead for many, many years. So they knew that person was no longer alive."[20] Even mailing a package of food was an involved process: after filling the box with tinned tuna, rice, coffee, and other food, Fran's family wrapped it in cloth, hoping to prevent theft as it passed through Poland's postal network, an attempt that did not always succeed, as the package often arrived ripped open.[21] Still, letters and parcels helped to maintain kinship ties, and allowed families to remain close, at least until the lines of communication were severed.

Most interviewees were conscious of a direct link between their Jewishness and the war effort. For example, Fran was very clear on the motivations of the Jewish community:

JENNIFER:	Was there a sense that the Jewish community had to be involved?
FRAN:	(emphatically) Oh, yes! Very much so.
J:	Because they felt a special responsibility?
F:	Their families were there, yeah. Their families were there.
J:	Because there's a scholar who says that Canadian Jews were far removed from what was happening –
F:	(flatly, and cutting me off) No.
J:	So you think there was a feeling among the Jewish community that –
F:	Oh, enormous, enormous. Every Jew.[22]

Later in the interview, Fran highlighted her desire to contribute to the war effort. She and her sister opened a lemonade stand, funnelling all the proceeds into the war effort, and she was involved in the common activities undertaken by girls, such as knitting, buying war stamps, and participating in patriotic concerts to raise money.[23]

In the years before and during the war, Canada's immigration policy was explicitly anti-Semitic. Indeed, in accepting Jewish refugees from the Nazi regime, Canada had the worst record of any Western country, admitting fewer than five thousand between 1933 and 1945.[24] However, many Jews refrained from protesting against the government's failure in this respect. As Fran stated, "Jews never did that. I think they were afraid ... if they criticized the government in any way, because they came from that kind of background, they would be sent back to Poland."[25]

Despite not being very vocal in protesting government policies, there was significant support for the war in the Canadian Jewish community, and not just because people wanted to save the lives of family and friends in Europe. The Canadian Jewish Congress, the national body that spoke for the community, encouraged Jewish men to enlist, and its Women's War Efforts Committee organized women and spearheaded projects to furnish recreation rooms for military bases across the country, eventually equipping over 1,400 rooms with everything from gramophones to writing tables to chess and checker sets.[26] The community undertook such work partially in the hope of counteracting anti-Semitism, overt displays of which had become increasingly common during the years leading up to the war. Fran vividly recalled such displays, describing the signs that read, "No dogs, no Jews," posted on the cottage gates near where she vacationed in the summer of 1939.[27] She also recalled a shoemaker her family had gone to for years, who, shortly before the outbreak of war, suddenly displayed his true colours. "I remember [him] saying to my mother, putting out his finger 'You just wait. Those Germans will get over here, and they'll kill every one of you.'"[28] Such stories were not uncommon, but by promoting enlistment and encouraging war work, the Jewish leadership hoped to demonstrate the community's unswerving dedication to the country – and to diminish the anti-Semitism. As Walker argues in his work on race and recruitment in the First World War, minority "communities encouraged, organized, and financed the enlistment of their young men, and those men volunteered in order to gain group recognition and to further the rights of whole communities."[29] Jewish support for the war would help to further the rights of the community, and women's participation in the war effort was key.

Like other Canadian women, many Jewish women took on paid employment – most for the very first time. As men enlisted and were sent overseas, a significant number of jobs became available and were filled by a massive influx of female workers. In addition, the mobilization of Canadian industry for war meant that the high unemployment of the 1930s gave way to the creation of entirely new occupations.[30] Women were recruited to fill these positions so that vital war materials and equipment could be produced; between 1939 and 1944, the number of working women doubled to approximately 1.1 million – part of the wider economic expansion discussed by Graham Broad in Chapter 6 of this volume.[31] Government propaganda stressed that women had a patriotic duty to work for the war effort. Their reasons for entering the labour force varied, however, and though some were inspired by patriotism, many others saw employment as a route to independence and freedom.[32]

Jewish women were no different in this regard. For many, salaried work constituted their first chance to exercise a degree of independence. Born in 1924, Ida Holtzkener was sixteen when she left school and embarked on a series of wartime jobs. Having moved to London, Ontario, from Toronto with her family in 1936, she was employed by a London furrier and then a cheesemaker before going back to Toronto around 1941 to work in a factory making air force uniforms. She recalled, "I missed Toronto so much and was a youngster,"[33] implying that a desire for excitement and the chance to be free of parental oversight were a big part of her decision to return to Toronto on her own. Eventually moving back to London to be with her family, Ida did what many women did during the war years – she applied to Central Aircraft Factory to work on military airplanes in 1942. Her incentive was money: "At that stage I was looking for

Figure 5.1

Ida Holtzkener (with plaid collar, shown here in about 1942) appreciated the financial freedom and independence from family supervision that came with her various wartime factory jobs. | Courtesy of Ida Holtzkener.

work, I was looking for something that pays well."[34] Achieving freedom and financial independence rather than helping the Jewish community was her motivation for undertaking war work.

Regardless of why they joined the labour force, Jewish women typically had to deal with discrimination at work. Many interviewees, often the only Jewish person in the factory or workplace, experienced anti-Semitism on the job. Ida said, "I don't remember the circumstances, but once it [a comment about her] was something to do with being Jewish, being a Jew. I was about the only one there, certainly in the department where I was."[35] She dismissed the incident by saying, "It got straightened out."[36] In skimming over the details, Ida confirms Sugiman's argument that nostalgia can soften the memory of difficult events. By contrast, Helen Mlotek was much more definitive about the anti-Semitism she faced: "If you went to a Gentile place for a job, they ask you what church you belong to, and if you say, 'Palmer Street Synagogue,' you're going to get 'we'll let you know.' You had to go to a Jewish place to get a job, more or less." She added that some businesses paid lip service to inclusivity: "They used to have a token Jew everywhere. Like, they could have had thirty or forty others, and let's say Eaton's or Simpson's or something and so, 'oh, we have one Jew, one Chinaman, one coloured.' So they can say, 'We've done our bit.'"[37]

However, as the war progressed, the supply of workers dwindled. Early in the conflict, married women, especially those with children, were discouraged from seeking paid employment. But by 1943, even they were being recruited to work in various industries, as the pool of single and childless women declined.[38] Thus, as Dionne Brand shows in the case of black Canadian women, the growing need for workers was hugely beneficial for minority women since jobs that had previously been closed to them were suddenly opened, providing exciting new opportunities.[39] Employers could simply no longer afford to turn away willing staff, so Jewish women were hired on. However, as was the case for most women,[40] their employment was a temporary measure, tolerated only because of the national emergency and expected to end when the men returned. Unlike other women, however, Jewish women faced a double restriction on their employment: not only did their gender keep them out of work, their religion narrowed their choices and probably meant that they would be among the first to be let go.

Their desire to enter the public sphere, whether to achieve personal goals or to support their community, could conflict with the expectations of their families. For instance, although most Jewish girls adhered to traditional gender norms that prevented them from pursuing higher education, others heeded the broader Jewish tradition that emphasized education and went on to earn university degrees. Most parents did not support such aspirations, but achieving a certain level of financial independence allowed one of my interviewees to attend university against the wishes of her parents. Like many women, Ruth Rischall took a variety of jobs during the war, first in the National Registration office, registering women to enter the workforce and then as a filing clerk in the Canadian government office of the Dominion Dairy Commissioner (now the Canadian Dairy Commission). She resigned from that position to work in the Postal Censorship Office. An excellent student, Ruth had taken German in high school and was the only person in the censorship office who did not have a post-secondary degree in languages. Her job entailed censoring the letters of German POWs being held in Canada. Like Ida Holtzkener, she stated specifically that her motivation for taking the job was the increased salary, which meant she could go to university: "When I went from the dairy products division to Postal Censorship, my salary doubled." She worked in the censorship office for a couple of years and then, "I had enough money to go to college and I resigned."[41]

Whereas work led to increased independence for some women, it could also generate anxiety for those who were trying to negotiate the sometimes complicated relationship between patriotism, independence, and faith. Some girls joined associations to contribute to the war effort, only to find themselves assigned tasks that contravened Jewish law. This led to a struggle between faith and religious identity, and the desire to aid the war effort and earn an independent living. For example, when Clara Halpern was elected president of the Junior Red Cross (JRC) chapter at her high school, she was very pleased: "I wanted that job so badly ... I tried to collect as much money as possible; we had maybe a bake sale."[42] However, Clara's involvement with the JRC caused some friction with her Jewishness. Organized through schools as an extracurricular activity, the JRC was an offshoot of the Canadian Red Cross Society and was meant to foster international co-operation by promoting mutual understanding and friendship. During the war, it focused on supporting the troops and raising money for humanitarian aid, and was thus seen as a patriotic endeavour, though it tried to avoid overt political statements.[43] Clara helped her chapter organize a school dance. Since JRC members were expected to raise money on their own and not to appeal to their parents or other adults, the dance would have been a major fundraiser for her chapter.[44] As president, she was expected to attend and give a few remarks. However, the dance was held on a Friday night, the beginning of the Jewish Sabbath, which was a cause for concern. Her family was observant – her father was an Orthodox rabbi – and in many ways her attendance contravened Jewish law.[45] "The dance was on Friday night," Clara recalled, "and I had to make an appearance. And I knew I was forbidden to go. And I had a talk with my father, and he said, 'Okay, I will allow you to go, but don't touch any money at all. Just go, talk, speak to them, and come back home.'"[46] Clara and her father found a way to make her support for the Red Cross and the war effort work within Jewish laws, demonstrating his support for both his daughter and the war effort.

Many of my Canadian Jewish women interview partners remember the war years as their first introduction to life outside the home and as providing them with a degree of fun and excitement, despite their knowledge of what was happening overseas. Ida Holtzkener moved to Toronto because she was "a youngster" looking for independence and adventure, and after she returned to London, she was part of a group that hosted dances for Jewish soldiers who came in from St. Thomas, the site of an air training base. Helen Mlotek was part of Hashomer HaTzair (the Young Guard), a Zionist group whose purpose was to train young Jews to become settlers in Palestine. Like the Girl Guides or the Boy Scouts, it was a social group, though it had the added bonus of being a mixed-gender organization, which the Guides and Scouts were not. Helen remembered, "Friday was co-ed; we did the horas [traditional Jewish dance] and we sat around [and] told stories." Her group also went on camping trips: "It was a fun group, and they rented space around Lake Simcoe ... We had baseball, we had running, anything to do with outside. Volleyball. And then we went swimming maybe twice a day."[47] Her participation in Hashomer during the war years was a highlight of her memories of that time, something she dwelt upon extensively during her interview. Fran Parnes was a member of Habonim, another Jewish youth group dedicated to Zionism, and she, too, attended mixed-gender Jewish summer camps, as well as putting on concerts and shows whose proceeds supported the war effort.[48]

Involvement in groups such as Hashomer HaTzair or Ida's dance-hosting organization for Jewish soldiers also helped to bolster Jewish identity.[49] Not only did these youth groups and their activities offer elements of escape from the anxieties and hardships of the time, they also encouraged relationships between Jewish individuals, which worked towards preventing intermarriage and assimilation, something much on the minds of Jewish community leaders who saw intermarriage as a threat.[50] The wider Jewish community shared this concern; as Jews became increasingly assimilated into Canadian society, Jewish-Gentile intermarriage rates grew from 4.9 percent of all weddings involving a Jewish bride or groom in 1926 to 12.4 percent in 1944.[51] Moreover, participation in Jewish youth groups, combined with the impact of the Holocaust as the extent and depth of Nazi atrocities were revealed, helped to fuel support for a Jewish homeland and drove many Jewish Canadians to raise money for charities dedicated to supporting Israel, especially after its founding in 1948. Helen and her husband, for instance, diligently raised money for the Jewish National Fund, an organization dedicated to maintaining and providing clean water and viable farmland, and to building infrastructure in Israel. So great was their support that the Toronto chapter of the national fund honoured them in the 1980s for their decades of service.[52] In this way, the wartime work done by many of my interview partners had lifelong repercussions and could extend well beyond Canada.

Oral history is about rediscovering those who have been left out of the historical record and allowing their voices to enrich our understanding of the past. The lives and experiences of the Jewish women whom I interviewed reveal much about how life on the home front was framed not only by gender, but also by faith and culture. Jewish Canadian women's reasons for participating in the war effort were more often grounded in a desire for financial independence and freedom than in simple patriotism. Nor did women seek an income for identical reasons: Ruth needed to fund her post-secondary studies, given the opposition of her parents. Along with these individual motives, women's involvement in wartime activities was also rooted in family or community reasons. Several interviewees participated because of family members left behind in Europe and the devastating knowledge of what that meant. The community was aware of what was happening through information gleaned from family and friends overseas and, as Margolis shows, via the Yiddish press.

Moreover, though Jewish women shared many of the same home front experiences as white Christian women, such as entering the workforce, organizing fundraising events, and writing letters to family overseas, they dealt with the added burden of anti-Semitism. Although labour shortages eventually opened the job market to them, this shift was widely seen as temporary. Such was the case for all women who undertook war work, but the "accommodation" was doubly fragile for Jewish women. Their identity as both women *and* Jews excluded them from post-war employment. Despite the shocking evidence of the Holocaust that surfaced at the conclusion of the war, anti-Jewish attitudes remained strong in Canada. The war was not a panacea for anti-Semitism; in 1946, a Canadian poll still listed Jews as the "second least desirable immigrants."[53] Nevertheless, anti-Semitism, though never disappearing, did begin to decrease in the aftermath of the Second World War, due in part to the Jewish community showing its commitment to Canada and the war effort. By demonstrating loyalty, Canadian Jews proved their right to be considered full citizens.

As a Jewish woman myself, it was fascinating, and occasionally surreal, to listen as my interview partners recounted their memories of the war years. It is even more surreal to realize that their stories have not been explored in depth before, despite the immense literature about Canada's war years. Their grief, anxiety, and sense of helplessness regarding what was happening to their families in Europe, as well as the overt anti-Semitism they faced, are practically unimaginable today. But I feel connected to them, and as Karen Olson and Linda Shopes state, "by researching subjects that are close to home, we have a greater opportunity – and perhaps feel a greater urgency – to communicate what informants have told us."[54] The life experiences of Ida, Clara, Fran, Ruth, and Helen show us that a treasure trove of information remains to be discovered, one that will provide a far more complete and nuanced understanding of Canada's war years.

Notes

1 Irving Abella, *A Coat of Many Colours: Two Centuries of Jewish Life in Canada* (Toronto: Lester and Orpen Dennys, 1990), 205–6.

2 Pamela Wakewich and Helen Smith, "The Politics of 'Selective' Memory: Re-Visioning Canadian Women's Wartime Work in the Public Record," *Oral History* 34, 2 (Autumn 2006): 58–59. Hurricanes were single-seater fighter planes developed in the United Kingdom during the Second World War. Elsie MacGill oversaw their production in Canada between 1939 and 1943. Her life and work were even turned into a comic book that was produced and distributed in the United States. Titled *Queen of the Hurricanes: Elsie MacGill,* it is reprinted in Pamela Wakewich, "'The Queen of the Hurricanes': Elsie Gregory MacGill, Aeronautical Engineer and Women's Advocate," in *Framing Our Past: Canadian Women's History in the Twentieth Century,* ed. Kate O'Rourke, Lorna R. McLean, and Sharon A. Cook (Montreal and Kingston: McGill-Queen's University Press, 2001), 398–99.

3 Ruth Roach Pierson, *"They're Still Women After All": The Second World War and Canadian Womanhood* (Toronto: McClelland and Stewart, 1986).

4 Kimberlé Crenshaw, "Demarginalizing the Intersection of Race and Sex: A Black Feminist Critique of Antidiscrimination Doctrine, Feminist Theory, and Antiracist Politics," *University of Chicago Legal Forum* 1 (1989): 139–67, https://chicagounbound.uchicago.edu/cgi/viewcontent.cgi?article=1052&context=uclf.

5 See, for example, Dionne Brand, "'We Weren't Allowed to Go," 171–91; Sandra Battaglini, "'Don't Go Down the Mine, Mamma!': Women in Production Jobs at Inco during World War II, 1942–1945," in *The Harvest of a New Life: Documenting, Thinking and Representing the Italian-Canadian Experience,* ed. Diana Iuele-Colilli (Welland, ON: Editions Soleil, 2002), 37–73; Pamela Sugiman, "'A Million Hearts from Here': Japanese Canadian Mothers and Daughters and the Lessons of War," *Journal of American Ethnic History* 26, 4 (2007): 50–68; Pamela Sugiman, "Memories of Internment: Narrating Japanese Canadian Women's Life Stories," *Canadian Journal of Sociology* 29, 3 (Summer 2004): 359–88; Pamela Sugiman, "'Life Is Sweet': Vulnerability and Composure in the Wartime Narratives of Japanese Canadians," *Journal of Canadian Studies* 43, 1 (Winter 2009): 186–218, doi:10.3138/jcs.43.1.186; and Pamela Sugiman, "'These Feelings That Fill My Heart': Japanese Canadian Women's Memories of Internment," *Oral History* 34, 2 (2006): 69–84.

6 Gerald Tulchinsky, *Branching Out: The Transformation of the Canadian Jewish Community* (Toronto: Stoddart, 1998), 209–10, 220–21, 228–29; and *Canada's Jews: A People's Journey* (Toronto: University of Toronto Press, 2008), 376. *Branching Out* was the second book in a two-part work; the first was titled *Taking Root: The Origins of the Canadian Jewish Community* (Toronto: Key Porter Books, 1992). Interestingly, though Tulchinsky

includes many quotations from Jewish men who served in the war, he includes none from women who were active on the home front. The only women whose voices we hear are those who write for information on injured or missing relatives. Moreover, many men are mentioned by name, but few women are, though this is partially due to the fact that women's first names were often not recorded. It should be noted that even on this one page in *Canada's Jews,* the focus is on Jewish women who joined the services, not on their contributions on the home front.

7 James Walker, "Claiming Equality for Canadian Jewry: The Struggle for Equality, 1930–1945," in *Nazi Germany, Canadian Responses: Confronting Antisemitism in the Shadow of War,* ed. L. Ruth Klein (Montreal and Kingston: McGill-Queen's University Press, 2012), 239. In an unpublished paper, I discuss the work of the Canadian Jewish Congress's Women's War Efforts Committee and the thousands of hours it devoted to creating the servicemen's centres, which hosted hundreds of thousands of visitors during their three years of operation. Jennifer Shaw, "'I Do Think We Can Carry On': The Women's War Efforts Committee of the Canadian Jewish Congress, 1939–1946" (unpublished paper, 2017).

8 Gendered analyses of the Holocaust are numerous. For a good overview, see Myrna Goldenberg and Amy H. Shapiro, eds., *Different Horrors/Same Hell: Gender and the Holocaust* (Seattle: University of Washington Press, 2013).

9 Joan Sangster, *Through Feminist Eyes: Essays on Canadian Women's History* (Edmonton: Athabasca University Press, 2011), 213.

10 Sugiman, "'These Feelings That Fill My Heart,'" 74.

11 Pierson, *"They're Still Women"*; Jeffrey Keshen, "Revisiting Canada's Civilian Women during World War II," *Histoire sociale/Social History* 30, 60 (1997): 239–66; Jeffrey A. Keshen, *Saints, Sinners, and Soldiers: Canada's Second World War* (Vancouver: UBC Press, 2004).

12 Franklin Bialystok, *Delayed Impact: The Holocaust and the Canadian Jewish Community* (Montreal and Kingston: McGill-Queen's University Press, 2000), 15.

13 Ida Holtzkener, interview by Jennifer Shaw, Toronto, 3 May 2016. All women included in this study consented to having their real names used.

14 Rebecca Margolis, "A Review of the Yiddish Media; Responses of the Jewish Immigrant Community in Canada," in Klein, *Nazi Germany, Canadian Responses,* 118. Margolis points out that the Yiddish press covered the Nazi campaign against the Jewish community, a source that many non–Yiddish speaking historians have ignored. At the time, more than 60 percent of Canadian Jews spoke Yiddish as a first language and would obviously have been able to read the Yiddish press.

15 Helen Mlotek, interview by Jennifer Shaw, Toronto, 3 May 2016.

16 Fran Parnes, interview by Jennifer Shaw, Windsor, 23 November 2016. "Bubbe" and "zaidy" are Yiddish for "grandmother" and "grandfather."

17 Jenny Hartley, "'Letters Are *Everything* These Days': Mothers and Letters in the Second World War," in *Epistolary Selves: Letters and Letter-Writers, 1600–1945,* ed. Rebecca Earle (Aldershot, UK: Ashgate, 1999), 183, 193.

18 Fran Parnes, interview by Jennifer Shaw, Windsor, 23 November 2016.

19 Hartley, "'Letters Are *Everything* These Days,'" 186.

20 Fran Parnes, interview by Jennifer Shaw, Windsor, 23 November 2016.

21 Ibid.

22 Ibid.

23 Ibid.

24 Irving Abella and Harold Troper, *None Is Too Many: Canada and the Jews of Europe, 1933–1948* (Toronto: Lester and Orpen Dennys, 1982), x. The title of this book comes

from an off-the-record comment made by a Canadian government official in 1945, who, when asked how many Jews would be allowed into the country, reportedly replied, "None is too many."

25 Fran Parnes, interview by Jennifer Shaw, Windsor, 23 November 2016.
26 Ellin Bessner, *Double Threat: Canadian Jews, the Military, and World War II* (Toronto: New Jewish Press, 2018), 2–3.
27 Fran Parnes, interview by Jennifer Shaw, Windsor, 23 November 2016.
28 Ibid.
29 James W. St. G. Walker, "Race and Recruitment in World War I: Enlistment of Visible Minorities in the Canadian Expeditionary Force," *Canadian Historical Review* 70, 1 (March 1989): 3.
30 Pierson, *"They're Still Women,"* 23. Pierson states that at the beginning of the war, 900,000 people were registered as unemployed, of a workforce of approximately 3.8 million.
31 Keshen, "Revisiting Canada's Civilian Women," 246.
32 Keshen, *Saints, Sinners, and Soldiers,* 247, 161.
33 Ida Holtzkener, interview by Jennifer Shaw, Toronto, 3 May 2016.
34 Ibid.
35 Ibid.
36 Ibid.
37 Helen Mlotek, interview by Jennifer Shaw, Toronto, 3 May 2016.
38 Pierson, *"They're Still Women,"* 27–30.
39 Brand, "'We Weren't Allowed to Go,'" 179.
40 Keshen, *Saints, Sinners, and Soldiers,* 163–65.
41 Ruth Rischall, interview by Jennifer Shaw, Skype, 21 September 2016. Ruth ended up at Queen's University. It was known to be more accepting of Jewish students than other prominent universities, such as the University of Toronto and McGill University, where quotas on Jewish enrollment were in place. However, it should be noted that anti-Semitism did occur at Queen's before, during, and immediately after the war. See Michael Brown, "On Campus in the Thirties: Antipathy, Support, and Indifference," in Klein, *Nazi Germany, Canadian Responses,* 144–82; and Randal F. Schnoor, "The Contours of Canadian Jewish Life," *Contemporary Jewry* 31, 3 (October 2011): 181, doi:10.1007/s12397-011-9075-6.
42 Clara Halpern, interview by Jennifer Shaw, 8 February 2017.
43 Sarah Glassford, "Practical Patriotism: How the Canadian Junior Red Cross and Its Child Members Met the Challenge of the Second World War," *Journal of the History of Childhood and Youth* 7, 2 (Spring 2014): 220–22, doi:0.1353/hcy.2014.0024.
44 Ibid., 229–30.
45 A full explanation of *halacha* – Jewish law – is beyond the scope of this chapter, but the rules for the Sabbath would not have permitted Clara to drive or accept a ride to her school, touch money while at the dance, or use a microphone when she addressed the students.
46 Clara Halpern, Skype interview by Jennifer Shaw, 8 February 2017.
47 Helen Mlotek, interview by Jennifer Shaw, Toronto, 3 May 2016.
48 Fran Parnes, interview by Jennifer Shaw, Windsor, 23 November 2016.
49 Tulchinsky, *Branching Out,* 283.
50 Ibid.
51 Ibid., 282. The Jewish community succeeded in bringing down the rate of intermarriage, though only briefly: in 1946, it dropped to 10.4 percent, but it increased steadily throughout the 1950s and 1960s. Intermarriage would spark even greater concerns during the 1960s, as Jews became more accepted in Canada, anti-Semitism diminished,

and both Jews and Christians were increasingly willing to marry outside their faiths. See Morton Weinfeld, "Intermarriage: Agony and Adaptation," in *The Canadian Jewish Mosaic,* ed. Morton Weinfeld, William Shaffir, and Irwin Cotler (Toronto: John Wiley and Sons, 1981), 365–82.

52 Helen Mlotek, interview by Jennifer Shaw, Toronto, 3 May 2016.

53 Tulchinsky, *Canada's Jews,* 402–3.

54 Karen Olson and Linda Shopes, "Crossing Boundaries, Building Bridges: Doing Oral History among Working-Class Women and Men," in *Women's Words: The Feminist Practice of Oral History,* ed. Sherna Berger Gluck and Daphne Patai (New York: Routledge, 1991), 199.

6

Shopping to Win the War

Female Consumers and Canada's Home Front

Graham Broad

In September 1940, as the Battle of Britain raged in the skies over southern England and the outcome of the war hung in the balance, Canada's most popular women's magazine, *Chatelaine,* published a remarkable issue devoted to "shopping to win the war." Canadian women, wrote columnist Alice Sharples, "have burned with a desire to do something towards waging and winning the war." But what could that be? As yet, there were no women's services in the armed forces or urgent calls for women to fill jobs in war industry, which had only just begun to produce munitions on a significant scale. Sharples's answer was one that *Chatelaine* editor, Byrne Hope Sanders (whose work for the Wartime Prices and Trade Board is discussed in Chapter 7 of this volume), promised to "hammer away at" for the duration of the conflict: that women should "shop to win the war."[1] Sharples put it this way: "It is our *duty* not to wear our old tweeds but to buy new ones ... not to make last year's frocks 'do' but to launch out in famous English prints; not to do without tea but to serve more tea than ever." Women would shore up the empire's economy by buying British and Canadian goods; they would maintain morale on the home front, with a smart appearance and thoughtful gifts; and they would model the latest fashions, especially for American tourists, whose hard US currency was needed north of the border. "Every woman a mannequin," Sharples proclaimed.[2] During the first two years of the war, nearly all the major women's organizations in Canada promoted this shop-to-win approach. The National Council of Women formally endorsed a "Buy British" and "Buy Canadian" platform at its annual congress in the summer of 1940.[3] Even groups such as the popular and influential Imperial Order Daughters of the Empire, whose leadership had at times expressed grave misgivings about the excesses of modern materialism, fully approved the "shop to win the war" ethos. It is my contention in this chapter that shopping to win the war, in one form or another, remained the foundation of consumer culture in Canada throughout the conflict. Patriotic groups, retailers, advertisers, and government agencies never stopped exhorting female consumers that buying the right thing in the right way was a vital contribution to the war effort.

This is not, perhaps, the image of consumerism that most readily comes to mind when the war is mentioned. The historical imagination tends to recall an era of penurious patriotism: rationing, shortages, scrap metal drives, carpooling, and make-do reviews, in which old clothes were made over into new. Canadians, the story goes, scrimped and saved, ate their rationed portions, planted their Victory Gardens, and bought their Victory Bonds, which they tucked away, awaiting a happier time. Undeniably, all this was part of life on the home front for at least the last half of the war. It is also true that the expanding war effort made shopping progressively more difficult for Canadian consumers, as resources were diverted to military needs.[4] But the overall picture is far more complicated. Hardly anyone in government or the press called for consumer restraint until well into 1941. Moreover, our understanding of wartime consumerism must be anchored to one inescapable fact: consumer spending in Canada went up during the Second World War, sometimes dramatically. Despite the emergence of shortages in late 1941 and the introduction of rationing in 1942, accompanied by a punishing *fifteen*-fold increase in personal taxation, retail sales grew by nearly 50 percent even after inflation is factored in – faster even than in the supposed consumer boom of the six years that followed the war. Jewellery, women's clothing, shoe, and drugstore sales doubled, beer consumption increased by two-and-a-half times, the restaurant business tripled, and paid admissions to movie theatres jumped from 137 million in 1939 to 215 million by 1945.[5] As one store owner put it in 1943, "My inventories are shrinking. Shelves are showing bare spots. Many lines of merchandise are in short supply, and business is booming."[6]

Canadian woman presided over a post-Depression consumer boom made possible by the rapid wartime growth in consumer purchasing power. With paid work available to almost anyone who wanted a job, per capita disposable incomes (adjusted to constant 1939 dollars) rose from $373 in 1939 to $587 by 1945, an increase of 57 percent. In roughly the same period, personal savings grew exponentially: from a meagre $18 per capita to $125 by 1944.[7] Spending and saving were largely the responsibility of female homemakers, who had become, as historian Cynthia Comacchio puts it, the "managers of household consumption" by the early twentieth century.[8] A 1939 trade journal advertisement for *Chatelaine* captured this idea succinctly, depicting a woman in her bridal gown under the tag line "Purchasing Agent (Just Appointed.)"[9] The ad copy went on: "The radiant girl you see is not only a bride. She is also a woman embarking on a lifetime career in the business of home making. Among other duties which she will now assume are those of purchasing agent for her new household." This was not just highly gendered hyperbole. In retail and advertising trade journals, it was an article of faith that women were responsible for about 85 percent of families' consumer spending (and had a good idea of what happened to the other 15, Byrne Hope Sanders liked to say), even exercising great leverage over the purchase of big-ticket items, such as major appliances and automobiles. Sanders was therefore perfectly sincere when, in the shop to win the war issue of *Chatelaine*, she urged Canadian women "not to take on too much work" outside the home, admonishing them gently that "your first loyalty and duty must be to your family."[10] Like many other boosters of the shop-to-win ethos, she saw no distinction between shopping responsibly for the family and supporting the war effort. As innumerable commentators noted at the time, the family was the moral foundation of the nation and the war itself a great moral struggle against a cruel and inhumane foe. It therefore followed that proper (or, in wartime, *patriotic*) consumerism fortified the family and the whole country in turn.

Nonetheless, considered in retrospect, the topic of consumer spending on Canada's home front might seem trivial in juxtaposition to such momentous events as the great campaigns fought to liberate Europe and the Pacific. But to contemporaries, the social significance of the emergence of a mass consumer society in the preceding generation and the vast scale of economic activity that it represented were anything but trivial. Politicians, journalists, academics, social reformers, novelists, poets, preachers, and ordinary Canadians added their voices to a chorus of discussion about buying things – a sustained conversation whose basic framework was established a century ago and continues today. The champions of the consumer society argued that modern mass consumerism generated prosperity and was democratizing and even civilizing; its critics, by contrast, fretted about materialism, vice, and moral decay. Finally, a relatively small number of Marxist or socialist critics (often contemptuously referred to by the business press as "university professors") contended that mass consumerism was homogenizing and stupefying, eroding working-class solidarity with false promises of emancipation. Admittedly, the world of middle-class consumption that was the subject of these debates was closed to many Canadians who, on the eve of war, remained poor, and to the hundreds of thousands who lived on farms without a steady supply of electricity, far from the shops and entertainments that were the hallmark of modern consumerism. But there can be little doubt that personal consumerism transformed the lives of millions of Canadians in the early twentieth century. They were the ones who could afford to indulge in the new consumer society, buying not just what they needed but also to satisfy a variety of non-material urges, as advertisers well knew. Certainly, Canadians owned the various accoutrements of middle-class existence (such as electrical appliances and automobiles) at a rate far exceeding anywhere else in the world except the United States.[11] In 1939, one Canadian in eight owned a car, twice the rate of ownership as in the United Kingdom and five times higher than in Germany. Even in Quebec, which had by far the lowest automobile ownership rates in the country, families were more likely to possess a car than anyone in Europe.[12]

Above all, personal consumption was the backbone of the economy, and it continued to be so even as the economy began its conversion to a wartime footing. This fact was one pillar of the shop-to-win argument: economic strength was the foundation of modern military power, and personal consumption was the foundation of the economy. Any study of consumers on the home front is therefore necessarily bound up in the history of the Canadian economy in wartime. One crude figure will illustrate the point: between 1939 and 1945, Ottawa spent approximately $19 billion on the war effort. During the same period, retail sales alone reached $25 billion.[13] So vast a quantity of economic activity in a time of war had to be regulated, as the government of Prime Minister William Lyon Mackenzie King understood. To that end, on 3 September 1939, a week before Canada formally declared war, King's government created a new agency, the Wartime Prices and Trade Board (WPTB), with a mandate to oversee the price and supply of food, fuel, and other commodities. For the next two years, however, the board operated on the periphery of an economy in which the war's impact on consumers had been mainly positive.[14] The second half of 1941 saw a major transformation in the economy, as military procurement plans established after the fall of France in June 1940 began to reach fruition. In addition, the continued growth of Canada's armed forces and the immense demands of the American rearmament program resulted in a large-scale diversion of raw materials, labour, and factory floor space for military needs.[15]

Only then did former supporters of the shop-to-win mantra start to preach a different gospel, one that favoured consumer restraint. Some commentators even began to allege that non-essential civilian consumption came at the expense of the war effort. In September 1941, the libertarian editor of the Canadian edition of *Liberty*, J.L. Rutledge, chastised Canadians for having "almost duplicated the fabulous spending jag of 1929" up to that point in the war. "We can either have more consumer goods or we can have more shells and more guns and more ships. The inescapable fact is that we can't have both," he wrote. One wonders what Rutledge thought of "September Shopping Spree," an article in the same issue that urged women to get out and buy, equipped with shopping lists and good shoes. "If you love nice things, you can't just wish for them! You *must* shop for them!" the article enthused.[16] During this transitional period between the initial consumer boom and the years of comparative austerity, such embarrassing juxtapositions were commonplace.

In any case, criticisms such as Rutledge's would ring out incessantly for the remainder of the war, even though the argument that civilian consumption undercut military production was not fully credible, as consumers must have realized. Under the War Measures Act, the government had the power to compel anything it wanted from the civilian economy. Canadian consumers faced shortages because resources were diverted for the war effort, but shortfalls in military requirements almost never arose due to non-essential civilian consumption. In one sense, however, the argument against non-essential consumption had merit: between growing wages and diminishing supply – especially of big-ticket items – the only possible outcome was inflation. As early as February 1941, the signs of an inflationary spiral had begun, and the National Council of Women urged the government to impose price controls on essential staple goods, including milk.[17] Then, between April and September, the cost of living index increased by an alarming 6 percent.[18] Rapid inflation of that kind threatened to do much more than undermine consumer purchasing power. Ottawa's total war expenditure for the fiscal year 1941–42 was projected to be $1.3 billion: ten times higher than in 1939–40 (and it would quadruple again by 1943–44).[19] With the government itself now a gigantic purchaser of goods, high inflation could potentially destabilize the country's entire military and economic program. More than anything else, this fact spurred King's government into action. In an October 1941 radio address to the nation, King announced that the WPTB would impose sweeping wage and price controls to combat inflation. Then, in language that was becoming increasingly familiar, he called on consumers to curtail their spending habits in favour of savings and thrift. "We must face the fact," he said, "that there are not enough materials to meet both the demands of consumers and the demands of war. We have no choice but to reduce our consumption of consumer goods. To us, too, has come the choice between guns and butter."[20]

The WPTB now assumed tremendous powers and responsibilities. Under the directorship of the formidable deputy governor of the Bank of Canada, Donald Gordon, it oversaw the implementation of broad-ranging price controls that froze the cost of nearly all goods and services beginning on 1 December 1941.[21] Over the next four years, the WPTB would become an omnipresent force in nearly every legal consumer transaction made in the country. Coupon rationing of sugar, coffee, tea, butter, and gasoline began in 1942. Meat rationing followed in 1943. When the United States entered the war, the supply of American component parts for civilian needs was cut off, and the production of most consumer durables, including electrical appliances, fell from record mid-1941 highs to a mere trickle. Civilian passenger car production halted altogether in early 1942, and the fabrication of tires for the civilian fleet plunged 95 percent. Orders from the WPTB required manufacturers to find additional economies in the production of goods still for sale, and retailers and consumers alike faced a ceaseless and often bewildering array of regulations governing buying and selling. Almost nothing escaped the board's attention. Administrators imposed a 25 percent "luxury" tax on non-essential goods and services, reduced store hours, cut the number of permissible deliveries, banned alcohol advertising, forbade bakeries from slicing bread, froze women's hat styles, removed the watch pocket from men's trousers, and even specified how many pins a retailer could use when pinning a folded shirt: twelve, down from the standard eighteen.[22] There were so many new regulations that the WPTB began publishing a periodical, *Consumers' News,* aimed largely at female shoppers, to help keep them informed. All this coincided with a deluge of new propaganda that discouraged needless spending in increasingly blunt and even confrontational language. Until late 1941, the government had been content to urge women to "serve by saving." In the next year, some propaganda went so far as to liken non-essential spending to treason. One striking mid-1942 advertisement produced by the National War Finance Committee depicts Adolf Hitler leaning over the shoulder of a woman who is about to go shopping. "Go on, spend it," he whispers into her ear. "What's the difference?" The copy went on, "The time has come when every nickel, dime and quarter you spend *needlessly* is money spent in the cause of our enemies!"[23]

The wage and price ceiling, coupled with the institution of coupon rationing, constituted an economic experiment of enormous and unprecedented complexity. Rules and regulations poured forth from WPTB offices in so vast a number that even their own officials had trouble keeping them all straight. Enforcing these rules was quite simply beyond WPTB capacity, as it lacked anything like the number of personnel required to ensure compliance. It was to the nation's homemakers, then, that Donald Gordon turned for help – a step explored in Chapter 7 of this volume. In a radio address delivered at the end of November 1941, Gordon warned of the dangers of inflation and appealed directly to housewives for support in maintaining the price ceiling:

> In this fight against inflation you cannot be neutral. You will either be helping to save yourself, your family, and your country from a terrible calamity, or you will be working for the enemy ... The housewife must be the real guardian of the law. Her job, for her country, will be to watch prices every day. She is the soldier in the battle line. She must battle against dishonesty, greed, stupidity – all the human weaknesses which are the allies of inflation and destruction.[24]

That month, Gordon met with the leaders of some eighteen women's voluntary groups and agreed to their proposal to create a liaison office between the WPTB and their organizations.[25] In a moment of inspiration, he chose none other than Byrne Hope Sanders, familiar to hundreds of thousands of Canadian women from her position at *Chatelaine,* to direct this new Consumer Branch. Almost overnight, it seemed, Sanders, along with the leaders of nearly every women's association in the country, converted to the new gospel of conservation and savings. And yet, Sanders had in some respects been correct when she had promised, in September 1940, to hammer away at the idea of shopping to win the war. Even as ever greater numbers of women took up paid employment, she never stopped insisting that their most important contribution to the war effort would be made in their traditional roles as wife, mother, homemaker, and principal consumer for the family: on the checkout line rather than the assembly line. They would report infractions of the price ceiling, black market dealings, and hoarding by retailers and unpatriotic neighbours; they would vow to follow the rules for rationing, buy only what they and their families needed, and plough the rest into Victory Bonds. Here was a ready-made job for women, of tremendous importance and not likely to ignite anxieties over transgressions of gender norms in the way that working in a factory or serving in uniform were wont to do.[26] "We women have been called in to wage a battle which is one of the most important ones in history," Sanders said in a March 1942 speech:

> Every one of us has our own patrol – the beat we tread on our shopping routes. Our weapons are our pencils and a list of prices. Our great and mobile defense line is the Wartime Prices and Trade Board. Our allies are our merchants; we know full well the horror of our foe – inflation ... So for the army on this home front, your country has picked soldiers who for years have been drilling for this work ... May we be worthy of this great hour in our history.[27]

Was all this, then, the beginning of the "penurious patriotism" of social memory? In part, perhaps. For the remainder of the war and into the early post-war period, shoppers had to choose from a narrower range of goods. Many consumer durables were completely unobtainable. Production of civilian radios, for instance, had fallen from half a million in 1940 to zero by 1944. There was a general decline in the availability of most semi-durables, too: department store stocks of clothing, to give another example, fell by about 20 percent.[28] Shopping for groceries could be an ordeal as well, with consumers never knowing what temporary or local shortages might suddenly arise. Those who bought more than they needed also faced the prospect of reproach from neighbours and friends. When Finance Minister J.L. Ilsley spoke to the National Council of Women in July 1943, he urged the members to "establish a code that frowns upon ostentation" and to bear in mind "that at this time a blatant spender should be considered a social outcast," to which they responded with enthusiasm, having complied already.[29]

But once again, we are confronted with the fact that despite shortages, rationing, and anti-spending campaigns, retail sales continued to rise throughout the war. Some contemporary critics and post-war historians argue that real inflation might have been higher than the official figure of about 3 percent from the imposition of price controls to the end of the war.[30] If this were the case, at least part of the apparent increase in consumer spending would be rendered illusory. However, such dramatic increases were not noted in various public opinion polls and surveys conducted during the war. Three Canadian Institute of Public Opinion polls (conducted in 1942, 1943, and 1945) found high levels of approval for the price ceiling and its effectiveness. Support for the ceiling grew over time, too, with the July 1945 poll finding that three-quarters of respondents favoured its continuation after the war – up from less than half in 1942. In addition, the WPTB's own surveys found generally high levels of endorsement for the price ceiling and its efficacy. Moreover, these surveys found that the income level of respondents produced remarkably little variation in that support, despite whatever anecdotal feedback the Women's Regional Advisory Committees of the Consumer Branch had managed to gather. Just 8 percent of lower-income consumers felt that the ceiling had failed to control prices. If, as some critics have charged, the retail sales boom was the effect of hidden inflation, it was not noted in contemporary surveys or polls, and we have no other reason to think that the official figures were very far off the mark.

The paradoxical impact of shortages combined with amplified consumer spending can be demonstrated by tracing the simultaneous increase in spending and savings. From 1939 to 1941 inclusive, Canadians spent, on average, just under 93 percent of their disposable income. From 1942 to 1945, that figure declined markedly to an average of just under 80 percent. During those years, however, total consumer spending grew from $4.7 billion to about $5.9 billion. In addition, as we have seen, per capita incomes rose sharply through the entire period. There are several remarkable facts to underscore here: first, Canadians had more money than ever, despite heavy taxation and the wage ceiling. Second, they *saved* more than ever. Third, they simultaneously *spent* more than ever, even though spending as a percentage of total disposable income declined by a hefty thirteen percentage points in the second half of the war. In short, for perhaps the only time in their history, Canadians on average had more money than they were able (or perhaps willing) to spend.

There are also good grounds for believing that most women saw the war's various impositions on them as consumers as comparatively minor, especially if they had suffered badly through the long years of the Great Depression. The cessation of civilian car and electrical appliance production, for instance, was of little consequence to the majority, who had never owned either, or even had electricity, in the first place. The case of rationing, too, is highly instructive. Only a handful of items were rationed and the WPTB's research revealed that rationing was not unpopular. Generally speaking, coupon rationing was implemented not merely to reduce consumption of a few staple foods (and gasoline) that were in short supply, but also to ensure equitable distribution. It was therefore socially levelling in ways that the free market was not. Indeed, direct action by women in the form of a near riot in Toronto helped establish butter rationing in late 1942. Moreover, rationing applied to a mere handful of goods for only part of the war, and the rationed portions were surprisingly generous. True, at a time when over 90 percent of Canadian households made their own preserves, the sugar allotment was generally felt to be inadequate, but the WPTB recognized the importance of canning and jarring to the food supply, so it arranged to release additional sugar. By contrast, meat rationing lasted only one year (it resumed for a time at war's end) and applied only to red meat, not pork, poultry, fish, or game. It was adopted in 1943 solely to help meet export requirements to Britain, and the rationed portions of up to *two pounds* per person – even for small children – could be *bigger* and more expensive than some families wanted. For inveterate coffee and tea drinkers, the ration of about a cup a day was barely sufficient, but they coped through such tricks as trading coupons with neighbours and friends, even though the rules initially prohibited this, and nothing prevented them from purchasing an extra cup at a canteen, lunch counter, or local restaurant. The restaurant business boomed during the war to accommodate the irregular schedules of shift workers, soldiers, and government employees, and also because a restaurant meal helped families to take the edge off rationing. To cope with other shortages, restaurants devised such novelties as meatless entrees and keeping sugar bowls off lunch counters (lest they be pocketed by customers seeking an extra ration), but restauranteurs struggled to find kitchen and waitstaff to contend with the swollen crowds. Finally, the gas ration provided the average car owner with enough fuel for about two thousand miles of driving per year. Farmers, doctors who made house calls, government officials, and others doing essential war work were permitted greater rations.

For the sixty percent of Canadian families who did not own a car, gasoline rationing was largely irrelevant; those who did own a car compensated for shortages by carpooling, busing, and taking trains between cities. Another way of coping, when coping was necessary, was by bending or breaking the rules. As with nearly all crimes, it is not clear how often people participated in the black market, as most infractions were not reported or prosecuted. There is evidence that a substantial black market arose in fake and reused ration coupons, but given the generous nature of food rationing and the fact that it affected only a few commodities, the black market may not have been especially sizable. Still, there were grey areas – technically illegal but seldom prosecuted – where friends and neighbours exchanged, bought, sold, and raffled coupons among themselves. One Ontario woman remembered, "Of course you could always trade with your neighbours. My shortage was always tea ... which meant I was always on the lookout for someone who wasn't quite so addicted."[31]

Government propaganda discouraging such behaviour as profligate spending features prominently in the historical imagination and is often reproduced in histories of the era. But the empirical fact is that Canadians received more commercial messages every day through advertising than they did from government efforts. In one of the country's most popular magazines, *Maclean's*, purely commercial advertising outnumbered government ads (propaganda, recruiting, and so forth) by a ratio of about thirteen to one, even at the peak of the war effort in 1944.[32] This was probably true of most other mass market magazines, and even a cursory scan of newspapers from the era reveals their continued reliance on local retail advertising, hawking all manner of goods.

Adworkers – that is, the writers of copy and the artists who illustrated ads – believed that they possessed unique insight into what made female consumers tick and adapted to wartime circumstances with alacrity.[33] They also felt that they played a critical role in the economy, using benevolent powers of suasion to aid consumers in making rational choices in their own best interests. They saw themselves as brokers in the vast commodity exchange of the modern era, and they never entirely abandoned the ethos of shopping to win the war. In 1941, advertisers began to unveil ingenious ways to convert wartime worries into rationales for continued consumption. Some of these methods were transposed from the First World War, whereas others – such as those that expressly equated political freedom with consumer choice – were new. As countless articles in their trade journals make clear, adworkers believed that advertising not only helped sell goods, but also carried and fostered a cultural ideal. It situated female consumers in the discourses of shopping patriotically to win the war and embraced what was valued about the past, including conventional understandings about a woman's role in society. At the same time, it advanced a modern and secular worldview in which better health, happiness, social status, prosperity, and even military victory and political freedom could be secured through personal consumption and the material progress it brought.

It is difficult to know how Canadian women understood the innumerable commercial impressions to which they were subjected every day, but there can be no doubting their ubiquity. In magazines and newspapers, on buses and streetcars, on the radio and in the movie theatre, in storefronts and from roadside billboards, female consumers were exposed to a ceaseless stream of advertising. Even the farm papers were jammed with ads. And, overwhelmingly, these appeals were directed at women, in recognition of the well-established fact that they handled most of the spending.

Broadly speaking, advertisements fell into three categories after 1940, when war themes began to appear in their illustrations and copy. The first type argued that the war gave women *additional* incentive to buy a given product. Such

Figure 6.1

Advertisers attempted to evade accusations of unpatriotic wastefulness by converting wartime anxieties into sales pitches. Here, Campana's Balm both protects a worker's hands and leaves them soft enough to charm a suitor. | "Your Hands Now Need Campana's Balm Protection *More Than Ever*!" *Maclean's*, 15 January 1944, 35.

objects were needed "more than ever," a phrase worn out by repetition. Usually, this was on the grounds that the product's qualities were more urgently needed in wartime than in peacetime: some products saved time (freeing it up for war-related work), some saved money (making it available for Victory Bonds), some safeguarded the family's health or promoted good nutrition (keeping the nation fighting fit), and so on. One example is an ad for a hand lotion called Campana's Italian Balm, in which the product is promoted for two practical purposes: it protects the hands of a female war worker from chapping and chafing, and renders them soft and lovely when a gentleman caller comes around later in the day.

The movement of hundreds of thousands of women into non-traditional jobs touched off what historian Ruth Roach Pierson calls widespread "jitters" about the war's impact on gender roles. These jitters were particularly evident in the case of some fifty thousand women who enlisted in the new women's auxiliaries of the army, navy, and air force. In her important study, Pierson detected a highly sexist backlash against these women, who, in the eyes of some traditionalists, stepped too far outside their proscribed social boundaries.[34] Whereas some historians argue that Pierson took her case too far, it is notable nonetheless how many wartime advertisements, like the Campana's ad discussed above, sought to assuage anxieties about changing gender roles. If war work and military service threatened to destabilize traditional female identities, a whole host of products promised to shore them up until circumstances could return to normal. As a corollary to the emphasis on beauty culture in munitions plants, which is explored in Chapter 12 of this volume, Palmolive sponsored a popular Miss War Worker beauty pageant.[35] Meanwhile, Helena Rubenstein cosmetics depicted a member of the Canadian Women's Army Corps (CWAC) under the tag line "Eager to serve – yet eager for beauty," reassuring readers that one need not come at the expense of the other.[36] And Blachford Shoe advertisements presented footwear specifically "made to fit the shapely feet of Canada's CWAC's, Air-women, and Wrens."[37]

Advertising depicted women both as capable and as the moral heart of the war effort, but also as particularly susceptible to a variety of infirmities: constipation, menstrual cramps, lack of knowledge about nutrition, and so forth. In peacetime, these were inconveniences, but now, adworkers suggested, they imperilled the entire war effort. One 1944 Kotex ad directed at war workers put the matter plainly: "Each time you stay at home – you keep our boys away from home, longer!"[38] Since the majority of women did not take up paid labour during the war, many ads referred to women as "house-soldiers," or some variation on the word, vesting their products with powers of transformation. A housewife in a Lysol ad calls on other women to "enlist for the war on germs!" Snapping a crisp salute, she says, "The housewife plays a vital part in National Defense. It is as important to protect health in the home as to protect the physical well-being of the army."[39] Similarly, Old Dutch cleanser depicted housewives marching down a residential street in lockstep with uniformed women.[40] A woman in an ad for Modess sanitary napkins proudly proclaims, "Everybody has a war job. Mine is in my house: shopping, mending, cleaning, cooking, looking after my family. To keep them healthy, well-fed, and happy is my contribution to victory." These tasks, of course, were made easier when certain other worries were eased by the "downy soft comfort of Modess."[41] Another of the company's ads in this vein can be seen in Figure 6.2.

The second category of wartime advertisement, of less interest to the present discussion, consisted of institutional ads placed by firms that, because of the conflict, no longer had anything to sell to civilians but sought to promote goodwill and brand name recognition for the post-war period. Ads in the third category, often related to the second, referenced not the present, but the future. They became more prominent late in the war, as Allied victory began to look assured. At their most extravagant, they heralded a future of rocket ships, flying cars, and domed cities, the stuff of Flash Gordon movie serials, made possible, or so the ads would claim, because of technological innovations unleashed during the war. By contrast, General Steel Wares portended something more plausible: a glittering "dream kitchen" of the future for happy housewives, dreamt up by the company's engineers while on breaks from designing war materials. Innumerable ads promised a future where, as one example put it, "Rosies stop riveting" and their dreams of "double drain-boards, swinging spout faucet, basket type strainer, and convenient storing cabinets" would come true.[42] Many ads envisioned a near future when families were reunited or sweethearts returned – accompanied by all the accoutrements of a consumerist domesticity. One popular Oneida Silverware ad, entitled "Back Home for Keeps," depicted a woman and her sweetheart, just returned from war, in a passionate embrace. "Crystal will gleam and silver will sparkle on a table set for two," the copy read. In the realm of advertising, the war was fought not just for democracy, but for a world of material abundance, of which Canadians could expect a hard-earned share.[43] It was, moreover, a world where pre-war gender expectations would be restored. The housewife of the future might have more free time, thanks to time-saving appliances, but she would certainly not seek freedom from domesticity. In one late war advertisement after another, fears of a post-war economic downturn or of a permanent transformation in familiar domestic (or economic) structures dissolved in a vision of material comfort.

Figure 6.2

In the world of advertising, and indeed from the perspective of the Wartime Prices and Trade Board, a housewife's foremost contribution to the war effort was to be a patriotic consumer for her family. In this ad, Modess sanitary napkins help a housewife consumer perform her duties during her (not-quite-defined) "difficult days." | "Like My Wartime Wagon?" Advertisement, *National Home Monthly*, April 1943, 45.

Figure 6.3

Late in the war, advertisers frequently depicted the glittering, high-tech "world of tomorrow." In a series of ads, General Steel Wares imagined post-war housewives, resplendent in their magnificent dream kitchens – thanks to the technological breakthroughs made by wartime engineers. | *Maclean's*, 15 October 1943, 30.

Did women really desire what advertisers promised? We cannot know for certain. However, the continued growth of consumer spending suggests a roughly parallel set of economic (if not cultural) interests between consumers and advertisers. The dramatic growth in consumer spending and retail sales also suggests that the social memory of wartime austerity is in many respects at odds with the facts. A safe conclusion would be that the war years were characterized by neither penurious patriotism nor guiltless mass consumption. With the advent of peace, even after years of full employment, many Canadians continued to live under economic circumstances that Magda Fahrni terms "rickety."[44] But even as thousands still lived in poverty, many had experienced a considerable and sometimes very great improvement in their standard of living during the war. Shopping on behalf of their families, Canadian women as a whole saved more than ever, but they also spent more than ever. There is every indication that, having done their bit through various forms of patriotic service, they also felt entitled to treat themselves to some non-essential shopping, a movie, or a meal out. For many women, this meant choosing to care for their families *and* for themselves – in a manner of *their* own choosing, no less – against the advice proffered by the WPTB and the various organizations to which they belonged or that professed to speak for them. Historians of Canada's home front in the Second World War have delved deeply into topics such as the rise of the Co-operative Commonwealth Federation, the development of the welfare state, and the possible alternatives offered by socialism. But they might do well to pay further attention to the "ism" whose wartime victory was decisive: consumerism.

Notes

1 This essay contains arguments made in Graham Broad, *A Small Price to Pay: Consumer Culture on the Canadian Home Front, 1939–45* (Vancouver: UBC Press, 2013).

2 Alice Sharples, "Shopping to Win the War," *Chatelaine*, September 1940, 38 (emphasis in original).

3 The National Council of Women of Canada (NCWC), *Yearbook* (Ottawa: NCWC, 1940), 29.

4 In this essay, I use the term "consumer" interchangeably with "shopper" and "buyer." One could argue that, strictly speaking, the consumer is one who actually *consumes* (uses) the product.

5 For retail sales and tax increases, see M.C. Urquhart and K.A.H. Buckley, eds., *Historical Statistics of Canada* (Cambridge: Cambridge University Press, 1965), Series T213–26 and Series H1–18. The rate of inflation was calculated using Bank of Canada, "Inflation Calculator," http://www.bankofcanada.ca/rates/related/inflation-calculator/.

6 *Drug Merchandising*, 1 October 1943, 26.

7 Urquhart and Buckley, *Historical Statistics*, Series E-66–78. Converted to constant 1939 dollars by the author.

8 Cynthia Comacchio, *The Infinite Bonds of Family: Domesticity in Canada, 1850–1940* (Toronto: University of Toronto Press, 1999), 150.
9 "Purchasing Agent," Advertisement, *Marketing*, 16 September 1939, 7.
10 Byrne Hope Sanders, "As an Editor Sees It," *Chatelaine*, September 1940, 60.
11 Canadian ownership rates from Dominion Bureau of Statistics, *Eighth Census of Canada, 1941*, vol. 9, *Housing* (Ottawa: King's Printer, 1941), Tables 12, 17, 18.
12 See *Facts and Figures of the Automobile Industry* (Canadian Automobile Chamber of Commerce, 1941), 15–19.
13 C.P. Stacey, *Arms, Men and Governments: Canada's War Policies* (Ottawa: Queen's Printer, 1970), 532–35; Urquhart and Buckley, *Historical Statistics*, Series T1–24.
14 The best administrative study of the WPTB is Christopher Waddell, "The Wartime Prices and Trade Board: Price Control in Canada in World War II" (PhD diss., York University, 1981).
15 On the transition of the Canadian economy to a war footing, see Michael Hennessy, "The Industrial Front: The Scale and Scope of Canadian Industrial Mobilization during the Second World War," in *Forging a Nation: Perspectives on the Canadian Military Experience*, ed. Bernd Horn (St. Catharines, Vanwell, 2002), 135–54. The impact of the American rearmament program on Canada's economy is discussed in James R. Warren, *Wartime Economic Co-operation: A Study of Relations between Canada and the United States* (Toronto: Ryerson Press, 1949).
16 J.L. Rutledge, "Editorial," *Liberty*, September 1941, 3; Bubbles Schanasi, "September Shopping Spree," *Liberty*, September 1941, 56 (emphasis in original).
17 Library and Archives of Canada (LAC), National Council of Women fonds, MG 28, vol. 79, file 19, NCW Resolutions and Correspondence, 1940–41.
18 Dominion Bureau of Statistics, *Cost of Living Index Numbers of Canada, 1941* (Ottawa: King's Printer, 1942).
19 Stacey, *Arms, Men and Governments*, 532.
20 William Lyon Mackenzie King, "Controlling the Cost of Living," CBC Radio, 18 October 1941, in William Lyon Mackenzie King, *Canada and the Fight for Freedom* (Toronto: Macmillan, 1944), 33.
21 On Gordon, see Joseph Schull, *The Great Scot: A Biography of Donald Gordon* (Montreal and Kingston: McGill-Queen's University Press, 1979).
22 The reduction in the number of pins is described in *Men's Wear Merchandising*, 1 July 1942, 19.
23 "Go On, Spend It," *Maclean's*, 1 July 1942, 28 (emphasis in original).
24 LAC, RG 64, vol. 6, file 145, Donald Gordon speeches.
25 LAC, RG 64, vol. 60, file 1, "A Brief Summary of the Origins and Development of the Consumer Branch of the Wartime Prices and Trade Board."
26 On gender norms in wartime Canada, see Ruth Roach Pierson, *"They're Still Women After All": The Second World War and Canadian Womanhood* (Toronto: McClelland and Stewart, 1986).
27 LAC, RG 64, vol. 1449, file A-10-29-16, Consumer Branch Administration, Address by Byrne Hope Sanders, March 1942.
28 See *Department Store Sales and Stocks, January 1941 to July 1948, by Months* (Ottawa: Dominion Bureau of Statistics, 1948).
29 "Speech by the Honourable J.L. Ilsley," in The National Council of Women, *Yearbook* (Ottawa: NCWC, 1943).
30 For example, E.J. Spence, "Wartime Price Control Policy in Canada" (PhD diss., Northwestern University, 1947); and Waddell, "The Wartime Prices and Trade Board," 211–314, 727–49. I investigate and reject the claim in Broad, *A Small Price to Pay*, 196–209.

31 Effie Donnell, quoted in Bill McNeil, ed., *Voices of a War Remembered: An Oral History of Canadians in World War II* (Toronto: Doubleday, 1991), 122.
32 See Tables 3.1 and 3.2 in Broad, *A Small Price to Pay*, 83–84.
33 The term "adworker" is Russell Johnston's, coined for his *Selling Themselves: The Emergence of Canadian Advertising* (Toronto: University of Toronto Press, 2001), which has also influenced my thinking about how members of the profession saw themselves.
34 Pierson, *"They're Still Women."*
35 "Me – Enter a Beauty Contest?" Advertisement, *National Home Monthly*, February 1943, 19. The contest winner was Dorothy Linham, a nineteen-year-old inspector at Research Enterprises Limited. Judging by the volume of coverage in the *Toronto Daily Star* – nearly a full page in total – this was no small competition. Linham's prize included a diamond watch and four hundred dollars, about equal to three months' pay. See various stories in the *Toronto Daily Star*, especially 20 July 1942, 3.
36 "Eager to Serve," Advertisement, *Echoes*, Spring 1942, 2.
37 "Made to Fit the Shapely Feet," Advertisement, *National Home Monthly*, April 1944, 68.
38 "I Don't Want to Be an Absentee," Advertisement, *National Home Monthly*, May 1944, 59.
39 "Enlist for the War on Germs," Advertisement, *Maclean's*, 15 July 1941, 28.
40 Old Dutch advertisement, reprinted in *Marketing*, October 1942, n.p.
41 "I Man the Home Front," Advertisement, *Maclean's*, 1 September 1942, 37.
42 "When Rosies Stop Riveting," Advertisement, *Canadian Homes and Gardens*, April 1944, 59.
43 For a thorough discussion of wartime advertising, see Broad, *A Small Price to Pay*, Chapters 2–5.
44 Magda Fahrni, "Counting the Costs of Living: Gender, Citizenship, and a Politics of Prices in 1940s Montreal," *Canadian Historical Review* 83, 4 (2002): 493.

7

Mrs. Consumer Goes to War

The Consumer Branch and Economic Policy Making

Joseph Tohill

In May 1944, more than seven hundred cities and towns across Canada took part in a national celebration of "that modest and in many respects reticent person, the Canadian housewife," for her role in fighting the battle against inflation. Organized by the Consumer Branch of the federal government's Wartime Prices and Trade Board (WPTB, also discussed by Graham Broad in Chapter 6 of this volume), "Mrs. Consumer Week" was timed to coincide with the end of both the third Victory Loan campaign and the women's club season. It featured widespread radio coverage, hundreds of newspaper and magazine advertisements and articles, thousands of meetings of women's groups, and countless window displays in retail stores. Editorialists called on "all mere males [to] pay tribute" to Mrs. Consumer, and a full-colour poster produced by the Wartime Information Board encapsulated the week's theme. Titled *Thank You Mrs. Consumer,* it depicts a smartly dressed, middle-aged woman who is clearly out on a shopping trip, her purse clamped under her arm as if to say she has a firm hold on her pocketbook. Around her, six men – a professional in a suit, a worker in overalls, a farmer, a sailor, a soldier, and an airman – salute her "for watching prices! Buying only what you need! Investing in war savings!" Effortlessly balancing three trim packages in one hand and her family's ration books in the other, she smilingly accepts their praise.[1]

Popular memory of and, to some extent, scholarly inquiry into women's contributions to the war effort are dominated by images of "Rosies of the North" and of members of the Canadian Women's Army Corps in uniform. However, Mrs. Consumer more accurately embodies the quotidian role that most women played in Canada's war. Roughly 50,000 of them served in the three branches of the armed forces, and over 260,000 took war production jobs. Yet many more engaged in the unpaid work of exercising their consumer citizenship. They watched prices, observed rationing regulations, conserved and remade clothing, canned produce, tended Victory Gardens, and invested in Victory Bonds and War Savings Stamps – all in the interests of channelling the 85 percent of consumer spending they were presumed to control in ways that prevented inflation. Much of this work took place under the auspices of the Consumer Branch, created in January 1942 by women whom the government and the WPTB called upon to police the retail price freeze imposed a month earlier.[2]

This chapter builds upon recent scholarship that focuses on the role that Canadian women, many of them working in tandem with the Consumer Branch, played in articulating a vision of economic citizenship that stressed the rights of consumers to a fair share at a fair price.[3] Yet it emphasizes the unconventional policy role that the Consumer Branch played in Canada's war. Conceived, organized, and run entirely by women, it rapidly mobilized a broad grassroots constituency through its nationwide web of voluntary Women's Regional Advisory Committees (WRACs). The WRACs tapped into virtually every women's association, consumer group, and labour auxiliary in the country, connecting the branch to a third of Canada's three million women. The women of the branch constituted a broad-based movement of consumers that drew support from across political, linguistic, and class lines. Under the leadership of *Chatelaine* magazine editor Byrne Hope Sanders, the Consumer Branch became a two-way conduit between the WPTB and Mrs. Consumer, promoting the board's programs to women and channelling their opinions and policy recommendations back to the board. But the branch's construction of Mrs. Consumer as a married, white, middle-class housewife left out many women, including working-class and young, single women, to whom the branch only belatedly reached out through a labour liaison program and a Miss Consumer Branch. Moreover, the claim to authority based on women's traditional role as housewives was a double-edged sword. Although it allowed women to carve out an unprecedented role for themselves in an important wartime undertaking, it also limited what consumer representatives could achieve in shaping public policy. Nevertheless, from its creation to the end of the war, the Consumer Branch gave Mrs. Consumer a genuine voice in economic policy making.

One Big War Job

Fearful of a repeat of the dramatic and disastrous inflation of the Great War and the subsequent deflation and depression, Ottawa created the WPTB a week before Canada went to war in September 1939, giving it a broad mandate to prevent undue rises in the cost of living. Although no consensus existed over the timing and extent of wartime controls, economists, policymakers, and politicians all generally agreed that avoiding the pitfalls of the last war would require management of supply, distribution, prices, wages, and even profits, as well as high taxes. Wartime policies embodied new understandings of the economy in which consumer spending played a vital role and therefore had to be managed along with the nation's productive resources. During its first two years, with an average monthly rise in the cost of living of less than 0.4 percent, the WPTB played a relatively minor role in the economy. By fall 1941, however, full employment and rising consumer spending were feeding an alarming

1 percent increase every month. In response, the government dramatically expanded the powers of the board and imposed a ceiling on wages and prices.[4]

To manage the demanding job of selling the price freeze to reluctant business people and anxious consumers, the government appointed Donald Gordon as the board's new chairman. A hard-drinking, outspoken, and unrefined workaholic and former Bank of Montreal executive, Gordon was deputy governor of the Bank of Canada and deputy chairman of the Foreign Exchange Control Board. A member of the so-called Ottawa Men, the tightly knit coterie of top civil service mandarins in External Affairs, Finance, and the Bank of Canada who shaped national policies from the mid-1930s to the mid-1950s, Gordon had helped plan the price freeze and convince the federal cabinet to implement it. As WPTB chairman, Gordon won the co-operation of business by filling the swelling echelons of commodity and industry administrators with appointees culled from the ranks of the industries being regulated. Allowing business a visible hand in formulating board policies and practices was the spoonful of sugar that made the bitter medicine of the price freeze go down. By contrast, Gordon rejected proposals for even an informal consultation process with labour, whose support he did not consider vital. His unsympathetic interactions with labour fostered distrust of the WPTB in that sector and complicated the government's efforts to win labour's support for wage controls.[5]

Consumers were another matter altogether. Their participation, Byrne Sanders later noted, was "inherent in the whole plan for price control." A complete freeze on retail prices left the board with the daunting task of administering and enforcing individual ceiling prices on over 1,800,000 items in 300,000 retail stores. Canada's price controllers saw women as their natural allies. Conventional wisdom held that they controlled consumer spending. Women's organizations had long been the most prominent advocates of consumer protection in Canada, and they were the first to call for wartime controls and to protest the rising cost of living.[6]

As the price freeze got under way in December 1941, Gordon and the WPTB enlisted Canada's most prominent women's groups at a well-publicized meeting in Ottawa. The delegates, representing eighteen English-speaking and three French-speaking bodies, expressed unstinting support for a plan involving the co-ordination of women's price watching through voluntary committees in each of the thirteen WPTB regions. As their liaisons with the board, they elected well-known women whom the board had recruited to help organize the meeting, Charlotte Whitton and Thérèse Casgrain. A massive publicity blitz followed. Full-page newspaper advertisements informed women that making the price ceiling work was the "one big war job that you alone can do." In national radio addresses on successive nights, Gordon and Whitton expanded the message, asserting that the "whole plan of your country's war economy" depended on "women who are the nation's shoppers." "Are you ready," Whitton asked dramatically, "to sign up in Canada's Household Corps as a guardian of the new Price Law?" The response was immediate and enthusiastic. Women's groups across the country pledged their support in letters and telegrams.[7]

Canada's Household Corps

Beyond the outlines of the basic plan, the WPTB gave women wide latitude to shape its policies regarding their participation. At the time, the board itself was rapidly expanding in an atmosphere of experimentation, trying things that it had never attempted before. Drawing inspiration from the Consumer Division of the United States Office of Price Administration, and with the backing of women's groups, Whitton and Casgrain seized this opportunity. The absence of a consumer voice in policy making, they informed Gordon, was a "deficiency" that the board needed to fix by founding, "as an integral part of its organization, a Consumer Representation Branch having a status similar to that of the Retail or Wholesale Trade Administration." The main purpose of the branch would be to create a direct two-way link between policymakers and consumers. Whitton and Casgrain insisted that the branch must be run exclusively by women, "who may be said to constitute the principal element in consumer requirements and interests."[8]

Reluctantly, Gordon and the board agreed. "When we considered the question of the consumer," he later confessed to WRAC leaders, "the last thing in my mind was that we should have an organization manned and staffed and controlled by women. I have always had a vast appreciation of women," he continued, "but I haven't really thought of them very much as organizers, and of [sic] business people, and as people who could do a job of work." The rest of the board shared Gordon's initial skepticism.[9] Nevertheless, the need to keep women onside with price watching outweighed any doubts. By the end of January, the WPTB had created the Consumer Representation Branch (subsequently shortened to the Consumer Branch) and appointed as director the well-known writer, magazine editor, and "authority on household economics," Byrne Hope Sanders.[10]

Even before Sanders was appointed, women's groups had begun to mobilize. At preliminary meetings in the board's thirteen regions, they elected organizing committees and drew up a constitution for a national network of Women's Regional Advisory Committees. Sanders and Casgrain addressed mass rallies in each region during February and March. The creation of the Consumer Representation Branch, Sanders told enthusiastic crowds totalling twenty-five thousand women, ensured that "Mrs. Consumer is an important part of our

Figure 7.1

A Consumer Branch exhibit at the Hamilton Public Library, c. 1944. These panels were part of a larger show sponsored by the Hamilton WRAC subcommittee, in co-operation with the library board and local merchants. The panel on the left advertises the popular WPTB-sponsored radio melodrama *Soldier's Wife* and its accompanying *Household Counsellor* segment. | Library and Archives Canada, 4238780.

wartime set-up." Women in every region elected a WRAC, each of which oversaw numerous local subcommittees. Liaison officers from each national, provincial, and local women's group in the region acted as a two-way link between organizations and the WRACs, and "corresponding members" connected small, rural communities to the committees.[11]

The WRAC network grew rapidly after the blitz of rallies in the winter of 1942, reaching three thousand women by late October 1942 and later surpassing Sanders's goal of having ten thousand members at the first anniversary of the branch. Membership reached over sixteen thousand by the end of 1944, eventually peaking at nearly seventeen thousand. Since most were liaison officers, each of whom represented an individual women's group, the reach of the branch was enormous. Liaison officers spoke at club meetings, distributed branch publications, and channelled the views of their organizations back to the WPTB. The monthly branch newsletter, *Consumer's News*, highly sought-after for both the latest price control information and its practical tips for homemakers, circulated in both French and English and reached at least 350,000 women monthly.[12]

The Consumer Branch did a better job of bridging Canada's linguistic divide than most other government departments and agencies at the time, including the WPTB. Despite francophone Quebec's somewhat less enthusiastic support for the national war effort – as demonstrated by Lisa Moore in Chapter 4 of this volume – and tensions produced by the conscription debate raging at the time of the branch's founding, francophone women joined it in numbers equal to their proportion of the Canadian population. Corrine de la Durantaye, its assistant director and former assistant to influential federal politician Ernest Lapointe, tirelessly cultivated connections with francophone communities across the country. She also ensured that the branch scrupulously avoided "the usual formula adopted in other government departments" – including the WPTB – whereby the release of French-language information lagged far behind the English and was characterized (according to Thérèse Casgrain) by often "appalling" or "laughable" translations that did not appeal "to the French speaking temperament." There was occasional friction, to be sure, particularly between Montreal's English- and French-speaking committees and in Trois-Rivières, where the minority anglophone committee complained of being "known as the meddling Englishwomen." Yet, overall, the branch was a model of English-French co-operation.[13]

However, its mass appeal was limited in other, largely self-imposed ways. It had difficulty moving beyond the predominantly white, middle-class orientation of the clubwomen who had helped found it. As one regional chairperson stated, clubwomen could be relied upon to provide "sane and sound leadership." Sanders and other branch leaders often mirrored Gordon's negative view of labour, and at first they made little effort to attract working-class women. Initially, such women played a significant role in creating the WRAC network only in cities, such as Toronto and Winnipeg, in which the militant Housewives Consumers' Association was well established or organized labour was an important force. This impeded price control since, as some local board representatives reported, working-class women assumed that the branch's middle-class women would be uninterested in reports of small price increases. Not until 1943 did the branch, pushed by female labour activists, such as Winnipeg WRAC member Christine White, and increasingly conscious of its failure to reach women outside of clubs, make serious attempts to recruit working-class women. It appointed White as chief labour liaison officer, with a mandate to establish a network of liaison officers among women's union auxiliaries.[14]

Both the WPTB and the branch also narrowed the branch's appeal by overselling the monitoring of price control as a housewife's job. Branch leaders occasionally perceived this as a potential weakness, but only belatedly did they reach out to women who were underrepresented by the clubs or not included at all in the board's image of a mature, married Mrs. Consumer. In late 1944, a youth wing, dubbed the Miss Consumer Branch, organized older high school girls in at least four cities, including Toronto, which elected sixty-five youth liaison officers. Across Canada, a special *High School Re-Make Revue* toured more than five hundred schools, and social studies and home economics classes added the branch's study kits, "Inflation Dangers Didn't End with V-J Day" and "Miracles of Make-Do," to their curriculum. This effort overlapped with a campaign aimed at young, unmarried women and centred on a new pamphlet, tellingly titled *What About Us?* In short order, the branch distributed 190,900 copies to "students, business girls, industrial workers, brides and brides-to-be" through employers, banks, high schools, church and youth groups (including the Girl Guides and YWCA), and women's auxiliaries of the armed services. (The impending demobilization of the latter had provided the impetus for the young women's campaign.) Despite consciously widening the branch's appeal to include working-class and young women, branch leaders never questioned the implicit whiteness of the Mrs. Consumer image.[15]

The Consumer Branch's explicit gendering of consumption also excluded men. Accepting the hackneyed assertion that women controlled the lion's share of consumer spending, the branch consistently couched its appeals and its claims to authority in terms of the commonplace ideal of the housewife as an efficient household manager who had "an intuitive understanding" of inflationary dangers. (This was the flipside of the profligate "hysterical housewife" stereotype, which also had considerable currency at the time.)[16] The announcement of Sanders's appointment, for example, gave as much weight to her experience as a housewife as to her professional qualifications. Sanders herself referred frequently to her "practical experience of running a household and bringing up a family" to legitimize or defend her authority. Branch publicity further reassured the public that "most of the women at Headquarters ... are married women who contrive to run their homes and look after husbands and children with little or no help."[17] Mrs. Consumer – featured in numerous radio broadcasts and propaganda posters – had become not only the iconic image of the branch, but also a stand-in for all consumers.

Only occasionally did the branch acknowledge that men, too, were consumers. Even then, its conception of itself as "essentially a women's division" obstructed its ability to respond to periodic demands from its committees that it should address itself to men. The exception was the extension in 1944 of

White's work with labour to include 1,600 male liaison officers from union locals and councils. WRAC women repeatedly complained that men did not pay attention to price control news because it appeared mostly in the women's pages of the newspapers, leading one wag to suggest that it be moved to the sports pages. Another woman sensibly suggested connecting with men through their service clubs. Only at war's end did the impact of the male shopper become a concern to the branch, when the imminent return of veterans – their pockets bulging with their demobilization pay and benefits – spurred an acknowledgment that "men are consumers, too." However, this came too late to change the impression that the branch represented women's interests only.[18]

An Army on the Home Front

Despite its limitations, the Consumer Branch successfully mobilized the nation's housewives to undertake a variety of tasks related to consumer protection. Soon after its creation, it demonstrated its capacity by organizing eighty thousand women in 106 locations to transcribe and distribute 12 million sugar ration cards. Branch women took part in the dissemination of all subsequent ration books and secured membership on most of the five hundred local ration boards established by the WPTB. In the face of severe housing shortages, the branch established forty-seven housing registries across the country and helped place over a hundred thousand people between 1942 and 1945. Its clothing conservation program, under well-known radio personality Kate Aitken, included the establishment of "re-make" classes for women in 183 centres, extensive publicity, the release of several popular pamphlets, and "travelling wardrobes" and re-make revues that strutted their way across the country for three years. Branch members also carried out a variety of educational programs on such issues as the government's anti-inflationary program, black markets, and shortages.[19]

But price checking remained the main activity of branch volunteers. "Women are an army on the home front," declared Sanders in April 1942, "each with her own patrol, the beat covered on shopping ... Her weapons are a list of prices, an understanding heart and an intelligent mind." Women responded enthusiastically to such calls for their help, and by mid-1942 the WPTB was receiving 1,500 price complaints monthly. With only a handful of paid investigators at the start, it relied almost wholly on consumer complaints.[20] The gradual increase in its enforcement staff decreased the relative importance of consumer complaints in policing price control, but women remained committed to monitoring prices. They responded eagerly to the creation of price study panels in 1944, which breathed new life into price checking.[21]

Despite its importance, price watching was secondary to what the Consumer Branch considered its central purpose – the representation of consumers at the policy-making level. Initially, it encountered considerable resistance from "a good many" WPTB administrators – only one of whom was a woman – who "looked at the whole Consumer Branch set-up with considerable distrust."[22] By 1943, however, Sanders could boast that the same administrators now realized that "as intelligent women we did not ask the impossible." Policymakers were increasingly turning to the branch for consumer opinion "on the practical working of any new order and regulation" and were amending regulations based on branch recommendations. The branch was the WPTB's best barometer of consumer opinion, Sanders asserted, serving as the equivalent of a "Gallup Poll with labour, rural, school, business and home-making women all represented."[23]

The nationwide WRAC network provided the basis of the branch's claim to be democratizing economic policy making. Sanders and WRAC leaders trumpeted the branch as a rare – perhaps unique – example of a "democratic organization" existing *within* a major government agency. It was truly a mass association that "stretched right down to the Canadian grass roots," boasted one press release. Its success would prove that a national consumers' organization could translate women's opinions into government policy.[24]

By the end of the war, the Consumer Branch could claim to have had a noteworthy impact on policy. "In every case where a major recommendation of consumers 'made sense,'" a post-war report claimed, "a way was finally found by the Board to put it into effect in spite of difficulties which were sometimes extensive." Often, the branch played the role of gadfly, pointing out where the WPTB was failing on its own terms. By documenting widespread complaints about shortages, quality deterioration, and price violations, the branch initiated investigations that led to new orders or punitive action against offenders. In some cases, branch recommendations led to the loosening of regulations, such as the initial prohibition on casual gifts or trading of rationed foods, which housewives felt was "a stupid regulation." A "continuous barrage of complaints" from the WRACs and individual consumers finally persuaded rationing officials to lift the ban.[25] The branch also succeeded in repealing counterproductive clothing conservation measures, such as the ban on pant cuffs, which prevented women from resizing clothing as children grew or for re-use. Thérèse Casgrain had pointedly asked Donald Gordon, who was six foot four, what his mother would have done had she not been able to let down his cuffs when he was a growing adolescent. After a public outcry that a bemused Gordon later noted had been one of the worst he had provoked during his long career as a top civil servant, the measure was repealed.[26]

More often, however, the branch was responsible for *increased* restrictions and regulations to ensure that consumers had access to a fair share at a fair price. Responding to complaints about shortages, for example, it pushed the WPTB to start butter rationing earlier than anticipated, implement preserves rationing, bring canned salmon under meat rationing, and include fresh fruits and vegetables (originally exempted from price control) under the price ceiling. It also rightly took credit for the requirement that retail butchers must standardize beef cuts and post ceiling prices, and for the ban on conditional sales – the practice by which a retailer made the sale of a scarce item contingent on the purchase of another.[27] Perhaps the most notable success was the board's creation of the Standards Administration, out of which came the post-war standards division of the federal Department of Trade and Commerce. Despite a growing chorus of protests about quality deterioration, especially in clothing, board administrators had been reluctant to admit that the problem was widespread. A campaign by the WRACs, focused on clothing and textiles, proved that it was, convincing administrators of the need for a dedicated body to regulate quality more closely in order to combat hidden cost-of-living increases.[28]

Plain Women with No Sense

Despite its many successes, the Consumer Branch had a more limited influence over policy than it generally admitted in *Consumer's News*, WRAC conferences, and annual reports. It failed to get the WPTB to agree to the two related price policy changes that were, by its own account, most important to women: standardized prices and mandatory price postings. The WRACs consistently demanded both. The price ceiling imposed in December 1941 had frozen individual retailers' prices at their highest level during a "base period," the month ending 15 October 1941. However, because retailers were not required to post what their ceiling prices had been, the base-period approach was not particularly useful in enabling consumers to determine whether stores were complying with the law. Despite WRAC and consumer demands for standardized prices, the WPTB stubbornly stuck to the original plan, unconvincingly claiming that changing course would look like an admission of a mistake and would undermine public confidence in price control. It also rejected as unworkable and unenforceable a requirement that retailers post their ceiling prices, another consistent consumer demand. In both cases, board officials pointed to problems encountered by the American Office of Price Administration (OPA), which had copied Canada's price ceiling in April 1942 and had run into difficulties when it experimented with such changes. By mid-1943, however, the OPA's successful and popular imposition of standardized "community prices" and widespread posting requirements negated the WPTB justification for inaction, as did the board's own requirement that butchers post their ceiling prices (a response to a growing black market in meat). The comparison between OPA and WPTB policies, Sanders noted, "is not to our benefit in the consumer's mind." In the end, the real problem with both policies was that retailers and their representatives in the WPTB opposed them, and Gordon's primary sympathies lay with this group.[29]

Other Consumer Branch recommendations also went unimplemented. Following the lead of its members, the branch was more enthusiastic about expanding rationing than were top WPTB officials, who rejected, for example, its call in early 1943 to follow the US lead in rationing canned goods. Rationing officials also rebuffed other restrictions urged by women, such as a ban on serving tea and sweets at club meetings, which seemed improvident when tea and sugar were rationed. As they had during the First World War, many women's groups had already adopted their own restrictions in the face of shortages, but rationing officials thought a formal ban unnecessary. When Sanders responded with a press release announcing a voluntary ban, one food official mocked, "Miss Sanders appears to be instituting a rationing system of her own."[30]

Even the branch's most notable policy success, the Standards Administration, had its limits. In the end, the administration passed few of the mandatory standards that consumers demanded, other than requiring manufacturers to include their WPTB licence and style number in every garment. In light of ongoing quality deterioration problems, a hidden form of price inflation, consumer groups and the WRACs consistently demanded more far-reaching and mandatory standards and labelling for all textiles and clothing, and they often rejected WPTB reassurances. Amid an outbreak of particularly vehement protests over the quality of children's shoes in the winter of 1944–45, senior branch official Christine White reported having cheap shoes "thrown at me in meetings in Trail, Kimberley, Edmonton, Flin Flon, Kenora, Fort William, London and Windsor."[31] Such actions represented grassroots frustration with the branch's inability to deliver on the promise of consumer representation.

Resistance encountered by the branch both in and out of the WPTB accounted for many of its disappointments. Retailers, especially, had greeted its creation with hostility. One food industry journal warned retailers that the goal of the branch's "three million price cops" was to "make their lives miserable." In the WPTB, the reaction of many administrators was similar. Resistance eventually softened somewhat, but out in the field the WRACs often complained that board officials treated them as if they were "plain women with no sense."[32]

Other limitations on the branch's influence were largely self-inflicted. Among them were the moderate consumerism of Sanders (explored in Chapter 6 of this volume) and other top branch officials (many of whom had ties to the governing Liberal Party), Sanders's conciliatory attitude toward business, and her tendency to see herself more as the board's champion than the consumer's.

Sanders perceived the branch's role as defending board policies against criticism from organized labour and more radical consumer groups, such as the Housewives Consumers' Association and the Edmonton Consumers' League, that advocated for more stringent controls over business. After the board's retail administrator and Simpson's executive Edgar Burton was grilled by Dr. Geneva Misener, the Edmonton league's vice-president, Sanders wrote Burton a sympathetic note, dismissing the league as "a very radical and energetic body ... always up in arms about something." Yet it was better to have Misener, also a member of Alberta's WRAC, within the fold so "we can educate her to understand *our* point of view." "Too many people are apt to think of the Branch as in there fighting against vague foes for the consumer," Sanders stated at one of its national conferences, when in fact "the whole board works for consumer protection." Her perceived accommodationist approach to asserting the consumer interest eventually prompted the Edmonton league to denounce her as "a $-a-year agent of anti-consumer big-business propaganda."[33]

Sanders's protectiveness over her fiefdom also led her to resist calls to expand consumer or women's representation into policy positions throughout the board. When the English-speaking Montreal WRAC passed a resolution in 1943, demanding that a woman be appointed to a policy-making position in the ration administration and nominated its chair, Mrs. Leslie J. Hodges, for the post, Sanders rebuffed it, reassuring Gordon that she did not share its view. "Montreal has delusions of grandeur," she wrote. "I have repeatedly put them in their place and shall continue to do so probably until the end of the story."[34]

Direct policy representation in fields with which the Consumer Branch was most concerned might have given it more influence. In principle, it was supposed to be consulted on every policy decision affecting consumers, but this was inconsistently applied. The branch maintained formal ties to the Ration and Foods Administrations, which may account for the fact that many of its policy successes were in these fields.[35] But only at the end of the war in Europe did it finally work out a relationship with the Information Branch, whereby Sanders and Durantaye would sit on the information policy committee. A similar arrangement with the Price Division or the Standards Administration might have given the branch more influence over policies in these areas. But Sanders did not seek such direct policy-making roles, preferring to rely on her direct line to Gordon and her seat at the table of the board's overall policy committee.[36]

Compounding these limitations were the small size of the branch's staff, its lack of an independent economic analysis unit, and its consequent reliance on experts in other departments. It simply was not oriented to an analysis of larger economic policy issues. Nor did it help that the branch's only economist was stationed in Toronto and focused more on advising the Toronto office and organizing price study panels than on advising the national office. Donald Gordon's biographer asserts that Sanders was sometimes lost during economic discussions in the board's policy committee meetings. If this were true, it probably resulted as much from the branch's lack of an independent economics staff as from the fact that she was a mere "journalist among economists and industrialists." The biographer's assessment may also reflect the sexism of the top policymakers upon whose memories he relied.[37]

Finally, staking the branch's claim to authority on the gendered notion of the consumer as housewife cut both ways. While maternalism spoke to the reality of many women's role in the home, it was also, more importantly, a useful language for activist women to assert their respectability and shield themselves from attack.[38] To be sure, it muted opposition to consumer representation within and outside the branch. In the hands of the branch leadership, this strategy was politically successful but perhaps limited the branch's potential to effect change, making it too easy to dismiss legitimate consumer concerns as coming from "plain women with no sense."

It is unlikely, of course, that the branch would have accomplished much more than it did had it asserted a wider role for itself, as such a role would surely have raised greater opposition both within and outside the WPTB. After the war, the branch would find its influence increasingly diminished as the pace of post-war decontrol accelerated. Certainly, the failure of the Consumer Branch, its post-war successor, the Canadian Association of Consumers, and the Housewives Consumers' Association to slow the rate of decontrol reveals how limited was consumer input into larger economic policy questions, especially when consumer interests ran counter to established government policies and powerful economic interests.[39]

Led by Sanders, the Consumer Branch embraced the image of the consumer as middle-class housewife and never aspired to more than a limited voice for consumers. Restricting its appeal to housewives reinforced the commonly held notion that consumer concerns were women's issues and therefore of little importance in economic planning. It also made Mrs. Consumer's wartime activism and policy-making influence appear to be a necessary deviation from the norm rather than a new normal, as the branch's leaders hoped it would be. The war politicized women's household duties, thrusting everyday acts of consumption into the public sphere and into the political limelight. Yet the idea that the branch's women were engaged in a temporary extension of their household duties created the expectation that, after the war, housewives would retreat to the private sphere, and society's gender order would be restored.

Notes

1 Ann Adam, "Today's Food," *Toronto Globe and Mail (G&M)*, 23 May 1944; Library and Archives Canada (LAC), RG 64, Wartime Prices and Trade Board, vol. 1566, file War Information Board Mrs. Consumer's, G. Fairbairn (Artist), *Thank You Mrs. Consumer*, Poster, n.d.; "'The Missus' Week," *G&M*, 23 May 1944. See also LAC, RG 64, vol. 432, file 10–29, vol. 3, Consumer Education, Jan 1/43 to Sept 10/45, "Report on 'Mrs. Consumer Week,'" n.d.; LAC, RG 64, vol. 1446, file A-10–29–7, Consumer Branch Educational Program, vol. 2, "General Summary," Report, n.d., and "Mrs. Consumer Week," Report, 22 June 1944.

2 The classic study on women in the workplace and the military is Ruth Roach Pierson, *"They're Still Women After All": The Second World War and Canadian Womanhood* (Toronto: McClelland and Stewart, 1986). This twin focus is maintained in Jeffrey A. Keshen, *Saints, Sinners, and Soldiers: Canada's Second World War* (Vancouver: UBC Press, 2004).

3 For recent studies addressing how the Consumer Branch helped women to develop a sense of economic citizenship, see Joy Parr, *Domestic Goods: The Material, the Moral, and the Economic in the Postwar Years* (Toronto: University of Toronto Press, 1999); Magda Fahrni, "Counting the Costs of Living: Gender, Citizenship, and a Politics of Prices in 1940s Montreal," *Canadian Historical Review* 83, 4 (December 2002): 483–504; Magda Fahrni, *Household Politics: Montreal Families and Postwar Reconstruction* (Toronto: University of Toronto Press, 2005); Graham Broad, *A Small Price to Pay: Consumer Culture on the Canadian Home Front, 1939-45* (Vancouver: UBC Press, 2013); and Ian Mosby, *Food Will Win the War: The Politics, Culture, and Science of Food on Canada's Home Front* (Vancouver: UBC Press, 2014).

4 Kenneth Norrie, Douglas Owram, and J.C. Herbert Emery, *A History of the Canadian Economy*, 3rd ed. (Toronto: Harcourt Brace, 2002), 266–71, 344–52; Christopher Waddell, "The Wartime Prices and Trade Board: Price Control in Canada in World War II" (PhD diss., York University, 1981), 17–51; Douglas Owram, *The Government Generation: Canadian Intellectuals and the State, 1900–1945* (Toronto: University of Toronto Press, 1986), 254–57.

5 "Straightening Out Control," *Financial Post*, 13 December 1941; Joseph Schull, *The Great Scot: A Biography of Donald Gordon* (Montreal and Kingston: McGill-Queen's University Press, 1979), 1–60; J.L. Granatstein, *The Ottawa Men: The Civil Service Mandarins, 1935–1957* (Oxford: Oxford University Press, 1982); Waddell, "The Wartime Prices and Trade Board," 221–24.

6 "Women Helpful as Vigilantes," *Hamilton Spectator*, 20 April 1943. See also Stephen Brobeck, ed., *Encyclopedia of the Consumer Movement* (Santa Barbara: ABC-CLIO, 1997), s.v. "Canadian Consumer Movement"; "Catholic Women Score Rising Prices in Food," *Hamilton Spectator*, 12 September 1939; LAC, RG 64, vol. 64, file W.P.T.B. Regional Offices Winnipeg Region, "The Wartime Prices and Trade Board: History of the Winnipeg Region," Draft history, n.d.

7 LAC, RG 64, vol. 1567, file W.P.T.B. – Posters (2), "To the Women of Canada: Here Is One Big War Job Which You Alone Can Do," Newspaper advertisement, n.d.; LAC, RG 64, vol. 6, file W.P.T.B. Speeches, Donald Gordon, 1941–43, Board History, "Radio Speech by Donald Gordon, Chairman, Wartime Prices and Trade Board, Ottawa," Transcript, 17 December 1941; "To the Homes of Canada: Radio Speech by Dr. Charlotte Whitton, a National Broadcast, December 18, 1941," Pamphlet, n.d., Fredericton Region Museum, CA FRM MS49–64.

8 LAC, RG 64, vol. 433, file 10–29–2, Consumer Education (Mme. Pierre Casgrain), Charlotte Whitton and Thérèse Casgrain to Donald Gordon, Memorandum, 9 January 1942, Ottawa. On the transnational aspects of women's consumer organizing, see Joseph

Tohill, "'A Consumers' War': Price Control and Political Consumerism in the United States and Canada during World War II" (PhD diss., York University, 2012).

9 LAC, RG 64, vol. 1447, file A-10–29–11, vol. 1, Consumer Branch Conferences, "Address of Mr. Donald Gordon ... before the Regional Women's Advisory Committee," Transcript, 23 September 1942; LAC, RG 64, vol. 60, file Consumer Branch I, "A Record of Consumer Branch Work in the Field of Consumer Problems and the Principal Problems Which Arose with Some Comments on Methods: Management of Consumer Problems Work," Manuscript, n.d.

10 LAC, RG 64, vol. 432, file 10–29, vol. 1, Consumer Education, Nov 1/39 to Aug 28/42, "Press Release No. 364," 30 January 1942; "Woman Editor Gets Key Post," *G&M*, 31 January 1942.

11 "A Democratic Movement," *Hamilton Spectator*, 11 March 1942. See also LAC, RG 64, vol. 1445, file A-10–9-2, vol. 1, Consumer Branch Women's Regional Advisory Committee (W.R.A.C.), Charlotte Whitton, "Constitution of Women's Regional Advisory Committee and Initial Mass Meeting, Central Ontario Region," Memorandum, 19 January 1942; and "Byrne Sanders Delighted with Response of Women," *Ottawa Citizen*, 12 March 1942. Estimated attendance comes from LAC, RG 64, vol. 1222, file 35–1, vol. 1, Consumer Representatives Generally, "Annual Report of Consumer Branch 1942," 1 December 1942.

12 LAC, RG 64, vol. 1445, file A-10–29–1, Consumer Branch Organization, "Report of Consumer Branch," Memorandum, 21 October 1942, and "Consumer Branch to November 1, 1945," Memorandum, n.d.; "Annual Report of Consumer Branch 1942"; LAC, RG 64, vol. 1447, file A-10–29–10, Consumer Branch Reports (Annual, Consumer, and Progress), "Annual Report of the Consumer Branch, Wartime Prices and Trade Board, 1944," n.d., and "Annual Report of the Consumer Branch, Wartime Prices and Trade Board, 1943," n.d.; LAC, RG 64, vol. 215, file Consumer Branch, "Press Release C-578 Consumer Branch," 14 May 1947.

13 LAC, RG 64, vol. 60, file Wartime Prices and Trade Board, Consumer Branch I, "A Brief Summary of the Origin and Development of the Consumer Branch, W.P.T.B.," Manuscript (draft), n.d.; LAC, RG 64, vol. 433, file 10–29–2, Consumer Education (Mme. Pierre Casgrain), Thérèse Casgrain to Donald Gordon, 7 February 1942, Montreal; LAC, RG 64, vol. 1447, file A-10–29–11, vol. 1, Consumer Branch, Conferences, "Report of Annual Conference, Sub-Regional Advisory Committees," 10 November 1943.

14 "Big Role by Women Seen in Price Control Success," *G&M*, 22 January 1946. See also LAC, RG 64, vol. 64, file W.P.T.B. Regional Offices: Winnipeg Region, "History of the Winnipeg Region," Manuscript, n.d.; LAC, RG 64, vol. 64, W.P.T.B. Regional Offices: Western Ontario, Mary Turner, "History of the Wartime Prices and Trade Board in Western Ontario," Manuscript, August 1947, 169–70; and LAC, RG 64, vol. 60, Christine White, "History of the Development of the Labour Relations Department of Consumer Branch," Manuscript, 8 October 1946.

15 "'Miss Consumer' Branch Joins Anti-Inflation Fight," *G&M*, 24 January 1945; LAC, RG 64, vol. 1447, file A-10–29–10, Consumer Branch, Reports (Annual, Consumer, and Progress), Harriet Parsons (Consumer Branch Educational Secretary), "Annual Report of the Toronto Office, 1945," n.d.

16 "The Consumer's Voice," *Toronto Daily Star*, 31 January 1942; "Sugar Hoarded So Peach Crop Rots on Trees," *G&M*, 14 September 1939. On the gendering of consumption, see Kathleen G. Donohue, "What Gender Is the Consumer? The Role of Gender Connotations in Defining the Political," *Journal of American Studies* 33, 1 (1999): 19–44.

17 LAC, RG 64, vol. 432, file 10–29, vol. 1, Consumer Education, Nov 1/39 to Aug 28/42, WPTB, "Press Release No. 364," 30 January 1942; LAC, RG 64, vol. 432, file 10–29, vol. 2,

Consumer Education, Oct 1/42 to Dec 31/43, Sanders to Cora Casselman (MP for Edmonton), 28 April 1943, Ottawa; "Consumers Are Asking," *Consumer's News*, 25 July 1943.

18 LAC, RG 64, vol. 1445, file A-10-9-2, vol. 1, "Minutes of a Meeting of Women's Regional Advisory Committee Held on Tuesday, May 16, 1944 in ... Montreal," Report, n.d.; "Consumer Branch Is Truly Representative," *Consumer's News*, April 1945. See also LAC, RG 64, vol. 1448, file A-10-29-11, vol. 3, Consumer Branch, Conferences, "Report of Ontario Conference, Consumer Branch, WPTB, King Edward Hotel, Toronto," Memorandum, 6 March 1945.

19 "Annual Report of Consumer Branch 1942"; "Annual Report of the Consumer Branch, Wartime Prices and Trade Board, 1944"; LAC, RG 64, vol. 1447, file A-10-29-7, Consumer Branch Educational Program, vol. 3, Kate Aitken, "Report on Remake Review," n.d., and Aitken and Irene Gougeon to Sanders, "Report on Conservation Programme," Memorandum, n.d.

20 "Canadian Women Help in Price Curb," *New York Times*, 25 April 1942. See also "Canadian Women Keep Prices at Ceiling: 1,500 Complaints a Month Are Investigated," *New York Times*, 4 June 1942.

21 LAC, RG 64, vol. 1445, file Consumer Branch Price Study Panels A-10-29-3, vol. 1, Toronto Consumer Branch Committee, "Report of the Price Study Panel for the Year Ending August 1944," Memorandum, August 1944.

22 "Address of Mr. Donald Gordon," 23 September 1942; "A Record of Consumer Branch Work in the Field."

23 "Report of National Conference, 17-21 January 1944"; LAC, RG 64, vol. 433, file 10-29-3, Consumer Education, Sanders to Gordon, Memorandum, 18 September 1942.

24 LAC, RG 64, vol. 1445, file A-10-29-1, Consumer Branch Organization, "The Consumer Branch: Wartime Prices and Trade Board," Memorandum, 1 June 1943; LAC, RG 64, vol. 215, file Consumer Branch, WPTB, "Press Release No. 0448, Consumer Branch Has 10,000 Officers," 31 March 1943.

25 "A Record of Consumer Branch Work in the Field"; LAC, RG 64, vol. 432, file 10-29, vol. 4, Consumer Education, Sept 20/45 to June 30/47, "Women – Partners in a War Epic: Radio Broadcast by Byrne Hope Sanders," Transcript, 28 October 1945.

26 Thérèse Casgrain, *Une femme chez les hommes* (Montreal: Éditions du Jour, 1971), 158-59.

27 "A Record of Consumer Branch Work in the Field"; "Annual Report of the Consumer Branch, Wartime Prices and Trade Board, 1943."

28 "A Record of Consumer Branch Work in the Field"; LAC, RG 64, vol. 35, file History of the Standards Administration, "History of the Standards Administration, Wartime Prices and Trade Board," Manuscript, 12 December 1946.

29 LAC, RG 64, vol. 1445, file Consumer Branch Price Study Panels A-10-29-3, vol. 1, Byrne Hope Sanders, "Report on Consumer Branch Program for Sending Information on Price Limits for Foods as Set by Special Board Order," Memorandum, n.d. See also Whitton, "Constitution of Women's Regional Advisory Committee and Initial Mass Meeting, Central Ontario Region," 19 January 1942; "Housewives Meet Protests Known Brands Disappearing," *Toronto Daily Star*, 22 April 1942; "Price Pegs Successful," *Windsor Daily Star*, 23 September 1942; "Address of Mr. Donald Gordon," 23 September 1942; and LAC, RG 64, vol. 421, file 10-15, Price Ceiling General Policy, vol. 4, Dec 1/43-Sept 21/44, A.F.W. Plumptre (WPTB Washington Representative) to Gordon, 1 April 1944.

30 LAC, RG 64, vol. 1222, file 35-1, vol. 1, Consumer Representatives Generally, J.M. Macdonald to Clive Planta, Memorandum, 10 September 1942. See also LAC, RG 64, WPTB, ser. 1010, vol. 10, file Weekly Progress Reports, 1-33, WPTB, "Weekly Progress Report,

Number 30," 28 January 1943. For an example of voluntary restrictions in the First World War, see Public Archives and Records Office of Prince Edward Island, ACC 3471 (Maple Leaf W.I., Travellers Rest fonds), series 1, vol. 2, PEI WI Minute Book, Maple Leaf Institute, 1915–17, Minutes of meeting held 19 April 1917.

31 LAC, RG 64, vol. 1446, file A-10–29–5, Consumer Branch Standards Division, Christine S. White to Sanders, "Special Report–Degradation of Shoes," Memorandum, 25 January 1945.

32 "Three Million Price Cops," editorial, *Food in Canada* 2 (May 1942): 4; "Report of Annual Conference, Sub-Regional Advisory Committees," 10 November 1943. See also "The Right Kind of Help," *Consumer's News,* 1 October 1943.

33 LAC, RG 64, WPTB, ser. 1030, vol. 433, file 10–29–3, Consumer Education, Sanders to E.G. Burton, 15 June 1942 (emphasis in original); "Report of National Conference, 17–21 January 1944"; LAC, RG 64, vol. 432, file 10–29, vol. 2, Consumer Education, Oct 1/42 to Dec 31/43, David Duncan (President, Edmonton Consumers' League) and Charles E. Nix (Secretary-Treasurer) to Cora Casselman (MP for Edmonton), 3 April 1943, Edmonton. On the radicalism of the Housewives Consumers' Association, see Julie Guard, *Radical Housewives: Price Wars and Food Politics in Mid-Twentieth Century Canada* (Toronto: University of Toronto Press, 2019).

34 LAC, RG 64, vol. 432, file 10–29, vol. 2, Consumer Education, Oct 1/42 to Dec 31/43, Sanders to Gordon, "Montreal Committee," Memorandum, 25 October 1943.

35 "A Record of Consumer Branch Work in the Field"; LAC, RG 64, vol. 432, file 10–29, vol. 4, Consumer Education, Sept 20/45 to June 30/47, Pauline Kennedy, "Annual Report of the Toronto Consumer Branch Committee, Wartime Prices and Trade Board, 1945," 20 December 1945.

36 LAC, RG 64, vol. 1448, file A-10–29–11, vol. 3, Consumer Branch, Conferences, WPTB Consumer Branch, "Report of National Conference, Consumer Branch, March 12–15, 1945," Minutes of meeting, n.d.

37 Schull, *The Great Scot,* 67.

38 On the use of maternalist claims to public authority, see, for example, Julie Guard, "A Mighty Power against the Cost of Living: Canadian Housewives Organize in the 1930s," *International Labor and Working-Class History* 77 (Spring 2010): 27–47.

39 By the late 1940s, consumer activism also ran afoul of the emerging Cold War's anti-communist crusade. On the fate of post-war consumer organizations, see Parr, *Domestic Goods;* Tohill, "'A Consumers' War'"; and Guard, *Radical Housewives.*

Part 3
Women and Overseas Humanitarian Work

It is most satisfying to know that I contributed in some small way to the war (and peace!) effort, and yet at the same time was able to enjoy every minute.

– Helen M. Egan, Canadian Red Cross Corps member[1]

During the First World War, tens of thousands of Canadian and Newfoundland women travelled overseas to Britain. A few went as journalists, and several hundred joined the Voluntary Aid Detachment, driving ambulances and assisting trained nurses. Most simply followed their officer husbands, sons, and brothers. Although many spent at least some of their time volunteering with a war charity or humanitarian organization, officials saw their unregulated presence as a nuisance. As a result, opportunities for Canadian and Newfoundland women to go overseas during the Second World War were severely restricted. Members of humanitarian organizations were among the few civilians who received government permission to travel to Britain.[2]

The provision of co-ordinated humanitarian aid on a large scale during wartime dates back to the mid-nineteenth century, and notable relief efforts were undertaken during the First World War by groups such as the Red Cross and the Save the Children Fund. However, the Second World War was the definitive turning point in the Western world's history of humanitarianism. The conflict and its immediate aftermath solidified the reputations of older aid organizations and gave birth to a multitude of new ones, including Oxfam and UNICEF. Initially focused primarily on suffering Europeans, they turned their attention to broader global misery once Europe was back on its feet.[3] The Second World War and its aftermath are therefore keys to understanding today's global humanitarian aid landscape. To date, however, most scholarship has concentrated on the political, economic, ideological, and organizational aspects of this history. Gender as a frame of analysis has not yet been widely applied, although age has been: children have featured as objects of aid and as iconic images of suffering since at least the First World War.[4]

At the same time, the scholarship and popular memory of Canadian and Newfoundland women's Second World War activities are limited almost exclusively to the home front. They also tend to focus on women's efforts to "back the attack" – to morally support and contribute to the waging of war in an explicitly pro-Allied context.

In this section, Marlene Epp and Sarah Glassford apply a gendered lens to the study of overseas humanitarian work by two prominent aid organizations in Canada. The Mennonite Central Committee and the Canadian Red Cross had very different relationships to military service, but shared a common organizational refusal to engage in overtly partisan action in wartime. Together, these chapters discuss the personal, emotional elements of young women's overseas wartime experiences and insert women's humanitarian work overseas into the narrative of Canada's Second World War. They also complicate the traditional temporal boundaries of war-related history, demonstrating that the cessation of hostilities merely expanded the opportunities for humanitarian service to suffering and displaced civilians in Europe, East Asia, and North Africa. As both volunteers and paid professionals, women would play central parts in post-war humanitarian relief and rehabilitation efforts.

Notes

1 Helen M. Egan, in *Women Overseas: Memoirs of the Canadian Red Cross Corps*, ed. Frances Martin Day, Phyllis Spence, and Barbara Ladouceur (Vancouver: Ronsdale Press, 1998), 220.

2 Debbie Marshall, *Firing Lines: Three Canadian Women Write the First World* War (Toronto: Dundurn Press, 2017); Linda J. Quiney, *This Small Army of Women: Canadian Volunteer Nurses and the First World War* (Vancouver: UBC Press, 2017); Jonathan Vance, *Maple Leaf Empire: Canada, Britain, and Two World Wars* (Don Mills, ON: Oxford University Press, 2012), 86, 93, 170; Sarah Glassford, *Mobilizing Mercy: A History of the Canadian Red Cross* (Montreal and Kingston: McGill-Queen's University Press, 2017).

3 Michael Barnett, *Empire of Humanity: A History of Humanitarianism* (Ithaca: Cornell University Press, 2011), Chapters 4 and 6.

4 Karen Dubinsky, "Children, Ideology and Iconography: How Babies Rule the World," *Journal of the History of Childhood and Youth* 5, 1 (2012): 5–13.

8

Responding to "War's Havoc"

The Relief Work of Mennonite Women

Marlene Epp

In 1948, Elfrieda Klassen Dyck (1917–2004) led approximately 750 refugees away from a Europe ravaged by the Second World War to new homes in South America. As a young, newly trained Mennonite nurse from Saskatchewan, Elfrieda had gone to England in 1942 to support war sufferers and distribute material aid. Later, she helped operate a refugee camp in the dangerous and provision-scarce city of Berlin. Her two-month crossing of the Atlantic Ocean, with one of the four shiploads she would accompany during the immediate post-war years, was beset with many difficulties, including sick and traumatized passengers and, not least of all, a mutiny by the crew. About her wartime relief work, she would later understatedly remark, "I can't believe I did this."[1] Alongside the daily tasks of food and clothing distribution to civilians, and the processing and shepherding of hundreds of refugees, Elfrieda made a profound statement for peace by acting in opposition to the suffering caused by war.

Throughout their history, when confronted with, and in the midst of, wars waged by states, Mennonites have taken their cue from biblical commands to love their enemies. Typically, they refer to their peace position as "nonresistance," from the New Testament passage that instructs Christians not to "resist evil." The label of "pacifism" was more commonly attributed to secular antimilitarists, although I will use these terms somewhat interchangeably. Historically, the most concrete expression of the Mennonite peace position was an unwillingness to participate in warfare, and thus the community expended much effort in securing exemption from military service and status as conscientious objectors (COs) for its men. During the Second World War, about 7,500 Canadian Mennonite men performed alternative service in lieu of military service for the state. This included building roads and highways, fire fighting and tree planting, and work in agriculture and industry, for example.[2]

Mennonite women also wanted to bring their own voice to the peace position. Indeed, they found themselves supporting it in much the same way that other Canadian women were aiding the war effort. They too prepared care packages, stocked with writing paper, envelopes, socks, gloves, and home baking, though these went to their own men in CO camps rather than to soldiers overseas. Wars often meant economic difficulty for CO women because their menfolk might be away from home for lengthy periods, either performing public service work or being held in prison. During both world wars, many women managed family farms on their own or took the unprecedented step of entering the paid workforce. Though other Canadian women improved their economic state during the Second World War, as Graham Broad demonstrates in Chapter 6 of this volume, the household income of Mennonite women declined, as CO wages above fifty cents a day were directed to the Red Cross. Also unlike the wives and mothers of soldiers, CO women often encountered public censure because their menfolk were seen as shirking their duty.[3]

Because they were not conscripted, women were excluded from the interrogation put to their menfolk regarding nonresistance – what the men "would not do" during war. Thus, they turned the question around and considered what they would do in the midst of conflict.[4] But they were not peace activists in the contemporary sense, or even in the tradition of the strong feminist anti-war movement of the First World War (which itself was more muted in the Second World War). They did not participate in marches or letter-writing campaigns or lobby governments in any organized manner. Their approach to pacifism was framed by an overall "quiet in the land" demeanour and belief, a phrase often applied to Mennonites, which referred to their agricultural background but also their chosen approach to political engagement.

Yet, Mennonite women did occasionally speak up. For instance, when the war broke out in 1939, Elizabeth B. Toews, a Manitoba woman with sons of conscription age, wrote to the federal government, reminding it of its promised military exemption for Mennonites. Her letter was returned with the request that it be written in English.[5] A 1945 Mennonite women's conference featured a paper on nonresistance delivered by Mrs. P.P. Rempel, who stressed "that it was an issue not only for men but also for girls."[6] In one family, it was apparently the mother who counselled her son, not yet a church member and thus not considered officially Mennonite, that his only grounds for seeking military exemption were that he was German and could not fight his German brothers.[7]

Far more commonly, Mennonite women actively and publicly offered relief – material and moral – to those who suffered from the violence of war. As members of a religious community that expressed its pacifism mainly through male non-involvement in a national project, these women chose active rather than passive resistance. They saw first-hand the effects of war and developed empathy for its civilian victims on both sides of the conflict. Because their peace position was grounded in their Christian beliefs, the language with which they described their anti-war activity was often religious in tone and reference.

This positive peacemaking took various forms, depending on time and place, and relief efforts were often generated within the home communities of

Mennonite women. For many, collecting used articles, sewing new clothing and quilts, and knitting socks and bandages became their unique non-militarist contribution to the nation. In 1939, Mennonite women in Ontario organized local sewing circles as part of the Nonresistant Relief Sewing Organization. Between 1941 and 1944, approximately $71,000 worth of clothing was sent under the auspices of the Mennonite Central Committee (MCC) from Canada to England, the main destination for relief supplies during the war years.[8] Mennonite relief workers in England suggested that women in North America should adopt the slogan "Non-Resistant Needles Knitting for the Needy" to underscore the "magnificent opportunity" that their work represented.[9] A 1940 report on the MCC relief clothing program for Europe described the relationship between relief and peace thus: "In the face of war's havoc there is need for a positive testimony of peace, love, and compassion toward the suffering."[10] The creation, collection, and delivery of relief goods were clearly positioned as an expression of peace, especially in this particular conflict, when direct opposition was extremely unpopular. Canadian Mennonite women spoke out through "the work of their hands" in this way.[11]

Even as they sent bale after bale of relief goods across the Atlantic Ocean, Mennonite women went themselves. Hoping to alleviate the suffering, they travelled overseas for extended periods, volunteering for various non-governmental organizations and the MCC in particular. Their desire for peace was literally embodied as they went overseas, during and after the war, to work in evacuation centres, distribute food and clothing, and staff refugee centres operated by government and church agencies. As historian Esther Epp-Tiessen comments, they were "on the forefront of women's involvement in ... service as a witness for peace."[12]

Through an analysis of their activities, their varied and collective motivations for going overseas, and their reflections on the experience we can gain an understanding of their unique statement as pacifist women. Useful sources include their diaries and memoirs, letters and newsletter reports sent to their home communities, and records of the church and relief agencies that oversaw their work. Although published profiles exist for some of the women, and a considerable amount of literature deals with church relief work during both world wars, there has been minimal effort to situate their travel and work within a framework of pacifist expression. As well, the published surveys of Mennonite relief work focus more on the men who led it than on the women who actually did it.[13] This chapter surveys a sampling of the Canadian women who served in England and the Continent during and after the war.

One of the first Canadian Mennonite women to go overseas was Edna Hunsperger, from Waterloo, Ontario. Edna completed her nurse training in 1937, and once Canada entered the war, she felt pressured to enlist as a nurse with the Royal Canadian Army Medical Corps, as many of her colleagues were doing. As she explained, "I certainly didn't feel comfortable joining the forces ... [I'd] be a part of the war machine ... Other nurses were signing up and I was thinking to myself that I would have some mud thrown at me for not doing anything because I knew they would not understand the conscientious objector point of view."[14] However, in 1940 she received a letter from a local minister, encouraging her to sign up with the MCC, which was beginning to respond to the need for wartime relief. It required workers in England, where Edna eventually spent almost four years. At the age of twenty-nine, she sailed to England from New York, with Elfrieda Klassen from Winnipeg. The two were among the approximately one hundred North American male and female MCC volunteers who performed relief work in Europe during and after the war. About 40 percent of them were single women, whereas the rest were married couples and single men.[15]

In England, the women were mainly assigned to a number of evacuation centres for children and seniors, which were situated outside the urban areas that were subject to bombing. They also worked at Shepherd's Hill in north London, where the MCC opened its relief headquarters in 1943. Elfrieda Klassen initially worked at a children's home in North Wales. As she stated,

> When I saw the first group of children arrive from the slums of Manchester and Liverpool, I knew I was needed and that I would love caring for those children. Some came straight from the hospital, others were sick due to malnutrition and poor environment, all of them in a run-down condition, some with skin infections and respiratory ailments, almost all of them infected with lice.[16]

Edna's first position was at a rural estate that had been converted to an evacuation centre for young children. She then moved to Woodlands, formerly an elite girls' school, near Birmingham, where she cared for elderly residents, many of whom had lost their homes and possessions in bombing raids. In 1943, she was relocated to Shepherd's Hill Mennonite Centre, where she became matron. The building functioned as a transit point and hostel for relief workers, as a distribution depot for clothing, and as temporary housing for displaced children who were waiting to be reunited with their families. It was built into a hill, and its basement was equipped with bunks for use during air raids.[17] The home for children was discontinued in November 1945.[18]

Mabel Cressman soon followed Edna overseas. Also a nurse from Kitchener-Waterloo, she "knew in her bones" that she should respond to the MCC invitation. She volunteered from 1944 to 1946 at Woodlands, at Shepherd's Hill, and at Taxal Edge boys' home (near Manchester). After her London work with children ended, Mabel wrote home, "I feel that I do not want to see children for a long time again." Given this, she was initially disappointed to learn that she would be sent to Taxal Edge.[19] Despite being tired of looking after children, Mabel was gratified to see the results of the care they received: "It is great joy to see these pale, thin lads gaining in weight and color as time goes on. All this due to the fresh air, regular and balanced diet, and the program of work and play during their stay at 'Taxal Edge.'"[20] Before returning to Canada in late summer 1946, Mabel spent two months in Holland, distributing food and clothing.[21]

Like other relief workers, Edna and Mabel had trained as nurses, but little of their assignment involved patient-care nursing. Instead, multi-tasking was demanded of everyone. Edna, for example, performed clerical chores in the MCC office, hosted guests, supervised the domestic side of the headquarters, distributed food and clothing, and attended to whatever was needed. She described in detail how she cared for children who were evacuated from war zones: "I assist with finding their clean clothes, doing admission baths, shampoos, treating spots, bumps, bruises, bites, scrapes etc. and clean heads, cut nails, label coats, sew on the missing buttons which have been overlooked and try to find a set of clothes to fit the new comers."[22] The multiplicity of tasks is suggested by one worker's comment that scrubbing floors seemed to be the first item on the relief program.[23] As well, Mabel Cressman commented on the large amount of mending that staff were expected to tackle at Taxal Edge: "When I first came to Taxal you should have seen the trousers and socks that had to be mended. Well I hardly think that I am stretching it when I say about 100 pr. of socks and 60 pr. of trousers all pilled [sic] up to be assorted and mended."[24] And later she noted that "if no one takes charge of this part of relief it just stacks up and waits for some one who takes an interest in it."[25] Some of the work was hard manual labour, such as when Dorothy Swartzentruber, who worked in Frankfurt after the war, joined teams to move rubble brick-by-brick from demolished buildings.[26]

Like nurses in the military, and the members of the Canadian Red Cross Corps Overseas Detachment discussed in Chapter 9 of this volume, pacifist relief workers often saw the results of war first-hand. Edna Hunsperger described the bombing attacks in graphic terms: "The flying bombs, when they touched ground the damage would fly up. The rockets were something else again; they went down, and they left a crater that you could put two double-decker buses in. We had one of the rockets drop within a mile of our place and we had quite a bit of glass damage and plaster falling."[27] Mabel Cressman, who had wondered whether being a "missionary nurse" might be dangerous in wartime, got an immediate answer upon docking at Liverpool. Due to bombing in London, her destination, she had to remain aboard ship for several days.[28] Arriving in London, she wrote in her diary about the sound of bombs and about going to pick up her gas mask.[29] The stark juxtaposition of mundane tasks with the dangers of life in a war zone stands out in some of Edna's diary entries: for example, on 18 July 1942, she "bought a gas mask case & some cherries."[30] As the household of staff and guests (referred to as family) went about their daily lives, an attack could strike at any minute:

> Did some mending & washing but was rudely disturbed by sirens in the midst 1:50 a.m. Planes, gunfire & bombs made a deathly din. Wave after wave of planes crossed over (bombers). Saw a few shells like rockets in the sky. Seemed to be heavier bombing than Mon. night and the air was tense & charged. Family all had tea.[31]

Despite the constant danger of death, the women's writing and reporting rarely expresses fear of it.

Although all of the women were motivated by a desire to do positive peacemaking through relief work, a few had personally received such assistance themselves, in the aftermath of war. Susan B. Peters from Winnipeg was one of thousands of Mennonites whose families had left the Soviet Union (present-day western Ukraine) in the 1920s, after the Great War, the Russian Revolution, and the civil war that followed brought violence, persecution, and starvation to their communities. A severe famine, accompanied by economic losses and disease, besieged the region in the early 1920s and saw many people die or suffer food deprivation. Founded in the United States in 1920 as a response to this situation, the MCC collected and distributed relief supplies, particularly food, to Mennonites and others in the Soviet Union.[32] The Peters family was the recipient of such aid, which partially inspired Susan to become an "adamant voice for peace" through relief,[33] answering a call for volunteers to help refugees in Europe after the Second World War. Accepted by the MCC, she was sent overseas for a two-year term, with maintenance, medical care, and ten dollars per month.

In August 1945, she arrived in England to work at Taxal Edge, and a year later she moved to London to help wind down the relief work at the Shepherd's Hill Mennonite Centre.[34] Not long after, Susan was transferred to Denmark, where she worked at an MCC-run refugee camp and advocated for the rights and needs of refugees. Thousands of ethnic Germans, expelled or displaced from their homes in Eastern Europe, had escaped the Soviet army by crossing the Baltic Sea to Denmark (many dying en route), where they were housed in barbed-wire-encircled barracks. Susan described these camps, noting the

Figure 8.1

Susan Peters (left) and Mabel Cressman, in England, 1945. | Mennonite Archives of Ontario, CA MAO 2000-1 63, photographer unknown.

numerous children whose parents had been killed or repatriated to the Soviet Union; many were recovering from injuries sustained during their flight from the Red Army.[35] Reflecting on their desperate plight, she wrote,

> One who is free to come and go anywhere, anytime of the day just cannot imagine what it is like to be behind barb wire for more than three years. Have you ever thought of it? Three years after the capitulation, civilians, mostly old folks, women and children are not free to go home. They must wait until the politicians have settled their squabbles or, God forbid, have started another war. How much longer?[36]

Her personal connection to her work is palpable: in a letter home, she wrote, "Having been a refugee myself, arriving penniless in Canada, I know in some measure what these people here have to go through."[37]

Working with refugees was probably what Susan had anticipated when she volunteered for overseas service. As the MCC evaluated its ongoing work in England after war's end, she expressed some concern that it was not assisting those who suffered the most:

> To me it seemed wrong to use money that had been given to us in good faith for – as I felt – the wrong people. I had in mind people at home, whom I knew personally, and who deny themselves necessities of life, just to be able to help suffering people over here. Again, feeling that if we could get the real needy children, they would benefit both ways – physically and spiritually. At the same time we would be doing what was expected of us by the people at home.[38]

Susan's sentiments were shared by other relief workers in England, who felt they were not responding directly to the most acute needs of the civilian population.

Although the MCC had done some initial work in Poland and France, by late 1942 it was disallowed in countries and regions under German occupation. However, by the fall of 1944, the Mennonite relief workers in England had begun to hope for transfer to the Continent. In a 1944 letter home, Mabel Cressman wrote, "Most of the rest of the M.C.C. here are planning and getting ready and waiting to go to France or Holland. So one never knows what might be next but if the door opens our group wants to be ready to go."[39] Soon, the door did open. Holland was the first destination outside England for Mabel, Edna, and Elfrieda, where distribution of food and clothing began in 1945. In her diary entries of spring 1946, Mabel listed the numbers of people served as they travelled throughout the country: on 8 May, they distributed meat to 2,347; on 17 May, they handing out clothing to 250 people daily; on 22 May, 820 people; on 6 June, 950 people; and on 12 June, they served beans to 3,500. On 21 June, Mabel wrote, "All day we distributed in Middleburg – we took care of 18,615 people. 1/2 lb. raisins and 5 kilo flour per person."[40] For the women who distributed food and clothing to thousands of civilians, their daily work was often summarized in numbers: precise accounting was crucial in ensuring that articles needed for survival were in good supply and dispersed equitably.

The greatest need for post-war relief was among the estimated 40 million people worldwide who had been displaced by the conflict. After the armistice, agencies such as the MCC facilitated the emigration of displaced Europeans and alleviated the suffering of those who could not be resettled. Many were

Germans – either by ethnicity or by citizenship – who were perceived as being in danger of starvation due to Allied policies regarding the enemy. MCC workers acknowledged that bringing aid to the enemy might be "incomprehensible" to others, but to them it was a moral imperative.[41] However, the MCC believed that its peace stance included neutrality toward all civilians who were in need. The relief workers who were eventually stationed in Germany frequently commented on the desperate state of people who came to their headquarters for food and clothing, most of whom would have been German by ethnicity or citizenship. In 1951, Dorothy Swartzentruber reflected on the situation:

> Germany has 14 million refugees. That is more than the total population of Canada. Consider then that still more than half of the living quarters are in ruins, and that little more than half the industry has been re-established, and you have a picture of the hopeless conditions. That is why, together with our spiritual witness and work, we need still some gifts of food and clothing to help the really needy people – a great many such people.[42]

Whereas Allied governments asserted that feeding the German people was important to enhance democracy and avoid communism in that nation, as Alice Weinreb argues, for Mennonites the rhetoric of feeding the enemy reinforced their self-identity as Christian pacifists.[43] Along with other Allied humanitarian organizations, the MCC poured significant amounts of food aid into Germany: between 1946 and 1963, this totalled 21,938,642 pounds; the next highest recipient was Holland, which received 4,073,717 pounds of food between 1945 and 1957.[44]

The hardship and poverty created by the war did not end with the Allied victory in 1945. Even as Edna Hunsperger was returning home in 1946, other women were just beginning to plan for overseas relief work. Twenty-nine-year-old Alice Snyder, from Waterloo County, arrived in Germany in the spring of 1948, where she witnessed the war's devastation.[45] She had already been active in war relief for a number of years, as she and her mother operated what was known as the Cutting Room, established by Mennonite women in Ontario in 1942. This project involved the purchase of large bolts of fabric that were cut into clothing patterns and sold to local women for sewing. Women returned the finished garments, which were then sent overseas to war sufferers.[46] Unlike her predecessors, Alice went directly to Germany, not only to distribute relief but also to aid Mennonites who had fled the Soviet Union and Poland during the war and were now displaced in various locales in Europe.

Another latecomer was Dorothy Swartzentruber, who spent about five years in Europe, beginning in 1949. She had started working at the Kitchener

MCC office in 1944, when she felt "the need to do something for somebody else."[47] She was secretary-bookkeeper during the years when the collection, packing, and sending of material goods were at their height. Having met many MCC workers who were going overseas, and being familiar with the work done there, she decided to join them. Dorothy was stationed in Frankfurt, where, among other administrative tasks, she helped co-ordinate MCC refugee work.

Those who were in Germany during the early 1950s witnessed the transition into the Cold War, with little alleviation of the desperate living conditions. In a 1953 letter to her family in Canada, Dorothy Swartzentruber lamented the ongoing tragedy:

> In Canada, except for isolated cases, the last war is something in text books – but here it is something the results of which must be endured weekly, daily, hourly. It is something from which one cannot escape – the emptiness in one's stomach, the loneliness, the poverty, and the otherwise deplorable conditions of a thousand various natures – keep memories alive, while new wounds are constantly inflicted by the Cold War now raging between East and West. And tears are still flowing, and hearts still bleeding![48]

Many of Dorothy's reflections on her refugee work appear in reports sent to Mennonites in North America. For example, in 1950 she wrote in a newsletter directed at women,

> We chose to distribute our allotted 500 bundles to children of families living in bunkers. These are huge, concrete, air-raid shelters which are being used as emergency homes for refugees and bombed-out folks. The conditions in these bunkers are pathetic because they are crowded, often with a family of six having but one room, and the lack of ventilation creates a depressing, sickening atmosphere.
>
> The children were tense with excitement and it was so thrilling to see their eyes sparkle and gleam as they received their bundles wrapped in colourful towels ... My mind also now goes back several weeks to our clothing distribution ... It was a wonderful experience to hand out a coat to a grandmother who had none ... overcoats and warm underwear to men who had just returned from a POW camp ... This experience, too, has left its indelible impression on our lives. How thankful we were for the blessed privilege of giving, of handing to the needy, those garments which you dear people had, in love, prepared for them.[49]

Dorothy's report illustrates the bonds between the relief workers who distributed clothing and the Canadian women who had made it. As nurse Edna Hunsperger wrote in a 1942 letter, she was delighted to recognize certain articles of clothing at the evacuation centre where she worked:

> Please tell Ida Brubacher that I saw her green afghan in the London depot, and recognized it immediately, as I think I saw it in the making. Also give her my love. I also saw the little pink sleeveless sweater I made last fall. Some of the other garments look familiar by the materials – some that I think I saw Mother and Stella work at.[50]

Mabel Cressman also wrote home to say that "I see a lot of our quilts here at London MCC."[51] The particularity of distributed goods also revealed women's roles as connectors, or "peace bridges," between their home communities in Canada and victims of the war. Dorothy Swartzentruber wrote, "The women's club from the [Mennonite] Church in Kitchener sent me 22 prs of children's mitts so I'll have a little distribution somewhere after all. We also have 12 cartons of raisins which we'll take to children's homes and 19 care packages and 50 lbs of wool (knitting)."[52] Far from being independent actors in the battle against suffering, women such as Dorothy served as conduits for the pacifist relief work of communities of women across North America.

What prompted young Canadian Mennonite women to undertake voluntary relief work far from home? The adventure of travel cannot be discounted as one motivating factor that pulled Mennonite and other women – some of whom had never left their communities – to cross the ocean and enter potentially dangerous situations.[53] In their book about Elsie Bechtel, an American peace church relief worker who was in France for three years after the war, M.J. Heisey and Nancy Heisey frame her journey as a "pilgrimage" in a long tradition of Mennonite mobility and religious travel.[54] In their reports, letters, and diaries, women occasionally refer explicitly to the excitement of travel and seeing new places. For example, Edna Hunsperger became an evacuee escort in 1944, accompanying children who had recovered from illness in hospitals in southern England to rejoin their families in the north. As she wrote home about herself, "this girl who loves travel, really enjoyed it!"[55] For women from relatively insular communities with social proscriptions and rigid gender roles, these types of peace pilgrimages also developed their vocational skill sets and broadened their worldviews. As historian T.D. Regehr interprets this, "Mennonites who participated in voluntary service projects came to see the outside world less as a hostile and threatening place to be avoided and more as a suffering, damaged, and violated place in desperate need of Christian love and compassion."[56]

Relief work could also bring romance. Much like the Canadian Red Cross workers discussed in Chapter 9 of this volume, single, twenty-something Mennonite relief workers, living and working together in intense and emotional situations, formed a variety of intimate relationships. Perhaps the best-known was that of Winnipeg nurse Elfrieda Klassen and Peter Dyck, an MCC administrator from Saskatchewan. Soon after reaching England, the two became engaged and married in October 1944. When the war ended, they went to Berlin to help with relief there and, in an oft-told account of danger and heroism, "rescued" Mennonite refugees from the Soviet-occupied zone in 1947.[57] When her good friend Freda became engaged, Edna Hunsperger wrote to her mother, "I am beginning to feel really unique in being the only one of our MCC workers not to be overcome by the tide of wartime romances!"[58] For her part, Susan Peters, working with refugees in Denmark, wrote about the flurry of weddings at home: "I am a confirmed old maid, or rather – single person. I like to live by myself as long as I have something worthwhile to do."[59] In other cases, diary entries and letters home offer vague suggestions of relationships that ended, though Dorothy Swartzentruber mentioned that "marriage doesn't seem so important right now," referring to the gender imbalance in post-war Germany that limited marriage prospects for millions of young, unmarried women.[60]

How MCC administrators felt about these liaisons is difficult to say. As historian Lucille Marr comments, the MCC "saw a single woman as 'the perfect worker,'"[61] and thus administrators might have feared that romantic interests could divert attention from the work at hand. Unencumbered by responsibility for children and husbands, single women could easily leave home for extended periods and be completely devoted to their work. Sources suggest that they were sometimes expected not only to do their assigned jobs, but also to perform domestic chores for the male workers with whom they shared accommodations. In a letter home, Mabel Cressman wrote about her boys' home co-worker Susan Peters, who had "told the male staff to do their own laundry since she was not able to get to the boy's [sic]."[62] Social norms of the day also meant that gendered power relations were apparent at times. This is illustrated, for example, in the relationship of Elfrieda Klassen and Peter Dyck. She had begun her relief work career independently and continued to make the decision to give of her time, but she was typically described as Peter's "assistant" after they married.[63] She was no mere assistant, displaying notable heroism while supervising four shiploads of over five thousand refugees from Europe to South America in 1947–48.[64]

What we now view as inappropriate conduct, even sexual harassment, may have occurred in contexts where unmarried women worked alongside and under the supervision of men (both single and married). Of working with a number of male leaders in a Frankfurt office, Dorothy Swartzentruber wrote in a letter, "Last night was discussion group again and I must say, these fellows are getting sorta fresh. They keep patting me, and rushing around in races to see who gets to the chair next to me ... I think they're sorta silly, really."[65] In a later letter, the situation appeared more than silly: "I will be glad to come home believe you me, especially when I get fed up with these fellows around here. They are good fellows but I wish they would treat us girls with more dignity and respect. I think it is an abnormal situation when boys and girls like we are put into a house and made to live like a family."[66] Despite the independence and ability that young Mennonite women demonstrated through their overseas work, they remained subject to prevailing male views of women's roles and characteristics.

In choosing to embark on overseas relief work, women were also motivated by deep convictions that taking life was wrong and that supporting life was good, which meant alleviating suffering. Although their letters, diary entries, and reports tend to be dominated by factual details of their daily work, they sometimes reflect on the values that underlay it and on the beliefs that informed their choices. In a speech given after she returned home, Mabel Cressman asked her listeners, "Can you picture yourself as the one who is able to comfort, cheer and bring happiness to drive away gloom and disappointment, to help alleviate pain, sooth [sic] the brokenhearted and allay fears of loved ones?"[67] Reporting on her work in Holland, she said,

> While living among people in this war torn country, one could feel and oftentimes hear the bitterness of hate caused by war. So we hope that our aim in showing by material gifts sent with a spirit of love will in time have its effect in these hearts and show them that there is still a God who can heal the bitterness of hate.[68]

Another woman commented on the "bonds of peace" that were created when Canadian Mennonite women sent material relief to war sufferers.[69]

Absolute pacifists of both world wars might have argued that engaging in relief work, such as supplying food and clothing, simply enabled the war machine. By making war "livable," such assistance could be seen as preventing people from experiencing its full consequences and thus lessening opposition to its horrific impact. In the sources available, there is no evidence that peace church women contemplated this logic. Of course, very few people, Mennonite or otherwise, opposed the fight against the Axis powers, known as the "good war." However, the relief work undertaken by Mennonite women who travelled to Europe and administered aid themselves, rather than simply sending it overseas, represented what some scholars describe as a new era of Mennonite peace "activism" that differed from the historic "quietism."[70] Women were responding out of a long anti-war tradition espoused by their religious community but actively expressing that stance through humanitarian aid.

Their efforts were rarely accompanied by ideological or philosophical speeches, and especially not by political campaigns or lobbying, but they did occasionally describe the meaning of their work. As she prepared to return home in early 1946, Edna Hunsperger wrote reflectively, indeed poetically, about her experience:

> In moments of insight, or in retrospect, I am reminded of joys and confidences shared, of the gratitude of the aged, of the love of a child, of friendly and unexpected letters and gifts, the beauty of nature or the song of a bird. *These,* not hatred, war, devastation, and misery, are the rays of the star in the east.[71]

The wartime and post-war work by pacifist women such as Edna was motivated, not by patriotism or a desire for vengeance, but by the unspoken assumption that providing food, clothing, and emotional support to the victims of war on all sides of the conflict was essential for creating conditions of peace. Thus, these remarkable young women experienced the Second World War in ways that differed markedly from those of so many Canadian women.

Notes

I am grateful for research assistance from Bethany Leis.

1 "Elfrieda Dyck Led Refugees out of Europe," *Canadian Mennonite,* 4 October 2004, http://legacy.canadianmennonite.org/vol08-2004/8-19/upclose.html. Elfrieda's story is also told in Peter Dyck and Elfrieda Dyck, *Up from the Rubble: The Epic Rescue of Thousands of War-Ravaged Mennonite Refugees* (Scottdale, PA: Herald Press, 1991).

2 Literature on the alternative service program includes Chapter 2, "Wartime Alternative and Military Service," in T.D. Regehr, *Mennonites in Canada, 1939–1970: A People Transformed* (Toronto: University of Toronto Press, 1996), 35–59; and "War and the Conscientious Objector," theme issue of *Journal of Mennonite Studies* 25 (2007).

3 For a fuller discussion of the impact of conscientious objection on Mennonite women in Canada, see Marlene Epp, "Alternative Service and Alternative Gender Roles: Conscientious Objectors in B.C. during World War II," *BC Studies* 105–6 (Spring-Summer 1995): 139–58. On the question of CO incomes, see also Sarah Glassford, *Mobilizing Mercy,* 176. Mennonite women in the United States were more involved than their Canadian counterparts in organized work programs for COs. See Rachel Waltner Goossen, *Women against the Good War: Conscientious Objection and Gender on the American Home Front, 1941–1947* (Chapel Hill: University of North Carolina Press, 1997).

4 Some of the material in this chapter is included in Marlene Epp, "Mennonite Women: Making Positive Peace," in *From Suffering to Solidarity: The Historical Seeds of Mennonite Interreligious, Interethnic, and International Peacebuilding,* ed. Andrew P. Klager (Eugene, OR: Wipf and Stock, 2015), 178–92. See also my *Mennonite Women in Canada: A History* (Winnipeg: University of Manitoba Press, 2008), especially Chapter 4. I am indebted to the published research on this topic by Lucille Marr, as cited in the notes.

5 Delbert F. Plett, *Johann Plett: A Mennonite Family Saga* (Steinbach, MB: Crossway, 2003), 197.
6 Esther Patkau, *Canadian Women in Mission, 1895–1952–2002* (Saskatoon: Canadian Women in Mission, 2002), 102.
7 Heidi Koop, comp., and Helga Dyck, ed., "'The Band Plays On': Mennonite Pioneers of North Kildonan Reflect" (manuscript, Mennonite Heritage Centre, Winnipeg, 1998), 60.
8 The Mennonite Central Committee is an independent, inter-Mennonite organization created in 1920 to deliver material relief to Mennonites and others suffering food shortages and famine in the Soviet Union. Today, its three-fold emphasis is peace, relief, and development. During the Second World War, it co-ordinated overseas relief work and negotiated the emigration of Mennonite refugees.
9 Mennonite Archives of Ontario (MAO), Conrad Grebel University College, Waterloo, "Mennonite Central Committee Relief Notes: London, England, Letter, January 28, 1941 from Claassen and Coffman," *Missionary News and Notes* (April 1941): 61. For an overview of Canadian Mennonite participation in wartime and post-war relief efforts in Europe, see Regehr, *Mennonites in Canada*, Chapters 3 and 4.
10 Quoted in Lucille Marr, *The Transforming Power of a Century: Mennonite Central Committee and Its Evolution in Ontario* (Kitchener, ON: Pandora Press, 2003), 41. See also Esther Epp-Tiessen, *Mennonite Central Committee in Canada: A History* (Winnipeg: CMU Press, 2013), Chapters 2–3.
11 Phrase borrowed from Gloria Neufeld Redekop, *The Work of Their Hands: Mennonite Women's Societies in Canada* (Waterloo: Wilfrid Laurier University Press, 1996).
12 Esther Epp-Tiessen, "Edna Hunsperger's Witness against War," Mennonite Central Committee Ottawa Office blog, 9 November 2016, https://mccottawaoffice.wordpress.com/tag/second-world-war/.
13 A detailed survey of MCC relief work through the war years makes virtually no mention of women, except in listings of volunteer workers. John D. Unruh, *In the Name of Christ: A History of the Mennonite Central Committee and Its Service, 1920–1951* (Scottdale, PA: Herald Press, 1952).
14 Quoted in Marcus Shantz, "Edna Hunsperger Bowman," *Ontario Mennonite History* 13, 2 (September 1995): 17. See also her profile in Lorraine Roth, *Willing Service: Stories of Ontario Mennonite Women* (Waterloo: Mennonite Historical Society of Ontario, 1992), 188–90. For a brief write-up about Edna, see Miriam Cressman, "Bowman, Edna Hunsperger (1912–2002)," December 2004, Global Anabaptist Mennonite Encyclopedia Online, https://gameo.org/index.php?title=Bowman,_Edna_Hunsperger_(1912–2002).
15 Marr, *The Transforming Power*, 99.
16 Dyck and Dyck, *Up from the Rubble*, 30.
17 Information from MAO, Edna Hunsperger Bowman collection, Hist. Mss. 1.154.12, Edna Hunsperger, "My Journey" (undated report).
18 Edna Hunsperger, "The London Centre Children's Home," *European Relief Notes* 1, 3 (November 1945): 4.
19 MAO, Hist. Mss. 1.216.2, Mabel Cressman to home, 15 and 25 October 1945.
20 Mabel Cressman, "From the Nurse, Mabel Cressman," *European Relief Notes* 1, 9 (May 1946): 4.
21 Mabel's story is told in Roth, *Willing Service*, 87.
22 MAO, Edna Hunsperger Bowman collection, Hist. Mss. 1.154.12, Edna Hunsperger to Mother and All, 1 April 1944, Blencathara.
23 Centre for Mennonite Brethren Studies (CMBS), Winnipeg, Susan B. Peters collection, vol. 1028, Susan B. Peters to friends and co-workers, 17 September 1945, Taxal Edge.

24 MAO, Hist. Mss. 1.216.2, Mabel Cressman to friends at the Dorcas Sewing Circle, 4 January 1946, Taxal Edge.
25 MAO, Hist. Mss. 1.216.2, Mabel Cressman to home, 8 March 1946, Taxal Edge.
26 MAO, Dorothy Swartzentruber Sauder collection, Hist. Mss. 1.286.1, Dorothy Swartzentruber to home, 29 March 1950.
27 Quoted in Shantz, "Edna Hunsperger Bowman," 19.
28 Roth, *Willing Service*, 86.
29 MAO, Hist. Mss. 1.216.2, Mabel Cressman, Diary, 28 and 29 August 1944.
30 MAO, Hist. Mss. 1.154.11, Edna Hunsperger Bowman, Diary, 18 July 1942.
31 Ibid., 29 July 1942.
32 For a history of these events and of the MCC, see, for example, Frank H. Epp, *Mennonite Exodus: The Rescue and Resettlement of the Russian Mennonites since the Communist Revolution* (Altona, MB: D.W. Friesen, 1962); and Epp-Tiessen, *Mennonite Central Committee*, Chapter 1.
33 Elizabeth Wittrig, "Susan B. Peters: An Adamant Voice for Peace," *Profiles of Mennonite Faith* 58 (Fall 2015), Mennonite Brethren Historical Commission, http://www.mbhistory.org/profiles/peters.en.html.
34 Susie Peters, "Thoughts on Closing London Center," *European Relief Notes* 2, 2 (October 1946): 3.
35 Susie Peters, "Denmark: Scenes in the Refugee Camps," *European Relief Notes* 4, 9 (May-June 1948): 4–5.
36 Ibid., 5.
37 Quoted in Wittrig, "Susan B. Peters: An Adamant Voice."
38 CMBS, vol. 1028, Susan B. Peters to S.J. Goering, 21 February 1946, Taxal Edge.
39 MAO, Hist. Mss. 1.216.2, Mabel Cressman to home, 1 December 1944, Wolverhampton, UK.
40 MAO, Hist. Mss. 1.216.2, Mabel Cressman, Diary, 8, 17, and 22 May 1946, 6, 12, and 21 June 1946.
41 Robert S. Kreider and Rachel Waltner Goossen, *Hungry, Thirsty, a Stranger: The MCC Experience* (Scottdale, PA: Herald Press, 1988), 71.
42 MAO, Hist. Mss. 1.286.1, Dorothy Swartzentruber to home, 28 November 1951.
43 For an analysis of the debates over post-war hunger in Germany, see Alice Weinreb, "'For the Hungry Have No Past Nor Do They Belong to a Political Party': Debates over German Hunger after World War II," *Central European History* 45, 1 (2012): 50–78.
44 John Hostetler, "Mennonite Central Committee and Material Aid, 1941–1969," *Mennonite Quarterly Review* 44, 3 (July 1970): 323.
45 Alice Snyder's experiences are chronicled in over a hundred letters she sent home from 1948 to 1950. See Lucille Marr with Dora-Marie Goulet, *Alice Snyder's Letters from Germany* (Kitchener: Pandora Press, 2009).
46 For details on the Cutting Room, see Marr, *The Transforming Power*, Chapters 2–3.
47 Quoted in Linda Hubert Hecht, "Legacy of Service: Dorothy M. Swartzentruber Sauder's Career in Church Work at Home and Abroad," *Ontario Mennonite History* 19, 2 (November 2001): 10.
48 MAO, Hist. Mss. 1.286.1, Dorothy Swartzentruber to home, 6 April 1953.
49 Dorothy Swartzentruber, "The Needs of Europe," *Women's Activities Letter*, 1 January 1950.
50 MAO, Edna Hunsperger Bowman collection, Hist. Mss. 1.154.11, Edna Hunsperger to home, (Dear Folks) from Auntie Edna, 23 July 1942, Wolverhampton, UK.
51 MAO, Hist. Mss. 1.216.2, Mabel Cressman to home, 1 December 1944, Wolverhampton, UK.

52 MAO, Hist. Mss. 1.286.1, Dorothy Swartzentruber to folks and Harold, 10 December 1950, Frankfurt.

53 For a discussion of the cultural adventures experienced by UNRRA (United Nations Relief and Rehabilitation Administration) workers in Europe, see Jessica Reinisch, "'Auntie UNRRA' at the Crossroads," *Past and Present* 218, supplement 8 (2013): 70–97.

54 M.J. Heisey and Nancy R. Heisey, *Relief Work as Pilgrimage: 'Mademoiselle Miss Elsie' in Southern France, 1945–1948* (Lanham, MD: Lexington Books, 2015), 2.

55 MAO, Edna Hunsperger Bowman collection, Hist. Mss. 1.154.12, Edna Hunsperger to Mother and All, 14 August 1944, Blencathara.

56 Regehr, *Mennonites in Canada,* 60.

57 Elfrieda and Peter's stories are told in Dyck and Dyck, *Up from the Rubble.*

58 MAO, Hist. Mss. 1.154.12, Edna Hunsperger to Mother and All, 14 August 1944, Blencathara.

59 CMBS, vol. 1028, Susan B. Peters to Helen, 24 April 1947, Copenhagen.

60 MAO, Dorothy Swartzentruber Sauder collection, Hist. Mss. 1.286.1, Dorothy Swartzentruber to folks and Harold, 10 December 1950, Frankfurt.

61 Arlene Sittler Woods, quoted in Marr with Goulet, *Alice Snyder's Letters,* 14.

62 MAO, Hist. Mss. 1.216.2, Mabel Cressman to friends at the Dorcas Sewing Circle, 4 January 1946, Taxal Edge.

63 "Elfrieda Klassen Dyck Transfers to Berlin," *European Relief Notes* 1, 12 (August 1946): 11.

64 For Elfrieda's obituary, see "Elfrieda Dyck, 87, Mennonite Who Helped Thousands Resettle, Dies," *New York Times,* 5 September 2004.

65 MAO, Dorothy Swartzentruber Sauder collection, Hist. Mss. 1.286.1, Dorothy Swartzentruber to Mibsie, 16 February 1950, Frankfurt.

66 MAO, Dorothy Swartzentruber Sauder collection, Hist. Mss. 1.286.1 Dorothy Swartzentruber to Mother, Dad and Harold, 3 October 1950.

67 MAO, Hist. Mss. 1.216.2, Mabel Cressman, "Nursing as a Vocation," Undated speech.

68 MAO, Hist. Mss. 1.216.2, Mabel Cressman, "Relief Work in Holland," Speech, 1946–47.

69 Arlene Sittler, "A Challenge to Mennonite Women," *Women's Activities Letter,* February 1946, 1–3.

70 See, for instance, Leo Driedger and Donald Kraybill, *Mennonite Peacemaking from Quietism to Activism* (Scottdale, PA: Herald Press, 1994).

71 Edna Hunsperger, "England," *European Relief Notes* 1, 4 (December 1945): 4 (emphasis in original). "The star in the east" refers to the Christmas star that guided the Magi to Bethlehem.

9

"It Keeps Our Spirits Up"

Emotional Labour and Resilience in the Canadian Red Cross Corps Overseas Detachment, 1943–47

Sarah Glassford

> *Excitement, fear, joy, sorrow, good times; bad times; companionship and laughter, touched us all.*
>
> – Nancy Laing[1]

"My British naval officer friend and I are here," explains Nancy Laing, indicating a fifty-year-old photo. Her gentle voice growing even softer, she adds: "He was killed." It is a quiet September afternoon in 1993, and former Canadian Red Cross Corps members Nancy Laing and Jane McGillivray are showing Nancy's mementoes of the Second World War to Red Cross librarian Ann Butryn. Ann tries to steer the conversation toward their work and uniforms, but Nancy and Jane keep circling back to the people they knew overseas. "This is another wedding we had," says Nancy, referring to a series of photos. "He was killed. Shoot, so many of the boys were killed."[2]

This simple but moving interplay between historical evidence and memory, captured on audio cassette, highlights the powerful personal and emotional dimensions of young women's overseas service with the Canadian Red Cross Corps (CRCC, also known as "the Corps"). To date, the historiography of women's relationships with Canadian men during that conflict has focused primarily on romance and sexuality in the forms of war brides and venereal disease.[3] This chapter expands that narrow view to include ties of blood, friendship, and nationality. And instead of asking whether the war was good for women, it asks how they coped – and helped men cope – with what was bad about the war.

The nuances of wartime societies cannot be truly understood without paying attention to the emotional lives of those who inhabited them.[4] "Adding emotions is like adding colour to a black-and-white image," writes Neta C. Crawford. "Work that reads world politics and war with emotions in the foreground ... offers ... lenses with a different prescription, that help us know what was already there, perhaps unseen."[5] Swati Parashar notes that there is a special value to studying women's emotions in wartime because too often they are reduced to stereotypes (the grieving wife/mother) or denied entirely.[6] Historians of sexuality have shown that women's emotions were implicated equally with their bodies in the waging of the Second World War.[7] Both women and emotions were central to the success of the Canadian Red Cross Society, which was itself a central part of the Canadian war effort in this period. Its overseas female volunteers are therefore a logical site for examining Canadian women's emotions in wartime. This chapter draws upon the letters, memoirs, and oral histories of members of the Corps, to examine some of the emotional dimensions of their wartime lives.

Most of the interviews and recollections left by CRCC members were produced many decades after the war and could be coloured by nostalgia or forgetfulness. As Carol Z. Stearns states, "to get the full flavor of a culture's emotional life without being there to observe is certainly a formidable, and ultimately impossible, task."[8] However, three sources in particular make it possible to attempt the feat: Jean Ellis's 1947 memoir and the extensive collections of wartime letters written by Lois MacDonald and Mary Macdonald (no relation).[9] From 1943 until shortly after the end of the war, all three women served first in England and later in northwestern Europe. Their writings serve as longitudinal case studies across several years of overseas work and offer a depth and intimacy that are missing from many of their peers' later recollections. Together with those recollections, the memoir and the letters paint a vibrant portrait of young women's voluntary service overseas for the Canadian Red Cross. After leaving Canada, they quickly created (and re-created) extensive networks of friendship, kinship, and romance. These emotional bonds became highly meaningful elements central to their wartime experiences, helping to sustain them and the servicemen whom they encountered through the most difficult elements of their time in Europe. In the face of stressful or traumatic experiences and the draining forms of emotional labour they provided to enlisted men, corps members shored up their own resilience through the relationships they established overseas or maintained from home and in the ways they spent their leisure hours.

Value-Added Volunteers: The Red Cross, the War, and the Corps

The Canadian Red Cross Society (CRCS) is steeped in potent ideals of compassion, caring, and service to suffering humanity. Formed in 1896 to aid the sick and wounded in war, it established a powerful relationship with Canadians through its relief effort for sick, wounded, and captured Canadian servicemen during the First World War.[10] During the Second World War, it was Canada's pre-eminent war charity, boasting a membership of more than 2.1 million adults and 900,000 youth.[11] Its humanitarian appeal crossed linguistic and religious lines, and even drew support from pacifist and nonresistant groups, such as the Mennonite community discussed by Marlene Epp in Chapter 8 of this volume.

CRCS overseas work included the provision of food parcels for Canadian and other Allied prisoners of war, supplementary medical and surgical items for military hospitals, visits and comfort items for Canadian servicemen in hospital, Maple Leaf Clubs for troops on leave in London, occupational therapy programs in military hospitals, and much besides.[12] By late 1942, a shortage of voluntary labour in Britain and a desire for specialist skills led the CRCS to begin importing members of the Canadian Red Cross Corps to help its overseas headquarters accomplish this work.

The CRCC was a wartime creation that was intended to harness the enthusiasm and energy of young women who sought more active roles than the knitting and fundraising that had to satisfy many of their mothers and grandmothers. First piloted in 1940, it eventually consisted of four sections: transport, nursing auxiliary, office administration, and food administration. Each section undertook relevant specialist training to provide emergency service in case of disaster or enemy attack. Members of the Corps were distinguished from ordinary Red Cross volunteers in Canada by their military-style uniforms, the hierarchical chain of command to which they were subject, and the military drill they practised. These three elements plus the mandated training courses and required volunteer hours produced a highly efficient organization with a strong esprit de corps. As of 1942, forty-five CRCC detachments were reported active across Canada, from Charlottetown to Victoria.[13] Some fifteen thousand women enrolled in the CRCC at some point during the war, with membership peaking in 1944, when six thousand sported the uniform. Their efficiency, dedication, and versatility soon made them essential to the home front CRCS.[14]

These same attributes made members of the Corps an ideal labour source for overseas Red Cross work. Accordingly, between December 1942 and December 1947, 641 CRCC members were sent to Britain, Italy, and northwestern Europe as part of a new Overseas Detachment – earning them the internal designation of "ODs."[15] As civilian volunteers, the ODs received about five dollars a week from the CRCS for basic necessities but were otherwise unpaid and self-supporting. Universally white and largely Anglo-Saxon, they included young women of modest means – many had held clerical jobs – as well as some from privileged backgrounds, such as Margaret Eaton of the Eaton's department store family. Overseas, since they often worked closely with members of the military, they were granted the courtesy of officer rank.[16]

On Duty: Emotional Labour and Resilience at Work

On the eve of her departure in August 1943, Ottawa's Mary Macdonald was praised by her hometown CRCC colleagues for her boundless energy, organizational skill, and creative ideas.[17] Yet, once overseas, ODs such as Mary found that more was required of them than practical tasks: as Red Cross representatives, and as women, they were *also* expected to perform emotional labour. In her pioneering work on emotional labour, Arlie Hochschild explains that "the world turns to women for mothering, and this fact silently attaches itself to many a job description."[18] Red Cross work was a prime example. Whether they were staffing a hospital, canteen, or club, driving an ambulance, or filling any other job that brought them in contact with servicemen, ODs performed emotional labour, deliberately behaving in certain ways so as to increase, decrease, or otherwise manage particular emotions in others.

Although not expressed in these terms at the time, the CRCS directed its Second World War humanitarian aid toward two complementary sets of needs: physical survival and psychological resilience. Food parcels, hospitals, ambulances, and medical supplies addressed the former; hospital visits, hometown newspapers, canteens serving home-style meals, and a diverse array of items

Figure 9.1

Corps members staffing a mobile canteen unit provide hot drinks and female conversation to servicemen, c. 1943–45. | Canadian Red Cross National Archive, Overseas Club collection, 22.4.

known as comforts (such as cigarettes, Christmas stockings, and small bags of personal hygiene items) were intended to support the latter. Twenty-first-century psychologists define resilience as "the process of adapting well in the face of adversity, trauma, tragedy, threats or significant sources of stress" and point out that a person's resilience is directly related to their behaviours, thoughts, and actions. Culture and personality influence which strategies work best for each person, but two of the most effective resilience-builders are personal connections with caring people and small acts of self-care.[19] Both were found in Red Cross efforts. Whether a warm sweater after being torpedoed and rescued at sea, or a sympathetic chat with a hospital visitor, each helped, in different ways, to reinforce a serviceman's ability to bounce back in the face of adversity.

The reason that women were recruited to provide these types of service was deeply rooted in the history of the CRCS. The First World War had established the Red Cross as a special channel for women's "mothering" work in wartime,[20] grounding this link in nineteenth- and early-twentieth-century beliefs about women's natural skills in the domestic realm. Although both men and women could express compassion for the suffering of others, compassion was often seen as "a distinctly 'feminine' emotion" because it was "elided with experiences of nurturing and care-giving associated with motherhood."[21] In both world wars, the Canadian government and military relied on voluntary organizations such as the Red Cross and the YMCA to connect servicemen to "their humanity and the family and community life for which they were fighting" because maintaining links between home front and battle front boosted morale on both sides.[22] When Jean Ellis of Victoria, British Columbia, landed in Normandy with the first group of ODs and Canadian nursing sisters, she recognized her role as a link between soldiers and civilians. The men whom they passed along the road barraged them with questions and wolf whistles, but she noticed that some had tears in their eyes (and became misty-eyed herself, in response). "We knew that we reminded the boys of their womenfolk at home, whom they missed so much," she recalled, "and they reminded us of boys we would never see again."[23] Supporting Jean's interpretation, Joshua Goldstein argues that when women play traditionally feminine roles in war zones, servicemen are powerfully reminded that "the battlefield is finite and the other world still exists."[24]

In a poem entitled "To a Red Cross Sister" – written in December 1944 at No. 12 Canadian General Hospital (CGH) in Belgium – serviceman Frankie Hamilton praised a CRCC member as steadfast, friendly, beautiful, and "wondrous kind." Her regular visits to the men in the wards "brighten up their day, / And faces, once so wracked with pain, light up, / When she appears to help them on their way." In "Our 'Sunshine Ray,'" written around the same time, Hamilton described the "cheery words and lovely smile" of another OD, who "makes us think of home / Of Sweetheart, Wife or Mother, / While we are so alone."[25] Both poems suggest that CRCC women's work in military hospitals and convalescent homes (and perhaps in other settings as well) was read by servicemen as a form of compassion. Defined as "individual feelings of empathy, expressed through actions," compassion "facilitates another's feeling of being cared for, joined, seen, felt, known, and not alone." It can therefore expedite mental and emotional healing or at least temporarily staunch those forms of pain and suffering.[26]

Ottawa native Lois MacDonald told her parents that making her daily rounds on the hospital wards took hours because of all the conversations she had, photos she looked at, and stories of home she listened to along the way.[27] Contemporary studies of male friendship suggest that men often find it easier to share their emotions with women than with other men.[28] This may be particularly true in military contexts, where, as Victoria Basham notes, "soldiers quickly learn the value of controlling and displaying their emotions; of when it is and is not appropriate to express emotions of one kind or another."[29] Until the 1990s and early 2000s, the Canadian military cultivated a stoic masculinity within its ranks that repressed emotions such as fear, pain, and guilt.[30] If emotional support were required, chaplains, nurses, voluntary agencies, or a soldier's family and friends were expected to supply it. Thus, when a Second World War serviceman could share his feelings or be emotionally vulnerable with a woman, it played an important part in helping him process and cope with physical or emotional trauma.

Emotional labour not only infused the work in which corps members engaged, it also shaped their larger place in the landscape of wartime society. As Ville Kivimäki and Tuomas Tepora write, "men were the actors of war, but women gave meaning to it; it was their role to encourage and support, to be admiring spectators, and to build up the scenery for heroism and sacrifice."[31] When CRCC women performed this type of encouraging, admiring behaviour, they were putting out an "unseen effort" of the kind that Hochschild compares to housework: it "does not quite count as labor but is nevertheless crucial to getting other things done."[32] More broadly, women mattered enormously to enlisted men: as highly sexualized creatures of fantasy in the form of pin-ups and conquests (real or imaginary), on the one hand, and as pure, idealized symbols of the best in life (loving mothers, faithful wives, sympathetic sisters), on the other.[33]

These contrasting roles figured in Lois MacDonald's assessment of the qualities that an OD needed to be a Red Cross welfare officer: "one would need to be a Master of Psychology, a glamour girl, a comedian, Dorothy Dix [an advice columnist], a Florence Nightingale, a Santa Claus, a Fount of Wisdom and Information, with the patience of Job, all rolled into one." The contradictions could be problematic. It was important, she wrote, "to let [the patients] treat you as a sister or girlfriend, and be gay and friendly," but not to the extent of letting them get fresh.[34] Like nursing sisters, the ODs promoted this sisterly rapport by referring to servicemen as "son," "our boys," or "the lads."[35] Notably, however, Lois also included being "gay and glamourous" in her imaginary job description.[36] In an article about Sir Archibald McIndoe's wartime work with facially disfigured airmen, Liz Byrski highlights the fact that McIndoe deliberately recruited attractive nurses and encouraged flirtations and relationships between them and the patients. Time and again, "the evidence that many women were able and willing to see through disfigurement to the person within" – and good-looking young women, at that – provided a psychological turning point in an airman's overall recovery.[37] The fraternizing encouraged in McIndoe's unit was unique, but the morale-boosting impact of attention from a pretty girl was also apparent to ODs such as Lois.

Research in the field of organizational behaviour suggests that both personality and environmental factors (notably, the existence or absence of social support) play important roles in the experience of emotional labour for the individual who performs it. A 1998 study of the caring professions, for instance, found higher levels of job satisfaction associated with strong social support and lower levels among those who had little social support.[38] It was therefore significant that most ODs felt their professional relationship with servicemen involved a supportive give-and-take on both sides. Lois MacDonald acknowledged that "one might get the impression that we are here ... giving a lot and getting little in return," but she cited the men's sacrifice of youth and health for the wartime cause as more than deserving of the effort, and she felt inspired by their courage and kindness. "Of course, they try our patience to the utmost," she admitted, but in the end she was convinced that "we really do little for them, in return for what they have given us."[39]

Yet, even emotionally meaningful work takes a toll on those who perform it. "I think I have aged ten years in the last two days," wrote an anonymous CRCC member in an article about her work in a Canadian hospital overseas.[40] A key element of Hochschild's concept of emotional labour lies in recognizing that managing the emotions of others is hard work. It can demand enormous effort and self-control – essentially subduing or otherwise managing one's *own* emotions – to achieve the desired effect in others while making it look effortless.[41] Projecting cheerfulness and high spirits required a woman to sublimate her own fatigue, anxiety, sadness, or frustration; displaying compassion, on the other hand, obliged her to "[surrender] to the pain of another" and convey her empathy in that moment.[42] Twenty-first-century studies show that over the long term, emotional labour – particularly when it involves suppressing one's own emotions – can harm one's physical and mental health and lead to burnout.[43]

For ODs on duty, interacting with servicemen in canteens and clubs certainly involved emotional labour, but the most harrowing experiences were reserved for those who drove ambulances or worked as welfare officers in military hospitals. OD Frances Martin Day recalled, "We went in with a ditty bag and had to be ho, ho, ho to keep their spirits up, but it was awful, horrible."[44] While handing out cigarettes to newly admitted stretcher cases in her hospital in Normandy, Jean Ellis similarly remembered "trying to be cheerful though it was a struggle not to burst into tears." "Saying things like 'Hi-ya chum. Anything we can do for you?' sounded slightly silly and very inadequate," she wrote, "but the boys appeared to like it."[45] Although ODs became accustomed to seeing men in pain, the scale and variety of the carnage must have remained shocking. Mary Macdonald, who served as a welfare officer at No. 12 CGH in Belgium from July 1944 to November 1945, saw more than 17,500 patients admitted over an eleven-month period, some 12,000 of them surgical cases. Only 58 of the surgical patients died,[46] but the steady stream of badly wounded, emotionally vulnerable men would have drained even the most ebullient young woman's reserve of cheerfulness.

It was the ODs' job to show that they cared – to pass out cigarettes and tea, write letters, stroke heads, adjust pillows, talk, or listen.[47] But caring was physically and emotionally exhausting, and sometimes traumatizing. Like many veterans,[48] OD Dorothy Falkner Burgoyne Dolittle never spoke of her feelings about what she had seen and done during the war, choosing instead to share amusing anecdotes with her children. However, the lasting emotional impact of her service is attested to by her daughters, who recalled that she could not bear to watch scenes of air raids or bombings in movies or television shows set in wartime. It is not difficult to connect this lifelong aversion with her experiences of nighttime air raids in London and later with the devastation she witnessed behind the Allied advance through Italy.[49] Being strafed by German planes and seeing the burned-out shells of military vehicles and bloated bodies of dead livestock made a similarly strong impression on the first ODs to land in Normandy.[50] Once their unit (No. 7 CGH) was established in France, the overwhelming volume of casualties meant that the three ODs, including Jean Ellis, were temporarily seconded to assist the nursing sisters. Assigned to the ward for patients with severe head wounds, Jean was deeply shaken by what she saw. On the first day, she left the tent to be violently ill, had no appetite by evening, and when "utter exhaustion produced sleep, ... awful dreams went with it."[51]

Work-related fatigue and emotional strain were not the only burdens borne by CRCC women overseas. Like other Canadians, many ODs carried a heavy weight of anxiety for loved ones and friends who were involved in the fighting.

In her 1947 memoir, Jean described listening to a BBC Radio report of the D-Day assault in the mid-morning of 6 June 1944, alongside the women and men of No. 7 CGH. Some were visibly excited, but Jean also remembered "several girls standing as if stunned, with tears running down their faces, or lips moving in prayer ... someone very close to their hearts must be in danger."[52] When Lois MacDonald learned that Robert "Spike" Rochon, a good friend from her teen years, had been killed, it finally broke her. "That seemed to be the last straw for all the tears I had stored up," she wrote to her parents. "Went back to our hotel, up to my room, threw myself down and sobbed. It was not just for Robert, but for the many friends, all the fine young men that have been lost." A little over a week later, on the night before the official V-E Day celebrations, Lois and many of her female hospital colleagues were subdued and restless. "The last years have been too tense," she mused, "and we have seen too much and lost too many friends, to forget it all so soon."[53]

ODs themselves were often in danger, and this, too, drained their reserves of resilience. First, the Atlantic crossing was tense and perilous, even though the threat of German submarines had peaked and begun to subside by 1943. While stationed in Britain, ODs were subject to the terror and nuisance of air raids and buzz bombs; one group was torpedoed en route to Italy, losing all their kit but escaping with their lives.[54] Those who were posted to Italy and Normandy with hospital units were at risk from bombings, landmines, and (potentially) a sudden pushback by enemy forces. The booming of artillery guns could seem shockingly close, and at times tin helmets were a must.[55]

Reflecting on the entire experience decades later, OD Phyllis Elder Matheson concluded, "If we knew what we were getting into, we probably would not have gone."[56] The letters and memoirs of CRCC members suggest that, as for front-line soldiers of the Great War, "the ability to endure, to take what the enemy dished out and 'stick it' for the duration" became the currency of courage.[57] It was a way to mimic the phlegmatic stoicism, not only of sick and wounded troops, but also of bombed and displaced civilians. But "sticking it" required resilience, and the women's reserves of that quality needed constant replenishment through specific actions, behaviours, and thought processes.

Off Duty: Resilience and Emotional Labour through Social Connection

Personal networks of support, and self-care through leisure activities, were critical to sustaining the ability of corps members to perform emotional labour for the benefit of servicemen, both on and off duty. The prospect of transatlantic travel and the coveted opportunity to provide hands-on volunteer service near the battle fronts made an overseas posting exciting for most CRCC women. But it also meant facing new challenges far from their established support networks of friends and loved ones. For some ODs, such as Mary Macdonald, the strain of separation materialized early. Normally an unflappable optimist, she admitted in an emotional letter that while riding the train east from Ottawa, she felt "lonesome" for her mother and sister.[58] Such feelings could resurface at any time, too, as Jean Ellis discovered while watching a movie with a Canadian soldier just before Christmas. When the actors onscreen sang "Holy Night," both Jean and her companion felt the aching pangs of homesickness. "He just grabbed my hand and hung on tightly," she wrote. "We didn't dare look at each other."[59]

Like the servicemen, ODs relied on contact with people from home to provide them with moral support.[60] Long-distance phone calls were prohibitively expensive, so correspondence played a vital role in maintaining those links. Lois MacDonald received around ninety individual parcels from her parents, friends, relatives, and former co-workers during her two years abroad, and she wrote three hundred letters to her parents alone. The Mary Macdonald fonds at Library and Archives Canada hold 126 of Mary's letters to relatives but not her weekly letters to her brother Neil in the RCAF or the letters and postcards she sent to friends. Jane Mersky Leder explains that in wartime women and their correspondents "substituted the intimacies shared in letters for those shared when living together."[61] As Mary wrote to her sister Catherine, known as Kay, in June 1945, "it doesn't really seem as long as two years because I have been right with you all along in your letters."[62] Details of daily life shared in both directions fostered a sense of security and stability: despite the distance and extraordinary circumstances, ODs remained connected to their traditional networks of emotional support. As a further way of maintaining these networks, Mary routinely ended her letters to her mother and sister with questions about friends and family, as well as a request that she be remembered to half a dozen people, to whom she lacked the time to write. Kay's descriptions of the weddings of two dear friends in Ottawa allowed Mary to vicariously enjoy the festivities and helped assuage her regret at not being there.[63]

For some, familiar social networks could be re-created in person. In Halifax, while awaiting transport to Britain, several ODs briefly reunited with an enlisted male relative or friend who was in port at the same time. One OD even recognized her brother's corvette as their convoy crossed the ocean. She was thrilled to have "an animated conversation [with him], with megaphones," mid-Atlantic.[64] The urge to reconnect merely increased in Britain. "Always so exciting when someone from home shows up," wrote Lois MacDonald.[65] OD Winifred Booth squeezed in a visit to her friend Vi between docking at Southampton and reporting to CRCC headquarters in London. On her first night in London, Mary Macdonald was telephoned by two Ottawa OD friends who had already arrived in the country and convinced a third to go out with her so she could experience the blackout. She spent part of the next day at RCAF headquarters, attempting to locate her brother Neil, who was stationed in England.[66] Many ODs also tried to stay in touch with their home corps detachment and with ODs who were transferred elsewhere or who returned to Canada. Irene Potter, stationed in London, wrote to Toronto corps leader Vida Peene that she and another OD friend "often talk about Toronto and the Corps."[67]

For some women of the corps, loved ones were integral to their decision to go overseas: either they volunteered to be near their husband or they sought a distraction from the grief of his death. Frances Martin did both. She joined the corps in 1943 when her husband, RCAF wing commander Norman Martin, was posted to England. Norman urged her "to move Heaven and earth" to join him, leaving their three-year-old son Grant in the care of relatives. "We were very young and very much in love," she recalled, adding that she would no longer make the same decision to leave their son. "It requires understanding how it was in wartime," she wrote, "living from day to day and grasping at straws of happiness when you could." Norman was killed before she left for Britain, but she decided to accept an overseas posting nonetheless, seeing it as a useful way to "bridge a difficult time."[68] OD Phyllis Elder Matheson recalled that some war widows accepted overseas postings "to get an atmosphere of the life they had not shared."[69] Yet, such proximity could be a double-edged sword. For Jean Ellis, landing in Normandy was a painful experience, as the carnage she saw there brought to mind her husband's death early in the war. She drew on her desire to do her job as well as the invading Allies had done theirs, to keep herself going.[70]

Lois MacDonald's friend Aileen Corkett benefitted from an overseas corps policy that gave first choice of hospital postings to married women, so they could be close to their husbands. Aileen was assigned to the No. 1 Canadian Neurological and Plastic Surgery unit in Basingstoke, Hampshire, where her husband, George, was a patient. When his health permitted it, they found nearby lodgings to share and celebrated their fourth wedding anniversary in England – the first they had ever spent together.[71] However, an overseas posting did not guarantee a happy reunion. OD Biddy Wilkins left Canada with the corps in July 1944 but arrived in Liverpool only to discover that her husband, Ron, had departed the same day, headed for Algiers. They were reunited in March 1946 – just in time to travel back to Canada together.[72] Aileen Corkett faced a crueller outcome. A few weeks after rejoining his regiment in Italy, George was killed in action, leaving her pregnant and far from home. Fortunately, the support network she had created in England came to her aid. Friends from her OD work in Basingstoke visited repeatedly and relayed the sad news to Lois MacDonald in Belgium, who sent a letter of condolence. The Red Cross arranged Aileen's return to Canada. Lois described the stoic Aileen as "a brick," saying she "certainly has what it takes."[73] Canadians of the 1940s admired this kind of "stiff upper lip" response to adversity – a resilience strategy in its own right – and the people in their lives helped them achieve it.

CRCC members left Canada with a strong sense of corps identity and bonded as new members of the Overseas Detachment en route to the war zone with others of their cohort. For many, the seeds of new friendships were planted as they travelled through Canada by train. The Atlantic crossing then developed them in earnest, through conversation and card playing, sing-songs, seasickness, storms, and the danger of U-boat attacks. Even women who were considered difficult to get along with found friends. Mary Macdonald's travel cohort included two women whom she called "duds" (due to their self-importance), who got along "beautifully" with each other.[74]

Corps House – three connected townhouses on Queensgate Terrace – was home to CRCC members who were stationed in London and others who were on leave or in transit. From 1943 to 1947, it housed up to a hundred women at a time. Overcrowded bedrooms, too few bathrooms, nightly air raids, and communal meals provoked outbursts of temper but also fostered bonds of friendship and camaraderie.[75] These attachments, rooted in shared space and communal living, mirror the experiences of women in the armed forces.[76] Similarly strong friendships often sprang up within the small groups of ODs who worked elsewhere in Britain or in continental Europe, and between ODs and the nursing sisters with whom they often worked and boarded. These new relationships with women who understood their struggles proved crucial to sustaining OD morale.

Anthropologist Daniel Hruschka notes that, across cultures, close friendships are marked not only by the enjoyment of one another's company, but by the provision of emotional support, sharing confidences, and talking over problems.[77] In her study of British women's oral histories of the Second World War, Penny Summerfield finds that during break times women in female-dominated workplaces engaged in supportive talk about sons, brothers, spouses, and friends: who was serving where, what they were doing, and what letters had been received.[78] Similarly, First World War combatants and the social scientists who studied them believed that close friendships made war endurable for the servicemen who were exposed to its worst horrors.[79] Jean Ellis reached much the same conclusion when she wrote in her memoir that "fear is a terrible thing when one is alone but it fades to some extent with company."[80]

The sheer number of Canadian servicemen in Britain (and then in Western Europe) meant that CRCC women encountered brothers, cousins, neighbours, schoolmates, family friends, and friends of friends with surprising frequency. Lois MacDonald reconnected with Flying Officer Harvey Fenton, an "old friend from home," during a mutual weekend leave in London and went with him to Buckingham Palace to see him receive the Distinguished Flying Cross from George VI.[81] Brand new mixed-gender friendships also sprang up overseas. Lois, an only child, cherished her friendship with Ad, a pharmacist at her hospital in Belgium, whom she came to regard as a brother.[82]

These male friends and social companions might be single but were equally likely to be married or otherwise spoken for. For the benefit of her late 1940s readers, Jean Ellis explained that "no eyebrows were lifted" when the women went on dates with their married male friends, because the wives were so far away and many had asked their husbands to look up corps girls whom they knew overseas. She added, reassuringly, "it wasn't all fun and frolic going out with homesick men who spent hours telling us how wonderful their wives and children were, but we felt it was part of our job to act as wailing walls once in awhile." Some married men were glad to be away from their wives, she admitted, but the best of them "soft-pedalled their married status and treated us as charming companions."[83] These mixed-gender friendships seem to have been especially important to servicemen as tensions built in the lead-up to D-Day. Jean noticed that the men put on a brave front in their letters home but more freely admitted their fears to the ODs – in her opinion, because they "knew we wouldn't think less of them."[84]

The abundance of lighthearted anecdotes in the written recollections of many ODs suggests that laughter was a common element of their overseas friendships with women and men alike. Charles McMoran Wilson's classic work on courage in the First World War concluded that humour was vital to sustaining servicemen's resilience,[85] and it seems reasonable to believe that the same was true for ODs. Humour cannot fix a bad situation, but it can help mitigate the impact and make it endurable, taking the sting out of unpleasant circumstances and offering a sense of control through reinterpretation of a situation.[86] Laughter provides temporary physiological, neurological, and psychological benefits, too, sending endorphins through the body and stimulating parts of the brain associated with pleasure, distracting from physical or emotional pain, and reducing anxiety, stress, and depression. Moreover, humour and laughter are usually shared with others, contributing to strong social bonds and helping to create friendships.[87]

ODs met and formed connections with people from many Allied nations and liberated countries during their time abroad. Lois MacDonald's New Year's Eve 1943 offers one example: she dined with "a rather cosmopolitan group" near Basingstoke – a British "RAF officer, two Canadian officers and three of the visiting Yankees."[88] Despite the international cast of ODs' social lives, however, fellow Canadians often earned special notice simply because of their nationality. In November 1943, Mary Macdonald described the happy exclamation "Hello Canada!" as "a familiar greeting by now."[89] Lois's landlady, Mrs. Simon, extended her hospitality to Lois's Canadian friends, who sometimes arrived in such numbers on weekends that "it is like a house party."[90] The British rail network, London's multitude of attractions, and a Canadian Red Cross hospitality arrangement scheme made it both attractive and convenient for ODs and their friends to visit one another and travel around Britain when they were off duty, and they accordingly took advantage of all three. Young Canadians abroad also occasionally went to great lengths to spend time together. Lois MacDonald and her corps colleagues at No. 12 CGH in Belgium became good friends with the officers of a regiment of Manitoba Dragoons that was stationed nearby, and when the dragoons moved on both groups travelled long distances to continue socializing and sightseeing together. One weekend, Lois and her friend Sheila hitchhiked to Holland to attend a dance with the dragoons; another time, the dragoons drove five hundred miles from Germany in a captured car to spend their leave time with Lois and Sheila. Such efforts contributed significantly to the resilience of young Canadians: after spending one forty-eight-hour leave with Sheila and the dragoons in Holland, Lois wrote that it left her "ready to start again tomorrow, with renewed vim and vigour."[91]

Jean Ellis, her fellow ODs Connie and Marj, and approximately fifty-seven Canadian nursing sisters landed in Normandy mere weeks after D-Day. As they made their way along the "Maple Leaf Up" highway, they received a riotous greeting from the army and air force units that were camped in fields and orchards along the route. From their initial landing on the beachhead, when "everyone cheered, everyone tried to shake our hands, and the Canadians pushed through to make sure they got a word in," until their arrival at the hospital, the women were barraged with questions from Canadian servicemen, who "asked any old thing just to get an answer in their own language, and of course there were the usual wolf-calls." For their part, the women immediately tried to re-establish connections, asking after the whereabouts and welfare of people whom they knew and units from their hometowns.[92] On one level, the Canadians represented "home" to each other – a potent, nostalgia-cloaked ideal in wartime.[93] On another level, this undiscerning identification with fellow Canadians also suggests the power of "imagined community" in a wartime context.[94] Passing through newly liberated parts of France, Lois MacDonald praised the fighting spirit of the entire Allied Expeditionary Force but told her parents that she was "more proud than ever to be Canadian."[95] The same nationalistic propaganda that urged men and women to enlist and to support the Canadian war effort could foster feelings of attachment to the nation-state and its cause. Fellow Canadians in the war zones became representatives of that ideal and could inspire an automatic attachment accordingly.[96]

Of all the friendships ODs formed overseas, those they developed with one another were among the strongest. This was apparent when some ODs joined, as passengers, the tens of thousands of war brides and children whom other CRCC members began escorting back to Canada in the waning months of the war in Europe. An anonymous OD's recollection of saying farewell to them was couched in terms of the relationships they had formed:

> One train load included several of our own girls, all of whom were pregnant and two of whom were already widows ... They were being sent home to have their babies in safety. They were also cutting ties – this wartime life in which they had loved and married, in which their friends had shared their happiness and their tragedy, was to be exchanged for the unreality of home, where everyone would be kind and no one would understand ... Their hands clung to ours and we stayed with them until the last possible moment.[97]

In many cases, the bonds of friendship and shared adversity outlasted the war by decades. The Overseas Club – born of a 1946 reunion dinner – was instrumental in this regard. Nancy Laing, one of the four co-founders, explained in 1984 that "many of the women who had returned from the wars had developed such close friendships that they felt they needed a special club ... to maintain close contact." For sixty years, the Overseas Club satisfied that need through local branches; memoir, museum, and fundraising projects; newsletters; and annual reunions. It held its final gala reunion in 2005, when most of its surviving members were in their eighties and nineties.[98] As Nancy put it, they had "shared so much – tears, fun and a lot of hard work, so the bond was in a way inevitable."[99]

In accounts of ODs' wartime social lives, it is not always clear which outings were romantic and which were just good fun with a platonic friend. Both provided important boosts to resilience, and dating did not necessarily spell romance. War widow Jean Ellis dined, danced, and dated regularly, for instance, but appears to have been too wrapped up in grief over her husband's death to seek anything more than friendship with the men she met overseas.[100] Moreover, Hruschka notes that the lines between friendship, romance, and sexual passion are fuzzy, and can easily overlap and shift. Importantly, all three are typically marked by some degree of "closeness, warmth, and love," as well as a tendency "to help each other from a genuine concern for the other's well-being."[101] Corps women spent some of their prime marriageable years overseas, surrounded by men who were equally eligible and/or willing to philander, so romance and its various outcomes were constantly in the air. As Goldstein writes of soldiers, "transitory love affairs ... are an escape, a distraction when the presence of death seems tangible."[102]

In Hollywood films of the 1930s and 1940s, the protracted contact offered by an ocean crossing was a classic romantic plot device, and some ODs did enjoy a shipboard flirtation. Jean Ellis's shipmate Sidney Thompson made the initial conquest of her cohort when the first officer of their Norwegian ship became infatuated with her.[103] The romantic opportunities increased dramatically upon arrival in England. Lois MacDonald wrote to her parents in March 1944 from Basingstoke that two servicemen had asked her out on Friday night and that she had received three separate invitations for each of Saturday and Sunday – although she already had a date with her favourite American officer, Gerry Phillips, for Sunday. "I seem to keep our household amused with my social life," she wrote. "With so many young men around and so few single girls, it is not surprising to be busy, but rather fun!"[104]

Military and civilian dances were staples of all ODs' lives and brought emotional labour into their off-duty hours.[105] The wish to avoid disappointing the men drove them to accept invitations to dances even when they were dog-tired after long, taxing workdays. American junior hostesses at the United Services Organization (USO) and Canadian nursing sisters both recalled the great effort required to be alternately charming, funny, or sympathetic (as the occasion required), as dance partners night after night.[106] But at their best, dances boosted everyone's morale: 1940s social dancing was a lively physical activity that tended to lift spirits while treading a careful line between respectability and tantalizing sexuality.[107] From her hospital in liberated Belgium, Lois MacDonald wrote that the ODs and nursing sisters all "realize that the young fellows we dance with have been on patrol and in battle all day, so really look forward to a little relaxation and fun." Tellingly, she added, "Also, it keeps our spirits up or we could drown in sorrow."[108]

Over the course of her overseas service, Lois balanced her many casual dates with three overlapping "steadies." In England, she regularly dated Gerry, an American infantry officer, and the pair kept in contact by letter when their postings diverged. She also saw Jack Cooper, a naval officer acquaintance from Canada who looked her up while he was in England and became an infrequent but valued date and correspondent. In Belgium, Lois went out with Ian, her favourite officer from the Manitoba Dragoons. Not surprisingly, when she told her friend Laura that she was engaged in May 1945, Laura "nearly collapsed and wondered who?" Jack Cooper had come to Belgium to convince Lois to marry him, and though she had spent more time with Gerry and Ian, she decided he was the one for her.[109]

A wave of weddings took place in the months immediately preceding the D-Day invasion of June 1944 (the imminence of which was signalled by the build-up of troops near the coast and cancellation of leave). Another wave followed the V-E Day celebrations.[110] Many couples, including Lois and Jack, decided to marry back home. However, eighty-six corps members could not wait and were married overseas. Once again, their support networks pitched in: friends helped with planning, loaned items of apparel, and attended as witnesses, members of the bridal party, or guests. If an OD married in London, the residents of Corps House put on a reception, complete with special food and decorations.[111] Such weddings were attempts to snatch a bit of happiness and to forge long-term relationships in the face of uncertainty and danger. But everyone knew that the happiness of the brides could prove short-lived. Lois MacDonald observed shortly after D-Day that "there are new widows [among the ODs] every day." As Aileen Corkett found, their overseas support networks helped them bear these bereavements, too.[112]

Corps memoirs, letters, and oral histories make no mention of lesbian relationships, but the anecdotal evidence for such romances in the women's armed forces and among military nurses suggests that at least a few ODs may have become involved with women whom they met overseas. The factors that, as Mersky Leder argues, allowed same-sex relationships to quietly exist among American servicewomen apply equally well to corps members: there were no psychological tests designed to weed out lesbian applicants, physical affection between women was socially acceptable at the time, and close camaraderie was encouraged as a means of building esprit de corps.[113]

The violence and disruption of total war increased many people's need to give and receive love, while loneliness, separation from home, fear of death, and uncertainty about the future all contributed to a dramatic increase in extramarital sex. Intense, short-term relationships that would be considered immoral in peacetime could now be recast as meaningful moments of connection – or simply escape.[114] A lighthearted December 1944 newsletter written by residents of Corps House contains a rare (albeit sidelong) glance at the presumed sexual activities of certain ODs. The "Items of Interest or Otherwise" column mentions a "high ranking officer" who "did not turn up until the night after the night before," as well as another who "went out one evening and was seen coming in at 8 a.m. the following day, shoes in hand – hair on end."[115] In general, however, corps members kept discreetly mum about sex as it related to themselves and other ODs. Their writing never mentions venereal disease,[116] and references to consensual sex are few, although pregnancies among the ODs made it obvious that some women were having it. Married ODs such as Aileen Corkett were honourably discharged if they got pregnant, but second-in-command OD Elizabeth Faessler recalled in 2001 that the Corps also "coped with six illicits" during the war. One unmarried OD who lived in Faessler's residence managed to disguise her pregnancy for seven months.[117]

Although downplayed in their writings, sexual harassment, sexual assault, and rape were real threats for ODs, as they worked and socialized with servicemen who were steeped in the hyper-masculine, aggressively heterosexual military culture of wartime.[118] Mary Macdonald was warned that it was not safe for respectable women to visit Piccadilly Circus at night. Jean Ellis feared rape when she got lost alone after dark in the Normandy countryside, and Lois MacDonald criticized the British officer class for its apparent belief that Canadian girls in uniform were "easy prey."[119] Nursing sisters and women in the armed forces had similar experiences. Thanks to persistent rumours that uniformed women were promiscuous, the danger emanated from enlisted men and male civilians of all nationalities. In wartime Britain, even a Salvation Army uniform was reputedly sufficient to suggest that its wearer was a loose woman.[120] Nighttime blackout conditions, overcrowded railway carriages, and dances could expose corps members to unwanted sexual advances, too. Some British servicewomen routinely concealed long, sharp hatpins in the lapels of their uniforms, for use on such occasions.[121]

When it came to non-corps sexuality, ODs had much more to say. In their written recollections, many mention the prostitution that flourished more or less openly in London during the blackout, sharing anecdotes about unexpectedly encountering couples in Hyde Park, Green Park, and Piccadilly Circus or being mistaken for amateur competition by professional ladies of the night. Lois MacDonald told her parents that "there seems much promiscuity" in Britain and continental Europe – including British women whom she disapprovingly described as "throw[ing] themselves" at North American troops.[122] In contrast, Mary Macdonald took a worldly attitude, wanting to see the famous "Piccadilly Commandos" (prostitutes and "good-time girls") for herself on her first evening in London.[123] Jean Ellis wrote frankly about distributing Red Cross layettes of baby supplies to the (often illegitimate) children of Canadian servicemen. As she explained to her 1940s readers, given the "awful tension" servicemen faced while awaiting the invasion, "it was natural for them to want love or a reasonable facsimile, and sometimes their feelings were genuine even when their intentions weren't honourable."[124]

In time, ODs' various ties of kinship, friendship, and romance spun themselves into webs of social interaction and support overseas – no matter how tenuous the individual threads would have seemed back in Canada. Winifred Booth's description of a single twelve-hour period during a visit to London offers a concise example. On her day off from hospital duty, she spent the afternoon with friend Johnny McGrath and his fiancée, viewing the waxworks at Madame Tussaud's. That evening, at the theatre, the threesome ran into a former patient of Winifred's, who joined them for a post-show dinner at the Waldorf Hotel. There, they met up with Johnny's cousin and her British officer date, spending the rest of the evening as a group of six.[125] Whether they lasted a lifetime or a single night and were engaged in first-hand or through letters, family relationships, friendships, romances, and sexual encounters filled the lives of the ODs. The best of these ties kept them going, replenishing their resilience through laughter, support, and connection.

Jan Plamper writes that "words often fall short of conveying the full, rich, complexity of what it was like to live through an event or time period."[126] Even so, the letters, memoirs, and oral histories left by the women of the Canadian Red Cross Corps Overseas Detachment offer a moving glimpse into the nature of their personal and professional lives. Their experiences testify to the persistence during the Second World War of layers of emotional and familial meaning, which are well documented for women's voluntary work in the First World War. Caring and connectedness were vital to both civilian and military morale, and ODs were tangible signifiers of home front support and care. Their emotional labour was understood as distinctively feminine, and – whether on duty or off – they themselves saw such work as a particular obligation of their gender in wartime.

In the face of destruction, separation, and loss, ODs created, maintained, and lived out intricate networks of kinship, friendship, and romance, and filled their leisure hours with activities that fostered social connection. These ties shaped their experiences and replenished their resilience, making bearable the demands of their work and the stresses of wartime. Looking back fifty years later, OD Nancy Tyrwhitt-Drake observed that her letters home "were all extremely happy." She attributed this in part to her passion for driving her Austin ambulance and to the emotional meaningfulness of transporting wounded servicemen between airfield and hospital, direct from the fighting in northwestern Europe. But, she added, the camaraderie she shared with her colleagues was important, too, tempering the all-night driving hours and the gruelling work schedule that granted her only a single twenty-four-hour leave per month. "It was a hard life," she concluded, "but a life together with other people."[127]

Notes

1 Canadian Red Cross National Archive (CRCNA), OCC-2.4, Nancy Laing, draft memoir submission, undated.

2 CRCNA, OCC-3.12, Nancy Laing, "Tape #1 Nancy Laing, Jane McGillvary [sic] Ann Butryn Talk about CRCC 10/9/93," side 2.

3 G.J. Casey and Maura C. Hanrahan, "Roses and Thistles: Second World War Brides in Newfoundland," *Newfoundland Studies* 10, 2 (1994): 240–49; Ben Wicks, *Promise You'll Take Care of My Daughter: The Remarkable War Brides of World War II* (Toronto: Stoddart, 1993); Linda Granfield, *Brass Buttons and Silver Horseshoes: Stories from Canada's British War Brides* (Toronto: McClelland and Stewart, 2002); Ruth Roach Pierson, "The Double Bind of the Double Standard: VD Control and the CWAC in World War II," *Canadian Historical Review* 62, 1 (1981): 31–58; James McCrostie, "'Women and Seamen Don't Mix': VD in Canada's Merchant Navy, 1942–1945," *Northern Mariner* 9, 4 (1999): 1–12; Peter Neary, "Venereal Disease and Public Health Administration in Newfoundland in the 1930s and 1940s," *Canadian Bulletin of Medical History* 15, 1 (1998): 129–51.

4 Linda Åhäll and Thomas Gregory, "Mapping Emotions, Politics and War," in *Emotions, Politics, and War*, ed. Linda Åhäll and Thomas Gregory (New York: Routledge, 2015), 2.

5 Neta C. Crawford, "Preface," in Åhäll and Gregory, *Emotions, Politics, and War*, xx.

6 Swati Parashar, "Anger, War and Feminist Storytelling," in Åhäll and Gregory, *Emotions, Politics, and War*, 72.

7 Ingrid Bauer and Renate Huber, "Sexual Encounters across (Former) Enemy Border Lines," *Contemporary Austrian Studies* 15 (January 2007): 65–101; Sabine Lee, "A Forgotten Legacy of the Second World War: GI Children in Post-War Britain and Germany," *Contemporary European History* 20, 2 (2011): 157–81; Mark McLelland, "'Kissing Is a Symbol of Democracy!' Dating, Democracy, and Romance in Occupied Japan, 1945–1952," *Journal of the History of Sexuality* 19, 3 (2010): 508–35.

8 Carol Z. Stearns, "'Lord Help Me Walk Humbly': Anger and Sadness in England and America, 1570–1750," in *Emotions: A Cultural Studies Reader*, ed. Jennifer Harding and E. Deidre Pribram (London: Routledge, 2009), 171.

9 Jean M. Ellis with Isabel Dingman, *Facepowder and Gunpowder* (Toronto: S.J. Reginald Saunders, 1947); Lois MacDonald Cooper, *Wartime Letters Home* (Ottawa: Borealis Press, 2005); Library and Archives Canada (LAC), R-11206, Mary Macdonald fonds. Mary knew and liked Jean when both worked for the Canadian Red Cross Society in London, and Mary and Lois spent some social time together when they were attached to the same hospital unit as welfare officers. For a photograph of Mary and Lois, see MacDonald Cooper, *Wartime Letters Home*, 132.

10 Sarah Glassford, *Mobilizing Mercy: A History of the Canadian Red Cross* (Montreal and Kingston: McGill-Queen's University Press, 2017), Chapters 1 (founding) and 3 (First World War).

11 Ibid., 163.

12 Ibid., 200–11.

13 Ibid., 196.

14 Ibid., 197.

15 Ibid., 205. A handful more were posted to Newfoundland, and perhaps as many as 110 performed escort duty on war bride transports at the end of the war. Their experiences differed in significant ways from those of the 641 and are not considered here.

16 Frances Martin Day, Phyllis Spence, and Barbara Ladouceur, eds., *Women Overseas: Memoirs of the Canadian Red Cross Corps* (Vancouver: Ronsdale Press, 1998), 14.

17 LAC, R-11206, Mary Macdonald fonds, vol. 1, file 1–7, "A Salute to Our Red Cross Friend," 24 August 1943.

18 Arlie Russell Hochschild, *The Managed Heart: Commercialization of Human Feeling* (1983; updated with a new preface, Berkeley: University of California Press, 2012), 170. See also Joshua Goldstein, *War and Gender: How Gender Shapes the War System and Vice Versa* (Cambridge: Cambridge University Press, 2001), 308–9; and Jean Bethke Elshtain, *Women and War* (New York: Basic Books, 1987), 183.

19 Lillian Comas-Diaz et al., "The Road to Resilience," American Psychological Association, APA Help Center, http://www.apa.org/helpcenter/road-resilience.aspx.

20 See Sarah Glassford, "'The Greatest Mother in the World': Carework and the Discourse of Mothering in the Canadian Red Cross Society during the First World War," *Journal of the Association for Research on Mothering* 10, 1 (Spring-Summer 2008): 219–32; and Glassford, *Mobilizing Mercy*, 92, 110, 120–22.

21 Julia Welland, "Compassionate Soldiering and Comfort," in Åhäll and Gregory, *Emotions, Politics, and War*, 115.

22 Meghan K. Winchell, *Good Girls, Good Food, Good Fun: The Story of USO Hostesses during World War II* (Chapel Hill: University of North Carolina Press, 2008), 23 (quotation); Glassford, *Mobilizing Mercy*, 121, 191; MacDonald Cooper, *Wartime Letters Home*, 211.

23 Ellis and Dingman, *Facepowder and Gunpowder*, 92.

24 Goldstein, *War and Gender*, 308–9. On women near the battlefields as a comfort and reminder of home, see Bethke Elshtain, *Women and War*, 183.

25 LAC, R-11206, vol. 1, file 1–9, Frank Hamilton, "To a Red Cross Sister," 12 December 1944; "Our 'Sunshine Ray,'" in MacDonald Cooper, *Wartime Letters Home*, 212, 245 (re: Frankie Hamilton).

26 Peter J. Frost et al., "Narratives of Compassion in Organizations," in *Emotion in Organizations*, 2nd ed., ed. Stephen Fineman (London: Sage, 2000), 27.

27 MacDonald Cooper, *Wartime Letters Home*, 240.

28 Geoffrey Greif, *Buddy System: Understanding Male Friendships* (New York: Oxford University Press, 2009), 123.

29 Victoria M. Basham, "Waiting for War: Soldiering, Temporality and the Gendered Politics of Boredom and Joy in Military Spaces," in Åhäll and Gregory, *Emotions, Politics, and War*, 128.

30 Allison Howell, "Making War Work: Resilience, Emotional Fitness, and Affective Economies in Western Militaries," in Åhäll and Gregory, *Emotions, Politics, and War*, 145.

31 Ville Kivimäki and Tuomas Tepora, "War of Hearts: Love and Collective Attachment as Integrating Factors in Finland during World War II," *Journal of Social History* 43, 2 (2009): 291.

32 Hochschild, *The Managed Heart*, 167.

33 Kivimäki and Tepora, "War of Hearts," 289–90. On wartime pin-up culture, see Philomena Goodman, *Women, Sexuality and War* (Basingstoke, UK: Palgrave, 2002), 110–14.

34 MacDonald Cooper, *Wartime Letters Home*, 263.

35 Cynthia Toman, *An Officer and a Lady: Canadian Military Nursing and the Second World War* (Vancouver: UBC Press, 2007), 110.

36 MacDonald Cooper, *Wartime Letters Home*, 263.

37 Liz Byrski, "Emotional Labour as War Work: Women Up Close and Personal with McIndoe's Guinea Pigs," *Women's History Review* 21, 3 (2012): 356.

38 Summarized in Joyce E. Bono and Meredith A. Vey, "Toward Understanding Emotional Management at Work: A Quantitative Review of Emotional Labor Research," in *Emotions in Organizational Behavior*, ed. Charmine E.J. Härtel, Wilfred J. Zerbe, and Neal M. Ashkanasy (London: Lawrence Erlbaum, 2005), 230.

39 MacDonald Cooper, *Wartime Letters Home,* 263, 265, 266. This idea of a reciprocal relationship between soldiers and civilians also appeared in CRCS blood donation advertising of the period. Glassford, *Mobilizing Mercy,* 200.
40 A Corps Member, "Hospital Duty after D-Day," *Despatch,* September–October 1944, 5.
41 Hochschild, *The Managed Heart,* 7–8.
42 Frost et al., "Narratives of Compassion," 27.
43 Robert S. Rubin et al., "A Reconceptualization of the Emotional Labor Construct: On the Development of an Integrated Theory of Perceived Emotional Dissonance and Emotional Labor," in Hartël, Zerbe, and Ashkanasy, *Emotions in Organizational Behavior,* 206–7. See also Hochschild, *The Managed Heart,* 202.
44 Frances Martin Day, quoted in Patrick Murphy, "Women Had to Smile throughout Carnage," *Victoria Times-Colonist,* 8 May 1995, 95.
45 Ellis and Dingman, *Facepowder and Gunpowder,* 100.
46 LAC, R-11206, vol. 1, file 1–8, *No. 12 Canadian General Hospital Year Book, 1943–44,* handwritten note on flyleaf; LAC, R-11206, vol. 1, file 1–10, "No. of Patients Admitted to No. 12 C.G.H. (September 1st to 30th Inclusive)."
47 Ellis and Dingman, *Facepowder and Gunpowder,* 101–2. Although nursing sisters sometimes performed these services, their time was often fully occupied with more medically important skilled nursing tasks.
48 Jonathan Vance, *Death So Noble: Memory, Meaning, and the First World War* (Vancouver: UBC Press, 1997), 75–77.
49 Janet Partridge and Harriet Lehnen, personal communication about Dorothy Falkner Burgoyne Dolittle, 13 April 2016.
50 Ellis and Dingman, *Facepowder and Gunpowder,* 92–93.
51 Ibid., 101.
52 Ibid., 80.
53 MacDonald Cooper, *Wartime Letters Home,* 290.
54 Miriam C. Mitchell and Florence C. Deacon, comps., *641: A Story of the Canadian Red Cross Corps, Overseas* (St. Catharines, ON: Canadian Red Cross Corps, 1978), 138–40.
55 For example, see Ellis and Dingman, *Facepowder and Gunpowder,* 95–98.
56 Phyllis Elder Matheson, quoted in Murphy, "Women Had to Smile," 95.
57 Edward Madigan, "'Sticking to a Hateful Task': Resilience, Humour, and British Understandings of Combatant Courage, 1914–1918," *War in History* 20, 1 (2013): 88.
58 LAC, R-11206, vol. 1, file 1–23, Mary Macdonald to Mother and Kay, [?] September 1943.
59 Ellis and Dingman, *Facepowder and Gunpowder,* 56.
60 For a discussion of the separation between home and war, and of the importance of links across that divide, see Goldstein, *War and Gender,* 304.
61 Jane Mersky Leder, *Thanks for the Memories: Love, Sex and World War II* (Westport: Praeger, 2006), 95.
62 LAC, R-11206, vol. 1, file 1–26, Mary Macdonald to Catherine Anne Macdonald, 12 June 1945.
63 LAC, R-11206, vol. 1, file 1–25, Mary Macdonald to Mrs. M.A. Macdonald, 24 August 1945, and Mary Macdonald to Mrs. M.A. Macdonald, 4 August 1944.
64 Mitchell and Deacon, *641,* 21.
65 MacDonald Cooper, *Wartime Letters Home,* 43.
66 LAC, R-11206, vol. 1, file 1–23, Mary Macdonald to Mrs. Mary A. Macdonald and Kay Macdonald, 12 October 1943; LAC, R-11206, vol. 1, file 1–26, Mary Macdonald to Fay, [late October?] 1943; LAC, R-11206, vol. 1, file 1–26, Mary Macdonald to Mrs. Mary A. Macdonald and Kay Macdonald, 16 December 1943.

67 LAC, Vida Peene fonds, MG 31-D26, vol. 2, file 2–2, Irene Potter to Vida Peene, 4 December 1945.
68 "Frances Martin Day O.D. #183," in *Memoirs: Women in War (1942–1947) (1952–1955)*, 3rd ed., comp. Frances Martin Day (Victoria, BC: 1993), 72–73, 79–80.
69 Phyllis Elder Matheson, quoted in Murphy, "Women Had to Smile," 95.
70 Ellis and Dingman, *Facepowder and Gunpowder*, 90.
71 MacDonald Cooper, *Wartime Letters Home*, 120.
72 "Biddy Wilkins O.D. #287," in Day, *Memoirs*, 81–82.
73 MacDonald Cooper, *Wartime Letters Home*, 200, 244, 280.
74 LAC, R-11206, vol. 1, file 1–26, Mary Macdonald to Dot, 25 September 1943.
75 CRCNA, OCC-23.4, "The Corpse – Bulletin No. 1," December 1944. This tongue-in-cheek newsletter contains doggerel that describes who shared which rooms at Corps House and pokes fun at food quality, wartime conditions, and the members' social activities.
76 Penny Summerfield, *Reconstructing Women's Wartime Lives: Discourse and Subjectivity in Oral Histories of the Second World War* (Manchester: Manchester University Press, 1998), 177.
77 Daniel J. Hruschka, *Friendship: Development, Ecology, and Evolution of a Relationship* (Berkeley: University of California Press, 2010), 51, 55–56. Hruschka defines friendships as "long-term relationships of mutual affection and support." Ibid., 2.
78 Summerfield, *Reconstructing Women's Wartime Lives*, 169. A similar phenomenon existed among American service wives on the home front. Mersky Leder, *Thanks for the Memories*, 94.
79 Joanna Bourke, *An Intimate History of Killing: Face-to-Face Killing in Twentieth-Century Warfare* (New York: Basic Books, 1999), 141–42.
80 Ellis and Dingman, *Facepowder and Gunpowder*, 102.
81 MacDonald Cooper, *Wartime Letters Home*, 49, 67–69.
82 Ibid., 275.
83 Ellis and Dingman, *Facepowder and Gunpowder*, 52.
84 Ibid., 61.
85 Lord Moran, *Anatomy of Courage* (London: Robinson, 2007), 152.
86 Stefan Meisiek and Xin Yao, "Nonsense Makes Sense: Humor in Social Sharing of Emotion at the Workplace," in Hartël, Zerbe, and Ashkanasy, *Emotions in Organizational Behavior*, 146.
87 Ibid.; Brian King, *The Laughing Cure: Emotional and Physical Healing – A Comedian Reveals Why Laughter Really Is the Best Medicine* (New York: Skyhorse, 2016), 193–96; Basham, "Waiting for War," 134.
88 MacDonald Cooper, *Wartime Letters Home*, 48.
89 LAC, R-11206, vol. 1, file 1–26, Mary Macdonald to Dot, 8 November 1943.
90 MacDonald Cooper, *Wartime Letters Home*, 62.
91 Ibid., 293, 300–7, 340–42, 215–16, 236.
92 Ellis and Dingman, *Facepowder and Gunpowder*, 91–92.
93 Goodman, *Women, Sexuality and War*, 19.
94 Benedict Anderson, *Imagined Communities: Reflections on the Rise and Spread of Nationalism* (London: Verso, 1991).
95 MacDonald Cooper, *Wartime Letters Home*, 150.
96 Kivimäki and Tepora make this argument in the Finnish case. Kivimäki and Tepora, "War of Hearts," 297.
97 Quoted in Mitchell and Deacon, *641*, 45.
98 CRCNA, OCC-17.11, Overseas Club, 60th Anniversary Reunion program, 2005.

99 Nancy Laing, quoted in "Overseas Club Part of the Red Cross Family," *Service*, March 1984, 5.
100 Ellis and Dingman, *Facepowder and Gunpowder*.
101 Hruschka, *Friendship*, 117, quotations on 77.
102 Goldstein, *War and Gender*, 310.
103 Ellis and Dingman, *Facepowder and Gunpowder*, 18.
104 MacDonald Cooper, *Wartime Letters Home*, 71.
105 LAC, R-11206, vol. 1, file 1–26, Mary Macdonald to Dot, 8 November 1943; Mitchell and Deacon, *641*, 147.
106 Winchell, *Good Girls*, 92; Toman, *An Officer and a Lady*, 102.
107 Winchell, *Good Girls*, 136–38.
108 MacDonald Cooper, *Wartime Letters Home*, 195.
109 Ibid., 328. The Coopers were married for more than fifty years, until Jack's death in 1997.
110 Ibid., 120. Jane Mersky Leder writes that "the immediate post-war spike in North American marriage rates speaks to the eagerness of women and men to attain an ideal of domestic life they envisioned during the war." Mersky Leder, *Thanks for the Memories*, 144.
111 MacDonald Cooper, *Wartime Letters Home*, 120; Mitchell and Deacon, *641*, 117–23.
112 MacDonald Cooper, *Wartime Letters Home*, 120–21.
113 Mersky Leder, *Thanks for the Memories*, 58–59. The overwhelming majority of Canadian nursing sisters were similarly silent about same-sex relationships, when interviewed. Toman, *An Officer and a Lady*, 114–15.
114 Goodman, *Women, Sexuality and War*, 130; Mersky Leder, *Thanks for the Memories*, x, xiv.
115 CRCNA, OCC-23.4, "Items of Interest or Otherwise," *The Corpse*, December 1944.
116 Even if corps members were not particularly concerned with VD, Allied governments, military brass, and social observers were; they stigmatized promiscuous women as spreaders of disease. Goodman, *Women, Sexuality and War*, 147–54; Mersky Leder, *Thanks for the Memories*, 102; Ruth Roach Pierson, "Ladies or Loose Women: The Canadian Women's Army Corps in World War II," *Atlantis* 4, 2 (1979): 245–66.
117 Shel Piercy, dir., *Love and Duty: Canadian Red Cross Women in WWII* (Vancouver: Infinity Films, 2001), VHS, 46 minutes, 45 seconds. Whether the OD concealed her pregnancy due to shame or a desire to keep working is unknown.
118 Goldstein, *War and Gender*, 333–34.
119 LAC, R-11206, vol. 1, file 1–26, Mary Macdonald to Fay, [late October?] 1943; Ellis and Dingman, *Facepowder and Gunpowder*, 123; MacDonald Cooper, *Wartime Letters Home*, 263, 258.
120 Toman, *An Officer and a Lady*, 113–15; Goodman, *Women, Sexuality and War*, 92–94; Roach Pierson, "Ladies or Loose Women," 245–66; Leisa D. Meyer, "Creating G.I. Jane: The Regulation of Sexuality and Sexual Behavior in the Women's Army Corps," *Feminist Studies* 18, 3 (1992): 581–602.
121 Goodman, *Women, Sexuality and War*, 145–46, 131, 94.
122 MacDonald Cooper, *Wartime Letters Home*, 258.
123 Mitchell and Deacon, *641*, 31; "Lois Goodwin Golding, O.D. #312," in Day, *Memoirs*, 84; LAC, R-11206, vol. 1, file 1–26, Mary Macdonald to Fay, [late October?] 1943. On wartime prostitution see Goodman, *Women, Sexuality and War*, 132–34. One Canadian soldier wrote, "I never saw so many whores in my life," and another serviceman described London's parks after dark as "a vast battlefield of sex." Paul Fussell, *Wartime: Understanding and Behaviour in the Second World War* (New York: Oxford University Press, 1989), 109.

124 Ellis and Dingman, *Facepowder and Gunpowder,* 53.
125 Western University, Department of History, Ley and Lois Smith War, Memory and Popular Culture Collection, Winifred Booth scrapbook.
126 Jan Plamper, *The History of Emotions: An Introduction,* trans. Keith Tribe (Oxford: Oxford University Press, 2015), 288.
127 Nancy Tyrwhitt-Drake, quoted in Patrick Murphy, "Nurse-Drivers Ignored Glamor and Danger," *Victoria Times-Colonist,* 19 March 1995, B13.

Part 4
Women in Wartime Nursing, Paid War Work, and the Armed Forces

It was an exciting time, and it seemed like the thing to do.

–Vicki Goodyear, Canadian Women's Army Corps member[1]

When Vicki Goodyear of St. John's, Newfoundland, joined the Canadian Women's Army Corps in 1943 at age eighteen, she had tried to enlist once before. Two years earlier, the Royal Canadian Air Force (Women's Division) had turned her away for being too young. Her 1943 enlistment was deeply upsetting to her mother, whose brother had died in the First World War. Now, not only was Vicki's brother Tim sailing the dangerous North Atlantic with the Merchant Navy, but Vicki herself was also leaving Newfoundland for war service. She served as a dispatch driver in British Columbia for the duration. Despite carrying the emotional weight of her mother's distress, Vicki loved her time in the army and was one of many Canadian and Newfoundland women who had no desire to relinquish their work after the end of the war.[2] This delight in the new opportunities for work, travel, and life experience resounds through the memoirs and oral histories of Canadian and Newfoundland women who participated in war-related occupations.

As discussed elsewhere in this volume, such opportunities were not open to all. Race, ethnicity, physical health, age, religious belief, and socio-economic class played key roles in determining women's options. And even as they revelled in wider horizons, many women workers were disappointed by the gendered limitations that still kept them from doing certain jobs or receiving higher wages and authority. Servicewomen who longed to go overseas often had to be content with a North American posting, and regardless of its location the work could be intensely boring, menial, or seemingly non-essential.[3]

Women's non-traditional paid labour and entry into the armed forces were two of the earliest subjects of interest to scholars of Canadian women and the

Second World War. With the addition of military nursing, these are some of the best-documented (and therefore well-studied) areas of Canadian and Newfoundland women's wartime experiences. Women's roles in the armed forces, military nursing, and paid work in war industries likewise dominate the Canadian popular memory of women and the Second World War. Decades after the first feminist historians became intrigued with these women, the empowering "We Can Do It!" Rosie the Riveter imagery still sparks the interest of undergraduate history students when essay-writing time rolls around. Nursing under wartime conditions, paid war work, and the armed forces likewise remain subjects of interest to scholars. The appeal may rest in the fact that these three roles allowed women to contribute directly to the military-industrial waging of the war – or simply that their service was made publicly visible by their uniforms, whether that meant brass buttons on a wool jacket or overalls and bandanas.

In this section, each author asks new questions and brings a fresh perspective to one of these familiar subjects. The military installation at Goose Bay, Labrador, quietly informs the civilian nursing experiences studied by Heidi Coombs. Sarah Hogenbirk uncovers the memorializing practices associated with servicewomen who died while on active duty. And finally, Sarah Van Vugt turns our attention to the embodied experiences of women in Canada's wartime industrial workplaces. Collectively, they open new paths for other scholars and demonstrate that several decades of scholarship in women's and gender history have yet to exhaust the questions that can be asked of women who engaged in these three high-profile wartime roles.

Notes

1 Emily Victoria (Goodyear) Luscombe, in Gene Quigley, *Voices of World War II: A Collection of Oral Histories* (St. John's: Jesperson, 2006), 70.

2 Ibid., 70–71.

3 Peg Cross Russell, an Ontario-born airwoman who was posted to Nova Scotia for the duration, quipped that "they also serve who only stand and wait" was "a good slogan because we did a lot of standing and waiting." Quigley, *Voices of World War II*, 77.

10

"War Comes to Labrador"

Nursing on the Home Front

Heidi Coombs

In 1939, the International Grenfell Association (IGA), or Grenfell Mission, was the only health care provider in northern Newfoundland and Labrador.[1] It ran a system of hospitals and nursing stations scattered throughout the region in small population centres and isolated coastal communities. The hospitals were administered by physicians and the stations by nurses, who were expected to defer to the former and to call upon them for advice and assistance in cases that were beyond their training. Despite the paternalistic structure of this system, it offered an element of independence to the nurses on the stations. In practice, since the stations were separated from the hospitals by hundreds of miles of rugged terrain and/or ocean, the nurses typically depended on their own judgment for daily patient care. During the tumultuous period of the Second World War – faced with persistent staff shortages, supply problems, and an increased patient population resulting from substantial military construction in the area and torpedoed ships off the coast – the mission relied more heavily than ever on the independent work of these nurses.

This chapter explores the provision of health care in northern Newfoundland and Labrador during the Second World War and the central place of nurses in maintaining the Grenfell system, focusing on the increased professional demands placed on them due to wartime conditions. The history of the Grenfell Mission has been the subject of academic research primarily in terms of biographical studies, especially those of Ronald Rompkey, which include *Grenfell of Labrador* and three edited collections of the letters of Eliot Curwin, Jessie Luther, and Harry Paddon, who were mission personnel.[2] Several historians highlight the history of nursing with the mission, and Jill Perry establishes that nursing there was "an exceptional female work experience."[3] A recently published collection of essays – *The Grenfell Medical Mission and American Support in Newfoundland and Labrador* – expands the historiography and focuses on the involvement of Americans in various aspects of the mission before the war, including their participation in the provision of medical services, administration, volunteer activities, sports, education, and clothing distribution.[4] The history of the mission during the war, however, has received far less academic attention. In fact, except for Steven High's article on the construction of military bases in Newfoundland and Labrador and

Figure 10.1

Mina Gilchrist Paddon nursed with the Grenfell Mission at North West River, Labrador, for many years, c. 1920s. | Courtesy of Dave Paddon.

Peter Neary's article on the Goose Bay Agreement of 1944, there has been little academic research on northern Newfoundland and Labrador during the war, and none that focuses on women.[5]

Fifty-two women nursed with the Grenfell Mission during the Second World War, including twenty-two Americans, thirteen Canadians, eleven Britons, three Labradorians, two Newfoundlanders, and one Dutchwoman. All filled a crucial gap in its services, either by staffing hospital or nursing station positions that were difficult to fill or by taking on the duties of physicians at one of the hospitals. At North West River, Canadian nurse Mina Gilchrist Paddon ran the hospital after the sudden death of her husband, Dr. Harry Paddon, in December 1939. Mina maintained the hospital throughout the war until her son, Dr. Anthony Paddon, completed service as a surgeon with the Royal Canadian Navy and returned to North West River to take over administration of the hospital. In 1940, with the assistance of British nurse Phyllis Wenyon, Mina treated 61 inpatients and 2,050 outpatients at the hospital (by comparison, during the same year, Dr. Garth Forsyth treated 100 inpatients and 1,500 outpatients at the Cartwright mission hospital, and Dr. Helen Hosmer treated 60 inpatients and 1,000 outpatients at St. Mary's River). Furthermore, in addition to the medical work, Mina supervised agricultural production at North West River and the preservation of fish, greens, and berries for use during the winter. Mina Paddon exemplified the realities of the Grenfell Mission during the war, in which nurses could take on more responsibility than ever before, to the point where their success in that capacity earned them accolades for heroism.[6]

The Grenfell Mission was founded in 1892, when British physician Wilfred Grenfell travelled to Labrador to explore the possibility of expanding the medical services of the Mission to Deep Sea Fishermen.[7] The widespread poverty of the people and the lack of basic health care inspired him to return the following year and establish permanent medical facilities. Before Grenfell arrived, medical services in Labrador were extremely limited. The only physician on the coast held a seasonal appointment – the Newfoundland government sent a physician north on a steamer every summer to provide basic services to the Newfoundland fishermen and their families who flooded the Labrador coast during the fishing season.[8] Grenfell's offer to furnish desperately needed care was a tremendous benefit to a government that could not afford to establish such services. It provided a small annual grant to aid in Grenfell's endeavours. However, the vast majority of funding, personnel, and tangible support for the mission came from external sources – especially the Grenfell-affiliated organizations in the United States, Canada, and Great Britain.[9] Under Grenfell's charismatic leadership, and with substantial help from these bodies, the mission became a long-lasting, paternalistic, and philanthropic system of health care in northern Newfoundland and Labrador.[10]

Immediate Impact of the War

The outbreak of the Second World War had an immediate impact on the Grenfell Mission's work, in both Britain and northern Newfoundland and Labrador. The Grenfell Association of Great Britain and Ireland (GAGBI), one of the IGA-supporting associations, recruited staff from Britain and raised money to help maintain mission activities. Its office was located at 66 Victoria Street in Westminster, an area of London that was heavily bombed during the Blitz. When war was declared, the GAGBI reduced its staff and removed its records and account books to Secretary Kate Spalding's home, in a safer part of London. The office at 66 Victoria was bombed several times, with the hit of May 1941 being particularly destructive. As Spalding wrote, "On the heavy raid on London last week end our offices were badly blitzed and narrowly escaped total destruction ... We really are most fortunate for we have one room undamaged (except for broken windows) in which we can carry on until it is possible for repairs to be made."[11] Spalding kept up the activities of the GAGBI throughout the war in exceptional circumstances, which sometimes involved co-ordinating transportation and logistics for several Newfoundland and Labrador women who were training as nurses in Britain. While training at the West Middlesex Hospital in London during the Blitz, Nora Noseworthy would "[pile] pillows over her head to shut out the blinding light and deaden the awful crash of bombs and buildings."[12] One night, the maternity block and the nurses' home in which she lived were bombed, and she woke to find that the roof was gone.[13] Discovering that Noseworthy had been upset by the experience and looked "very sadly shaken," Spalding encouraged her to take a holiday before starting her midwifery training.[14] However, Noseworthy continued with her training and graduated in April 1943; in August, Spalding arranged her documents and transportation home, where nurses were desperately needed.[15]

Meanwhile, on the coast, the mission retained salaried staff under formal contracts and also retained volunteers, who worked for room and board only. With the outbreak of war, its medical superintendent, Dr. Charles Curtis, permitted staff to break their contracts and return home to contribute to the war efforts of their own countries; many left immediately. After returning to Britain in the fall of 1939, one such volunteer described the mission's response at St. Anthony on the Northern Peninsula, which was the headquarters of the mission on the coast: "There are tremendous changes on account of the war and the anticipation of lack of funds. Directly war was declared Dr. Curtis sent as many of the Staff home as could possibly be spared including of course all summer volunteers and even people with contracts had to go."[16] All voluntary workers at St. Anthony had left on the last boat by October 1939, the mission's Industrial Department was closed, and orders for raw materials from Britain were cancelled.[17] The national emergency and shortage of nurses in Britain drew many nurses back home voluntarily, whereas several other salaried staff had their contracts broken but remained on the coast, working without pay.[18] Some criticized Curtis for taking these extreme measures, but Cecil Ashdown, executive director of the IGA, explained,

> When war came Curtis acted as he felt best and I think perhaps he went a little far. I confess the outlook did look black and what worried him most was the

> possible lack of supplies early next summer and he felt that every person whose presence was not really necessary should return and so save coal and supplies, and make them last longer next summer. We shall have difficulties in getting shipping facilities at a reasonable cost next spring and shall have to rely largely on the "Cluett" [the mission's ship] ... Newfoundland is east of long.66° so it is outside the scope of U.S. boats and neutral vessels are scarce and expensive.[19]

The mission relied heavily on imported food, coal, and other provisions for the large and dispersed staff on the coast, and Curtis's reaction to the war reflected its vulnerability in this regard.

The war also significantly increased the cost of food, fuel, medications, hospital equipment, and supplies; the mission could not afford to maintain its pre-war budget.[20] As a cost-saving measure, it introduced "a campaign of rigid economy."[21] Thus, it cancelled the printing of its annual report and cut all salaries by 10 percent for the duration of hostilities.[22] In March 1941, Curtis reported to the IGA board of directors that the mission's total running expenses were down $25,000 from the previous year, most of the savings being in salaries ($9,000), food ($5,000), freights ($2,000), fuel ($2,000), and travel costs ($2,000).[23] Due to the cut in wages, the mission was unable to appoint physicians during the war, so North West River was turned into a nursing station under the authority of Mina Paddon.[24] Furthermore, when Dr. Helen Hosmer resigned from St. Mary's River and Dr. Donald Hodd retired from Harrington Harbour, nurses took over administration of both hospitals – British nurse Dorothy Jupp and American nurse Laura Nels Thompson, respectively.[25]

Recruitment and Staffing

Nurses were integral to the Grenfell Mission and the services it provided. However, Newfoundland- and Labrador-born nurses were in short supply, especially in rural areas. By 1939, Newfoundland had three nursing schools (all in St. John's), but most graduates practised in the city or in rural communities and cottage hospitals on the island.[26] To staff the Grenfell hospitals and stations, the mission recruited the vast majority of its nurses from outside Newfoundland. Those with midwifery training were especially essential for the stations, where so much of the work related to childbirth and pre- and post-natal care. Most nurses at the stations were Britons who had formal midwifery training and were certified through the Central Midwives Board.[27] Those who lacked such training were typically posted to one of the mission hospitals, where physicians performed obstetric services, or they worked as second nurses at a station under the supervision of a nurse-midwife.

Recruiting staff was one of the greatest challenges that the Grenfell Mission faced during the Second World War. Once the war began, the numbers of British staff with the mission drastically declined. Many returned home to contribute to the war effort there. Furthermore, recruitment of British nurses declined as travel out of Britain was no longer permitted and obtaining a release from war service could be difficult.[28] Any British nurse who wished to work with the mission could not sign a contract and leave home without being officially released from national service by the British Ministry of Labour, permission that was hard to obtain due to the demand for nurses in Britain.[29] In fact, the Ministry of Labour required all nurses to re-register, and it decided where and in what capacity they would work, based on their training. For example, though nurse Margaret Ormerod wanted to return to midwifery while she was home in England, she was required to continue with health visiting because she had taken the health visitor's course and there was a shortage of such nurses in Britain.[30] The ministry finally granted her release on 25 June 1945, more than a year after she applied for it.[31]

But this was not the final hurdle. The next step was to obtain an exit permit from the Passport Authorities and then, with the assistance of the London Grenfell office, arrange transatlantic transportation, which was uncertain, expensive, and risky.[32] U-boat attacks on ships in the North Atlantic made everyone nervous, especially the families of Grenfell staff who were crossing the Atlantic.[33] However, one nurse, at least, relished the excitement and adventure of the voyage and recalled her "delightful journey" from London to Labrador: "I travelled in a very fine ship, but the presence of guns, men in uniform, and life belts continually reminded one that this was no pleasure trip. The first two days we were escorted by a couple of destroyers, but then we were left to carry on alone ... Blackout followed us to New York."[34]

With such difficulties in recruiting British staff, the mission turned to nurses from the United States and Canada to fill the void.[35] As Figure 10.2 shows, the numbers of American nurses did increase for a short period, but they dropped from ten to five after the United States entered the war. In April 1942, Kathleen Young of the Staff Selection Committee published an appeal for workers in the mission's quarterly magazine, *Among the Deep Sea Fishers:*

> Since hostilities started we have only had two staff members come out from England and far fewer from Canada than normally. Consequently, for the past two years we had come to rely almost entirely on Americans to fill vacancies. This year Americans too are fast becoming absorbed into war work. Many of the doctors, dentists, and nurses of the type and age to whom our work makes the strongest appeal are now serving in the armed forces or Red Cross ... We appeal

to all alumni, and other friends of the Mission, to remember and bring to the notice of their friends the opportunities for real service to humanity that exist in Labrador and Newfoundland.[36]

However, this appeal had limited success, and by 1943 the staffing situation had worsened. American and Canadian staff who handled recruitment found that candidates initially expressed interest but often backed out at the last minute. Writing from Ottawa, Ethel Graham voiced their frustrations to Kate Spalding in London:

> Poor Kathleen [Young] made the remark not so long ago that if one more nurse backed out she was leaving herself. Since then one by one the applicants seem to find some good reason why a trip to the Coast is impossible. Those on the Coast seem to discover illness in their families or some other calamity necessitating their return.[37]

After the United States went to war, Canadian nurses began increasingly meeting the staffing needs on the coast, and by 1945 they outnumbered nurses of any other nationality at the mission. Despite these financial, operational, and staffing challenges, only one station shut its doors due to lack of personnel, and three hospitals that could not retain physicians were administered by nurses.[38]

Figure 10.2

Nationalities of Grenfell nurses, 1939–46.

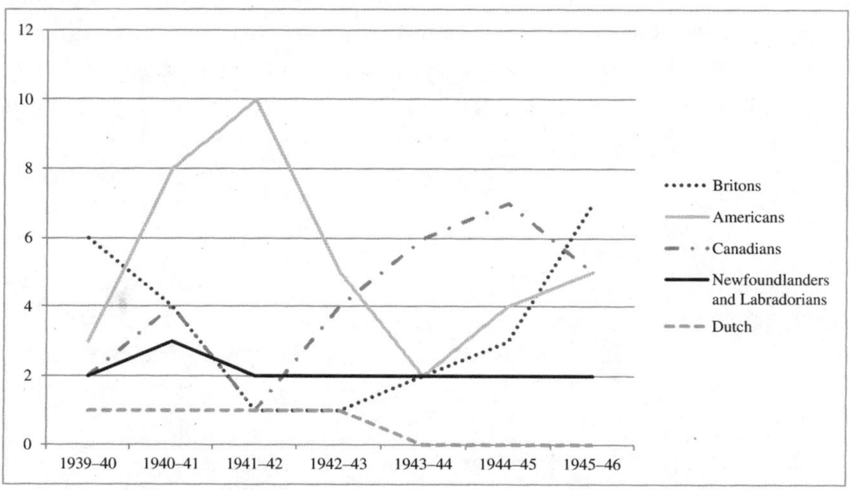

Source: "Report of the Staff Selection Committee," *Among the Deep Sea Fishers* 37, 2 (July 1939) to 43, 3 (October 1945).

The Backbone of This Mission

On the coast, mission nurses performed a variety of nursing and non-nursing duties, much like outpost nurses in rural and remote areas of Canada during the same period.[39] These included operating the dispensary and treating out-patients, ensuring the physical and emotional comfort and health of patients, and performing pre- and post-natal health and midwifery/obstetrics (if they had midwifery training).[40] They also handled first-aid and dealt with medical emergencies, conducted public health information sessions, administered vaccinations, pulled teeth, ran the station, grew vegetables, bottled preserves, managed the clothing store and donations, and treated animals. These responsibilities were not uniform across the stations and hospitals or throughout the twentieth century – they often depended on period, location, and available amenities. During the war, many stations were small and their amenities primitive, such as the Flowers Cove station, which had "no basement, no lighting system, no running water, only one small room for patients and in winter five stoves were needed to keep it tolerably warm."[41] A nurse's experience and level of responsibility depended on the features of the building in which she worked and the size and constitution of the staff. And in these circumstances, nurses proved so valuable to the mission during the war that Curtis described them as "the backbone of this Mission."[42]

Although the nurses devoted much of their time to fundamental nursing duties, they exercised a significant amount of professional responsibility and authority. With no physician present, they saw all cases that came to the stations, determined their needs, diagnosed their conditions, and prescribed treatment. They handled any and every medical emergency in the region and pragmatically tackled whatever tasks were necessary to remedy a situation. For Curtis, having these women meet medical emergencies was crucial to maintaining the Grenfell system during the war. Many emergencies involved maternity cases, such as the one that faced Canadian nurse Ella Hewitt at Forteau in 1944. In *Among the Deep Sea Fishers,* Curtis explained that Hewitt was called to a complicated obstetrical case, "which would defy the skill of any obstetrician in any obstetrical hospital with plenty of nurses and assistants and means for blood transfusions. Miss Hewitt was alone and had no chance to get a doctor's aid in this emergency. Alone in a fishing house, with no one to help her but a local midwife."[43] Two days after the birth, Curtis contacted Hewitt to ask about the patient – both mother and baby were doing well.

Whenever possible, it was customary and expected for nurses to wire the doctor for advice on the treatment of a patient, as Hewitt did in this situation. The physician would provide valuable medical information, suggest next steps for treatment, and if necessary, arrange to visit the station/community or to have the patient brought to the hospital. Nurse Laura Thompson, who was put in charge of the Harrington Harbour hospital when Dr. Donald Hodd retired, followed this protocol. One week after assuming responsibility at Harrington, she wired Curtis about "a patient with a strangulated hernia,"[44] informing him of the treatment she had administered and asking for advice. Curtis approved of her treatment and replied that it "was all that could be done. The next day she was able to wire [him] that she had succeeded in reducing the hernia and the patient was out of danger and comfortable."[45] This incident epitomized the ideal of a Grenfell nurse – Thompson was competent enough to treat the patient on her own, but she still sought the advice, confirmation, and approval of a Grenfell physician, whose education and skills were typically more advanced.

Grenfell hospitals and stations also dealt with a significant number of work-related accidents arising from the local fishing and logging industries. Canadian nurse Alice Phillips was stationed at Roddickton during the war, where the primary industry was forestry. In the winter of 1945, "she had to deal with every sort of emergency that can occur among people working in the lumber woods," including a man whose leg had been severed above the knee.[46] Phillips dosed him with "intravenous glucose, tied off the bleeding vessels, sprinkled the wound with sulfa powder, and wrapped the stump in sterile dressings."[47] She then took him to the hospital at St. Anthony, travelling with him for twelve hours in an open motorboat. In his articles for *Among the Deep Sea Fishers*, Curtis referred to nurses like Phillips as "heroines" and admitted that even at the hospitals, they sometimes had to "take on the duties of a doctor" for four- to six-week periods when the resident physician was away on medical trips to northern Labrador. He described them as courageous and "truly heroic women."[48]

Although Newfoundland and Labrador were distant from the battlefields of the Second World War, the direct effects of war landed at the doorstep of the St. Mary's River mission hospital on 27 August 1942. That day, an American transport ship, the SS *Chatham*, was torpedoed by German U-boat 517 in the Straits of Belle Isle. The ship was en route from Sydney, Nova Scotia, to Goose Bay, Labrador, and then on to Greenland, carrying 428 passengers, 106 crew, and 28 navy personnel. It sank close to the Labrador coast, south of Henley Harbour, and most passengers managed to row ashore in lifeboats and rafts or were rescued by the United States Coast Guard, the Canadian navy, or the Canadian air force (RCAF).[49] Dr. Helen Hosmer and British nurse Dorothy Jupp were on duty at St. Mary's River, and together they expertly treated the victims of the explosion. In her article "War Comes to Labrador," Hosmer

Figure 10.3

The Grenfell Mission hospital at North West River, Labrador, in the 1930s. | The Rooms, Provincial Archives Division, Fred Coleman Sears fonds, VA 114–20.

recalled that the worst cases were brought to the hospital first and that there was much to do

> in applying the protective dye to blistered areas, and in carrying out the necessary measures to give them rest and some degree of comfort. One man, the radio operator, had no intact skin up to well above his elbows, and very little on his face. But his plight was better than that of his comrade, a big muscular chap, who had slid down a rope to the life boat with his blistered hands, removing so deep a layer that the nerve ends were exposed. Even morphia only lessened his suffering and we had to use an anesthetic the next morning to complete his dressings. These two men had been talking on a lower deck just above where the torpedo had exploded, and they had no memory of how they had gotten out.[50]

The next day, several more survivors of the *Chatham* were brought to the hospital, those with broken bones and sprained joints. Such was the increased strain on the hospital's facilities that Hosmer and Jupp had to put beds in the operating room and the hallway. They recruited a slightly injured survivor, who had been a hospital orderly, to assist with night duty. The burn cases were then air-lifted to the base hospital at Goose Bay.[51]

Military Construction at Goose Bay, Labrador

Newfoundland and Labrador became geographically and tangibly involved in the war after the United States and Britain concluded the Destroyers for Bases Agreement in September 1940. The country's location in the North Atlantic made it strategically valuable, from a defence perspective, to Canada, Britain, and the United States. In particular, it became an important stopover point for transatlantic flights and shipping convoys between North America and Europe. To protect this valuable link, Britain entered into arrangements with the Canadian and American governments pertaining to the increased defence of the island and Labrador. In June 1940, the British government turned over to Canada the airport at Gander and the seaplane base at Botwood, Newfoundland, both of which had been built during the late 1930s. Canada also constructed air bases at Torbay (near St. John's) and at Goose Bay.[52] Under the Destroyers for Bases Agreement with the United States, Britain acquired fifty obsolete US naval destroyers in exchange for permitting the Americans to lease base sites and build military installations in Newfoundland and Labrador, as well as other territories in the western hemisphere.[53] The construction of the Canadian and American air force bases at Goose Bay in 1941–42 prompted Cecil Ashdown, executive director of the IGA, to declare, "we are right in the defense areas of this continent, and helping the Mission is undoubtedly war work, even if we are some thousands of miles from the conflict on land."[54]

These developments ushered in a building boom across Newfoundland and Labrador, which disrupted the socio-economic order of the coast. Securing waged employment in construction and later as civilian staff on the bases, local residents began to turn away from their traditional resource sector jobs. Writing from North West River in 1941, nurse Penelope Barnard noted that "all the men [were] going to work there instead of trapping."[55] Salaried employment introduced cash in communities that had previously functioned on the credit system. According to Steven High, "people used their earnings to pay old debts, to make long-needed repairs to their homes and to purchase new fishing equipment. In fact, hundreds of homes in each district received badly needed repairs and a fresh coat of paint. Newfoundlanders also bought foodstuffs and consumer goods that had been beyond their means only a few months previously."[56] In short, the war substantially changed the economy and society in northern Newfoundland and Labrador. Employment on the bases, combined with wartime improvements in the fishing economy, boosted the standard of living for many families. At the same time, the presence of American and Canadian military personnel increased residents' exposure to North American culture and a consumer society. The military personnel became a fixture in the region and an important part of the community, contributing to the work of the mission and local churches while developing close friendships and, sometimes, marriages with residents and Grenfell staff.[57]

Situated near Goose Bay, the town of Happy Valley appeared almost overnight, when three families from the north coast of Labrador arrived in September 1943 for work on the base. They pitched tents on the banks of the Hamilton River, five miles from the base, and built homes there. During the following months, another twenty-five families arrived, building homes "here, there and everywhere, all shapes and sizes. The place was called Refugee Cove. Medical care was given by the American and Canadian Doctors."[58] Before the base had its own hospital, the civilians of Happy Valley were treated by Mina Paddon at the North West River hospital.[59] Paddon always had a second nurse on staff, including Briton Phyllis Wenyon (1940–41), American Doris Willard (1941–42), Dutchwoman Louise Slob (1942–43), and Labradorian Florence Goudie (1943–45). With the rapid development of Happy Valley, Goudie also took on the medical care of approximately seven to eight hundred people living there, while Paddon maintained medical services at North West River. Since the health and well-being of its civilian staff were important to the base, Goudie was able to call on RCAF or United States Air Force doctors during emergencies.[60]

The Second World War was a turbulent time for the Grenfell Mission. Although the region in which it operated lay far from the front lines, the conflict disrupted communications between the IGA and the various transnational associations in London, New York, Boston, Ottawa, and St. John's that supported it. The GAGBI office in London was particularly hard hit, and recruiting British nurses became extremely difficult, with the unsurprising result that the mission was plagued by staff shortages throughout the war. The remaining nurses were obliged to cope with both heightened complexity in their work and greater numbers of patients. To maintain its services, the mission entrusted them with more professional responsibility and sometimes relied on them to manage its hospitals without physicians. Fortunately, Dr. Charles Curtis could count on fifty-two exceptional nurses to fulfill the mission's staffing needs, meet the health requirements of the public, and uphold the Grenfell system in northern Newfoundland and Labrador.

Notes

1 In this chapter, "northern Newfoundland and Labrador" refers to the two geographic areas in which the Grenfell Mission operated – on the northern peninsula of Newfoundland and in mainland Labrador.

2 Ronald Rompkey, "Elements of a Spiritual Autobiography in Sir Wilfred Grenfell's 'A Labrador Doctor,'" *Newfoundland Studies* 1, 1 (1985): 17–28; Ronald Rompkey, *Grenfell of Labrador: A Biography* (Toronto: University of Toronto Press, 1991); Ronald Rompkey,

ed., *Labrador Odyssey: The Journal and Photographs of Eliot Curwen on the Second Voyage of Wilfred Grenfell, 1893* (Montreal and Kingston: McGill-Queen's University Press, 1996); Ronald Rompkey, ed., *Jessie Luther at the Grenfell Mission* (Montreal and Kingston: McGill-Queen's University Press, 2001); Ronald Rompkey, ed., *The Labrador Memoir of Dr. Harry Paddon, 1912–1938* (Montreal and Kingston: McGill-Queen's University Press, 2003).

3 Jill Samfya Perry, "Nursing for the Grenfell Mission: Maternalism and Moral Reform in Northern Newfoundland and Labrador, 1894–1938" (Master's thesis, Memorial University of Newfoundland, 1997); Heidi Coombs-Thorne, "Nursing with the Grenfell Mission in Northern Newfoundland and Labrador, 1939–81" (PhD diss., University of New Brunswick, 2010); Heidi Coombs-Thorne, "'I Am Sure She Thinks of Herself as a Doctor Rather than a Nurse': Conflict and Resistance to Paternalism – Nursing with the Grenfell Mission in Newfoundland and Labrador," in *Caregiving on the Periphery: Historical Perspectives on Nursing and Midwifery in Canada*, ed. Myra Rutherdale (Montreal and Kingston: McGill-Queen's University Press, 2010), 210–42; Heidi Coombs-Thorne, "'Mrs. Tilley Had a Very Hasty Wedding!': The Class-Based Response to Marriages in the Grenfell Mission of Newfoundland and Labrador," *Canadian Bulletin of Medical History* 27, 1 (2010): 123–38; Heidi Coombs-Thorne, "'Such a Many-Purpose Job': Nursing, Identity, and Place with the Grenfell Mission, 1939–1960," *Nursing History Review* 21 (2013): 89–96.

4 Jennifer J. Connor and Katherine Side, eds., *The Grenfell Medical Mission and American Support in Newfoundland and Labrador, 1890s–1940s* (Montreal and Kingston: McGill-Queen's University Press, 2019).

5 Steven High, "'From Outport to Outport Base': The American Occupation of Stephenville, 1940–1945," *Newfoundland and Labrador Studies* 18, 1 (Spring 2002): 84–113; Peter Neary, "The Diplomatic Background to the Canada-Newfoundland Goose Bay Agreement of October 10, 1944," *Newfoundland and Labrador Studies* 2, 1 (Spring 1986): 38–61. Several works discuss naval history and/or the city of St. John's during the Second World War, including Steven High, ed., *Occupied St. John's: A Social History of a City at War, 1939–1945* (Montreal and Kingston: McGill-Queen's University Press, 2010); and Paul W. Collins, *The "Newfyjohn" Solution: St. John's, Newfoundland as a Case Study of Second World War Allied Naval Base Development during the Battle of the Atlantic* (Calgary: Write Advice Press, 2014). For more on the broader history of women in Newfoundland and Labrador during the war, see Jessica Steffler, "Morals and (Im)morality in Second World War Newfoundland: American Servicemen's Relations with Local Newfoundland Women, 1941–1945" (Master's thesis, Memorial University of Newfoundland, 2018); Jennifer Flight, "'We Are All in the Front Line This Time': The Patriotic Association of the Women of Newfoundland during the Second World War" (Master's research report, Memorial University of Newfoundland, 2007); Ruth E. Haywood, "'Delinquent, Disorderly and Diseased Females': Regulating Sexuality in Second World War St. John's, Newfoundland" (Master's thesis, Memorial University of Newfoundland, 2002); and Katherine Lind, "'A Share of the Sacrifice': Newfoundland Servicewives in the Second World War" (PhD diss., Memorial University of Newfoundland, 2001).

6 Charles S. Curtis, "Heroines," *Among the Deep Sea Fishers (ADSF)* 43, 1 (April 1945): 3.

7 The Mission to Deep Sea Fishermen (later the Royal National Mission to Deep Sea Fishermen) was a British organization that provided spiritual guidance and medical aid to the fishermen of the North Sea fleets.

8 The Moravian Mission provided basic medical services to the Inuit in northern Labrador, although it had no trained medical personnel. For more, see *Moravian Beginnings in Labrador: Papers from a Symposium Held in Makkovik and Hopedale, Labrador,*

Occasional Publication, Newfoundland and Labrador Studies No. 2 (St. John's: Memorial University of Newfoundland, 2009).

9 For more on the early structure and financial history of the mission and the foundation of the IGA (1914), see Heidi Coombs-Thorne, "To Prevent 'the Otherwise Inevitable Catastrophe': American Philanthropy and the Creation of the International Grenfell Association, 1905–14," in Connor and Side, *The Grenfell Medical Mission and American Support*, 77–99.

10 Before the establishment of the Cottage Hospital System by the Commission of Government in 1935, medical services across Newfoundland and Labrador were, according to historian J.T.H. Connor, "totally fragmented and underdeveloped." J.T.H. Connor, "Rural Medical Lives and Times," *Newfoundland and Labrador Studies* 23, 2 (Fall 2008): 233. For more on the Cottage Hospital System, see Gordon S. Lawson and Andrew F. Noseworthy, "Newfoundland's Cottage Hospital System: 1920–1970," *Canadian Bulletin of Medical History* 26, 2 (2009): 479; and Heidi Coombs-Thorne, "A Credit to All Concerned: Community Involvement and the Bonne Bay Cottage Hospital," *Newfoundland Quarterly* 107, 2 (2014): 43–47.

11 The Rooms Provincial Archives Division (RPA), International Grenfell Association collection MG 63, file 100, Kate Spalding (London) to Cecil Ashdown (Bermuda), 15 May 1941.

12 "Northern Nurses," *ADSF* 42, 2 (July 1944): 39.

13 RPA, MG 63, file 1329, Nora Noseworthy (London) to Kate Spalding (London), 7 January 1941; "Northern Nurses," 39.

14 RPA, MG 63, file 27, Kate Spalding (London) to Ethel Graham (Ottawa), 16 May 1941.

15 RPA, MG 63, file 27, Kate Spalding to Ethel Graham, 16 April and 21 August 1943.

16 Quoted in RPA, MG 63, file 238, Henry Richards (London) to Cecil Ashdown (Bermuda), 8 January 1940.

17 RPA, MG 63, file 1496, folder 1, Pansy Rowbotham to Kate Spalding, 19 October 1939; RPA, MG 63, file 520, Kate Spalding to Ethel Currant, 4 October 1939.

18 RPA, MG 63, file 1552, Kate Spalding to the Matron of Queen Alexandra's Imperial Nursing Service, 16 February 1942; RPA, MG 63, file 238, Henry Richards to Cecil Ashdown, 8 January 1940.

19 RPA, MG 63, file 238, Cecil Ashdown (Bermuda) to Henry Richards (London), 26 January 1940.

20 H.M. Richards, "The Grenfell Association of Great Britain and Ireland," *ADSF* 41, 1 (April 1943): 26.

21 RPA, MG 63, file 100, folder 2, Garth Forsyth to Kate Spalding, 17 July 1942.

22 RPA, MG 63, file 520, Kate Spalding to Ethel Currant, 4 October 1939.

23 RPA, MG 63, file 113, folder 2, "Report Submitted by Dr. Curtis to the I.G.A. Board of Directors, March 1941," March 1941.

24 Rompkey, *Grenfell of Labrador*, 293. See also [Charles S. Curtis], "The Superintendent Reports," *ADSF* 42, 1 (April 1944): 16.

25 Curtis, "Heroines," 3; Charles S. Curtis, "Heroines (Concluded)," *ADSF* 43, 2 (July 1945): 45.

26 Joyce Nevitt, *The Early Days of Nursing in Newfoundland, 1794–1922* (St. John's: Newfoundland Historical Society, 1977); Joyce Nevitt, *White Caps and Black Bands: Nursing in Newfoundland to 1934* (St. John's: Jesperson Press, 1978).

27 For more on midwifery in Britain, see Jean Towler and Joan Bramall, *Midwives in History and Society* (London: Croom Helm, 1986); and Robert Stevens, "The Midwives Act 1902: An Historical Landmark," *Midwives* 5, 11 (2002): 370.

28 RPA, MG 63, file 113, folder 2, Kate Spalding (London) to Charles Curtis, 26 May 1944.

29 RPA, MG 63, file 1543, Kate Spalding to Margaret Seaman, 26 March 1945.

30 RPA, MG 63, file 1313, Margaret Ormerod to Kate Spalding, 24 May 1944. See also RPA, MG 63, file 428, Penelope Banard to Kate Spalding, 24 September 1942. For more on the history of health visiting in Britain, see G.M. Owen, "Health Visiting," in *Nursing, Midwifery and Health Visiting since 1900,* ed. Peta Allan and Moya Jolly (London: Faber and Faber, 1982), n.p.
31 RPA, MG 63, file 1313, Ministry of Labour and National Service to Mrs. Collins, 25 June 1945.
32 RPA, MG 63, file 1585, folder 3, Mrs. Collins to Jean Smith, 25 May 1944.
33 RPA, MG 63, file 100, Kate Spalding (London) to Garth Forsyth (Cartwright), 8 September 1939.
34 Lydia Veitch, "London to Labrador," *ADSF* 43, 1 (April 1945): 16.
35 Kathleen Young, "Our Staff," *ADSF* 40, 2 (July 1942): 41.
36 Kathleen Young, "Labrador Calling," *ADSF* 40, 1 (April 1942): 7.
37 RPA, MG 63, file 27, Ethel Graham (Ottawa) to Kate Spalding (London), 17 June 1943.
38 RPA, MG 63, file 113, folder 2, Charles Curtis to Kate Spalding, 4 October 1943.
39 On outpost nursing in Canada, see, for example, Cynthia Comacchio Abeele, "'The Mothers of the Land Must Suffer': Child and Maternal Health in Rural and Outpost Ontario, 1918–1940," *Ontario History* 80, 3 (1988): 183–205; Jayne Elliott, "Blurring the Boundaries of Space: Shaping Nursing Lives at the Red Cross Outposts in Ontario, 1922–1945," *Canadian Bulletin of Medical History* 21 (2004): 303–25; Jayne Elliott, "A Negotiated Process: Outpost Nursing under the Red Cross in Ontario," in Rutherdale, *Caregiving on the Periphery,* 245–77; Edgar House, *The Way Out: The Story of NONIA in Newfoundland, 1920–1990* (St. John's: Creative, 1990); Linda Kealey, "Delivering Health Care in Rural New Brunswick: Outpost Nursing in the Twentieth Century," in *Medicine in the Remote and Rural North, 1800–2000,* ed. J.T.H. Connor and Stephan Curtis (London: Pickering & Chatto, 2011), 183–98; Linda Kealey, "On the Edge of Empire: The Working Life of Myra (Grimsley) Bennett," in Rutherdale, *Caregiving on the Periphery,* 84–105; Kathryn McPherson, "Nursing and Colonization: The Work of Indian Health Service Nurses in Manitoba, 1945–1970," in *Women Health and Nation: Canada and the United States since 1945,* ed. Georgina Feldberg et al. (Montreal and Kingston: McGill-Queen's University Press, 2003), 223–46; Laurie Meijer Drees and Lesley McBain, "Nursing and Native Peoples in Northern Saskatchewan: 1930s–1950s," *Canadian Bulletin of Medical History* 18 (2001): 43–46; Linda J. Quiney, "'Suitable Young Women': Red Cross Nursing Pioneers and the Crusade for Healthy Living in Manitoba, 1920–30," in *Place and Practice in Canadian Nursing History,* ed. Jaybe Elliot, Meryn Stuart, and Cynthia Toman (Vancouver: UBC Press, 2009), 91–110; and Linda White, "NONIA," *Newfoundland Quarterly* 100, 1 (2007): 3–6.
40 For more on the history of midwifery and the Central Midwives Board, see Stevens, "The Midwives Act 1902"; and Towler and Bramall, *Midwives in History and Society.*
41 Charles S. Curtis, "New Nursing Station at Flowers Cove," *ADSF* 46, 4 (January 1949): 103. See also Lesley Diack, *Labrador Nurse* (London: Victor Gollancz, 1963), 61; and Anne Robinson Hopkins, "Island Summer," *ADSF* 48, 4 (January 1951): 102.
42 Charles S. Curtis, "Medical Work," *ADSF* 44, 3 (October 1946): 81.
43 Curtis, "Heroines," 6.
44 Curtis, "Heroines (Concluded)," 45.
45 Ibid.
46 Ibid., 47.
47 Ibid.
48 Ibid., 48.

49 Most of the passengers were construction personnel, on their way to Bluie West One, Greenland. For more on the SS *Chatham,* see Kevin Griffin, Chapter 8, "Clarke Ships Go to War – And War Comes to the St Lawrence," in "St Lawrence Saga: The Clarke Steamship Story," 73–74, https://clarkesteamship.wordpress.com/2014/03/13/chapter-8-clarke-ships-go-to-war-and-war-comes-to-the-st-lawrence/; and uboat.net, "Ships Hit by U-Boats: Chatham, American Steam Passenger Ship," http://uboat.net/allies/merchants/2093.html.

50 Helen R. Hosmer, "War Comes to Labrador," *ADSF* 41, 2 (July 1943): 35–36.

51 Ibid., 36.

52 See Peter Neary, "'A Mortgaged Property': The Impact of the United States on Newfoundland, 1940–49," in *Twentieth-Century Newfoundland: Explorations,* ed. James Hiller and Peter Neary (St. John's: Breakwater, 1993), 180–81.

53 Ibid., 183.

54 RPA, MG 63, file 238, Cecil Ashdown (Bermuda) to Sir Henry Richards (London), 4 June 1943. For more on Ashdown, see "In Memoriam – Cecil S. Ashdown," *ADSF* 46, 3 (October 1948): 68–70.

55 RPA, MG 63, file 428, Penelope Barnard to Kate Spalding, 1 December 1941.

56 Steven High, "Working for Uncle Sam: The 'Comings' and 'Goings' of Newfoundland Base Construction Labour, 1940–1945," *Acadiensis* 32, 2 (Spring 2003): 90. The author argues that labour turnover rates on the American bases and in primary industries were high, due at least partially to the actions of the Commission of Government, which urged fishers and loggers to return to their seasonal work and attempted to keep base construction wages low. As a result, it "encouraged Newfoundlanders to combine base work with other traditional activities." Ibid., 107. High also points out that the majority of Newfoundlanders returned to fishing when construction work ended, though the fishery was now based on a cash economy.

57 Gordon W. Thomas, *From Sled to Satellite: My Years with the Grenfell Mission* (Toronto: Irwin Law, 1987), 78.

58 Alice Perrault, "History of Happy Valley: Part One," *Them Days* 1, 1 (1975): 22. See also "The War Years," *Them Days: On the Goose* 12, 4 (1987): 43.

59 Bella McLean Shouse, "NWR and RCAF Helped Each Other," *Them Days: On the Goose* 12, 4 (1987): 46.

60 Curtis, "Heroines," 3.

11

They Died so That Men May Fight

Depictions of Female Military War Dead

Sarah Hogenbirk

A FEW DAYS after the death of Section Officer Rose Goodman, her hometown newspaper, the *New Glasgow News*, paid tribute to her sense of dedication:

> With her university training, Miss Goodman, – it is hard to think of her in military terms – could have chosen a less risky, but still useful vocation; or she could have chosen the so-called "social" world and done not much anything other than seeking her own pleasure. She could have disdained service in the ranks. She made her choice; she has given her life for her country.[1]

Goodman, who served with the Royal Canadian Air Force (Women's Division) – RCAF (WD) – had died in an RCAF plane crash outside Claresholm, Alberta, on 26 January 1943. Her story provides a window into an overlooked part of Canadian history: the female military dead of the Second World War.

The newspaper's reluctance to refer to Goodman by her military rank reflects the widespread uneasiness regarding women who joined the women's services of the Canadian army, navy, and air force. The 1941 decision to recruit women produced fears about their safety in the masculine domain of the military. Canadians worried about what might happen to young women who were placed in proximity to young men in an institution whose purpose was to turn boys into men. They also worried about whether women would be put in harm's way. As historians such as Ruth Roach Pierson document, defence officials felt the need to reassure the public that servicewomen would be kept morally and physically safe, working and living under careful supervision and remaining feminine. Officials also upheld gender norms that positioned men as warriors abroad, protecting the women who took on supportive roles at home: a long-standing gendered binary of male combatant and female non-combatant. Wartime authorities insisted that women would be stationed far from the front and would perform solely supportive functions to free up men for combat.[2]

Nonetheless, some servicewomen were exposed to physical risk and died because of it, as Goodman's story reveals. Scholars have argued that, although they were officially non-combatants, Canadian, British, and American servicewomen were involved in "combat or near combat" situations.[3] Pierson notes that a Canadian Women's Army Corps (CWAC) "mobile office unit close behind the front lines in Belgium in late 1944" came across "booby traps left behind by the retreating German army."[4] Members of this unit were also injured by German V2 rockets. Most Canadian servicewomen who were stationed overseas risked death or injury by Axis torpedo, naval shell, bomb, or to a lesser extent, by artillery shell.[5]

Although scholars have documented the physical risks that servicewomen faced, they have paid limited attention to female military war dead, choosing instead to focus on the male combatant. Most references merely state briefly that some women lost their lives. Even scholarship on the women's services concentrates on whether the war improved women's rights and, as such, overlooks female casualties.[6] Nor do servicewomen have much place in the commemoration of the Second World War: remembrance ceremonies privilege the male combatant and the grieving mother.[7] Cynthia Toman documents the silencing of nursing casualties and argues that First World War military nurses have overshadowed their Second World War counterparts in social memory. The former are memorialized twice in Ottawa: on the National War Memorial and on the National Nurses Association War Memorial, located in the Hall of Honour within the Centre Block of Parliament. Dianne Dodd asserts that these memorials minimize the contributions of nurses because the example in the Hall of Honour "is generic in nature and avoids direct acknowledgement of nurses' sacrifice of life" and because the nurses on the National War Memorial lack the tools of their profession.[8]

Of the estimated 44,090 Canadian military personnel who died in the Second World War, roughly 91 were in the women's services.[9] However, this tally is incomplete: for example, it excludes the women who lost their lives while working as nurses, doctors, or foreign operatives in the Canadian and Allied forces. Similarly, this chapter omits military nurses, because their status as professional women, their lengthier presence in the forces, and greater exposure to physical risk differentiated them from the 91 women studied here.[10] Although they represent a tiny fraction of the war dead, an examination of how they died, how they have been remembered, and how they have been forgotten expands our understanding of what it meant to be a uniformed woman during the war and of the wartime society in which they lived.

Through an examination of newspaper articles, service files, and various post-war commemorations, this chapter explores how servicewomen died and how their deaths were portrayed during and after the war, ultimately addressing the question of which women's sacrifices have been remembered and which forgotten. At the time, the treatment of the subject was a complex phenomenon. On the one hand, the military bureaucracy was ill-equipped to handle such deaths, and remembrance was highly selective as they were contained by the gendered binary of male combatant and female non-combatant, which predominated in 1940s Canada and beyond. On the other hand, servicewomen and servicemen were subject to many of the same physical dangers, and the armed forces applied standardized commemorative practices to all military personnel. In the handling of their deaths, servicewomen were not treated entirely unequally, but the meaning of their sacrifices seems to have differed from that of their male counterparts and to have afforded different levels of recognition.

Circumstances of Servicewomen's Deaths

The deaths of servicewomen reflect the nature of their duties. They were non-combatants, and most served as cooks and clerks in Canada. Of the ninety-one dead discussed here, forty-three were with the CWAC, thirty-seven had worn the RCAF (WD) uniform, and eleven belonged to the Women's Royal Canadian Naval Service (WRCNS, or Wrens). These numbers correspond with the respective size of the women's services: the CWAC was largest, with approximately twenty-two thousand members, the RCAF (WD) had just over seventeen thousand, and the WRCNS had close to seven thousand. Women from all three died in remarkably similar ways.

For those who were stationed in Europe, German bombs were a common threat. Stories of injuries and near fatalities from bombs are scattered throughout their accounts, but only one account has been found so far which mentions an individual who died from wounds inflicted during a bombing raid.[11] As RCAF (WD) veteran Nano Pennefather-McConnell wrote in her memoir, "Airwoman Curtis ... was hit by a stone that fell from a building hit by a V2 Rocket. She died some time later as a result of her injuries."[12] Interestingly, the documents in Leading Aircraftswoman Elizabeth Curtis's service file do not match this version of events. According to the file, Curtis died of tuberculosis peritonitis while stationed overseas, and there is no report that she was hurt during a bombing. She was one of the few women who died and was buried overseas.[13]

More typically, servicewomen died in much the same ways as civilian women. In 1942, the five most common causes of mortality for Canadian women between the ages of fifteen and forty were tuberculosis, "maternal deaths," heart disease, cancer, and "violent or accidental deaths."[14] Servicewomen did not escape these trends, but some deaths were recorded in ways that suggest officials tried to protect the reputation of the women's services. For example, Wren Ruth Floyd's death was attributed to tuberculosis, Corporal Annie Gyles succumbed to cancer, and Private Patricia Cooney died of a cerebral hemorrhage.[15] Several committed suicide, and one was murdered by her husband.[16] Airplane crashes took the lives of Rose Goodman (as mentioned above), as well as others. Some died in automobile accidents or from injuries they sustained in these accidents. Several drowned.[17] In her history of the CWAC in Waterloo County, Ruth Russell cites the testimony of a veteran who recalled that an eighteen-year-old CWAC died after she visited a "back-street abortionist in London, Ontario."[18] Her death does not correspond to the details in the official CWAC service files examined here. In another potential sanitization, though servicewomen were discharged for becoming pregnant, "maternal death" was never listed as the cause or contributing factor of mortality. For instance, Olive Clegg had tuberculosis when she gave birth by caesarean section on 2 April 1944, before she died on 17 June 1944, but though Acting Surgeon Lieutenant Commander J.F. Elliott stated his "opinion [that] pregnancy was the chief reason for the flare up of tuberculosis," her record cites "tuberculosis" as cause of death.[19] The armed forces handled pregnancy quietly, even it seems, to the extent of managing personnel records, because of widespread rumours that the women's divisions were subject to high rates of out-of-wedlock pregnancies. These rumours were a problem, partly because they hurt recruitment. Such reporting discrepancies aside, the deaths of servicewomen and their civilian sisters follow similar patterns.[20]

In some ways, servicewomen were safer than their civilian counterparts because they had better access to medical care. Improved health care for civilians was recommended during the war, but its implementation had to wait until later.[21] However, though military personnel enjoyed better care, one must guard against uncritically accepting the evidence offered for this. In an effort to defend the reputation of the armed forces, officers emphasized in their letters to grieving relatives that the deceased had received the best possible care. Even so, their claims do have a certain basis in reality. For example, as Toman explains, military personnel took precedence when it came to the limited supply of penicillin. She notes that the drug became widely available to civilians only in March 1945.[22] Enlistment afforded better protection to some women, even as it exposed others to greater risk.

Like that of other female war workers, servicewomen's employment could place them in greater danger than they would have encountered had they not signed up. Unlike servicemen and military nurses, they were not killed in enemy attacks, but their work entailed dangers that were not associated with combat. For example, they were often required to travel to their basic training and postings in a time when automotive safety research was in its early stages and before the use of seatbelts became mandatory.[23] Some women died in vehicle accidents while on duty. For instance, Jean Grant reportedly lost control of an army jeep after it skidded on the road.[24] Andrew Iarocci writes that many Allied soldiers and civilians were injured or killed in vehicle crashes. Cynthia Toman reports that accidents of various types as well as illness took the lives of at least eleven military nurses and that one died after enemy fire destroyed the ferry she was on. According to Timothy Balzer, accidents and illness accounted for the majority of Canadian army casualties until the end of November 1940. Daniel Byers notes that some male trainees died due to certain diseases, such as meningitis, that spread easily in heavily populated training camps. Since Canadian involvement in the war effort included the training of pilots and aircrew under the British Commonwealth Air Training Plan, plane crashes were common. Servicewomen's work could place them in dangerous situations.[25]

Journalists suggested that Section Officer Rose Goodman and Section Officer Irene Watson, who was also killed in a plane crash, died while performing their duty. The editor of the *New Glasgow News* linked Goodman's death to her military service by stating that she gave her life for her country.[26] However, the RCAF determined that the accident did not occur "in the performance of air force duty."[27] On 10 November 1943, a *Toronto Telegram* article entitled "Lakeshore Woman Believed Killed in Crash" reported that Irene Watson's family had been informed that she was missing and was presumed dead. According to the *Telegram*, the Watsons were aware that she "had been stationed in Newfoundland where her duties required considerable travelling by plane."[28] Watson's service file reveals that she was a passenger on an aircraft that crashed while on a transportation flight.[29] While the press concluded that both Goodman and Watson died because of their wartime employment, officials declared only certain plane crashes as service related, thereby hinting that not all war deaths were viewed the same.

The Canadian Pension Commission, the federal government body that administered the Pension Act, concluded that the deaths of some servicewomen were caused by military service, whereas others were not. For example, the commission declared that Ruth Floyd's death by tuberculosis and Annie Gyles's death by cancer were "related to military service."[30] By contrast, it stated that in the case of Patricia Cooney's cerebral hemorrhage, "the condition which resulted in death was incurred during service in Canada subsequent to May 21st, 1940, but not pensionable as it did not arise out of, nor was it directly connected with, military service."[31] There were precedents for these differing conclusions. In her study of First World War nursing casualties, Dianne Dodd documents that military physicians typically labelled nurses' deaths by illness as war-related but deemed some cancer cases as unconnected to service.[32] Officials linked some deaths to wartime employment.

Unfamiliarity with Female War Dead

Even though military nurses had died in the First World War, Second World War depictions portrayed female military dead as a new phenomenon. Journalists framed their deaths in terms of novelty and innovation. Coverage of

Airwoman Mary Heysel's funeral mentioned that she was the first female RCAF casualty.[33] The *New Glasgow News* stated that Rose Goodman was the "first Canadian girl to give her life in the service of her country in the crash of one of His Majesty's planes."[34] The *Toronto Globe and Mail* article on the funeral for Wren Margaret McGill bore the headline "First Wren Dies on Overseas Duty."[35] The war, journalists wrote, exposed servicewomen to the ultimate sacrifice: like servicemen, they, too, might die for their country.

Such press articles simultaneously challenged and reinforced the gendered binary that identified men as protectors on the battle front and women as subject to protection on the home front. Simply by reporting on servicewomen's deaths at home and overseas, journalists revealed that they were not always kept safe. As discussed below, officials assumed that women would be safe and therefore did not draft the necessary paperwork for the handling of their deaths. But even as journalists challenged some aspects of the social narratives of the war, their coverage of servicewomen's deaths also upheld gender hierarchies. For example, the *Toronto Daily Star* announced the death of Leading Aircraftwoman Elizabeth Shaw with the headline "Girl Veteran Dies at Christie Street." Shaw was twenty-five at the time. In her day, the word "girl" was not restricted to individuals of a specific age in colloquial speech but was applied according to status: children, teens, unmarried women, female office staff, and factory workers were all "girls." Calling Shaw a girl maintained gendered power relations by modifying and minimizing her standing as a veteran. Her death was also framed in familial terms. The article shifted attention away from her military work by focusing on the fact that, despite their best efforts, her parents could not be at her bedside when she died.[36]

The *New Glasgow News* emphasized that Goodman died in a non-combative supportive role, thus containing the challenge to gender boundaries that were inherent in a servicewoman's death. According to the editor, Goodman "served – and died – that men may fly. That we may win this war." This tribute was a slight modification of the RCAF (WD) motto: "We Serve That Men May Fly." By invoking these words, the editor attempted to present Goodman's death as a noble sacrifice. Yet, though Goodman was portrayed as a heroine, the use of the motto reminded readers that piloting (and combat too) remained the preserve of men.

Those who administered servicewomen's estates also upheld the category of military war dead as primarily male, as they demonstrated in voicing their expectations regarding the deceased. While handling the estate of CWAC Florence Fowler, the manager of the Ordinary Claim Department at Prudential Insurance wrote to the administrator of estates at the Department of National Defence, acknowledging his company's inexperience with such a situation. The manager wrote, "Inasmuch as this is the first occasion we have had to consider a claim on a Canadian woman in service we are interested to know whether they, as a general rule, execute military Wills."[37] In response, Lieutenant R.G. Phelan admitted that the Estates Branch could not answer the question, because it, too, had little experience with CWAC casualties.[38] Although the forces had an established procedure for casualty notification, and much experience with handling men's estates, officials seemed unsure of how the practices applied to servicewomen. Phelan pursued the matter of military wills with the CWAC commanding officer, asking her to determine whether most servicewomen lacked military wills and, if that were the case, to have them write one.[39] The question was eventually forwarded to the army's director of administration, who replied that women, like men, could choose whether they left a will. Officials clearly saw the existence of the female war dead as an unusual phenomenon.[40]

Other archival evidence suggests that defence officials did not expect servicewomen to die during the war and were ill-equipped to respond when they did. The service files for several women contain paperwork that was designed for male personnel and modified to apply to them. For example, in a typed request by the Department of Veterans Affairs for the documents of Wren Olive Irene Clegg, the word "man's" has been crossed out and replaced with "Wren's."[41] Errors in the official correspondence sent to relatives of deceased servicewomen further demonstrate the Estates Branch's assumption that the dead would naturally be male. In several cases, defence officials misgendered the dead women. Letters to CWAC Mary Gallant's parents refer to "your son" and "his estate." Gallant was listed as part of the army, not the CWAC, its women's service. An official letter incorrectly referred to Kathleen Moore's sister Mary Harkans as her son.[42] Such careless mistakes were probably grounded in the fact that male casualty figures significantly outnumbered those for women, which meant that the forces had much more experience with the administration of male fatalities. The exclusion of servicewomen from combat made their cases less common and less likely to register with busy defence staff. The sheer volume of paperwork may also have contributed to the clerical errors. Timothy Balzer writes that the military administered thousands of cases, and that mistakes occurred despite its best efforts.[43]

Still, the misgendering probably added to the grief of the family. A letter from Mrs. W.J. Young illustrates that one grieving relative was bothered by such errors. She acknowledged the Department of National Defence's reply to her "application for my daughters [sic] gratuity but I think you have made a mistake as you refer to 'my son.' And I have lost no son."[44] Young also pointed out that her son was very much alive: in fact, he had provided her with information as to the possible location of her daughter's will. Despite her polite phrasing, she thought it was important to correct any misunderstanding. An Estates Branch official apologized, writing that it "sincerely regret[ted]" the error.[45] Young's insistence that the Estates Branch accurately refer to her daughter's sacrifice reminds us of the personal impact of each death.

Other mothers criticized the administration of their daughters' estates. For example, Florence Ellis, who lost her son and her daughter during the war, complained that the officials failed to provide her with the same amount of information for her daughter, Rosella Henry, as they had for her son. In October 1945, she wrote to Rosella's commanding officer, Lieutenant Louise Leslie, demanding a fuller account of Rosella's death. She explained that a British nurse had written her a detailed account of her son's "case from day of entering Hosp. and the 3 wks until his death" overseas. She stressed that she valued the nurse's letter and then asked that, since "Rosella only lived such a short time surely you could tell me more than you have."[46] Several months later, she again objected to the lack of information, writing that "no mention has been made as to what monies she had at time of accident, statement very brief, not as one rec'd of my dear son."[47] From her letters, Mrs. Ellis felt that army officials awarded less importance to her daughter's death than to her son's. Rosella's service file complicates the story. She had died only two days after being admitted to hospital and thus had less opportunity to be noticed by a nurse. Subsequent correspondence reveals that she received a high level of care (she was given penicillin) and that officials responded to Mrs. Ellis's request for information.[48] Her complaints are another reminder of the personal trauma of each death and an expression of understandable frustration with a bureaucracy that was unprepared to handle female war dead.

Tributes and Commemoration

Military deaths are both public and private losses. In their study on Western perceptions of war dead, Luc Capdevila and Danièle Voldman argue that "even if they [soldiers] often remained anonymous, their death became both public and individual during the First World War."[49] These insights are equally applicable to the Second World War. Public recognition has included naming the war dead and making their names accessible. The names of Canadian military personnel who lost their lives are recorded in the *Second World War Book of Remembrance* and the *Newfoundland Book of Remembrance*, which are housed in the Memorial Chamber of the Peace Tower on Parliament Hill. Interested parties can learn when individuals died and where they are buried by searching online registries, such as the Canadian Virtual War Memorial and that of the Commonwealth War Graves Commission (CWGC).[50]

Whereas servicewomen's deaths were sometimes handled differently from those of servicemen, the memorialization of the two groups does display similarities. Those who have an unknown or have a hard-to-reach grave have been recorded on monuments. For example, after Sergeant Pamela Bennett died in a plane crash on 13 July 1945, Wing Commander W.R. Gunn informed her mother that her name would be inscribed on a memorial in Ottawa, commemorating RCAF personnel who had no "known" or "accessible" grave. Bennett had been a passenger on an RCAF Liberator that crashed in what Gunn described as a "mountainous region of Vancouver Island."[51] Corporal Nora Johnson and Leading Aircraftwoman Margaret Mann also died in the crash, which claimed the lives of fourteen personnel. Their names, along with that of Section Officer Irene Watson, are inscribed on the Ottawa Memorial, which "commemorates those of the Air Forces of the British Commonwealth who lost their lives while serving in units operating from bases in Canada, the British West Indies and the United States of America, or while training in Canada and the U.S.A."[52]

Figure 11.1

This panel on the Ottawa Memorial includes Section Officer Irene Watson. She, along with Sergeant Pamela G. Bennett, Corporal Nora Johnson, and Leading Aircraftwoman Margaret Mann are among the eight hundred men and women whom the memorial commemorates. | Photograph by Sarah Hogenbirk.

Similarly, the federal government and the armed forces officially included servicewomen among the military dead. Wartime sources show that many had military funerals. For example, a newspaper article on Wren Margaret McGill's funeral stated that she was "buried with full naval honors" in Brookwood Military Cemetery, in the United Kingdom, one of the many cemeteries under the care of the CWGC.[53] Ottawa and the armed forces also awarded certain honours from the First World War to mothers of female military dead in the Second World War. The Memorial Cross was established in 1919 "as a memento of personal loss and sacrifice on the part of the mother and widow of a sailor or soldier of Canada or Newfoundland who laid down his life for his country."[54] Mothers of servicewomen who died on active duty were awarded the Memorial Cross, which is also known as the Silver Cross medal. Regardless of whether the deceased were male or female, government officials used the same language of sacrifice when they informed mothers that they would "receive a Silver Memorial Cross given by the Canadian government as a slight token of appreciation of the sacrifice you have made."[55] Mrs. Julia Labbé valued the gesture: she informed the minister of national defence that she was "greatly moved by this token of appreciation for the services rendered to the country by my daughter whom I shall never forget."[56] Her words reflect both the personal and public nature of her daughter's death.

Many family members wanted permanent recognition that their daughter, sister, or wife had died in uniform. Service files reveal that several families accepted an offer from the Imperial War Graves Commission to mark their relative's grave with a publicly funded headstone for military personnel.[57] On the headstones, collective and individual expressions of grief overlap. Uniform in size, material, and lettering, all are marked with the emblem for the relevant division, the individual's name, service number, and unit, a cross or other symbol of his or her religion, and an optional personal passage.[58] They are not differentiated by gender. For example, when Rosella Henry's mother asked that the CWAC crest appear on her tombstone, army officials informed her that they could not grant her request. As they explained, the maple leaf, which was the emblem of the army, "has been adopted for use on all headstones provided to mark the graves of deceased members of the Canadian Army who served during the war 1939–45."[59] Viewed from a distance, servicewomen's headstones are indistinguishable from those of servicemen. Only the inscription signals the individual's gender.

Certain grieving relatives and war dead received different types of acknowledgment. Emilie Buchanan's husband was entitled to her medals but not the Memorial Cross. That recognition of sacrifice went to Emilie's mother.[60] Suzanne Evans writes that fathers became eligible for the Memorial Cross in 1976 "but only if there were no mother, widow, or child of the soldier."[61] Other deaths have been singled out by the armed forces and postwar publications. A plaque and cairn honour the fourteen people who died in the Liberator crash on Vancouver Island.[62] In *Athene, Goddess of War,* Hugh Conrod recognizes several CWAC war dead as going "beyond the call of duty."[63] Conrod honours these women slightly differently, depending on how they died. For instance, he states that Jean Grant was "killed during the performance of duty" but that "former CWAC Private Rita Labbé ... died after a lengthy illness."[64] Les Allison and Harry Hayward similarly differentiate between types of death in their tribute to RCAF personnel who died during the war: victims of accidents were "killed," whereas those who succumbed to illness died "by natural causes."[65]

Although commemoration was a public recognition of loss, it often coexisted with personal and familial efforts to come to terms with the death. Some families took refuge in silence to cope with their loss. In 1994, Bev Huston contacted the National Archives of Canada, seeking information about her aunt, Margaret Victoria Hart. Admitting that she knew very little about Hart, Huston explained that "unfortunately I come from a family who refuse to tell my Mother (or anyone else) anything about Margaret's service or her life."[66] Huston's mother was five when Hart died. Some information and Hart's medals had been passed down through the family, and in a 2014 piece for the *Alaska Highway News,* Huston noted that "growing up we were told that my Aunt was the first female casualty of war."[67] This family story, however, was incorrect. Hart was not the first servicewomen to die. Huston's incomplete knowledge of her aunt's passing echoes the scanty public commemoration of female war dead after the Second World War. As mentioned above, Canadian scholars have echoed these public values, largely ignoring female deaths.

The study of female military war dead invites further discussion of what it means to die while on active service. Although servicewomen were not exposed to the dangers of front-line combat, they died from many of the same causes as servicemen. Both were killed in accidents and by illness. Military service could place women in dangerous situations, and some, such as Jean Grant and Irene Watson, died while performing their duties. The male death in combat was one example of military sacrifice, but it was not the only one. The intention here is not to diminish such deaths, but rather to prompt a more inclusive remembrance. The handling and commemoration of servicewomen who died during the Second World War were complicated affairs. Gendered expectations that they would be protected on the home front shaped their treatment and remembrance. Officials seem genuinely to have expected that they would not be harmed and sometimes blundered in administering their deaths. Yet, the practices designed for male fatalities were also applied to those of women. Like their male colleagues, women responded to their country's call to service. Also like the men, some lost their lives.

Notes

1 Editorial, *New Glasgow News*, 29 January 1943, quoted in extract of David Rome, ed., *Canadian Jews in World War II* (Montreal: Canadian Jewish Congress, 1948), 31, as reproduced in Veterans Affairs Canada, Photo of Rose Goodman, "Section Officer *Rose Jette Goodman*," Digital Collection, Canadian Virtual War Memorial (CVWM), 2019, http://www.veterans.gc.ca/eng/remembrance/memorials/canadian-virtual-war-memorial/detail/2687659?Rose%20Jette%20Goodman#inline_content_modal_3.

2 Ruth Roach Pierson, *"They're Still Women After All": The Second World War and Canadian Womanhood* (Toronto: McClelland and Stewart, 1986), 129–86; Jeffrey A. Keshen, *Saints, Sinners, and Soldiers: Canada's Second World War* (Vancouver: UBC Press, 2004), 172–93.

3 Stephen J. Dienstfrey, "Women Veterans' Exposure to Combat," *Armed Forces and Society* 14, 4 (Summer 1988): 551–56; Judy M. Iseke and Leisa A. Desmoulins, "Critical Events: Metis Servicewomen's WWII Stories with Dorothy Chartrand," *Canadian Journal of Native Studies* 33, 2 (2013): 44–45; Carolyn Gossage, ed., *Greatcoats and Glamour Boots: Canadian Women at War (1939–1945)*, rev. ed. (Toronto: Dundurn, 2001), 205; Gill Abousnouga and David Machin, *The Language of War Monuments* (London: Bloomsbury, 2013), 181–88. The quoted phrase comes from Dienstfrey, "Women Veterans' Exposure to Combat," 551.

4 Pierson, *"They're Still Women After All,"* 111.

5 W. Hugh Conrod, *Athene, Goddess of War: The Canadian Women's Army Corps, Their Story* (Dartmouth, NS: Writing and Editorial Services, 1983), 196–202, 258–59, 350.

6 Sarah Hogenbirk, "Women inside the Canadian Military, 1938–1966" (PhD diss., Carleton University, 2017), 4–42. For examples of this limited scholarship see: Pierson, *"They're Still Women After All,"* 129–86; Keshen, *Saints, Sinners, and Soldiers*, 172–93; Serge Durflinger, "'I Regret to Inform You …': Next-of-Kin Notification and Official Condolences – The Case of Flight Lieutenant George J. Chequer, RCAF," *Canadian Military History* 9, 4 (Autumn 2000): 45; Jonathan F. Vance, "An Open Door to a Better Future: The Memory of Canada's Second World War," in *Canada and the Second World War: Essays in Honour of Terry Copp*, ed. Geoffrey Hayes, Mike Bechthold, and Matt Symes (Waterloo: Wilfrid Laurier University Press, 2012), 462, 468; Directorate of History and Heritage, Department of National Defence, Ottawa, 90/447, file 104, Research Branch of the Library of Parliament, "History of the RCAF (Women's Division), 1941–1971" (manuscript, Ottawa, 1971), 9.

7 Debra Marshall, "Remembering Women: Envisioning More Inclusive War Remembrance in Twenty-First Century Britain," in *Lest We Forget: Remembrance and Commemoration*, ed. Maggie Andrews (Stroud, UK: History Press, 2011), 197–202; Abousnouga and Machin, *The Language of War Monuments*, 163–88; Suzanne Evans, "History of the Silver Cross Medal," *Canadian Military History* 19, 1 (2010): 42–49; Suzanne Evans, "Marks of Grief: Black Attire, Medals, and Service Flags," in *A Sisterhood of Suffering and Service: Women and Girls of Canada and Newfoundland during the First World War*, ed. Sarah Glassford and Amy Shaw (Vancouver: UBC Press, 2012), 219–40.

8 Cynthia Toman, *An Officer and a Lady: Canadian Military Nursing and the Second World War* (Vancouver: UBC Press, 2007), 190–99; Dianne Dodd, "Commemorating Canadian Military Nurse Casualties during and after the First World War: Nurses' Perspectives," in *Routledge Handbook on the Global History of Nursing*, ed. Patricia D'Antonio, Julie A. Fairman, and Jean C. Whelan (New York: Routledge, 2013), 55–71. The quotation comes from Dodd, "Commemorating Canadian Military Nurse Casualties during and after the First World War: Nurses' Perspectives," 55–56.

9 Most women were identified using the search function of the CVWM registry, which has the option of searching by unit/regiment. The totals of Second World War military

dead vary by source. The 44,090 cited here is taken from Library and Archives Canada (LAC), Ottawa, "Service Files of the Second World War – War Dead, 1939–1947," http://www.bac-lac.gc.ca/eng/discover/military-heritage/second-world-war/second-world-war-dead-1939-1947/Pages/files-second-war-dead.aspx.

10 Toman, *An Officer and a Lady*, 72–77, 190–99.

11 For example, see "Blown Out of Bed" and "Buzz Bombs," quoted in Jean Bruce, *Back the Attack! Canadian Women during the Second World War – At Home and Abroad* (Toronto: Macmillan, 1985), 50; Conrod, *Athene, Goddess of War*, 195–204, 258–59; and Nano Pennefather-McConnell, *We Never Stopped Dancing: An Airwoman's Scrapbook* (Shawville, QC: Life Profiles, 2002), 67–68, 108, 133–36.

12 Pennefather-McConnell, *We Never Stopped Dancing*, 133.

13 LAC, R112, vol. 30632, Service file for Curtis, Elizabeth Audrey, Official Royal Canadian Air Force casualty notification form for Curtis, Elizabeth Audrey, 19 November 1945.

14 LAC, MG 30, E386, Jean Flatt Davey fonds, Folder Questionnaires, Statistics, N.D., 1942–43, Untitled sheet listing ten leading causes of death for women aged fifteen to forty in Canada, 1942, and other data on Canadian wartime births and maternal deaths, n.d.

15 LAC, RG 24, vol. 29056, Service file for Floyd, Ruth, H.B. Money, Cdr. (S), Royal Canadian Naval Reserve, Director of Personnel Records, to the Secretary, Department of National Defence (DND) for Naval Service, 19 September 1945; LAC, RG 24, vol. 26028, Service file for Gyles, Annie Kathleen, Memorandum from E. Lackey, Canadian Pension Commission (CPC), to Deputy Minister, DND, 31 May 1947; LAC, RG 24, vol. 25634, Service file for Cooney, Patricia Jane, Report of death of a soldier for Patricia Cooney, 29 June 1942.

16 Conrod, *Athene, Goddess of War*, 245.

17 Ibid., 245, 258–61; Research Branch of the Library of Parliament, "History of the RCAF (Women's Division), 1941–1971," 9; Les Allison and Harry Hayward, *They Shall Grow Not Old: A Book of Remembrance* (Brandon: Commonwealth Air Training Plan Museum, 1992), 21–22, 42, 46, 82, 122, 169, 236, 270, 320, 358, 364, 395, 403, 462, 543, 564, 584, 675, 679, 684, 690, 788, 793, 798, 804, 828.

18 Ruth Russell, *Proudly She Marched: Training Canada's World War Women in Waterloo County*, vol. 1, *Canadian Women's Army Corps* (Waterloo: Canadian Federation of University Women, Kitchener-Waterloo, 2006), 161.

19 LAC, RG 24, vol. 29037, Service file for Clegg, Olive Irene, Copy of D.J. Coulter, Executive Director of Children's Aid Society of Cape Breton, to F.E. MacKinnon, Director of Child Welfare, 27 June 1949; Service file for Clegg, Olive Irene, Copy of C.M. Drury, Deputy Minister of Department of Public Welfare to Director of Child Welfare, 18 June 1949; Service file for Clegg, Olive Irene, Author unknown to the Administrator of Estates, Naval Services, 22 July 1944; Service file for Clegg, Olive Irene, J.F. Elliott, Acting/Surgeon Lieutenant Commander, R.C.N.V.R., "Report of Surgeon Lieutenant Commander J.F. Elliott, R.C.N.V.R. on Disability of Olive Irene Clegg, W.R.C.N.S., O.N. W-1396," n.d.; Service file for Clegg, Olive Irene, Memorandum from E. Lackey, for Canadian Pension Commission, to Director of Records, Canadian Agency, Imperial War Graves Commission, 12 March 1945. Some records, such as the memorandum by Lackey cite "tuberculosis and fecal fistula" as the official cause of death, while others such as the letter to the Administer of Estates simply list "military tuberculosis."

20 Pierson, *"They're Still Women After All,"* 169–87. As Pierson argues, the pregnancy rumours were false, revealing more concern about the social consequences of women's new role than actual "immoral" behaviour.

21 Jacques Bernier, *Disease, Medicine and Society in Canada: A Historical Overview*, Canadian Historical Association Historical Booklet 63 (Ottawa: Canadian Historical Association, 2003), 21–23.

22 Toman, *An Officer and a Lady,* 130–33.
23 Ibid., 72–87; Keshen, *Saints, Sinners, and Soldiers,* 172–93; Christopher Dummitt, *The Manly Modern: Masculinity in Postwar Canada* (Vancouver: UBC Press, 2007), 127–37, 142–49; Amy Gangloff, "Safety in Accidents: Hugh DeHaven and the Development of Crash Injury Studies," *Technology and Culture* 54, 1 (January 2013): 42–53.
24 LAC, RG 24, vol. 25997, Service file for Grant, Jean, Court of Inquiry – Death for Pte. Grant, J., 20 January 1945; Conrod, *Athene, Goddess of War,* 260.
25 Andrew Iarocci, "Dangerous Curves: Canadian Drivers and Mechanical Transport in Two World Wars," in Hayes, Bechthold, and Symes, *Canada and the Second World War,* 121, 127–29; Toman, *An Officer and a Lady,* 75–76; Timothy Balzer, "'Canada's Roll of Honour': Controversy over Casualty Notification and Publication during the Second World War," *Canadian Military History* 20, 1 (2011): 36; Daniel Byers, *The Zombie Army: The Canadian Army and Conscription in the Second World War* (Vancouver: UBC Press, 2016), 144; Keshen, *Saints, Sinners, and Soldiers,* 129; Mary Teresa Ziegler, *We Serve That Men May Fly: The Story of the Women's Division Royal Canadian Air Force* (Hamilton, ON: RCAF (WD) Association, 1973), 127.
26 Editorial, *New Glasgow News,* quoted in extract of Rome, as reproduced in Veterans Affairs Canada, Photo of Rose Goodman.
27 LAC, RG 24, vol. 27614, Service file for Goodman, Rose Jette, Officer or Airmen – Report on accidental or self-inflicted injuries or immediate death therefrom for Goodman, Rose Jette, 27 January 1943.
28 "Lakeshore Woman Believed Killed in Crash," *Toronto Telegram,* 10 November 1943.
29 LAC, RG 24, vol. 28901, Service file for Watson, Irene, Official Royal Canadian Air Force casualty notification for Watson, Irene, 19 June 1944.
30 LAC, Service file for Floyd, Ruth, Memorandum from E. Lackey, CPC, to Deputy Minister, DND, 24 August 1946; LAC, Service file for Gyles, Annie Kathleen, Memorandum from E. Lackey, CPC, to Deputy Minister, DND, 31 May 1947.
31 LAC, Service file for Cooney, Patricia Jane, Memorandum from B. O'Meara, CPC, to the Officer i/c Records, DND (Army), 14 August 1942.
32 Dianne Dodd, "Canadian Military Nurse Deaths in the First World War," *Canadian Bulletin of Medical History* 34, 2 (2017): 340–47.
33 LAC, RG 24, vol. 27732, Service file for Heysel, Mary Kathryn, "Full Military Honors," undated newspaper clipping.
34 Editorial, *New Glasgow News,* quoted in extract of Rome, as reproduced in Veterans Affairs Canada, Photo of Rose Goodman.
35 "First Wren Dies on Overseas Duty," *Toronto Globe and Mail,* 29 May 1945.
36 "Girl Veteran Dies at Christie Street," *Toronto Daily Star,* 13 October 1945; Jane Nicholas, *The Modern Girl: Feminine Modernities, the Body, and Commodities in the 1920s* (Toronto: University of Toronto Press, 2015), 10–11.
37 LAC, RG 24, vol. 25896, Service file for Fowler, Florence May, Manager of Ordinary Claim Department Prudential Insurance Company of America to Administrator of Estates, DND, 11 June 1943.
38 LAC, Service file for Fowler, Florence May, Copy of Lieutenant R.G. Phelan on behalf of Lieutenant-Colonel L.M. Firth, Administrator of Estates, to Prudential Insurance Company of America, 15 June 1943.
39 LAC, Service file for Fowler, Florence May, Copy of Lieutenant R.G. Phelan on behalf of Lieutenant-Colonel L.M. Firth, Administrator of Estates, to Commanding Officer, CWAC, Ottawa, 15 June 1943.
40 LAC, Service file for Fowler, Florence May, Memorandum from Director of Admin to Administrator of Estates, 24 June 1943.

41 LAC, Service file for Clegg, Olive Irene, E. Ferris, Supervisor, Stenographic and Document Section, Department of Veterans Affairs, to the Secretary of the Naval Board, Naval Service Headquarters, 27 October 1944.

42 LAC, RG 24, vol. 25927, Service file for Gallant, Mary Margaret, Copy of Colonel L.M. Firth, Director of Estates, to Mrs. Mary M. Gallant, 11 April 1947; LAC, RG 24, vol. 25927, Service file for Gallant, Mary Margaret Copy of Colonel L.M. Firth, Director of Estates, to Mr. Reginald J. Gallant, 11 April 1947; LAC, RG 24, vol. 26057, Service file for Harkans, Mary Evelyn, Copy of letter sent on behalf of Brigadier A.R. Mortimore, Paymaster-General, to Mrs. Kathleen Moore, 21 July 1945.

43 Balzer, "'Canada's Roll of Honour,'" 32–33.

44 LAC, RG 24, vol. 27395, Service file for Young, Margaret Ada, Mrs. W.J. Young to DND (Army), 3 December 1945.

45 LAC, Service file for Young, Margaret Ada, Copy of Captain [blank] for Director of Estates to Mrs. W.J. Young, 10 January 1946.

46 LAC, RG 24, vol. 25990, Service file for Henry, Rosella Bernice, Copy of Mrs. Florence H. Ellis to Lieutenant Louise Leslie, 9 October 1945.

47 LAC, Service file for Henry, Rosella Bernice, Mrs. Florence Henry Ellis to DND, Estates Branch, 27 March 1946.

48 LAC, Service file for Henry, Rosella Bernice, Copy of Lieutenant Louise Leslie for CWAC to Mrs. F.H. Ellis, 25 October 1945; LAC, Service file for Henry, Rosella Bernice, Mrs. Florence Henry Ellis to DND (Army), 19 November 1945; LAC, Service file for Henry, Rosella Bernice, Copy of Lieutenant Louise Leslie to Mrs. Ellis, 28 August 1945.

49 Luc Capdevila and Danièle Voldman, *War Dead: Western Societies and the Casualties of War,* trans. Richard Veasey (Edinburgh: Edinburgh University Press, 2006), 52.

50 Veterans Affairs Canada, "Books of Remembrance," http://www.veterans.gc.ca/eng/remembrance/memorials/books; Commonwealth War Graves Commission – Official Site, "Find War Dead," https://www.cwgc.org/find/find-war-dead.

51 LAC, RG 24, vol. 24839, Service file for Bennett, Pamela Gladys, Copy of Wing Commander W.R. Gunn, RCAF Casualties Officer, for Chief of the Air Staff to Mrs. Gladys A. Bennett, 24 October 1955.

52 Allison and Hayward, *They Shall Grow Not Old,* 46, 364, 462, 798; Veterans Affairs Canada, "Sergeant (Women's Division) Pamela Gladys Bennett," 2019, http://www.veterans.gc.ca/eng/remembrance/memorials/canadian-virtual-war-memorial/detail/2622450?Pamela%20Gladys%20Bennett/. The quotation comes from Veterans Affairs Canada, "Sergeant (Women's Division) Pamela Gladys Bennett."

53 "First Wren Dies on Overseas Duty," *Toronto Globe and Mail,* 29 May 1945. For other examples, see LAC, Service file for Heysel, Mary Kathryn, "Full Military Honors"; and Conrod, *Athene, Goddess of War,* 260–63.

54 Privy Council Order 2374, 1 December 1919, quoted in Evans, "History of the Silver Cross Medal," 43.

55 LAC, RG 24, vol. 27024, Service file for Shearer, Agnes Jeanie, Copy of A.C. Chadwick for A/Director, War Service Records, to Mrs. Jeanine R. Shearer, 23 March 1948.

56 LAC, RG 24, vol. 26287, Service file for Labbé, Rita, Translation of letter from Mrs. Julia (Roméo) Labbé to Minister of National Defence, 14 May 1945.

57 For example, see LAC, RG 24, vol. 26931, Service file for Roney, Lillian LeVerna, Secretary Treasurer for Village of Imperial, Saskatchewan, to Officer in Charge of Records, DND (Army), 7 June 1943; and LAC, RG 24, vol. 24794, Service file for Bamsey, Dora Marion, Wing Commander T.K. McDougall, RCAF Records Officer, to Officer i/c Records, DND, 15 July 1949.

58 LAC, RG 24, vol. 26417, Service file for McBride, Mona Ethelyn, Copy of Form H.Q. 1772-45-8; Julie Summers, *Remembered: The History of the Commonwealth War Graves Commission* (London: Merrell in association with the Commonwealth War Graves Commission, 2007), 22–28, 37–38.
59 LAC, Service file for Henry, Rosella Bernice, H/Major R. Essex, District Chaplain (P) for M.D. 13, to War Graves Commission, National Defence Headquarters, 5 July 1946; LAC, Service file for Henry, Rosella Bernice, F.[?]B. Radin for Colonel C.L. Laurin, Director of Records for Adjutant-General, to Mrs. Florence H. Ellis, 14 August 1946.
60 LAC, RG 24, vol. 25272, Service file for Buchanan, Emile [sic], Form listing Awards – Canadian Army (Active) (1484) for Buchanan, Emilie, n.d.
61 Evans, "History of the Silver Cross Medal," 47.
62 Veterans Affairs Canada, "Sergeant (Women's Division) Pamela Gladys Bennett."
63 Conrod, *Athene, Goddess of War,* 259–61.
64 Ibid., 260.
65 Allison and Hayward, *They Shall Grow Not Old,* 21–22, 42, 46, 82, 122, 169, 236, 270, 320, 358, 364, 395, 403, 462, 543, 564, 584, 675, 679, 684, 690, 788, 793, 798, 804, 828.
66 LAC, RG 24, vol. 26069, Service file for Hart, Margaret Victoria, Bev Huston to National Archives of Canada, 16 March 1994.
67 Bev Huston, "Huston: Everything They Fought For," Opinion, *Alaska Highway News,* 6 November 2014, http://www.alaskahighwaynews.ca/opinion/columnists/huston-everything-they-fought-for-1.1526958.

12

"Keep Your Mind on Your Job"

Women Workers, Beauty Culture, and Dangerous Bodies in the Wartime Industrial Workplace

Sarah Van Vugt

In a 1942 newsletter editorial written specifically for war plant employees, columnist Mildred Heywood argued that the uniforms of female munitions workers granted women a special kind of appeal:

> The woman war worker. How very important she is to-day. In bandana, smock and flat-heeled shoes each girl looks very much like the girl beside her. But they are all in uniform and every uniformed person acquires a certain glamour. Most people agree that the woman war worker belongs to the élite as far as labour's social scale is concerned. Two years ago we might have thought twice about entering a factory to work. To-day, we are proud of the work we are doing in one of Canada's largest factories.[1]

Heywood suggested that the woman war worker was an alluring and important figure, despite her plain, dour uniform. This glamorous gloss legitimized a symbol that also represented gendered wartime disruption.

During the Second World War, the beautiful woman war worker became an iconic visual symbol of the complications that wartime labour created for prevailing ideas about gender in Canada. Her practical uniform and safety gear, as well as the occasionally rough nature of the factory environment, existed in tension with ideas about womanliness and beauty. Canadians closely scrutinized women workers for any evidence of ugliness or manliness, and they strongly encouraged these women to maintain their femininity. By making an active effort to beautify, women could continue looking feminine and feeling attractive, thus retaining their heterosexual appeal. This would minimize the wartime disruption to patriarchal power, preserve ideas about the connection between beauty and womanhood, and ensure the future formation of procreative families based on heterosexual coupling. Worries about the bodies of women workers were not limited to concerns about protecting them and keeping them beautiful, however. War plant management also perceived women's bodies as potentially dangerous: women's vanity might lead them to disregard safety rules, and their beauty and sex appeal might distract male workers. In the wartime industrial workplace, women's bodies seemed to pose a gendered risk, one inflected by the youth, whiteness, class status, heterosexuality, fertility, femininity, and beauty of imagined, idealized female bodies. Young, white, middle-class women's presence in the industrial workplace raised the spectre of a twofold peril: they were both vulnerable to existing workplace dangers and creators of new ones. For this reason, plant management and Canadian society more broadly framed them as requiring care and containment in equal measure.

Even though working-class women had long been involved in factory labour, their influx into industrial jobs during the Second World War was viewed as novel. While the majority came from working-class backgrounds, public imagery and discourse imagined women war workers as mostly middle class, patriotically and temporarily joining the workforce for the first time. This inaccurate but powerful narrative sparked concerns: Was the rough and masculine world of the factory an appropriate place for women? Should society accept them as munitions workers? Would their bodies become more masculine, and less beautiful, as a result of their labour? Evidence in print media, including war plant newsletters (*The Commando*, *Fusilier*, and *Mosquito*), magazines (*Chatelaine*, *Maclean's*, and *Saturday Night*), and newspapers (*The Globe and Mail* and *The Toronto Star*), suggests that as long as women workers remained attractive and feminine, their labour would be patriotically sanctioned and socially acceptable. For this reason, visual representations frequently emphasized their womanly bodies and heterosexual appeal, diverting attention from their role as labourers. Cartoons and poems framed them as unique and temporary workers whose most notable qualities were glamour and beauty.

In response to concerns that war work could masculinize women, and to make it seem more appealing, an iconic visual representation of the woman war worker emerged in both Canada and the United States. She was depicted as young, white, and conventionally beautiful, often wearing blue coveralls or slacks and a blouse, as well as a bandana or kerchief over her hair – perhaps the most iconic element of the war worker look. Print media presented a remarkably consistent image: an hourglass figure (or at least a trim waist), tidy, styled hair (one perfect curl often emerging from the bandana), clean, soft hands (frequently with polished nails), and an attractive face enhanced by cosmetics. The pervasiveness of this imagery underscored the existence of simmering fears about the potentially transformative effects of war work. These images reassured North American society about the appropriateness of women's industrial war work, while pressuring women workers to beautify themselves and match the symbolic standard. Bodily beauty was considered a respectable and worthy goal in wartime: women were regularly reminded that being beautiful was itself an act of patriotism. Magazine advertising for beauty products featured headlines such as "Your Country Needs Your Loveliness," "Beauty Answers the Bugle," and "The Brave

Deserve the Fairest."[2] Even during a period of global crisis, women's physical beauty was framed as a tangible and valuable contribution to the war effort.

The iconic, beautiful woman war worker appeared in a variety of print media, including newspapers, magazines, and advertisements, as well as company newsletters created by and for individual war plants. Although evidence from newspapers and magazines informs the analysis in this chapter, it focuses on the newsletters of three plants, all in southern Ontario: Defence Industries Limited (DIL), a shell-filling plant with over nine thousand employees at its peak, located in Ajax; the General Engineering Company, or GECO, which produced fuses in Scarborough; and DeHavilland Aircraft, which built Mosquito airplanes in Toronto.[3] DIL published *The Commando,* GECO the *Fusilier,* and DeHavilland the *Mosquito*. Managers and employers supervised the creation of these newsletters, with employees explicitly identified as the intended audience: for example, the front cover of the *Fusilier* always carried the subtitle "Issued in the interests of employees by the General Engineering Company (Canada) Limited, Purveyors of head-aches for axis assassins."[4] Combined with magazines and newspapers, these newsletters clearly show the celebration of beauty culture in war plants but also reveal the conflicted position of the woman worker's body: simultaneously vulnerable to the dangers of the factory floor and a threat to the safety of men.

Unlike the remarkably homogeneous images of war workers that appeared in print media, real women workers and their wartime experiences were diverse – the Jewish Canadian women discussed in Chapter 5 of this volume are only one example. As they accepted factory jobs in unusually high numbers, women encountered both special opportunities and gendered challenges.[5] The woman war worker was a complex figure, shaped not only by her gender and job, but also by class, sexuality, age, race, and family status. Joan Sangster, Pamela Sugiman, Susanne Klausen, and Takaia Larsen show that the beauty of women workers in non-munitions industries was closely scrutinized.[6] Helen Smith, Pamela Wakewich, and Patrizia Gentile's work addresses the engagement of women workers with ideas and expectations about feminine bodies. While Smith and Wakewich use oral histories to connect women's diverse perceptions of their experiences as wartime workers, Gentile contextualizes questions about women and beauty in wartime by considering them alongside the wider history of beauty and beauty pageants in Canada.[7] The present discussion reveals the ways that the beautiful and feminine bodies of women workers were central both to their perceived value and to what made them dangerous in the eyes of plant management and Canadian society more broadly. Applying the insights of body history shows that women workers were viewed primarily through the lens of their bodies and that beauty culture was a major force in war plants.

Uniforms represented an undeniable tension between the desire for women to be beautiful and the need for safety in the plants. Because they played such a visible role in reshaping the woman war worker's body, factory uniforms and other safety gear became a key focus of debate among ordinary Canadians around labour and beauty in the context of wartime work. Coveralls, safety shoes, hair coverings, and even specific undergarments were all common requirements for war workers, but these concessions to safety were perceived to impair women's ability to perform femininity. Furthermore, factory labour in munitions plants menaced women's bodies in other ways: to shapeless, masculine clothing could be added dirty or grimy hands, rough skin, and flat, dry hair. In other words, war work threatened to transform women's bodies in a variety of unacceptable ways.[8]

Although the appearance of work uniforms might seem a trifling concern during a time of global conflict, the femininity and appearance of women war workers attracted national attention. In a 1945 episode of the CBC Radio program *Servicemen's Forum,* which dealt with women's work, several Canadian servicewomen, and one man, debated the looks of women workers. In serviceman Roy Robertson's opinion, factory attire *did* make women less attractive: "A lot of women working in factories are becoming too masculine," he asserted. "You see them walking down the street in a pair of coveralls and a dirty old turban wound around their head, and carrying a chipped old lunch pail. And while I've no grudge against women working, I'd like to see them retain their femininity. Of course that's just speaking for a mere male."[9] Both women's uniforms and their dirtiness were, apparently, objectionable. Notably, Robertson complains not just about women's masculinity, but also about a perceived lack of care and attention to appearance: he describes both the turban and the pail as old, and the pail as chipped. Like many others, Robertson associated femininity with the exertion of substantial thought and effort in crafting the proper physical presentation. Only constant vigilance in this regard could keep factory work from unsexing women's bodies.

While Robertson felt that women's factory attire was unattractive, or at least unorthodox, employers and social commentators in print media frequently suggested that women looked good in their workwear. Failing that, they at least tried to reassure prospective female employees that industrial safety clothing could be pretty, fun, and fashionable. The frequency of such cheerful assurances suggests the equally persistent concern that Canadian women's bodies were being masculinized by their war jobs and perhaps also a shared conviction that the uniforms were far from attractive.

The tension between seeing factory uniforms and safety gear as either ugly-but-necessary or safe-and-feminine persisted throughout the war years, alongside the claim that women cared how they looked – and, perhaps more importantly, that their appearance affected their ability to work. Lotta Dempsey and other journalists made this claim in several magazine articles. In a September 1942 *Chatelaine* article featuring women's descriptions of their war work, Dempsey reported that

> they talk about smart uniforms to work in, and do better when they have them. And about comfortable rest-rooms where they can relax, and wash and make-up before they go off duty. And the hair-dos and pretty dresses they wear after work. And how they wish everybody would realize that they wear their slacks to work to save time for the job.[10]

Commenting on the differences between male and female workers in 1943, Dempsey asserted, "How a woman looks is a matter of concern because it affects her efficiency."[11] In *Chatelaine*'s special September 1942 war worker issue, Jean Alexander wrote confidently about working women's continuing attractiveness: "What if they do wear slacks and shirts and bandannas, instead of skirts and slips! That doesn't mean that our women in war industry have lost interest in keeping up appearances. Far from it! They know that health, cleanliness, good looks and careful grooming are just as essential to them now as in former days."[12] In loudly dismissing the suggestion that war work was undermining femininity and eroding beauty, Canadian media communicated the actual depth of concern.

While print media uniformly praised workers' appearance and explained away any evidence of problematic masculinity, the women themselves reacted in diverse ways to the rules around workwear. Oral history suggests that women who worked in factories held complex and conflicting perspectives on safety gear. In her study of Ontario auto workers, Pamela Sugiman documents the ways in which women at General Motors pushed back against the rules on workplace attire, from spending time on the shop floor styling one another's hair to ignoring or subverting increasingly rigid requirements to keep all hair covered.[13] In their work on CanCar, a Canadian aircraft manufacturer, Smith and Wakewich report that women recalled struggles around uniforms and instances of resistance, as well as examples of pleasure and the exercise of agency. As at many other plants, at Cancar, Smith and Wakewich's interviewees recalled that hair and hair coverings were a primary site of tension and resistance between women workers and management; some women resisted by wearing their prescribed hats and headscarves in unapproved ways, even though they might be sent home as a result.[14] In her interviews with women who worked at DeHavilland Aircraft and Victory Aircraft, Valerie Endicott discovered that some did not feel particularly constrained by their unfeminine uniforms, though others recalled co-workers who tried to dress in a more sexy and feminine way – actions that provoked censure from supervisors.[15] Still others felt that factory uniforms were part of their much-needed patriotic service and happily wore whatever was assigned to them.[16] The complexity and diversity of women's reactions to factory uniforms remind us that ideals, though powerful, could be ignored.

Celebrating women's uniforms as fashionable and interesting may also have been intended to counter the possibility that ugly uniforms discouraged women from pursuing munitions employment. In August 1943, attempting to showcase work uniforms in a lighthearted and fun way, the Toronto Local Council of Women, the National Selective Service, and Toronto War Industries sponsored a war industries show in Toronto's Eaton Auditorium. Promotional material promised that the display would answer women's questions about wartime employment, including "What does a war worker wear?" by demonstrating "what the well-dressed war worker should wear at work."[17] The day after the show, a *Toronto Globe and Mail* article described this part of the event as "a fashion parade of war-plant uniforms and off-duty dresses." The event also gave job-seekers a chance to meet women with war jobs attired in their workwear, including representatives from GECO, who dressed in "smart two-piece outfits of immaculate white."[18] Modelling cleanliness, femininity, and beauty, these GECO employees no doubt proved that accepting war work did not necessitate abandoning feminine allure.

To defuse the gendered threat posed by safety clothing, the coveralls and jumpsuits worn by women were tailored to differ markedly from the men's versions. When possible, women workers were assigned dresses or skirts to wear – this was most frequently an option for laboratory, transportation, and inspection staff. Women's coveralls had narrower waists than men's did, and although men often wore caps, women's hair coverings were more elaborate and customizable. The expertly tied bandana became a key element of the iconic war worker look, and it allowed women to exercise some control over their appearance on the job without breaking safety regulations. A *Toronto Globe and Mail* article even credited the women workers of the John Inglis Company with developing the signature style. Women at Inglis were assigned to wear hairnets attached with elastic, and then fishnet turbans, both of which were unpopular. Cotton bandanas, in contrast, were more palatable.[19] The remedy, then, to the challenge of ugly, unfeminine uniforms was to reframe, reimagine, and tweak women's apparel until it could be argued that it was uniquely womanly, reducing the tension between beauty and safety. With care and attention to the shape of uniforms and the styling of bandanas, the threat to gender norms posed by women's factory attire could be reduced.

In tandem with efforts to construct women workers' uniforms and safety gear as appropriate and even pretty, plants also deployed beauty culture as a solution to the gendered disruptions of wartime. Women workers were tasked with caring for their bodies and enthusiastically working to achieve a more feminine appearance. Factory managers presented beautification efforts, including an on-site hair salon, company-sponsored glamour classes, and beauty advice columns in the plant newsletter, as ways to defuse the explosive potential of factory work to defeminize. Encouraging women workers to care about and pursue beauty and femininity also extended expectations about middle-class women's interests, activities, and consumption habits to working-class women. At DIL, for example, a beauty salon was opened and it operated on the plant grounds, focusing specifically on beauty and hair treatments for its women workers.[20] The shop offered oil steam treatments, oil shampoos, manicures, and finger waves (a fashionable hairstyle), treatments which proved popular enough that they were awarded as prizes in the bingo games played by women workers living in residence at DIL.[21] The existence of a beauty shop in a gated plant compound, directly serving female staff, may be compelling evidence that women's bodies were perceived to require active specialist care to overcome the gendered risk of war work. Alternatively, the salon can be seen as proof that the workers themselves valued convenient access to a beauty business: perhaps it served as a unique draw for valuable employees living far from the conveniences of a larger city.[22] Proprietor Winnie Heyd was an experienced beautician who studied and trained in Toronto before coming to DIL. To "learn all she could about her prospective customers," Heyd worked on the line before opening her shop. She discovered that, despite the supposedly fashionable and protective effects of the iconic war worker's bandana, it could have disadvantages: "working among explosive fumes and having a bandana tied tightly on the head for eight hours does not tend to keep the hair attractive."[23] Echoing Heyd's concerns about the bandana, and underscoring the potential risk war work posed to a woman's appearance, the September 1943 issue of *The Commando* reminded women at length that the bandana should entirely cover their hair, lest ill effects ensue: "Your bandanna is meant to cover all your hair, not just a part of it. If you continue to leave your hair uncovered, it is very apt to become dull and discolored and may even fall out. Beauty begins with your hair."[24]

In response to the bandana-hair problem, Heyd consulted an expert and apparently found a crème solution that resulted in successful styling. Professional hair care helped to erase the evidence of long shifts spent in safety clothes, at least on a woman's so-called crowning glory. Heyd's beauty shop, then, addressed problems particular to women war workers' bodies and created by their industrial work. While prosaically serving as reading material for those waiting for service at the salon, company newsletters highlighted the threat that women's work posed to their bodies and advanced beauty culture as the solution. The DIL, GECO, and DeHavilland newsletters regularly covered beauty issues, reflecting a perceived interest in and undoubted public scrutiny of women war workers' bodies and beauty.[25] Between October 1943 and April 1944, *The Commando* published five articles on the theme of "Beauty on the Job." Appearing on the "Of Interest to Women" page, the brief columns provided cautions and advice about protecting, maintaining, and improving women war workers' bodies, including the hands, nails, face, and hair. They expressed both concern about the damaging effects of war work and confidence that with a little effort and some helpful tips, women could look and feel feminine and attractive despite their labour. Beautifying the war worker, the articles argued, was an arduous but valuable and enjoyable activity. "Might as well face it," one article told women workers, "you must go in for a more rigid and faithful beauty routine than you kept when you were ladies of leisure. Your skin and hands are taking a beating all the time you're on the job, so you must acquire new beauty habits to ward off the ill effects."[26] The first "Beauty on the Job" column, focusing on skincare, explained the destructive effects of "millions of flying particles of dust and abrasives that fill the air of most factories," and recommended frequent washing and the use of "protectives" as remedies.[27]

Subsequent installments detailed other parts of an ideal war worker's beauty regimen and provided tips, information, and encouragement. In a discussion of nail lacquer, readers were advised that, though some beauty products had become scarce because of the war, "there shouldn't be any fingernail dimout if we practice a few economies." These included, for example, tightly closing the bottle to avoid waste. Creativity was also encouraged: partial bottles of undesirable colours could simply be saved and then mixed together – "stir well, and pour yourself a brand-new shade."[28] Just as with foods, clothing, and other domestic materials, women were reminded to exercise their creativity and resourcefulness in wartime beauty endeavours. A column on hair problems suggested treatments for both dry and oily hair, as well as frequent brushing to "make your hair a shining glory."[29] Another piece was dedicated to beauty masks for those who "want to look 20 when you feel like 100." It offered recipes that included oatmeal, almond meal, milk, lemon juice, and peroxide, explained application procedures, and concluded, "go see if you don't find a more radiant vision in the mirror. A beauty on the job."[30] Each article shared a common tone and perspective on beauty as a pleasurable pursuit, suggesting that women would be happier when they looked good.

The "Beauty on the Job" series went beyond facial cleansers and hair treatments, also tackling the topic of colour cosmetics. In the March 1944 issue, readers were reminded that "nothing is as bad as it seems when you look as pretty as you can in the right make-up" and were urged, "aside from the real protective benefits choose make-up to glorify your own beauty and lift your spirits."[31] Encouraging the use of foundation, face powder, rouge, lipstick, brow pencils, and mascara, one column promised that makeup could protect skin from "the dirt and grime of the day," as well as providing a psychological boost and increased confidence. The idea that makeup could be transformative, protective, and able to promote self-esteem was not unique to the Second World War or to women war workers.[32] However, the inclusion of beauty tips and cosmetics advice in a staff newsletter suggests that women were expected to maintain their physical beauty, despite the additional challenges and stresses of wartime.

Advice and hands-on instruction in beauty culture were also available to war workers in classes offered as part of plant recreational programs. DIL announced a multi-session "Seven Steps to Beauty" course, sponsored by the Ajax Health and Culture Club.[33] A quiz in *The Commando* promoted the course and signalled contemporary beauty ideals at the same time, asking readers,

1. Is your hairdo suitable to your particular type?
2. Are you wearing clothes that make you look your best, giving you that slender, chic appearance?
3. Are you being kind to your skin?
4. Do you know everyday, proper etiquette?
5. Do you possess grace and poise?
6. Do you know what gives you personal charm?
7. Do you know how to develop your personality?[34]

Organized by Mr. H.S. Rumball of the DIL Recreation Department and open to "all girls in Residence and all women in the Village," the course promised to reveal "how to make yourself more attractive" through presentations by professionals and experts.[35] The establishment of a beauty course may show that women workers were expected to try to protect their bodies from the gendered threat of war work by seeking to look beautiful and glamorous. Alternatively, we can see beauty courses offered as part of a workplace recreational program as evidence of the power that women exerted as valuable staff whom the plants were keen to retain: to satisfy these employees, the plants made space for beauty.

Like DIL, Scarborough's GECO also offered "glamour classes," which combined instruction in fitness and beauty. In the 23 October 1943 issue of GECO's *Fusilier*, the advertisement that announced the classes presumed the importance of an attractive body. "Let's be honest, girls, we're all looking for it!" the author enthused. "Personality – beauty – poise – in the movies they call it 'glamour.' You've got to have glowing vitality, a graceful carriage and radiant good health to qualify."[36] The assertion that all women wanted to acquire glamour signals broad pressure to participate in beauty culture and an association between femininity and attractiveness. At the cost of ten cents per class, women could take part in "easy, graceful motions that sooth [sic] tired limbs and relax muscles" – with the important qualification that the exercises would be neither strenuous nor "muscle-forming."[37]

Despite constant reminders to beautify and critical attention to any hint of masculinization, the beautiful bodies of women workers were also subject to suspicion and stigma. Ironically, even while being encouraged to participate in beauty culture, women workers were warned against caring *too* much about their appearance: vanity could fuel a dangerous disregard for safety rules. The belief that women would prioritize looking good over being safe suggests that their bodies were perceived as a gendered risk in the industrial workplace. This manifested primarily as concern about accidents related to their hair. Women's apparent dislike of unattractive head coverings led to frequent reminders about hair and safety. Though there is some evidence that women workers resisted regulations by adjusting their bandanas to show some carefully styled locks, prescriptive safety materials contained exaggerated warnings about the dangers of women's hair at work.[38] In the April 1945 issue of *The Commando,* the "Safety Sam Sez" column argued that unsafe work practices were akin to gambling: "There's only one way to beat the odds – protect yourself and do things the safe way. And remember poor Lulu: Lulu Dripp was a gorgeous blonde; No cap confined her hair, A drill machine peeled Lulu's bean, Now Lulu wears a spare."[39] The amusing tone of the poem is at odds with the grisly nature of the scalping accident.[40] By keeping her "gorgeous blonde" hair uncovered, Lulu risked being violently disfigured. Warnings, like this poem, reminded women to observe uniform-related safety regulations but also connected factory floor accidents specifically with attractive women and their hair-related vanity.

In the DeHavilland *Mosquito,* safety cartoons and poems warned readers about strikingly similar accidents. In one issue, a poem in the "Safety Lines" column read, "A cute little lady named Hannah / Who discarded her scarlet bandannah / Got close to a pulley / And her hair, though quite wooly / Was shorn in a horrible mannah."[41] Similarly, in a three-panel cartoon, also published in the *Mosquito,* a woman with long blonde hair stands beside a sign that reads "Cover your hair"; the second panel shows her screaming, her hair trapped in a machine. In the final panel, nearly bald, she looks at a sign that says, "Don't comb your hair inside plant."[42] Another issue of the *Mosquito* identified *blonde* hair as especially risky, claiming that "blonde people, particularly women, store up more electricity than brunettes." An anecdote about a tire manufacturer whose facility was prone to fires caused by static electricity followed, with the conclusion that "a blonde girl worker was the cause, and upon her removal and the removal of the other blondes from this Department, the fires have ceased." The same article reminded readers that "girls in Canadian shell filling plants" were required to wear only cotton underwear, not silk, to reduce the risk of static sparks.[43] While male workers did not need special reminders about keeping their bodies safe, women's hair, underwear, and desire for beauty were depicted as uniquely dangerous and gendered forces in the workplace.[44]

Gendered safety hyperbole did not end with warnings about hair-related disfigurement. Instead, women's bodies were perceived to be so alien, and so inherently sexual, that just by existing in the workplace they constituted a distracting danger to men. A safety poster in the *Fusilier* speaks directly to male workers: it shows a deep-sea diver whose entire body and head are covered by a diving suit and helmet, sitting next to a wrecked ship at the bottom of a body of water. A cable rises from the diver's suit to the surface, and a fish severs this line, oxygen bubbles escaping as a result. On the diver's lap sits a topless mermaid with light flowing hair. The mermaid and diver have their arms around one

Figure 12.1

This 1943 cartoon from the *Fusilier* reminds both male and female war workers that women's bodies could be dangerously distracting. | Archives of Ontario, General Engineering Company (Canada) fonds, F 2082, box 3, folder F2082-1-1-11, "Carelessness Brings Trouble," GECO *Fusilier: A Powder Magazine* 2, 11 (28 August 1943): 4.

another. The caption drives home the visual point: "Carelessness brings trouble / keep your mind on your job." In this image, the gender roles are clear: the male diver is distracted; the female mermaid is the distractor. The implications are anything but subtle: attractive women could "bring trouble" to the workplace. The power of alluring female bodies, combined with assumptions about the enthusiastic heterosexuality of all workers, comprised a potentially dangerous situation. Thus, the greatly increased presence of women (often young and single) in wartime factories produced not only repeated encouragement for women to keep themselves beautiful, but also frequent reminders that their male co-workers must be vigilant against the distractions of that beauty.

Sending a related message about men's gaze and the temptation of looking at women's bodies, a comic in the *Mosquito* shows a blonde woman whose sweater is caught in a machine. As it unravels from the hem upward, five smiling men stand by and watch, their hands in their pockets or on their hips. The alarmed woman asks for help: "Well, don't just stand there. Do something!" In this comic, the men's interest in seeing a woman worker's attractive body stops them from helping her remove her tangled, disintegrating clothing from a machine – they *want* her sweater to continue unraveling and expose her further. Their heterosexual desire is so powerful that they choose to put a fellow worker at risk rather than give up the opportunity to leer at a young and beautiful female body. This image, intended as humour, highlights the fact that, despite uniforms and bandanas, women workers were viewed through the lens of their bodies – as sexualized women first and workers second.

In a 1945 issue of the *Fusilier,* the connection between men's attraction to women and the potential for workplace casualties is made even more directly and dramatically. A cartoon, accompanied by a poem, identifies flirting as the cause of one man's careless accident. In the black and white drawing, a man approaches a blind corner in a hallway. He looks behind him, smiling, with eyebrows raised, at a woman worker wearing a white uniform and turban. She returns his gaze. Around the corner, another worker, also a woman, approaches. All three are moving quickly – lines around each figure suggest speed. A poem makes the meaning unmistakable: "Giddy Jack Horner / Barged round a corner / Heedless of danger ahead / If while he was flitting / He'd attended his knitting / He'd've avoided the man in red." The *Mosquito* addressed the same theme in its safety cartoons. One example in its "I. Maida Mistake" series (subtitled "The Plant Menace") shows a male employee stepping off the top of a false staircase because he is looking at a pretty worker. A speech bubble indicates he is saying, "M-m-m-m Gosh! Nice eh?" A woman's face and upper torso, including large breasts, appears at the bottom right. The drawing is accompanied by an explanatory verse: "Everyone knew he'd say 'GEE GOSH' / When he met with Dolly

Figure 12.2

This image from a 1945 issue of the *Mosquito* suggests the power of the male gaze and male desire, as well as the novelty and spectacle of women's bodies in the industrial workplace. | Archives of Ontario, Fred W. Hotson fonds, F 4531, box 3, file F 4531-25-2-6, "Well, Don't Just Stand There," *Mosquito* 3, 1 (1 August 1945): 8.

Dash, / But we didn't think he'd be in a spot / Where he'd fall and break his – er – Neck." Again, the message is clear: women war workers are perceived as real threats to the health and safety of male workers, whose heterosexuality and susceptibility to a pretty face or curvy figure are taken for granted.

Figure 12.3

In this 1945 cartoon from the *Fusilier,* a beautiful worker distracts her male co-worker so much that he ignores plant safety procedures and ends up causing an accident. | Archives of Ontario, General Engineering Company (Canada) fonds, F 2082, box 3, folder F 2082–1–1–11, "Giddy Jack Horner," GECO *Fusilier: A Powder Magazine* 4, 2 (14 May 1945): 8.

Both because they were vulnerable to the perils of work in a war plant and because the mere presence of their sexualized bodies could endanger their male colleagues, the bodies of women war workers were believed to create significant gendered risks in the wartime workplace. Journalists sunnily affirmed that, despite worries to the contrary, war work and factory uniforms were not masculinizing Canada's new womanpower. Recreation departments offered structured opportunities in which women could learn how to manage the additional challenges to beauty posed by industrial work and how to present themselves most attractively for themselves, their men, and their country. In the process, they were targeted by contradictory messages: they were to look attractive, but not so attractive that they distracted male co-workers. In short, their (beautiful) bodies were central

Figure 12.4

Another cartoon from the *Mosquito,* this one from 1942, highlights in especially stark terms the potential for the bodies of women workers to endanger their male counterparts. | Archives of Ontario, Fred W. Hotson fonds, F 4531, box 3, file F 4531–25–2–1, "I. Maida Mistake," *Mosquito* 1, 10 (November 1942): 5.

to how they were perceived and represented in the wartime workplace. Focusing on women as possessors and cultivators of beauty set them apart from male staff and constantly reminded everyone of the rigidity of the gender binary that prevailed during the period. Women might enter masculine spaces such as the factory and take on masculine jobs, but their bodies perpetually signalled their difference. The idea that women's bodies and beauty were a problematic presence in industrial settings added another dimension to arguments that they should vacate their factory jobs when male veterans returned at the end of the war. Their presence might be tolerated and accommodated during the crisis, but perhaps women workers were simply too dangerous to remain in factories in peacetime.

Notes

This essay is adapted from Sarah Van Vugt, Chapter 4, "'Through These Clocks Pass Canada's Most Glamorous War Workers': Beauty Culture in the Wartime Workplace," in "Beauty on the Job: Visual Representation, Bodies, and Canada's Female War Workers, 1939–1945" (PhD diss., University of Victoria, 2016).

1 Mildred Heywood "Midge," "Powder Puffs," *The Commando* 1, 3 (5 August 1942): 4.

2 "Your Country Needs Your Loveliness," Vita-Ray advertisement, *Saturday Night,* 13 March 1943, 22; "Beauty Answers the Bugle," Harriet Hubbard Ayer advertisement, *Saturday Night,* 6 March 1943, 28; "The Brave Deserve the Fairest," Dorel advertisement, *Saturday Night,* 3 October 1942, 22. Note that these ads are aimed at Canadian women in general, not specifically at war workers.

3 For DIL, see Ken Smith, *Ajax: The War Years, 1939/45* (Oshawa, ON: K. Smith, 1989), 4; Archie McDonald, ed., *A Town Called Ajax* (Ajax, ON: Ajax Historical Board, 1995), 34–36. For GECO, see "Introduction," Typescript, *The Story of Scarboro/Canada 1941 to 1945 Inclusive,* Allied War Corporation Project No. 4, Fonds 2, Series 1243, Subseries 5, File 1, Toronto City Archives. For DeHavilland, see Fred Hotson, *De Havilland in Canada* (Toronto: Canav Books, 1999); Fred Hotson, *The De Havilland Canada Story* (Toronto: Canav Books, 1983).

4 See, for example, Archives of Ontario (AO), Fred W. Hotson fonds, F 4531, box 3, folder F 4531-25-2-1, front cover, *Mosquito,* February 1942, 1.

5 Ruth Roach Pierson, *"They're Still Women After All": The Second World War and Canadian Womanhood* (Toronto: McClelland and Stewart, 1990); Jennifer Stephen, *Pick One Intelligent Girl: Employability, Domesticity, and the Gendering of Canada's Welfare State, 1939–1947* (Toronto: University of Toronto Press, 2007); Jeffrey A. Keshen, *Saints, Sinners, and Soldiers: Canada's Second World War* (Vancouver: UBC Press, 2004); Emily Spencer, *Lipstick and High Heels: War, Gender and Popular Culture* (Kingston, ON: Canadian Defence Academy Press, 2007).

6 Joan Sangster, *Earning Respect: The Lives of Working Women in Small-Town Ontario, 1920–1960* (Toronto: University of Toronto Press, 1995); Pamela Sugiman, *Labour's Dilemma: The Gender Politics of Auto Workers in Canada, 1937–1979* (Toronto: University of Toronto Press, 1994); Susanne Klausen, "The Plywood Girls: Women and Gender Ideology at the Port Alberni Plywood Plant, 1942–1991," *Labour/Le Travail* 41 (Spring 1998): 199–235; Takaia Larsen, "Sowing the Seeds: Women, Work and Memory in Trail, British Columbia during and after the Second World War" (Master's thesis, University of Victoria, 2007).

7 Helen Smith and Pamela Wakewich, "'Beauty and the Helldivers': Representing Women's Work and Identities in a Warplant Newspaper," *Labour/Le Travail* 44 (Fall 1999): 71–107; Helen Smith and Pamela Wakewich, "Regulating Body Boundaries and Health during the Second World War: Nationalist Discourse, Media Representations and the Experiences of Canadian Women War Workers," *Gender and History* 24, 1 (2012): 56–73; Helen Smith and Pamela Wakewich, "Trans/forming the Citizen Body in Wartime: National and Local Public Discourse on Women's Bodies and 'Body Work' for Women during World War II," in *Contesting Bodies and Nation in Canadian History,* ed. Patrizia Gentile and Jane Nicholas (Toronto: University of Toronto Press, 2013), 305–27; Patrizia Gentile, "Queen of the Maple Leaf: A History of Beauty Contests in Twentieth-Century Canada" (PhD diss., Queen's University, 2006).

8 Note that there was a similar debate concerning the uniforms of the Canadian Women's Army Corps and men's and women's roles in society more broadly during the war. See, for example, Pierson, *"They're Still Women,"* and Tina Davidson, "'A Woman's Right to Charm and Beauty': Maintaining the Feminine Ideal in the Canadian Women's Army Corps," *Atlantis* 26, 1 (Fall/Winter 2001): 45–54.

9 "What Is the Role of Women after the War?" *Servicemen's Forum*, CBC Radio, 22 March 1945, CBC archives, http://www.cbc.ca/archives/entry/second-world-war-women-after-the-war.
10 Lotta Dempsey, "What the Girls Say of the Job," *Chatelaine*, September 1942, 16.
11 Lotta Dempsey, "What They've Found Out about Us," *Chatelaine*, September 1943, 16.
12 Jean Alexander, "Keeping Fit for the Job," *Chatelaine*, September 1942, 29. It is ironic that Alexander described female war workers as "careerists," since deskilling and job segmentation meant most were unable to remain in the same fields after the war ended. Further, they were constantly framed as temporary workers, serving the war effort but ultimately destined for lives as homemakers.
13 Sugiman, *Labour's Dilemma*, 73–77. For more on how women exercised agency around factory uniforms, see Van Vugt, "'Through These Clocks,'" 195–203.
14 See Smith and Wakewich, "Regulating Body Boundaries," 63–64.
15 Valerie Endicott, "Woman's Place (was) Everywhere: A Study of Women Who Worked in Aircraft Production in Toronto during the Second World War," (Master's thesis, Ontario Institute for Studies in Education, 1991), 53–55.
16 See Van Vugt, "'Through These Clocks,'" especially 196–97 and 202–3.
17 "War Industries Display," *Toronto Globe and Mail*, 30 August 1943, 3.
18 "War Industries Display Is Challenge to Women," *Toronto Globe and Mail*, 31 August 1943, 10. Undoubtedly, their colour helped them to look especially clean, countering Robertson's concern about dirtiness.
19 "Munition Workers' 'Badge' of Skillfully Tied Bandana Originated in Toronto," *Toronto Globe and Mail*, 2 November 1942, 15.
20 "Powder Puffs," *The Commando* 1, 2 (20 July 1942): 4. Some American plants, such as Lockheed, also had on-site salons. See Melissa A. McEuen, *Making War, Making Women: Femininity and Duty on the American Home Front, 1941–1945* (Athens: University of Georgia Press, 2011), 168. There was also a salon at the Canadian Women's Army Corps training centre in Kitchener, Ontario. See Pierson, *"They're Still Women,"* 156.
21 "Ajax Beautician Solves Girls' Hair-Do Problem," *The Commando* 1, 10 (15 January 1943): 5; "Fran Sez," *The Commando* 1, 8 (5 December 1942): 8.
22 DIL was built on expropriated farmland. Workers either lived in an on-site compound or commuted from nearby communities.
23 "Ajax Beautician Solves Girls' Hair-Do Problem," 5.
24 "Keep Your Hair Covered," *The Commando* 2, 2 (September 1943): 5.
25 The employee newsletter for the John Inglis Company, *The Shotgun*, also included a regular fashion and beauty column, entitled "Pot Shots at Style and Beauty." David Sobel and Susan Meurer, *Working at Inglis: The Life and Death of a Canadian Factory* (Toronto: J. Lorimer, 1994), 73.
26 "Beauty on the Job," *The Commando* 2, 3 (October 1943): 5.
27 Ibid.
28 "Beauty on the Job," *The Commando* 2, 4 (November 1943): 5.
29 "Beauty on the Job," *The Commando* 2, 9 (April 1944): 5.
30 "Beauty on the Job," *The Commando* 2, 6 (January 1944): 5.
31 "Beauty on the Job," *The Commando* 2, 8 (March 1944): 5.
32 In her crucial book on beauty culture in America, Kathy Peiss writes, "Makeup promised personal transformation, a pledge that sounded deeply in American culture – from conversion experiences and temperance oaths to the appeals of medicine men and faith healers. Beauty culturists had proclaimed the mutual transformation of external appearance and inner well-being." Kathy Peiss, *Hope in a Jar: The Making of America's Beauty Culture* (New York: Henry Holt, 1999), 144.

33 "Girls Take Keen Interest in Seven Steps to Beauty," *The Commando* 2, 9 (April 1944): 5.
34 "Quiz Questions," *The Commando* 2, 8 (March 1944): 3.
35 "'Seven Steps to Beauty' Shows How to Make Yourself More Attractive," *The Commando* 2, 8 (March 1944): 4.
36 AO, General Engineering Company (Canada) fonds, F 2082, box 3, folder F 2082-1-1-11, "Classes Being Formed to Acquire 'Glamour,'" GECO *Fusilier: A Powder Magazine* 2, 15 (23 October 1943): 6.
37 For more on idealized women's athletic bodies, the emphasis on femininity and heterosexuality among female athletes, and especially the social preference for beauty over power in mid-twentieth-century women's sporting culture, see M. Ann Hall, *The Girl and the Game: A History of Women's Sport in Canada* (Toronto: University of Toronto Press, 2002), especially Chapter 4, "Sweetheart Heroines: Athletic and Lovely," 104–34.
38 For an American assessment of the value of and risk posed by women's hair in factory settings, including a poster series on hair and safety featuring actress Veronica Lake, see McEuen, *Making War, Making Women,* 166–71. For Canadian examples of resistance to wearing hair coverings, see Smith and Wakewich, "Regulating Body Boundaries," 64–65.
39 "Safety Sam Sez," *The Commando* 3, 9 (April 1945): 7.
40 For further documentation of gory hair-related wartime injuries, including scalping, see Sugiman, *Labour's Dilemma,* 75; and McEuen, *Making War, Making Women,* 167.
41 AO, Fred W. Hotson fonds, F 4531, box 3, file F 4531-25-2-4, Howard Pyke, "Safety Lines," *Mosquito* 1, 8 (1 December 1944): 7.
42 AO, Fred W. Hotson fonds, F 4531, box 3, file F 4531-25-2-6, "Hair Today and Gone Tomorrow," *Mosquito* 2, 5 (15 March 1945): 10.
43 AO, Fred W. Hotson fonds, F 4531, box 3, file F 4531-25-2-1, "Gentlemen Prefer Blondes?" *Mosquito* 1, 3 (April 1942): 8.
44 For another example of the same theme, see AO, Fred W. Hotson fonds, F 4531, box 3, file F 4531-25-2-2, "Think Safety," *Mosquito* 2, 1 (February 1943): 12.

Conclusion
Making the Best of It

Sarah Glassford and Amy Shaw

> *It was like a chunk out of my life that had no connection with anything that happened before or afterwards.*
>
> – Former member, Royal Canadian Air Force (Women's Division)[1]

For some women, the Second World War felt like an aberration, a period of heightened emotion and new actions and responsibilities that had little connection to what came before or after. The isolation and privations of the Great Depression and the domestic concerns of suburban motherhood during the baby boom both seemed far away from playing a personal role in the life-and-death struggles of democracy and fascism. The natural distance between war and peace was also increased by government and military policies that pushed women out of the workforce and closed down day nurseries when the conflict ended. Government policies were supported by advertising and popular sentiment that promoted a post-war return to "normalcy," which included reinstating women in their familiar domestic, maternal roles and limiting their options for work and public life. "Normal" family life, greatly reliant on the gender-appropriate behaviour of the heterosexual wife and mother at home, also became an ideological battleground in the Cold War between capitalist democracy and communism, which had emerged by 1947. The chapters in this collection demonstrate the significant degree to which post-war reconstruction and the return to normalcy were central elements in women's experiences of the Second World War. Many seem to have accepted this return to domestic life with little immediate regret.

A return to (so-called) normalcy may have been the general aim of Canadian and Newfoundland society, but it was neither desirable nor possible for everyone. Some women lamented the loss of their wartime independence and the rewards of meaningful employment, chafing under an enforced return to domestic roles. Others who lost family members, or saw them return home damaged in body, mind, or spirit, could not move smoothly into the post-war ideal of cheerful, competent, and highly gendered participation in the workforce and the raising of children. Nor did the ordeal of interned Japanese Canadians end with the Allies' defeat of imperial Japan. Denied permission to reconstitute their pre-war

Pacific coast communities, they were instead given the options of moving east of the Rockies or being "repatriated" to a devastated and (for many) unfamiliar Japan.[2] Also trying to rebuild in an unfamiliar place and with few supports were new immigrants to Canada. The war brides and their children were made much of, but they were outnumbered by refugees, mainly Europeans, who had been displaced by the destruction of their homelands or the geopolitical realignments that preceded, featured in, and followed the war years. Facing prejudice, financial strictures, and cultural differences from mainstream Canadian society, these newcomers encountered a lived reality that was a far cry from the popular image of post-war consumerism and suburban bliss.[3]

Even among those for whom ethnicity did not mean repression, and whose experience of the war adhered more closely to the patriotic narratives produced by the National Film Board of Canada, making a sharp distinction between "war" and "post-war" was sometimes impossible. In the realm of humanitarian

Figure C.1

Scottish war brides and children of members of the Newfoundland Overseas Forestry Unit pose with Lady Walwyn, wife of the governor (front row, fifth from left) at Government House in St. John's. Adjusting to Canadian society and peacetime married life after a whirlwind wartime romance could be challenging. | The Rooms, Provincial Archives Division, Newfoundland Tourist Development Board photograph collection, VA 15b–55.2.

work, the need for relief initially *increased* with the cessation of hostilities, as the extent of civilian suffering became apparent and the former war zones were once again accessible. For years afterward, Mennonite women continued their support for refugees and people displaced by the war. Canadian Red Cross Corps members stayed in Europe and Britain to attend to the needs of sick and wounded troops, former POWs, civilians, and war brides until 1947.[4] The home front consumer and domestic activities that marked many women's contribution to the conflict also carried over into the post-war period. And despite the push for women to return to domestic life, some managed to parlay their experience and qualifications gained through voluntary, paid, or military work into new employment opportunities. In other words, female experiences of the war were not always governed by the temporal boundaries of the actual conflict. The war had many fronts, and it did not end for everyone in August 1945.

The Second World War was a time of tension and contradiction for many Canadian women and girls – some of them more visible in retrospect, others readily apparent at the time. Interviewed in the late 1980s, one former Canadian airwoman explained, "it used to gnaw at my conscience that I was having such a good time because there was a war on – it could never have happened otherwise – and because of the war, other people were dying and suffering horrors beyond my imagining. It seemed a terrible price to pay for my happiness."[5] This sense of guilt for her access to fun and adventure was a significant part of her emotional experience of the war. When historians consider whether women's wartime work led to expanded opportunities in the longer term – whether the Second World War was beneficial for them – that guilt should not be overlooked. In the first place, it is a curious question to ask. Even when the war is understood as necessary, it must also be seen as a catastrophically terrible moment in human history. Millions died horrible deaths; others lived through brutal violence and inhumanity, lost loved ones, or saw them permanently impaired. Families and communities were destroyed, interned, uprooted. The war laid bare the worst in human nature – its cruelty, violence, and intolerance – even as it also called forth humanity's better qualities of compassion, courage, and endurance. Any gains that it might have conferred on North American women and girls were purchased at an extraordinarily high price.

Perhaps the only way to make sense of such contrasts – the thrill of adventure and of meaningful new opportunities alongside destruction and crushing grief – is to regard the Second World War not as a single event, but as millions of smaller ones, tragedies and triumphs large and small orbiting around the nucleus of a set of geopolitical events like so many electrons. If we set aside the notion of the war as a simple narrative of good or bad, liberation or oppression, the many contradictions, tensions, and paradoxes inherent in its repercussions may appear more clearly. In terms of its impact on women and girls, the war can be understood in much the same way that Charles Dickens famously described the French Revolution: "It was the best of times, it was the worst of times ... it was the season of Light, it was the season of Darkness, it was the spring of hope, it was the winter of despair."[6] It was a complicated six years, and whether, on balance, a person's experience of it leaned more strongly toward positive or negative depended not only on her membership in various communities, but also upon her individual circumstances and personality.

Ruth Pierson's groundbreaking monograph, *"They're Still Women After All,"* has shaped the Canadian historical conversation about women and the Second World War for decades. Her conclusion – that the war did not usher in greater equality for women – challenged the widely accepted narrative of the day, which linked demonstrations of female ability in the 1940s to the women's liberation movement of the 1970s. Pierson showed that accommodations for women's war work were limited and always intended to be temporary, and her analysis of government discourse around women and women's issues highlighted regressive and sexist attitudes.[7] More recently, with the benefit of greater distance from the events, some historians have wondered if Pierson's definition of what constituted positive change for women was perhaps too stark. Jeffrey Keshen notes that the messages women received were more varied than the limited changes emphasized by the government:

> Media content and government propaganda not only influenced but also reflected popular trends and ideas. They lauded women for successfully assuming unconventional and highly skilled roles in the workplace and the military, as well as for running all aspects of the wartime home in the absence of men and managing monumental volunteer activities. Furthermore, both during and after the war, women often stressed their sense of accomplishment, growing confidence, importance, and independence.[8]

And if most women returned to the domestic sphere when the war ended, they nevertheless raised daughters who were far less comfortable with the idea of centring their career ambitions around homemaking. Of course, it is difficult to be precise about cause and effect. But treating the activism of the 1960s and 1970s as absolutely separate from the limited advances of the 1940s seems just as problematic as seeing a direct and causal link between the war and second-wave feminism. Understanding the relationship between women's Second World War experiences and all that later unfolded requires us to embrace ambiguity and to recognize that change is often partial, incremental, and subject to periods of regression.

Perhaps the most valuable contribution we can make to this long-standing historiographical conversation is to stress the importance of listening to individual women as they voice their experiences and of giving their assessments as much analytical weight as the hopes or expectations that governments, or Canadian society more broadly, held for them. For a case in point, we need look no further than Christine Hamelin's article about young people in Ottawa high schools during the war. There, Hamelin describes the Lisgar Girls' Rifle Club, established by the girls of Lisgar Collegiate as an adjunct to the school's male-only cadet corps. In its coverage of the club, a local newspaper displayed the widely held attitudes of the day that Pierson and other historians have noted. "Friday is the day that the comely young misses, dressed in warm ski slacks, gather during the lunch hour," wrote the reporter, "to lend their feminine charms to the firing of the cadet corps' B.S.A.'s [air rifles] at targets some 20 yards away," as taught by "a lady teacher." The trivializing language emphasizes that these girls with their guns were no threat to familiar notions of feminine difference. But a student whom the journalist quoted had a different perspective on what the club was all about. "We'll be able to lick the Hun if he ever comes," she proudly claimed.[9] Official and journalistic sources commonly offer one view, whereas women and girls themselves present quite another. As Jonathan Vance writes in his history of East Flamborough township during the First World War, "the voices of the past will tell us what was important to them; our job is to avoid assuming that we know better than they do."[10]

In this vein, it is worth noting that most women and girls in Canada and Newfoundland seem, at the time, to have interpreted their work as a valuable contribution to the war effort. They also seem not to have abandoned this view as the years wore on. The relative abundance of autobiographies and memoirs of the war years by women who lived through them indicates that, as the decades passed, they came to consider their stories as worthy of a place in the larger narrative of Canada's and Newfoundland's Second World War. As was the case for many male veterans, women's wartime experiences frequently became important elements of their post-war identities, the stuff of dinner-table reminiscences, as well as more formal memoirs. This tendency was strengthened by the friendships and communities forged in wartime that continued after its conclusion. Editor Amy Shaw's maternal grandmother, Millie, provides a characteristic example. She was a member of the Women's Royal Canadian Naval Service (colloquially known as "Wrens") during the war, and being a Wren was a key aspect of her social life long after it concluded. For years she kept up her friendships with other Wrens and travelled to attend Wren reunions. When she died in 2016, at the age of ninety-six, one female funeral guest was unknown to the family. The woman explained that she was there to honour Millie on behalf of the Wrens. Although the surviving Wrens were all nonagenarians by that point, they maintained such a strong sense of collective identity (seventy years after the war ended!) that they felt the need to perform this last duty to each other: there would always be a Wren at the funeral of another Wren. These bonds of individual friendship and community identity had a profound significance in the lives of many women and serve as a central theme across the primary literature on the war as well as in this collection.

The Second World War deeply marked the lives of the girls and women who lived through it – some for the better, some for the worse – and imprinted a generation with memories of a time unlike any other. For many, it brought adventure, excitement, and intensity, a sense of purpose and meaning, stronger bonds of community, and a host of new opportunities. But every good thing came at a price – a steep price – and the benefits were unevenly distributed. Even if the changes wrought by the war *had* been intended to advance women's place in society (which Pierson and her successors have convincingly disproven), the cost of that liberation, measured in death, destruction, social injustice, and lasting trauma on a global scale would have been a truly terrible price to pay. The women and girls of Canada and Newfoundland did not want war in 1939 and certainly did not expect it to improve their lives, but in frequently unsung instances of resilience, ingenuity, and determination – whenever and wherever they could – they made the best of it.

Notes

1 Quoted in Carolyn Gossage, ed., *Greatcoats and Glamour Boots: Canadian Women at War (1939–1945)*, rev. ed. (Toronto: Dundurn, 2001), 166.

2 Maryka Omatsu, *Bittersweet Passage: Redress and the Japanese Canadian Experience* (Toronto: Between the Lines, 1992); Pamela Hickman and Masako Fukawa, *Japanese Canadian Internment in the Second World War* (Toronto: Lorimer, 2011); Yuukichi Niwayama, "Caught In-between: The Life History of a Japanese Canadian Woman Deportee," *Journal of American and Canadian Studies* 28 (2010): 3–28.

3 Joan Sangster, "The Polish 'Dionnes': Gender, Ethnicity, and Immigrant Workers in Post–Second World War Canada," *Canadian Historical Review* 88, 3 (2007): 469–500; Lubomyr Luciuk, *Searching for Place: Ukrainian Displaced Persons and the Migration of Memory* (Toronto: University of Toronto Press, 2000); Veronica Strong-Boag, "Home Dreams: Women and the Suburban Experiment in Canada, 1945–60," *Canadian Historical Review* 72, 4 (1991): 471–504; Mona Gleason, "Psychology and the Construction of the 'Normal' Family in Postwar Canada, 1945–1960," *Canadian Historical Review* 78, 3 (1997): 422–77.

4 Sarah Glassford, *Mobilizing Mercy: A History of the Canadian Red Cross* (Montreal and Kingston: McGill-Queen's University Press, 2017).

5 Quoted in Gossage, *Greatcoats and Glamour Boots*, 90.

6 Charles Dickens, *A Tale of Two Cities* (New York: Charles Scribner's Sons, 1898), 1.

7 Ruth Roach Pierson, *"They're Still Women After All": The Second World War and Canadian Womanhood* (Toronto: McClelland and Stewart, 1986).

8 Jeffrey A. Keshen, *Saints, Sinners, and Soldiers: Canada's Second World War* (Vancouver: UBC Press, 2004), 6.

9 Christine Hamelin, "A Sense of Purpose: Ottawa Students and the Second World War," *Canadian Military History* 6, 1 (1997): 40.

10 Jonathan F. Vance, *A Township at War* (Waterloo: Wilfrid Laurier University Press, 2018), xi.

Selected Bibliography

The following list of secondary sources and memoirs pertaining to women and girls of Newfoundland and Canada during the Second World War demonstrates the preoccupations and growing diversity of the field and may serve as a useful starting point for scholars who are researching this period.

Newfoundland

Baldwin, Douglas O., and Gillian Poulter. "Mona Wilson and the Canadian Red Cross in Newfoundland, 1940–1945." *Newfoundland and Labrador Studies* 20, 2 (2005): 281–311.

Barrett, Barbara, and Eileen Dicks, eds. *We Came from over the Sea: British War Brides in Newfoundland*. Portugal Cove: British War Brides Association of Newfoundland and Labrador in co-operation with ESP Press, 1996.

Bartlett, Jessica Robyn. "Women, Waged Labour and the Second World War, in St. John's Newfoundland." Honours diss., Memorial University of Newfoundland, 2005.

Buss, Helen M. "War: Mother's Child." In Helen M. Buss, *Memoirs from Away: A New Found Land Girlhood,* 29–51. Waterloo: Wilfrid Laurier University Press, 1999.

Casey, G.J., and Maura C. Hanrahan. "Roses and Thistles: Second World War Brides in Newfoundland." *Newfoundland Studies* 10, 2 (1994): 240–49.

Collins, Daphne. *Crossing the Narrows*. St. John's: Print Three, 2001.

Cullum, Linda. "'It Was a Woman's Job, I 'Spose, Pickin' Dirt outa Berries': Negotiating Gender, Work, and Wages at Job Brothers, 1940–1950." *Newfoundland and Labrador Studies* 23, 2 (2008): 185–213.

–. "'It's Up to the Women': Gender, Class, and Nation-Building in Newfoundland, 1935–1945." In *Creating This Place: Women, Family, and Class in St John's, 1900–1950,* ed. Linda Cullum and Marilyn Porter, 179–201. Montreal and Kingston: McGill-Queen's University Press, 2014.

Doran, Barbara. "Women's War Efforts – First and Second W.W. in the Women's Patriotic Association of Newfoundland." Paper submitted for History 3813, Centre for Newfoundland Studies, Memorial University of Newfoundland, 1982.

English, Christopher, and Sara Flaherty. "'What Is to Be Done about Failed Marriages?' The Supreme Court and the Recovery of Jurisdiction over Marital Causes in Newfoundland in 1948." *Newfoundland Studies* 19, 2 (2003): 297–321.

English, Leona M. "Adult Education on the Newfoundland Coast: Adventure and Opportunity for Women in the 1930s and 1940s." *Newfoundland and Labrador Studies* 26, 1 (2011): 25–54.

Evans, Janine. "The War Effort Put Forth by Newfoundland Women during World War II." Paper submitted for History 1001, Centre for Newfoundland Studies, Memorial University of Newfoundland, 1982.

Flaherty, Sara. "'Out of Date in a Good Many Respects': Newfoundland's Fight for Judicial Separation and Divorce in the 1940s." In *Weather's Edge: Women in Newfoundland and Labrador – A Compendium,* ed. Linda Cullum, Carmelita McGrath, and Marilyn Porter, 222–34. St. John's: Killick, 2006.

Flight, Jennifer. "A Time of Great Change: Women and Social Change in St. John's, Newfoundland, during the Second World War." Honours diss., Memorial University of Newfoundland, 2006.

–. "'We Are All in the Front Line This Time': The Patriotic Association of the Women of Newfoundland during the Second World War." Master's research report, Memorial University of Newfoundland, 2007.

Haywood, Ruth E. "'Delinquent, Disorderly and Diseased Females': Regulating Sexuality in Second World War St. John's, Newfoundland." Master's thesis, Memorial University of Newfoundland, 2002.

High, Steven, ed. *Occupied St. John's: A Social History of a City at War, 1939–1945*. Montreal and Kingston: McGill-Queen's University Press, 2010.

House, Edgar. *The Way Out: The Story of NONIA in Newfoundland, 1920–1990*. St. John's: Creative, 1990.

Kochan, Pearl Collis, with Kevin Quirk. *To Johnnie with Love*. St. John's: Flanker Press, 2003.

Ling, Katherine Anne. "A 'Share of the Sacrifice': Newfoundland Servicewives in the Second World War." PhD diss., Memorial University of Newfoundland, 2001.

Lorenzkowski, Barbara. "The Children's War." In *Occupied St. John's: A Social History of a City at War, 1939–1945*, ed. Steven High, 113–50. Montreal and Kingston: McGill-Queen's University Press, 2010.

McGee, Anita, dir. *Seven Brides for Uncle Sam*. Montreal: National Film Board of Canada, 1997.

Morris, Anne. "Women and Work, 1935 to 1951." Course paper submitted to Sociology Department, Centre for Newfoundland Studies, Memorial University of Newfoundland, c. 1980s.

Richard, Agnes M. *Threads of Gold: Newfoundland and Labrador Jubilee Guilds, Women's Institutes*. St. John's: Creative, 1989.

Stanbridge, Karen. "Framing Children in the Newfoundland Confederation Debate, 1948." *Canadian Journal of Sociology* 32, 2 (2007): 177–201.

Stanbridge, Karen, and Jonathan Luedee. "Thrift and the Good Child Citizen: The Junior Thrift Clubs in Confederation-Era Newfoundland." In *Creating This Place: Women, Family, and Class in St. John's, 1900–1950*, ed. Linda Cullum and Marilyn Porter, 202–20. Montreal and Kingston: McGill-Queen's University Press, 2014.

Canada

Abella, Irving, and Harold Troper. *None Is Too Many: Canada and the Jews of Europe, 1933–1948*. Toronto: University of Toronto Press, 2012.

Ambrose, Linda McGuire. *For Home and Country: The Centennial History of the Women's Institutes in Ontario*. Guelph, ON: Federated Women's Institutes of Ontario, 1996.

Arney, Ada. *Here Come the Khaki Skirts – The Women Volunteers: A Pictorial Review of the Canadian Women's Army Corps during the Second World War*. Cobalt, ON: Highway Book Shop, 1988.

Arnold, Gladys. *One Woman's War: A Canadian Reporter with the Free French*. Toronto: J. Lorimer, 1987.

Auger, Geneviève, and Raymonde Lamothe. *De la poêle à frire à la ligne de feu: La vie quotidienne des Québécoises pendant la guerre '39–'45*. Montreal: Boréal Express, 1981.

Auger, Lauren Beth. "'That's My Story': Unpacking Canadian War Bride Veterans' Life Histories." PhD thesis, University of Brighton, 2017.

Axelrod, Paul, and Charles Levi. "Universities, Students, and the Conduct of War in Canada and Britain: A Comparative Perspective." In *Cultures, Communities and*

Conflict: Histories of Canadian Universities and War, ed. Paul Stortz and E. Lisa Panayotidis, 253–71. Toronto: University of Toronto Press, 2012.

Backhouse, Constance. "Sexual Assault and Disability: Saskatchewan, 1942." In Constance Backhouse, *Carnal Crimes: Sexual Assault Law in Canada, 1900–1975*, 131–64. Toronto: Osgoode Society for Canadian Legal History, 2008.

Baillargeon, Denyse. *A Brief History of Women in Quebec*. Waterloo: Wilfrid Laurier University Press, 2014.

Baker, Marilyn. "The Later Years: Women Instructors at the Winnipeg School of Art in the 1940s." *Atlantis* 30, 2 (2006): 50–62.

Banister, Lisa, ed. *Equal to the Challenge: An Anthology of Women's Experiences during World War II*. Ottawa: Department of National Defence, 2001.

Barris, Ted, and Alex Barris. *Days of Victory: Canadians Remember: 1939–1945*. Toronto: Macmillan, 1995.

Barry, Francine. *Le travail de la femme au Québec: 1940–1970*. Montreal: Les Presses de l'Université du Québec, 1977.

Beeby, Dean. "Ontario Women in the C.C.F., 1940–1950." *Ontario History* 74, 4 (1982): 258–83.

Belisle, Donica. "Sexual Spectacles: Saleswomen in Canadian Department Store Magazines between 1920 and 1950." In *Feminist History in Canada: New Essays on Women, Gender, Work, and Nation*, ed. Catherine Carstairs and Nancy Janovicek, 135–58. Vancouver: UBC Press, 2013.

Bérubé, Louise. "Les femmes québécoises durant la deuxième guerre mondiale." Master's thesis, Université de Montréal, 1979.

Bilson, Geoffrey. *The Guest Children: The Story of the British Child Evacuees Sent to Canada during World War II*. Saskatoon: Fifth House, 1988.

Bingley, Lindsey. "From Overalls to Aprons? The Paid and Unpaid Labour of Southern Alberta Women, 1939–1959." Master's thesis, University of Lethbridge, 2006.

Birnie, Lisa Hobbs. *In Mania's Memory*. Vancouver: Read Leaf, 2010.

Bland, Susan M. "Henrietta the Homemaker and 'Rosie the Riveter': Images of Women in Advertising in Maclean's Magazine, 1939–50." *Atlantis* 8, 2 (1983): 61–86.

Bowman, Phyllis. *We Skirted the War!* Prince Rupert, BC: privately printed, 1975.

Brand, Dionne. "'We Weren't Allowed to Go into Factory Work until Hitler Started the War': The 1920s to the 1940s." In *We're Rooted Here and They Can't Pull Us Up: Essays in African Canadian Women's History*, ed. Peggy Bristow, Dionne Brand, Linda Carty, Afua P. Cooper, Sylvia Hamilton, and Adrienne Shadd, 171–91. Toronto: University of Toronto Press, 1994.

Brandon, Laura. "Women Artists and the 1944 Canadian Army Art Exhibition." *Canadian Military History* 18, 1 (2009): 48–54.

Brandt, Gail Cuthbert, Naomi Black, Paula Bourne, and Magda Fahrni. *Canadian Women: A History*. 3rd ed. Toronto: Nelson Education, 2011.

Broadfoot, Barry. *Six War Years, 1939–1945: Memories of Canadians at Home and Abroad*. Don Mills, ON: PaperJacks, 1974.

Brookfield, Tarah. "Children as 'Seeds of Destiny': Nation, Race, and Citizenship in Post-War Foreign Relief Programs." In *Bringing Children and Youth into Canadian History: The Difference Kids Make*, ed. Mona Gleason and Tamara Myers, 377–90. Don Mills, ON: Oxford University Press, 2017.

Bruce, Jean. *Back the Attack! Canadian Women during the Second World War – At Home and Abroad*. Toronto: Macmillan, 1985.

–. "Canadian Women in the Second World War." *Canadian Oral History Association Journal* 6 (1983): 16–20.

Bryce, Gladysann. *First In, Last Out: The RCAF, Women's Division and Nursing Sisters in World War II*. Toronto: University Women's Club of Toronto, 2010.

Buch, Mary Hawkins, with Carolyn Gossage. *Props on Her Sleeve: The Wartime Letters of a Canadian Airwoman*. Toronto: Dundurn Press, 1997.

Burn, Hazel, and Heather Northcott, eds. *The Women's Canadian Club of Edmonton Remembers: World War II Vignettes*. Seba Beach, AB: Purple Wolf, 1996.

Burns, Patricia, ed. *They Were So Young: Montrealers Remember World War II*. Montreal: Véhicule Press, 2002.

Campbell, J. *My Experiences on the S.S. Athenia (Torpedoed Sept. 3rd, 1939)*. [London, ON?: privately printed?, 1939?].

Cancian, Sonia. *Families, Lovers, and Their Letters: Italian Postwar Migration to Canada*. Winnipeg: University of Manitoba Press, 2010.

Carter, Doris V. *Never Leave Your Head Uncovered: A Canadian Nursing Sister in World War Two*. Waterdown, ON: Potlatch, 1999.

Casgrain, Thérèse. *Une femme chez les hommes*. Montreal: Éditions du Jour, 1971.

Cash, Gwen. *A Million Miles from Ottawa*. Toronto: Macmillan of Canada, 1942.

Charles, Aline. "Women's Work in Eclipse: Nuns in Quebec Hospitals, 1940–1980." In *Women, Health and Nation: Canada and the United States since 1945*, ed. Gina Feldberg, Molly Ladd-Taylor, Alison Li, and Kathryn McPherson, 264–91. Montreal and Kingston: McGill-Queen's University Press, 2003.

Choko, Marc H. *Canadian War Posters, 1914–1918, 1939–1945*. Montreal: Éditions du Méridien, 1994.

Christie, Kay. "Behind Japanese Barbed Wire: A Canadian Nursing Sister in Hong Kong." *Royal Canadian Military Institute Year Book*, 11–13. Toronto: Royal Canadian Military Institute, 1979.

Colter, Erica. "The Homefire Women: Organized Volunteer Work in Halifax and Dartmouth during World War II." Honours thesis, Mount Saint Vincent University, 2002.

Comacchio, Cynthia. *The Dominion of Youth: Adolescence and the Making of Modern Canada, 1920 to 1950*. Waterloo: Wilfrid Laurier University Press, 2006.

Conrod, W. Hugh. *Athene, Goddess of War: The Canadian Women's Army Corps, Their Story*. Dartmouth, NS: Writing and Editorial Services, 1983.

Cooper, Lois MacDonald. *Wartime Letters Home*. Ottawa: Borealis Press, 2005.

Csinos, David M. "'What Can I Say to Them?' Messages about War and Peace in a Mennonite Children's Periodical during World War II." *Journal of Mennonite Studies* 31 (2013): 11–30.

Danys, Milda. *DP, Lithuanian Immigration to Canada after the Second World War*. Toronto: Multicultural History Society of Ontario, 1986.

Davidson, Tina. "'A Woman's Right to Charm and Beauty': Maintaining the Feminine Ideal in the Canadian Women's Army Corps." *Atlantis* 26, 1 (2001): 45–54.

Davis, Donald F., and Barbara Lorenzkowski. "A Platform for Gender Tensions: Women Working and Riding on Canadian Urban Public Transit in the 1940s." *Canadian Historical Review* 79, 3 (1998): 431–65.

Day, Frances Martin, Phyllis Spence, and Barbara Ladouceur, eds. *Women Overseas: Memoirs of the Canadian Red Cross Corps*. Vancouver: Ronsdale Press, 1998.

Dickson, Barbara. *Bomb Girls: Trading Aprons for Ammo*. Toronto: Dundurn Press, 2015.

Draper, Paula J. "Surviving Their Survival: Women, Memory, and the Holocaust." In *Sisters or Strangers? Immigrant, Ethnic, and Racialized Women in Canadian History*, ed. Marlene Epp, Franca Iacovetta, and Frances Swyripa, 399–414. Toronto: University of Toronto Press, 2004.

Drinkwater, Catherine Knight. *Letters to Edgewood Farm from a Canadian Girl in World War II*. Calgary: Bunker to Bunker, 2002.

Durflinger, Serge Marc. *Fighting from Home: The Second World War in Verdun, Quebec*. Vancouver: UBC Press, 2006.

Egener, Fred, and Norah Egener. *A Time Apart: Letters of Love and War*. Owen Sound, ON: Ginger Press, 1995.

Ellis, Jean M., with Isabel Dingman. *Facepowder and Gunpowder*. Toronto: S.J. Reginald Saunders, 1947.

England, Kim, and Kate Boyer. "Women's Work: The Feminization and Shifting Meanings of Clerical Work." *Journal of Social History* 43, 2 (2009): 307–40.

Epp, Marlene. "Alternative Service and Alternative Gender Roles: Conscientious Objectors in B.C. during World War II." *BC Studies* 105–06 (1995): 139–58.

–. "'United We Stand, Divided We Fall': Canadian Mennonite Women as COs in World War II." *Mennonite Life* 48, 3 (1993): 7–10.

–. *Women without Men: Mennonite Refugees of the Second World War*. Toronto: University of Toronto Press, 2000.

Evans, Suzanne. "Coming in the Front Door." *Canadian Military History* 19, 2 (2010): 55–62.

–. "Culinary Imagination as a Survival Tool." *Canadian Military History* 22, 1 (2013): 38–49.

Fahrni, Magda. "The Romance of Reunion: Montreal War Veterans Return to Family Life, 1944–1949." *Journal of the Canadian Historical Association* 9 (1998): 187–208.

Falconer, Tasha. "Mac at War: Women's Work and Education at the Macdonald Institute during the First and Second World Wars." *Studies by Undergraduate Researchers at Guelph* 9, 1 (2016): 40–47.

Florence, Elinor. "Young Women Trained to Defend the Home Front." *British Columbia History* 49, 4 (2016): 5–8.

Forestell, Diane G. "The Necessity of Sacrifice for the Nation at War: Women's Labour Force Participation, 1939–1946." *Histoire sociale/Social History* 22 (1989): 333–48.

–. "The Victorian Legacy: Historical Perspectives on the Canadian Women's Army Corps." PhD diss., York University, 1986.

Fortune, Gabrielle. "'Mr Jones' Wives': War Brides, Marriage, Immigration, and Identity Formation." *Women's History Review* 15, 4 (2006): 587–99.

Freeman, Barbara M. "Mother and Son: Gender, Class and War Propaganda in Canada, 1939–1945." *American Journalism* 12, 3 (1995): 260–75.

Freund, Alexander. "Contesting the Meanings of Migration: German Women's Immigration to Canada in the 1950s." *Canadian Ethnic Studies* 41, 3 and 42, 1 (2009–10): 1–26.

Freund, Alexander, and Laura Quilici. "Exploring Myths in Women's Narratives: Italian and German Immigrant Women in Vancouver, 1947–1961." *BC Studies* 105–06 (Spring 1995): 159–82.

Galloway, Orpha E. *Women of the War Years: Stories of Determination and Indomitable Courage*. Gladstone, MB: privately printed, 2000.

Galloway, Priscilla, comp. *Too Young to Fight: Memories from Our Youth during World War II*. Toronto: Stoddart, 1999.

Glassford, Sarah. "Mobilisées, organisées, et aptes à s'occuper des autres: le travail sanitaire des femmes de la Croix-Rouge au Canada au XXe siècle." In *L'incontournable caste des femmes: Histoire des services de santé au Québec et au Canada*, ed. Marie-Claude Thifault, 59–78. Ottawa: Les Presses de l'Université d'Ottawa, 2012.

–. *Mobilizing Mercy: A History of the Canadian Red Cross*. Montreal and Kingston: McGill-Queen's University Press, 2017.

–. "Practical Patriotism: How the Canadian Junior Red Cross and Its Child Members Met the Challenge of the Second World War." *Journal of the History of Childhood and Youth* 7, 2 (2014): 219–42.

Goldberg, Adara. *Holocaust Survivors in Canada: Exclusion, Inclusion, Transformation, 1947–1955*. Winnipeg: University of Manitoba Press, 2015.

Gossage, Carolyn. *The Accidental Captives: The Story of Seven Women Alone in Nazi Germany*. London: I.B. Tauris, 2012.

–, ed. *Double Duty: Sketches and Diaries of Molly Lamb Bobak, Canadian War Artist*. Toronto: Dundurn Press, 1992.

–. *Greatcoats and Glamour Boots: Canadian Women at War (1939–1945)*. Rev. ed. Toronto: Dundurn, 2001.

Granfield, Linda. *Brass Buttons and Silver Horseshoes: Stories from Canada's British War Brides*. Toronto: McClelland and Stewart, 2002.

Greer, Rosamond. *The Girls of the King's Navy: Rosamond "Fiddy" Greer*. Victoria, BC: Sono Nis Press, 1983.

Gregor, Frances. "The Women of the St. John Ambulance Brigade: Volunteer Nursing Auxiliaries in War-Time and Post-War Halifax." *Journal of the Royal Nova Scotia Historical Society* 8 (2005): 17–34.

Grypma, Sonya Joy. *China Interrupted: Japanese Internment and the Reshaping of a Canadian Missionary Community*. Waterloo: Wilfrid Laurier University Press, 2012.

Hacker, Carletta. "The Bluebirds Who Went Over." *Canadian Nurse* 65, 11 (1969): 31–34.

Halladay, Laurel. "'It Made Them Forget about the War for a Minute': Canadian Army, Navy, and Air Force Entertainment Units during the Second World War." *Canadian Military History* 11, 4 (2002): 20–35.

–. "A Lovely War: Male to Female Cross-Dressing and Canadian Military Entertainment in World War II." *Journal of Homosexuality* 46, 3–4 (2004): 19–34.

Halstead, Claire. "Dangers Behind, Pleasures Ahead: British-Canadian Identity and the Evacuation of British Children to Canada during the Second World War." *British Journal of Canadian Studies* 27, 2 (2014): 163–80.

–. "From Lion to Leaf: The Evacuation of British Children to Canada during the Second World War." PhD diss., University of Western Ontario, 2015.

Hamilton, Margaret Claire. *It's a Galley, Not a Kitchen, You Landlubber!* Fredericton: ACH Press, 2013.

Harzig, Christine. "MacNamara's DP Domestics: Immigration Policy Makers Negotiate Class, Race and Gender in the Aftermath of World War II." *Social Politics: International Studies in Gender, State and Society* 10, 1 (2003): 23–49.

Hawker, Harriet. *It Was Her War Too*. Edmonton: privately printed, 1996.

Henkenhaf, Heidi Jane. "Women in the Canadian Federal Civil Service during World War II." Master's thesis, Memorial University of Newfoundland, 1994.

Hernandez, Jon. "'You Just Lived for the Moment': Meet One of the Last Surviving Female Pilots Who Served in the Second World War." CBC News, 5 August 2018. https://www.cbc.ca/news/canada/british-columbia/second-world-war-female-pilot-jaye-edwards-1.4772568.

Hibbert, Joyce. *Fragments of War: Stories from Survivors of World War II*. Toronto: Dundurn Press, 1985.

–, ed. *The War Brides*. Toronto: PMA Books, 1978.

Hoyt, Marguerite Elizabeth. "You Have a Date with a (Blond) Bond: Women in Anglophone World War II Poster Art." PhD diss., Johns Hopkins University, 2003.

Hummelt, Bob. "Trouble on the Home Front: Perspectives on Working Mothers in Winnipeg, 1939–1945." Master's thesis, University of Manitoba, 2001.

Humphreys, Lewis. "Women and Government Intervention in the Canadian Labour Force, 1941–1947." Master's thesis, Dalhousie University, 1986.

Hutton, Anne van Arragon. *Uprooted: The Story of Dutch Immigrant Children in Canada, 1947–1959*. Kentville, NS: North Mountain Press, 2001.

The Imperial Order Daughters of the Empire: Golden Jubilee, 1900–1950. Toronto: Imperial Order Daughters of the Empire, 1950.

Iseke, Judy M., and Leisa A. Desmoulins. "Critical Events: Metis Servicewomen's WWII Stories with Dorothy Chartrand." *Canadian Journal of Native Studies* 33, 2 (2013): 29–54.

Jarratt, Melynda. *Captured Hearts: New Brunswick's War Brides*. Fredericton: Goose Lane Editions and New Brunswick Military Heritage Project, 2008.

–. *War Brides: The Stories of the Women Who Left Everything Behind to Follow the Men They Loved*. Toronto: Dundurn Press, 2009.

Jean, Michèle. *Québécoises du 20e siècle*. Montreal: Quinze, 1977.

Johnson, Sara E. *To Spread Their Wings*. Spruce Grove, AB: Sarabond Productions, 1990.

Kelsey, Marion. *Victory Harvest: Diary of a Canadian in the Women's Land Army, 1940–1944*. Montreal and Kingston: McGill-Queen's University Press, 1997.

Keshen, Jeffrey A. "Revisiting Canada's Civilian Women during World War II." *Histoire sociale/Social History* 30, 60 (1997): 239–66.

–. *Saints, Sinners, and Soldiers: Canada's Second World War*. Vancouver: UBC Press, 2004.

Kiefer, Nancy, and Ruth Roach Pierson. "The War Effort and Women Students at the University of Toronto, 1939–1945." In *Youth, University, and Canadian Society*, ed. Paul Axelrod and John G. Reid, 164–74. Montreal and Kingston: McGill-Queen's University Press, 1989.

Kimber, Stephen. *Sailors, Slackers and Blind Pigs: Halifax at War*. Toronto: Doubleday Canada, 2002.

Kitagawa, Muriel. *This Is My Own: Letters to Wes and Other Writings on Japanese Canadians, 1941–1948*. Edited by Roy Miki. Vancouver: Talonbooks, 1985.

Klassen, Pamela E. *Going by the Moon and the Stars: Stories of Two Russian Mennonite Women*. Waterloo: Wilfrid Laurier University Press, 1994.

Klausen, Susanne. "The Plywood Girls: Women and Gender Ideology at the Port Alberni Plywood Plant, 1942–1991." *Labour/Le travail* 41 (Spring 1998): 199–235.

Lachapelle-Poirier, Mariette. *Liens d'amour*. Montreal: Bellarmin, 1978.

Ladouceur, Barbara, and Phyllis Spence, eds. *Blackouts to Bright Lights: Canadian War Bride Stories*. Vancouver: Ronsdale Press, 1995.

Lambert, Barbara Ann. *War Brides and Rosies: Powell River and Stillwater, B.C.* N.p.: Trafford, 2012.

Lambton, Gunda. *Sun in Winter: A Toronto Wartime Journal, 1942 to 1945*. Montreal and Kingston: McGill-Queen's University Press, 2003.

Landells, E.A., ed. *The Military Nurses of Canada: Recollections of Canadian Military Nurses*. 3 vols. N.p.: privately printed, 1995–99.

Langford, Tom. "Why Alberta Vacillated over Wartime Day Nurseries." *Prairie Forum* 28, 2 (2003): 173–94.

Laprise, Andrée. *Coupables d'être étrangères: le camp de femmes de Kingston, 1939–1943*. Outremont: Athéna Éditions, 2010.

Larsen, Takaia. "Sowing the Seeds: Women, Work and Memory in Trail, British Columbia during and after the Second World War." Master's thesis, University of Victoria, 2007.

Latta, Ruth. *The Memory of All That: Canadian Women Remember World War II*. Burnstown, ON: General Store Publishing House, 1992.

Leah, Ronnie. "Women's Labour Force Participation and Daycare Cutbacks in Ontario." *Atlantis* 7, 1 (1981): 36–44.

LeBas Howe, Margaret. *Call Me Ma'am: Captain Margaret LeBas Howe, M.A.* London, ON: Ley and Lois Smith War, Memory, and Popular Culture Collection, Department of History, University of Western Ontario, 2015.

Lemire, Daniel Lachapelle. "Bittersweet Memories: Narratives of Japanese Canadian Children's Experiences before the Second World War and the Politics of Redress." *BC Studies* 192 (Winter 2016–17): 71–104.

Lewis, Norah. "'Isn't This a Terrible War?': The Attitudes of Children to Two World Wars." *Historical Studies in Education* 7, 2 (1995): 193–215.

Light, Beth, and Ruth Roach Pierson. *No Easy Road: Women in Canada, 1920s–1960s.* Toronto: New Hogtown Press, 1990.

Lindström, Varpu. "Propaganda and Identity Construction: Media Representation in Canada of Finnish and Finnish-Canadian Women during the Winter War of 1939–1940." In *Sisters or Strangers? Immigrant, Ethnic, and Racialized Women in Canadian History,* ed. Marlene Epp, Franca Iacovetta, and Frances Swyripa, 287–313. Toronto: University of Toronto Press, 2004.

Ling, Katherine Anne. "Servicewives in Wartime Halifax, 1939–1945." Master's thesis, Dalhousie University, 1994.

Ling, Kathy Anne. "Prince Edward Island Women and World War II." Honours thesis, University of Prince Edward Island, 1992.

Lloydlangston, Amber. "Applying to Be 'Industrial Soldiers': The Letters of Young Women Wanting to Train as Chemistry Laboratory Technicians, 1942–1944." *Historical Studies in Education* 26, 2 (2014): 30–47.

–. "Molly Lamb Bobak." *Canadian Military History* 23, 2 (2014): 1–9.

Lounder, Barbara. "(Some) Canadian Women and War." *Atlantis* 12, 2 (1987): 86–89.

MacPherson, Hélène de la Hitte. *Letters to Leon.* Victoria, BC: Sono Nis Press, 1984.

Maddison, Johnnene, with Madeline Lennon and Aldona Sendzikas. *Over Here: Women, Work and WWII.* Ontario, 2004.

Maitland, Beatrice McMillan, and Gayl Veinotte. *Put on Your Tin Helmet and I'll Tell You Some War Stories.* Calgary: privately printed, 2004.

Mann, Jessica. *Out of Harm's Way: The Wartime Evacuation of Children from Britain.* London: Headline, 2005.

Marshall, Dominique. "Reconstruction Politics, the Canadian Welfare State, and the Ambiguity of Children's Rights, 1940–1950." Reprinted in *Histories of Canadian Children and Youth,* ed. Nancy Janovicek and Joy Parr, 255–70. Don Mills, ON: Oxford University Press, 2003. Originally published 1996.

Martz, Fraidie. *Open Your Hearts: The Story of the Jewish War Orphans in Canada.* Montreal: Véhicule Press, 1996.

Mathews-Klein, Yvonne. "How They Saw Us: Images of Women in National Film Board Films of the 1940's and 1950's." *Atlantis* 4, 2 (1979): 20–33.

Matrix, Sidney Eve. "Mediated Citizenship and Contested Belonging: Canadian War Brides and the Fictions of Naturalization." *Topia* (York University) 17 (2007): 67–86.

McCrostie, James. "'Women and Seamen Don't Mix': VD in Canada's Merchant Navy, 1942–1945." *Northern Mariner* 9, 4 (1999): 1–12.

McCullough, Steve. "Narrativity and Uniqueness in Canadian Women's Holocaust Memoirs." PhD diss., Dalhousie University, 2006.

McDonald, Sharon. "Hidden Costs, Hidden Labours: Women in Nova Scotia during Two World Wars." Master's thesis, St. Mary's University, 1999.

McIntosh, Terresa. "Other Images of War: Canadian Women War Artists of the First and Second World Wars." Master's thesis, Carleton University, 1990.

McKenzie, P. Gayle. *Our Women in Uniform*. Edmonton: Institute for the Advancement of Aboriginal Women, 2003.

McNeil, Bill. *Voices of a War Remembered: An Oral History of Canadians in World War II*. Toronto: Doubleday Canada, 1991.

McWilliams, Caitlin. "Camaraderie, Morale, and Material Culture." *Canadian Military History* 19, 4 (2010): 21–30.

Medelsohn, Farah. "Challenge to Mars: Essays on Pacifism from 1918–1945." *Quaker History* 89, 1 (2000): 62–67.

Mitchell, Miriam C., and Florence C. Deacon, comps. *641: A Story of the Canadian Red Cross Corps, Overseas*. St. Catharines, ON: privately printed, 1978.

Moniz, Tracy. "A Woman's Place Is in the News." *Journalism History* 42, 2 (2016): 81–90.

Morriss, Geraldine, ed. *The Most Important Available Reserve of Manpower: A Series of Wartime Recollections by Members and Friends of the University Women's Club of Winnipeg*. Winnipeg: privately printed, 1996.

Morton, Suzanne. *Wisdom, Justice, and Charity: Canadian Social Welfare through the Life of Jane B. Wisdom, 1884–1975*. Toronto: University of Toronto Press, 2014.

Mosby, Ian. "Administering Colonial Science: Nutrition Research and Human Biomedical Experimentation in Aboriginal Communities and Residential Schools, 1942–1952." *Histoire sociale/Social History* 46, 91 (2013): 145–72.

–. *Food Will Win the War: The Politics, Culture, and Science of Food on Canada's Home Front*. Vancouver: UBC Press, 2014.

Mosher, Marial M. *Remembering: One Woman's World War II Story*. Halifax: Glen Haven Press, 2008.

Muir, Gladys. *Yûn-nan, South of the Clouds: My Life in Southwest China from 1939–1951*. White Rock, BC: privately printed, 1989.

Murray, Sylvie. "Quand les ménagères se font militantes: La Ligue auxiliaire de l'Association international des machinistes, 1905–1980." *Labour/Le travail* 29 (Spring 1992): 157–86.

Muzzin, Linda J., Maija Saari, and Maria Athina Martimianakis. "Wonder Drugs, Working Women, and the War: The Education and Careers of 1940s Pharmacy Graduates in Ontario, Canada." *Pharmacy in History* 47, 4 (2005): 127–42.

Nash, Mary Teresa. "Images of Women in National Film Board of Canada Films during World War II and the Post-War Years (1939 to 1949)." PhD diss., McGill University, 1982.

Neary, Peter, and Shaun Brown. "The Veterans Charter and Canadian Women Veterans of World War II." *British Journal of Canadian Studies* 9, 2 (1994): 249–77.

Nicholson, G.W.L. *Canada's Nursing Sisters*. Toronto: Hakkert, 1975.

Niwayama, Yuukichi. "Caught In-between: The Life History of a Japanese Canadian Woman Deportee." *Journal of American and Canadian Studies* 28 (2010): 3–28.

O'Hara, Peggy. *From Romance to Reality*. Cobalt, ON: Highway Book Shop, 1983.

Oikawa, Mona. *Cartographies of Violence: Japanese Canadian Women, Memory, and the Subjects of Internment*. Toronto: University of Toronto Press, 2012.

Ouellet, J. Maurice. *Les combattants du Madawaska durant la seconde guerre mondiale, 1939–1945*. Edmunston, NB: J.M. Ouellet, 1993.

Pasolli, Lisa. "'I Ask You, Mr. Mitchell, Is the Emergency Over?': Debating Day Nurseries in the Second World War." *Canadian Historical Review* 96, 1 (March 2015): 1–31.

Peate, Mary. *Girl in a Sloppy Joe Sweater: Life on the Canadian Home Front during World War II*. Montreal: Optimum, 1988.

Pedersen, Diana. "Exhibit Review: 'Women and War' at the Canadian War Museum, Ottawa, July 1984–September 1985." *Atlantis* 10, 2 (1985): 162–67.

Pennefather-McConnell, Nano. *We Never Stopped Dancing: An Airwoman's Scrapbook*. 2nd ed. Shawville, QC: Life Profiles, 2002.

Pickles, Katie. *Female Imperialism and National Identity: Imperial Order Daughters of the Empire*. Manchester: Manchester University Press, 2002.

Piercy, Shel, dir. *Love and Duty: Canadian Red Cross Women in WWII*. Burnaby, BC: Infinity Films, 2002.

Pierson, Ruth. "'Home Aide': A Solution to Women's Unemployment after World War II." *Atlantis* 2, 2 (1977): 85–97.

–. "Women's Emancipation and the Recruitment of Women into the Canadian Labour Force in World War II." *CHA Historical Papers* (1976): 141–73.

Pierson, Ruth Roach. "Archival Research as Refuge, Penance, and Revenge." *Queen's Quarterly* 114, 4 (2007): 490–99.

–. "Canadian Women and Canadian Mobilization during the Second World War." *Revue internationale d'histoire militaire* 54 (1982): 181–207.

–. *Canadian Women and the Second World War*. Ottawa: Canadian Historical Association, 1983.

–. "The Double Bind of the Double Standard: VD Control and the CWAC in World War II." *Canadian Historical Review* 62, 1 (1981): 31–58.

–. "'Jill Canuck': CWAC of All Trades, But No 'Pistol-Packing Momma.'" *CHA Historical Papers* (1978): 106–33.

–. "Ladies or Loose Women: The Canadian Women's Army Corps in World War II." *Atlantis* 4, 2 (1979): 245–66.

–. *"They're Still Women After All": The Second World War and Canadian Womanhood*. Toronto: McClelland and Stewart, 1986.

Pilkington, Gwen Evans. *Time Remembered: A Woman's Story of World War II*. Burnstown, ON: General Store, 1993.

Porter, Ann. "Women and Income Security in the Post-War Period: The Case of Unemployment Insurance, 1945–1962." *Labour/Le travail* 31 (Spring 1993): 111–44.

Pottie, Laura. *Their Dreams, Never Ending: A History of Women's Institutes in PEI*. Charlottetown: Federated Women's Institutes of PEI, 2000.

Poulin, Grace. "Invisible Women: WWII Aboriginal Servicewomen in Canada." Master's thesis, University of Manitoba, 2006.

Prentice, Susan. "Workers, Mothers, Reds: Toronto's Postwar Daycare Fight." *Studies in Political Economy: A Socialist Review* 30 (1989): 115–41.

Pringle, Sherry J. *Extraordinary Women, Extraordinary Times: Canadian Women of WWII*. Ottawa: Borealis Press, 2015.

Rains, Olga. *Voices of the Left Behind: Project Roots and the Canadian War Children of World War Two*. Toronto: Dundurn Group, 2006.

Rankin, Diana L. "The Mobilization and Demobilization of Canadian Women in the World Force during the Second World War." Master's thesis, University of Western Ontario, 1986.

Redstone-Lewis, Julie Anne. "The Creation of the Women's Royal Canadian Naval Service and Its Role in Canadian Naval Intelligence and Communications, 1939–45." Master's thesis, Wilfrid Laurier University, 2007.

Reimers, Mia. "The Glamour and the Horror: A Social History of Wartime Northwestern British Columbia, 1939–1945." Master's thesis, University of Northern British Columbia, 1999.

Richardson, Evelyn May Fox. *B ... Was for Butter and Enemy Craft*. Halifax: Petheric Press, 1976.

Roe, Kathleen Robson. *War Letters from the C.W.A.C.* Toronto: Kakabeka, 1975.

Roelens-Grant, Janine. *Fighting for Home and Country: Women Remember World War II*. Guelph: Federated Women's Institutes of Ontario, 2004.

Roth, Lorraine. "Conscientious Objection: The Experiences of Some Canadian Mennonite Women during World War II." *Mennonite Quarterly Review* 66, 4 (1992): 539–45.

Routier, Simone. *Adieu Paris!: Journal d'une évacuée canadienne, 10 mai–17 juin 1940*. Ottawa: Éditions du "Droit," c. 1940.

Roy, Patricia E. "Mona Okiwawa, Cartographies of Violence: Japanese Canadian Women, Memory, and the Subjects of Internment." *Canadian Ethnic Studies* 46, 1 (2014): 221–23.

Russell, Ruth Weber. *Proudly She Marched: Training Canada's World War II Women in Waterloo County*. Waterloo: Canadian Federation of University Women, Kitchener-Waterloo, 2006.

Sage, Elsie Mills Dunnet. *Battlefield Nurse: Letters and Memories of a Canadian Army Overseas Nursing Sister in World War II*. Edited by W.D.M. Sage. Vancouver: Sage Family, 1994.

Sager, Eric W. "Women in the Industrial Labour Force: Evidence for British Columbia, 1921–53." *BC Studies* 149 (Spring 2006): 39–62.

Savoie, Chantal. "Femmes, mondanité et culture dans les années 1940: l'exemple de la chronique 'Ce don't on parle' de Lucette Robert dans La Revue populaire." *International Journal of Canadian Studies* 48 (2014): 105–17.

Saxberg, Kelly, dir. *Rosies of the North*. Montreal: National Film Board of Canada, 1999.

Schaap, Tanya. "'Girl Takes Drastic Step': Molly Lamb Bobak's 'W110278 – The Diary of a C.W.A.C.'" In *Working Memory: Women and Work in World War II*, ed. Marlene Kadar and Jeanne Perreault, 171–90. Waterloo: Wilfrid Laurier University Press, 2015.

Scheinberg, Ellen. "The Tale of Tessie the Textile Worker: Female Textile Workers in Cornwall during World War II." *Labour/Le travail* 33 (Spring 1994): 153–86.

–. "Women, War, and Work: Female Textile Workers in Cornwall, Ontario, 1936–1946." Master's thesis, Queen's University, 1990.

Scott, Ruth. *Keeping the Home Fires Burning: A Story of Fredericton, New Brunswick in World War II*. Fredericton: privately printed, 1996.

Sheftel, Anna. "'We Started Over Again, We Were Young': Postwar Social Worlds of Child Holocaust Survivors." *Urban History Review* 39, 1 (2010): 20–30.

Simpson, Suzanne, Doris Toole, and Cindy Player. "Women in the Canadian Forces: Past, Present, and Future." *Atlantis* 4, 2 (1979): 267–83.

Smith, Helen, and Pamela Wakewich. "'Beauty and the Helldivers': Representing Women's Work and Identities in a Warplant Newspaper." *Labour/Le travail* 44 (Fall 1999): 71–107.

–. "Regulating Body Boundaries and Health during the Second World War: Nationalist Discourse, Media Representations, and the Experiences of Canadian Women War Workers." *Gender and History* 24, 1 (2012): 56–73.

Smuin, Dorothy. *The Farmer's Daughter: Wartime Letters Home, 1941–1942*. Penticton, BC: privately printed, 2005.

"A Snapshot in Time: Saskatchewan Women during World War II." Regina, Status of Women Office, 2005. http://library2.usask.ca/gp/sk/ws/wWIInapshot05.pdf.

Spencer, Emily. *Lipstick and High Heels: War, Gender and Popular Culture*. Kingston, ON: Canadian Defence Academy Press, 2007.

Spencer, Hanna. *Hanna's Diary, 1938–1941: Czechoslovakia to Canada*. Montreal and Kingston: McGill-Queen's University Press, 2001.

Starns, Penny. *Oceans Apart: Stories of Overseas Evacuees in World War 2*. Stroud, UK: History Press, 2014.

Stephen, Jennifer A. "Balancing Equality for the Post-War Woman: Demobilising Canada's Women Workers after World War Two." *Atlantis* 32, 1 (2007): 122–32.

–. *Pick One Intelligent Girl: Employability, Domesticity, and the Gendering of Canada's Welfare State, 1939–1947*. Toronto: University of Toronto Press, 2007.

Stevenson, Michael D. *Canada's Greatest Wartime Muddle: National Selective Service and the Mobilization of Human Resources during World War II*. Montreal and Kingston: McGill-Queen's University Press, 2001. Especially Chapter 8, "Female Primary Textile Labour and Nurses."

Stewart, Lee. "The Politics of Women's Education: Establishing Home Economics at the University of British Columbia, 1914–1949." *Historical Studies in Education* 1, 2 (1989): 261–81.

Strong-Boag, Veronica. "Canada's Wage Earning Wives and the Constructions of the Middle-Class, 1945–60." *Journal of Canadian Studies* 9, 3 (1994): 5–25.

–. "Home Dreams: Women and the Suburban Experiment in Canada, 1945–60." *Canadian Historical Review* 72, 4 (1991): 471–504.

Sugiman, Pamela. "'Days You Remember': Japanese Canadian Women and the Violence of Internment." In *Not Born a Refugee Woman: Contesting Identities, Rethinking Practices*, ed. Maroussia Hajdukowski, Nazilla Khanlou, and Helene Moussa, 113–34. New York: Berghahn Books, 2008.

–. *Labour's Dilemma: The Gender Politics of Auto Workers in Canada, 1937–1979*. Toronto: University of Toronto Press, 1994.

–. "'Life Is Sweet': Vulnerability and Composure in the Wartime Narratives of Japanese-Canadians." *Journal of Canadian Studies* 43, 1 (2009): 186–219.

–. "Memories of Internment: Narrating Japanese Canadian Women's Life Stories." *Canadian Journal of Sociology* 29, 3 (2004): 359–88.

–. "'A Million Hearts from Here': Japanese Canadian Mothers and Daughters and the Lessons of War." *Journal of American Ethnic History* 26, 4 (2007): 50–68.

–. "Passing Time, Moving Memories: Interpreting Wartime Narratives of Japanese Canadian Women." *Histoire sociale/Social History* 37, 73 (2004): 51–79.

–. "'These Feelings That Fill My Heart': Japanese Canadian Women's Memories of Internment." *Oral History* 34, 2 (2006): 69–84.

Svarc, Rose Ickovits Weiss. *Forces of Darkness: Personal Diary of Rose Ickovits Weiss Svarc from 1938 to 1946*. Montreal: Montreal Institute for Genocide and Human Rights Studies, 2000.

Swinton, Marion. *A Duffle Bag, Close Friends and Lots of Memories: The Photo Diary of Marion Swinton, W.R.C.N.S.* Edited by Michelle Fowler. Waterloo: Laurier Centre for Military, Strategic and Disarmament Studies, 2009.

Thiessen, Edna Schroeder, and Angela Showalter. *A Life Displaced: A Mennonite Woman's Flight from War-Torn Poland*. Kitchener, ON: Pandora Press, 2000.

Thomas, Patricia J. "Women in the Military: America and the British Commonwealth: Historical Similarities." *Armed Forces and Society* 4 (1978): 623–46.

Thompson, Jerry, and Bette Thompson, dirs. *The 13th Mission: One Lancaster Bomber, the Women Who Built It, and the Men Who Flew It into History One Week after D-Day*. Toronto: CBC Home Video, 2004.

Thrift, Gayle. "This Is Our War Too." *Alberta History* 59, 3 (2011): 2–12.

Tierney, Ruth. *Petticoat Warfare*. Belleville, ON: Mika, 1984.

Toman, Cynthia. "Blood Work: Canadian Nursing and Blood Transfusion, 1942–1990." *Nursing History Review* 9 (2001): 51–78.

–. "Frontlines and Frontiers: War as Legitimate Work for Nurses, 1939–1945." *Histoire sociale/Social History* 40, 79 (2007): 45–74.

–. *An Officer and a Lady: Canadian Military Nursing and the Second World War*. Vancouver: UBC Press, 2007.

–. "'An Officer and a Lady': Shaping the Canadian Military Nurse, 1939–1945." In *Out of the Ivory Tower: Feminist Research for Social Change*, ed. Andrea Martinez and Meryn Stuart, 89–115. Toronto: Sumach Press, 2003.

Trzcinska-Croydon, Lilka. *The Labyrinth of Dangerous Hours: A Memoir of the Second World War*. Toronto: University of Toronto Press, 2004.

Turnbull, Elsie G. "Women at Cominco during the Second World War." In *Not Just Pin Money: Selected Essays on the History of Women's Work in British Columbia*, ed. Barbara K. Latham and Roberta J. Pazdro, 429–34. Victoria, BC: Camosun College, 1984.

Turnbull Caton, Susan. "Fashion and War in Canada, 1939–1945." In *Fashion: A Canadian Perspective*, ed. Alexandra Palmer, 249–69. Toronto: University of Toronto Press, 2004.

Van Vugt, Sarah. "Beauty on the Job: Visual Representation, Bodies, and Canada's Women War Workers, 1939–1945." PhD diss., University of Victoria, 2016.

Veterans Review and Appeal Board. *My Grandmother's Wartime Diary/Le journal de guerre de ma grand-mère*. Charlottetown: Veterans Affairs, 1999.

Wade, Susan. "Joan Kennedy and the British Columbia Women's Service Corps." In *Not Just Pin Money: Selected Essays on the History of Women's Work in British Columbia*, ed. Barbara K. Latham and Roberta J. Pazdro, 407–28. Victoria, BC: Camosun College, 1984.

Wakewich, Pamela, and Helen Smith. "The Politics of 'Selective' Memory: Re-Visioning Canadian Women's Wartime Work in the Public Record." *Oral History* 34, 2 (Autumn 2006): 56–68.

Ward, Sue. *One Gal's Army*. Prince George, BC: Caitlin Press, 1996.

Warren, Vi, and Arnold Warren. "Flying with the ATA: A Girl Air Transport Auxiliary Pilot Recalls Her Wartime Experiences." *C.A.H.S.: The Journal of the Canadian Aviation History Society* 37, 3 (1999): 84–99.

Waterston, Elizabeth Hillman. *Blitzkrieg and Jitterbugs: College Life in Wartime, 1939–1942*. Montreal and Kingston: McGill-Queen's University Press, 2012.

Weiller, Karen H., and Catriona H. Higgs. "Living the Dream: A Historical Analysis of Women Professional Baseball Players 1943–1954." *Canadian Journal of the History of Sport* 23, 1 (1992): 46–54.

White, Mary M. *Hello War, Goodbye Sanity*. Surrey, BC: privately printed, 2002.

Wicks, Ben. *Promise You'll Take Care of My Daughter: The Remarkable War Brides of World War II*. Toronto: Stoddart, 1993.

–. *When the Boys Come Marching Home: True Stories of the Men Who Went to War, and the Women Who Took Them Back*. Toronto: Stoddart, 1991.

Williamson, Marie. *Just a Larger Family: Letters of Marie Williamson from the Canadian Home Front, 1940–1944*. Waterloo: Wilfrid Laurier University Press, 2011.

Ziegler, Mary Teresa. *We Serve That Men May Fly: The Story of the Women's Division Royal Canadian Air Force*. Hamilton, ON: RCAF (WD) Association, 1973.

Contributors

Graham Broad is an associate professor of history at King's University College at Western University. The author of *A Small Price to Pay: Consumer Culture on the Canadian Home Front* (UBC Press, 2013) and *One in a Thousand: The Life and Death of Captain Eddie McKay, Royal Flying Corps* (University of Toronto Press, 2017), he is also co-director (with Jonathan Vance) of the website Wartime Canada, http://wartimecanada.ca/.

Heidi Coombs is a research associate with the Faculty of Medicine at Memorial University of Newfoundland. She has a PhD in history, specializing in nursing with the Grenfell Mission in northern Newfoundland and Labrador, and has completed post-doctoral research on the negotiation of medical encounters between the mission and the Southern Inuit of Labrador. Heidi has presented her research to numerous academic and public audiences and is currently president of the Newfoundland and Labrador Historical Society.

Marlene Epp is a professor of history and peace and conflict studies at Conrad Grebel University College at the University of Waterloo. She is the author of *Women without Men: Mennonite Refugees of the Second World War* (University of Toronto Press, 2000), *Mennonite Women in Canada: A History* (University of Manitoba Press, 2008), and in 2017, a Canadian Historical Association booklet titled *Refugees in Canada: A Brief History*. She has also co-edited essay collections on Canadian food history and immigrant women.

Sarah Glassford is an archivist in the University of Windsor's Leddy Library and a social historian of modern Canada. She is the author of *Mobilizing Mercy: A History of the Canadian Red Cross* (McGill-Queen's University Press, 2017) and co-editor with Amy Shaw of *A Sisterhood of Suffering and Service: Women and Girls of Canada and Newfoundland during the First World War* (UBC Press, 2012).

Claire L. Halstead is a social and cultural historian who specializes in modern British and Canadian history. She currently holds a post-doctoral research fellowship in the Department of History at St. Mary's University, Halifax. Claire earned her PhD from the University of Western Ontario, with a dissertation that focused on British children who were evacuated to Canada during the

Second World War. As a digital historian, she is the creator of the British Child Evacuee database and HExD, the Halifax Explosion database.

Sarah Hogenbirk is a researcher and historian who specializes in the histories of Canada, military women, and wartime. She earned her PhD in Canadian history from Carleton University in 2017.

Barbara Lorenzkowski is an associate professor of history at Concordia University, Montreal. She is the author of *Sounds of Ethnicity: Listening to German North America* (University of Manitoba Press, 2010). Her current research project explores the social spaces of childhood in wartime Atlantic Canada, children's mobility in the city, and children's sensuous geographies.

Lisa Moore holds Bachelor's and Master's degrees from Concordia University. Her Master's thesis explores aspects of Catholic private schooling for girls in twentieth-century Montreal. Now a PhD student, she is currently preparing a doctoral dissertation on gender and juvenile justice in post-war Quebec. Lisa also has extensive professional experience in the history and heritage sector, including as a Concordia-based editorial and research assistant and as a researcher for the Montreal Museum of Fine Arts.

Lisa Pasolli is an assistant professor of history at Queen's University, where she researches and teaches the history of social policy, women and gender, and the politics of childcare in twentieth-century Canada. She is the author of *Working Mothers and the Child Care Dilemma: A History of British Columbia's Social Policy* (UBC Press, 2015).

Amy Shaw is an associate professor of history at the University of Lethbridge. She is the author of *Crisis of Conscience: Conscientious Objection in Canada during the First World War* (UBC Press, 2009) and the co-editor, with Sarah Glassford, of *A Sisterhood of Suffering and Service: Women and Girls of Canada and Newfoundland during the First World War* (UBC Press, 2012).

Jennifer Shaw is a PhD candidate in the Department of Women's Studies and Feminist Research at the University of Western Ontario. Her doctoral work blends oral history and archival research to explore the lives and experiences of Canadian Jewish women on the home front during the Second World War and how such women attempted to claim space in both the Jewish community and wider Canadian society.

Joseph Tohill is the co-editor of *Shopping for Change: Consumer Activism and the Possibilities of Purchasing Power* (Between the Lines, 2017). He has a PhD from York University and writes about and teaches twentieth-century

American and Canadian history, including the history of public policy, consumer politics, and consumer activism, at York University and Ryerson University.

Sarah Van Vugt has a PhD in history from the University of Victoria, where she completed her dissertation, "Beauty on the Job: Visual Representation, Bodies, and Canada's Women War Workers, 1939–1945," in 2016.

Index

Note: Page numbers with (f) refer to illustrations; (t) refers to tables.

Studies In Canadian Military History

John Griffith Armstrong, *The Halifax Explosion and the Royal Canadian Navy: Inquiry and Intrigue*

Andrew Richter, *Avoiding Armageddon: Canadian Military Strategy and Nuclear Weapons, 1950–63*

William Johnston, *A War of Patrols: Canadian Army Operations in Korea*

Julian Gwyn, *Frigates and Foremasts: The North American Squadron in Nova Scotia Waters, 1745–1815*

Jeffrey A. Keshen, *Saints, Sinners, and Soldiers: Canada's Second World War*

Desmond Morton, *Fight or Pay: Soldiers' Families in the Great War*

Douglas E. Delaney, *The Soldiers' General: Bert Hoffmeister at War*

Michael Whitby, ed., *Commanding Canadians: The Second World War Diaries of A.F.C. Layard*

Martin F. Auger, *Prisoners of the Home Front: German POWs and "Enemy Aliens" in Southern Quebec, 1940–46*

Tim Cook, *Clio's Warriors: Canadian Historians and the Writing of the World Wars*

Serge Marc Durflinger, *Fighting from Home: The Second World War in Verdun, Quebec*

Richard O. Mayne, *Betrayed: Scandal, Politics, and Canadian Naval Leadership*

P. Whitney Lackenbauer, *Battle Grounds: The Canadian Military and Aboriginal Lands*

Cynthia Toman, *An Officer and a Lady: Canadian Military Nursing and the Second World War*

Michael Petrou, *Renegades: Canadians in the Spanish Civil War*

Amy J. Shaw, *Crisis of Conscience: Conscientious Objection in Canada during the First World War*

Serge Marc Durflinger, *Veterans with a Vision: Canada's War Blinded in Peace and War*

James G. Fergusson, *Canada and Ballistic Missile Defence, 1954–2009: Déjà Vu All Over Again*

Benjamin Isitt, *From Victoria to Vladivostok: Canada's Siberian Expedition, 1917–19*

James Wood, *Militia Myths: Ideas of the Canadian Citizen Soldier, 1896–1921*

Timothy Balzer, *The Information Front: The Canadian Army and News Management during the Second World War*

Andrew B. Godefroy, *Defence and Discovery: Canada's Military Space Program, 1945–74*

Douglas E. Delaney, *Corps Commanders: Five British and Canadian Generals at War, 1939–45*

Timothy Wilford, *Canada's Road to the Pacific War: Intelligence, Strategy, and the Far East Crisis*

Randall Wakelam, *Cold War Fighters: Canadian Aircraft Procurement, 1945–54*

Andrew Burtch, *Give Me Shelter: The Failure of Canada's Cold War Civil Defence*

Wendy Cuthbertson, *Labour Goes to War: The CIO and the Construction of a New Social Order, 1939–45*

P. Whitney Lackenbauer, *The Canadian Rangers: A Living History*

Teresa Iacobelli, *Death or Deliverance: Canadian Courts Martial in the Great War*

Graham Broad, *A Small Price to Pay: Consumer Culture on the Canadian Home Front, 1939–45*

Peter Kasurak, *A National Force: The Evolution of Canada's Army, 1950–2000*

Isabel Campbell, *Unlikely Diplomats: The Canadian Brigade in Germany, 1951–64*

Richard M. Reid, *African Canadians in Union Blue: Volunteering for the Cause in the Civil War*

Andrew B. Godefroy, *In Peace Prepared: Innovation and Adaptation in Canada's Cold War Army*

Nic Clarke, *Unwanted Warriors: The Rejected Volunteers of the Canadian Expeditionary Force*

David Zimmerman, *Maritime Command Pacific: The Royal Canadian Navy's West Coast Fleet in the Early Cold War*

Cynthia Toman, *Sister Soldiers of the Great War: The Nurses of the Canadian Army Medical Corps*

Daniel Byers, *Zombie Army: The Canadian Army and Conscription in the Second World War*

J.L. Granatstein, *The Weight of Command: Voices of Canada's Second World War Generals and Those Who Knew Them*

Colin McCullough, *Creating Canada's Peacekeeping Past*

Douglas E. Delaney and Serge Marc Durflinger, eds., *Capturing Hill 70: Canada's Forgotten Battle of the First World War*

Brandon R. Dimmel, *Engaging the Line: How the Great War Shaped the Canada–US Border*

Meghan Fitzpatrick, *Invisible Scars: Mental Trauma and the Korean War*

Patrick M. Dennis, *Reluctant Warriors: Canadian Conscripts and the Great War*

Frank Maas, *The Price of Alliance: The Politics and Procurement of Leopard Tanks for Canada's NATO Brigade*

Geoffrey Hayes, *Crerar's Lieutenants: Inventing the Canadian Junior Army Officer, 1939–45*

Richard Goette, *Sovereignty and Command in Canada–US Continental Air Defence, 1940–57*

Geoff Jackson, *The Empire on the Western Front: The British 62nd and Canadian 4th Divisions in Battle*

Steve Marti and William John Pratt, eds., *Fighting with the Empire: Canada, Britain, and Global Conflict, 1867–1947*

Steve Marti, *For Home and Empire: Voluntary Mobilization in Australia, Canada, and New Zealand during the First World War*

Peter Kasurak, *Canada's Mechanized Infantry: The Evolution of a Combat Arm, 1920–2012*

Alex Souchen, *War Junk: Munitions Disposal and Postwar Reconstruction in Canada*

Studies In Canadian Military History
Published by UBC Press in association with the Canadian War Museum